REAL WORLD
PRINT
PRODUCTION

with Adobe Creative Suite Applications

D0624340

REAL WORLD
PRINT
PRODUCTION

with Adobe Creative Suite Applications

CLAUDIA McCUE

PEACHPIT PRESS
BERKELEY, CALIFORNIA

REAL WORLD PRINT PRODUCTION WITH ADOBE CREATIVE SUITE APPLICATIONS
Claudia McCue

Copyright © 2009 by Claudia McCue

This Adobe Press book is published by Peachpit.
For information on Adobe Press books, contact:

Peachpit
1249 Eighth Street
Berkeley, CA 94710
510/524-2178
510/524-2221 (fax)

For the latest on Adobe Press books, go to www.adobepress.com
To report errors, please send a note to errata@peachpit.com
Peachpit is a division of Pearson Education

Project Editor: Susan Rimerman
Production Editor: Lisa Brazieal
Copy Editor: Anne Marie Walker
Technical Editor: Premedia Systems
Proofreader: Cathy Caputo, Elaine Merrill
Compositor: WolfsonDesign
Indexer: James Minkin
Cover design: Charlene Charles Will

Notice of Rights
All rights reserved. No part of this book may be reproduced or transmitted in any form by any means, electronic, mechanical, photocopying, recording, or otherwise, without the prior written permission of the publisher. For information on getting permission for reprints and excerpts, contact permissions@peachpit.com.

Notice of Liability
The information in this book is distributed on an "As Is" basis without warranty. While every precaution has been taken in the preparation of the book, neither the author nor Peachpit shall have any liability to any person or entity with respect to any loss or damage caused or alleged to be caused directly or indirectly by the instructions contained in this book or by the computer software and hardware products described in it.

Trademarks
Adobe InDesign, Adobe Photoshop, Adobe Illustrator, and Adobe Acrobat are registered trademarks of Adobe Systems, Incorporated in the United States and/or other countries. All other trademarks are the property of their respective owners. Many of the designations used by manufacturers and sellers to distinguish their products are claimed as trademarks. Where those designations appear in this book, and Peachpit was aware of a trademark claim, the designations appear as requested by the owner of the trademark. All other product names and services identified throughout this book are used in editorial fashion only and for the benefit of such companies with no intention of infringement of the trademark. No such use, or the use of any trade name, is intended to convey endorsement or other affiliation with this book.

ISBN-13 978-0-321-63683-6
ISBN-10   0-321-63683-X

9 8 7 6 5 4 3

Printed and bound in the United States of America

For my North Star

CONTENTS AT A GLANCE

Introduction...xv

Chapter One: Life Cycle of a Print Job...1

Chapter Two: Ink on Paper...27

Chapter Three: Binding and Finishing..51

Chapter Four: Preparing Raster Images...77

Chapter Five: Vector Graphics...97

Chapter Six: Fonts..107

Chapter Seven: Cross-Platform Issues...119

Chapter Eight: Job Submission..125

Chapter Nine: Photoshop CS4 Production Tips...143

Chapter Ten: Illustrator CS4 Production Tips..169

Chapter Eleven: InDesign CS4 Production Tips...203

Chapter Twelve: Acrobat Production Tips...259

Appendix: Print Production Resources...297

Index..313

TABLE OF CONTENTS

Introduction...**xv**

   Who Should Read This Book xvi

   What This Book Is *Not*..xvii

   About the Author xvii

   Acknowledgments xviii

Chapter One: Life Cycle of a Print Job...**1**

   The Olden Days 1

   Brave New World: Desktop Publishing 3

   Job Submission..4

   Scenic Tour of a Typical Printing Plant 4

      Sales 6

      Customer Service 6

      Planning, Estimating, and Scheduling.....................................6

      Preflight..8

      Prepress 8

         Production 8

         Digital Photography 9

         Scanning..9

         Image Work...10

         Raster Image Processor (RIP)...10

         The Adobe PDF Print Engine 11

         Trapping 11

         Imposition..12

         Proofing..12

         Corrections 13

      Creating Plates..13

      Pressroom 14

      Digital Printing..15

      Finishing 15

         Trimming 15

         Folding 15

         Stitching...16

         Die Cutting...16

         Binding...16

         Gluing 17

      Fulfillment and Shipping...17

      Glossary of Printing Terms..18

Chapter Two: Ink on Paper **27**

  Fundamentals of Black-and-White Printing 27

  Fundamentals of Color Printing 30

    Limitations of CMYK 33

    Spot Colors 34

    Approximating Spot Colors with Process 35

  Press Issues 36

    Registration 36

    Trapping 37

    Large Ink Coverage Areas 39

      Rich Black 39

      Problem Inks 40

      Specialty Inks 41

      Custom Mixed Inks 42

      Coatings and Varnishes 42

  Digital Printing 43

    Digital Printing Advantages 43

      Short Runs 44

      Variable Data 44

    Digital Printing Issues 44

      Registration 45

      Spot Colors on Toner-Based Digital Presses 45

      Paper Requirements and Limitations 46

      Cracking and Flaking 46

      Resolution and Screen Ruling 46

  Your Monitor is Not Made of Paper 47

    A Quick Overview of Color Management 47

    Control Your Environment 48

    Realistic Expectations 49

    Contract Proofs 50

Chapter Three: Binding and Finishing **51**

  One Size Does Not Fit All 51

    Rule Number One: Build to the Correct Trim Size 52

    Rule Number Two: Provide Bleed 54

    Rule Number Three: Stay Away from the Edge 55

    Rule Number Four: Follow the Print Specifications 55

  Folding: High-Speed Origami 56

Imposition..58
    Basic Imposition 59
    Multipage Imposition...60
Binding Methods 65
    Saddle Stitching..65
    Perfect Binding and Case Binding..66
    Comb Binding...67
    Coil Binding 68
    Other Binding Methods 69
Moving Beyond Two Dimensions 69
    Die Cutting...72
    Embossing...74
    Foil Stamping...75

Chapter Four: Preparing Raster Images **77**
Ancient Times: B.P. (Before Pixels)...77
Now: A.P. (All Pixels, All the Time)..78
    Scanners 78
    Digital Cameras 79
    Imaging Software..79
Resolution and Image Fidelity...80
    Bitmap Images 81
    Scaling Up 81
    Scaling Down 82
    Planning Ahead...83
    Digital Photographs..85
    Cropping and Transforming Images 85
        Cropping..85
        Rotating Images 86
        Where to Transform: Image Editor versus Page-Layout Application..............................86
Appropriate Image Formats for Print..87
    TIFF 87
    Photoshop EPS 88
    Photoshop Native (PSD)..88
    Photoshop PDF...89
    Moving to Native PSD and PDF 90
    Special Case: Screen Captures...91
        Converting Screen Captures to CMYK......................................93
    RGB versus CMYK...94
Inappropriate Image Formats for Print..95

Chapter Five: Vector Graphics **97**

    Vector File Formats 97

        Encapsulated PostScript (EPS) 97

        Native File Formats..99

        Adobe PDF 100

        Vector Formats Not Appropriate for Print 100

            Microsoft Windows Metafile Format (WMF)..100

            Enhanced Metafile Format (EMF)...100

            Raster Formats...101

    Handling Text..101

        Embedding Fonts 101

        Outlining Text 102

    Incorporating Images into Vector Files 103

    Avoiding Unnecessary Complexity...104

        Simplify Your Paths 104

        Recommended Approaches to Document Construction 105

            It's a Drawing Program 105

Chapter Six: Fonts **107**

    Font Flavors..107

        PostScript (Type 1) Fonts...107

        TrueType Fonts 108

        OpenType Fonts 109

        Macintosh OS X System Fonts 111

        Windows System Fonts...112

        Multiple Master Fonts 112

        Substituting One Font Species for Another 113

    Activating Fonts in the Operating System..113

        Apple Font Book 113

        Windows Control Panel..114

    Font-Management Programs 114

        Automatic Font Activation..115

        Font Conflicts..115

    Font Licensing Issues 116

        End User License Agreements (EULAs) 116

        Embedding Fonts in PDFs 117

        Converting Text To Outlines...118

        Sending Fonts to the Print Service Provider 118

Chapter Seven: Cross-Platform Issues 119

Crossing The Great Divide 119
Naming Files 120
    Let's Have a Lot of Brevity 120
    Filenames Don't Need Punctuation. Period. 121
    Watch Your Language 122
    Include File Extensions 122
Fonts 123
Graphics Formats 124

Chapter Eight: Job Submission 125

Preparations During the Design Process 125
Talking with the Printer 126
Planning for Print 128
    Checking Raster Images 129
    Checking Vector Artwork 130
    Checking Page Layout Files 131
Sending Job Files 132
    Submitting PDF Files 133
    Submitting Application Files 134
        Platform Issues 135
        Sending Files 136
Preparing for Proofing Cycles 136
    Checking Image Proofs 137
    Checking Page Proofs 138
    Checking Corrections 140
    Checking Imposed Bluelines 140
    Signing Off on Proofs 140
Attending a Press Check 140

Chapter Nine: Photoshop CS4 Production Tips 143

Off to a good start 143
    Know the Fate of the Image 143
    Image Resolution 145
    Color Space 145
    Converting RGB to CMYK 146

Working in Layers 146
    Don't Erase that Pixel! 146
    Color Corrections with a Safety Net 147
    Smart Objects 149
    Clipping Masks 150
    Should You Flatten a Layered File? 151
Transparency 151
Silhouettes and Masking 153
    Creating a Path: Right and Wrong 153
        Path Flatness Settings 155
        Paths that Aren't Clipping Paths 156
    Alternative Silhouetting Methods 157
    Non-Destructive Mask Edits 159
Beyond CMYK 160
    Creating Duotones 160
    Adding Spot Color to a CMYK Image 161
    Creating a Spot Varnish Plate 162
Beyond Pixels 163
    Vector Elements 163
    Saving as a Photoshop PDF 165
Saving for Other Applications 167

Chapter Ten: Illustrator CS4 Production Tips **169**
Document Profile and Color Mode 169
Artboards 170
    Creating Artboards 172
    Modifying Artboards 173
    Bleed Settings 174
    Please Don't Call Artboards "Pages" 174
Using Symbols 175
Simplifying Complex Artwork 177
Live Effects 179
    Why Filters Are Gone 179
        Using Effects 180
        Document Raster Effects Settings 181
Using the Appearance Panel 183
Creating 3D Artwork 185

Transparency 186

Flattening Transparency 187

Linked and Embedded Images 189

Blended Objects 190

Spot Colors 191

Pantone Goe System 193

What About My Old Pantone Guides? 193

Separations Preview 194

Why Versions Matter 194

Saving for Other Applications 198

Saving Files with Multiple Artboards 198

Saving Artboards to Older Versions 199

Saving as EPS 200

Including Bleed in Export 200

Creating PDF Files 200

Saving to PDF 201

Opening PDF Files in Illustrator 202

Chapter Eleven: InDesign CS4 Production Tips **203**

Graphics 203

Placing Graphics 203

There's *Good* Drag and Drop… 205

… and There's *Bad* Drag and Drop 206

Embedding and Unembedding Graphics 207

Updating Missing or Modified Graphics 208

Finding Missing Graphics 211

Updating Modified Graphics 211

Replacing Current Graphics 211

Editing Graphics 212

Transforming Graphics 213

Using Native Files 214

Photoshop Native Files (PSD) 214

Drop That Shadow 214

Object Layer Options 216

Illustrator Native Files (AI) 218

InDesign Files as Artwork 219

PDF Files as Artwork 220

Swatches 220
  Stubborn Swatches 222
  What to Do About All Those Extra Swatches 223
  Ink Manager 224
  Colorizing Images 226
Converting Legacy QuarkXPress and PageMaker Files 227
  Preparing for Conversion 227
  What to Expect 228
    PageMaker Conversion Issues 229
    QuarkXPress Conversion Issues 230
    Cleaning Up 231
    When *Not* to Convert Legacy Files 231
Miscellaneous Document Tips 232
  IDLK Files 232
  Automatic Recovery 232
  Going Back in Time 233
    Cautions About Backsaving 233
  Reducing File Size 233
  Let It Bleed 234
  One Size Fits All: Layout Adjustment 235
  Checking Out of the Library 235
  Why Is My Text Two Sizes? 236
  Getting Smart 237
    Smart Guides 237
    Smart Spacing 238
    Smart Guide Preferences 239
    Smart Text Reflow 239
Transparency 239
  Transparency Flattening 240
    Put Text on Top 241
    Choose the Appropriate Transparency Blend Space 241
    Choose the Appropriate Transparency Flattener Preset 242
    Invoking Transparency Flattener Presets 244
    Special Case: Spot Color Content 245
    Spot Colors and Transparency: Overprinting at the Print Service Provider 247
    Drop Shadows: The Sun Never Moves 247

Finding & Fixing Problems 248
    Forensic Tools...248
    Info Panel...251
    Live Preflight 252
        Creating a Custom Preflight Profile 253
        Importing and Sharing a Preflight Profile..............................255
    Packaging the File...255
PDF Creation Methods 256
PDF Creation Settings..257

Chapter Twelve: Acrobat Production Tips.................................**259**

Acrobat Product Line..260
Where Do PDFs Come From? 260
Creating PDF Files...261
    Determining Which Type of PDF You Should Create...................261
    PDF Settings and Some Important Standards...............................262
    Export vs. Distiller..264
    Acrobat Distiller 265
    Handling Image Content...268
        Resolution Settings...269
        Compression Settings 270
    Font Embedding...271
Editing PDF Files...271
    Editing Text...272
    Editing Graphics...273
Comment and Review 275
    Reader Users Can Play, Too 278
    Collaborating with Others...279
        Email-based Reviews...279
        Shared Reviews...279
        Collaborate Live..280
    Collecting and Summarizing Comments......................................281
        Exporting Comments...281
        Importing Comments...281
        Summarizing Comments...282
    ConnectNow...283
        Sharing Your Screen with Adobe ConnectNow 283
    Acrobat.com..284

Print Production Toolbar 284
    Forensic Tools: What's Wrong with This PDF? 285
        Output Preview 285
        Preflight 287
    Repair Tools 290
        Ink Manager 290
        Convert Colors 290
        Add Printer Marks 291
        Crop Pages 292
        Fix Hairlines 293
        Transparency Flattener Preview 294
        PDF Optimizer 295
        Trap Presets 295
        JDF 295
Using External PDF Editors 296

Appendix: Print Production Resources **297**
    Organizations 297
    Conferences and Trade Shows 302
    Design and Printing Books 304
    Software-Specific Books 307
    Publications 310
    Destinations 311

Index **313**

INTRODUCTION

I am not a designer.

I can place type and graphics in a respectable arrangement on a page, but that's about it. I can't conjure up compelling concepts and award-winning designs. But that's fine; I'm not *supposed* to be a designer

I'm a printing geek; I spent half my life in prepress, troubleshooting, fixing jobs, and meeting impossible deadlines. And I loved it. I still love it. I love the heavy rhythm of presses, the smell of the chemicals, the beehive bustle of a pressroom. I love to see paper roll in one end of the press, and printed sheets fly out the other end. You know you've been in printing a long time if:

- Your grocery list has hanging indents.

- Your driver's license lists your eye color as PMS 5757.

- Your shoe size is 6½ plus ⅛-inch bleed.

- You refer to painting your house as a two-color job.

- You decide to write a book called *Real World Print Production with Adobe Creative Suite Applications.*

WHO SHOULD READ THIS BOOK

If you are a designer or a production artist who would like a better understanding of the pitfalls you encounter in using popular software, you'll find lots of pointers in this book to help you avoid problems. Almost all software provides options that are tempting to choose, but are dangerous under some circumstances. It's good to know which buttons *not* to push. And it's valuable to know *why* those buttons shouldn't be pushed.

As graphics software gives us increasingly powerful tools, it's also important to realize that each application is part of an ecosystem. Choices you make in Photoshop can limit your options when you place the image in InDesign. Options you choose in InDesign can affect the quality of the PDF you create. And so on. You need an aerial view of the programs' capabilities so you can anticipate the outcome. It would help if you were psychic, too, but that's another book entirely.

In addition, the more designers know about the physical requirements of the printing process, the more easily they can avoid problems and missed deadlines. This book can explain why your printer sometimes asks you to modify your designs for print. Better yet, you can beat them to it, and they will compliment you on how well-prepared your jobs always are. Besides, working within limitations can sometimes lead to imaginative solutions and more interesting designs.

If you are a prepress production operator, you'll find many reminders of subtle problems that can lurk in images, page layouts, and illustration files. If you're new to printing, you'll find beneficial insights into what's happening on the other side of the pressroom door. And if you're looking for a gentle way to educate clients who keep submitting nightmare jobs, well, a book always makes a nice gift, doesn't it?

As the lines between *designer* and *printer* become more blurred, some professionals don't fall clearly into a single category. Many organizations are responsible for both design and output, and it's especially important to know the whole story if you're going to shoulder such a wide responsibility.

WHAT THIS BOOK IS *NOT*

If you're in the market for a hot tips-and-tricks book, this isn't it. It's not a guide for wow-your-friends special effects, unless you consider it a special effect to get your job to print as expected. And, although this book demonstrates how to do some useful things in the most popular desktop publishing programs, it isn't strictly a how-to book either. In fact, there's quite a bit of how-*not*-to.

Are there any prerequisites for using this book? Only two, really. First, you should have basic proficiency with your computer and operating system, as well as the basics of InDesign, Illustrator, and Photoshop. The other requirement is arguably more important: You should have a healthy curiosity about the printing process and a desire to build problem-free files.

ABOUT THE AUTHOR

You never know where you'll end up. I was a chemistry major. Really. But I had a knack for illustration, and I took some college art classes for extra credit. One of my instructors (Michael Parkes, who has since become a well-known fine artist in Europe), suggested that I change my career path from chemistry to commercial art. I thought, "Well, I'll try it for a while," and took a job at a printing plant that summer. A funny thing happend: I fell in love with printing, and never went back to the lab. (Thanks, Michael.) Printing turned out to be the ideal environment for someone who held the dual titles of Class Clown and Science Student of the Year in her senior year of high school.

As a prepress production person, I always enjoyed troubleshooting, discovering new techniques, and sharing those discoveries with coworkers. I started in conventional paste-up, and then moved into film stripping. (It's not what you think. See the glossary in Chapter One, "Life Cycle of a Print Job.") And I was extremely fortunate (or cursed) to be one of the very early operators of color electronic prepress systems in the United States, so I've been pushing pixels around for a *long* time. Then, because it could perform the same magic as a Scitex or Crosfield system (minus the million-dollar price tag), Adobe Photoshop lured me to desktop computers.

I always believed in educating customers so they wouldn't be intimidated by the mysteries of printing. Not surprisingly, that led to my second career as a trainer, consultant, writer, and presenter at industry conferences. It's truly invigorating to answer questions, illuminate software mysteries, and solve problems for clients and conference attendees.

ACKNOWLEDGMENTS

I'm passing on to you some of the Basic Printing Truths imparted to me by a number of fine old printing curmudgeons. Count yourself truly lucky if you're befriended by a craftsman like Rick Duncan, who came up through the ranks, learned how to do everything the old-fashioned way, and who was always patient with a kid asking too many questions.

I'm also fortunate to be part of an informal fraternity of graphic arts aficionados. While we each have our specialties, our common bond is the love of learning and sharing new tricks. David Blatner, Scott Citron, Sandee "Vector Babe" Cohen, and Anne-Marie Concepción are my InDesign brethren (and sistren), going back to the days when we were considered page-layout rebels. Mordy Golding's passion for Illustrator is contagious, and he shares my devotion to enlightening designers in the mysteries of print. Dan Margulis is my long-time Photoshop color-correction hero, and I'm grateful to Chris Murphy for putting color management into mere-mortal language. These are some of the brightest (and funniest people) I know.

It's priceless to have friends on the inside at Adobe Systems: Dov Isaacs and Lonn Lorenz have been generous with their dry humor and no-nonsense advice on PostScript and PDF for years. And Noha Edell has long provided inspirational support and encouragement. "PDF Sage" Leonard Rosenthol has frequently enlightened me on arcane Acrobat mysteries, and he always knows where the best restaurant is (as well as the longest, most interesting route to get there).

I'm pleased to have the opportunity to update this book for Creative Suite 4; it's sort of like reincarnation. It's truly gratifying that the first edition is being used as a textbook in some schools, and I trust this version will continue the tradition. I hope it plays a part in creating designers who appreciate the technical underpinnings of the design craft. I have to thank Pam Pfiffner for convincing me (rightly) that writing the first edition would be fun.

I'm grateful to my technical editors, Jim Birkenseer and Peter Truskier of Premedia Systems, Inc., for taking time from their brutal schedules to poke through my words and ensure that I wasn't spreading any myths. In addition to knowing the inner workings of printing technology, they are responsible for the automation that made the stellar series of *America 24/7* books possible, as well as the engine under the hood of the wonderful FOLDRite InDesign plug-in.

And for applying the last coat of varnish and polishing this book to a sheen, I must thank Owen Wolfson for his design and composition work, and James Minkin for crafting the index so you can actually *find* the information in this book.

CHAPTER ONE

Life Cycle of a Print Job

People who aren't involved in the graphic arts industry probably have no idea where all that stuff in their mailbox comes from. They're blissfully unaware of the design process and give not a whit about those poor guys on third shift in the printing plant trying to troubleshoot a problem file. They don't think about the electronic design environment or the mechanical process of printing. All they think is, "Wow! That really looks good! I should buy this!" But as a designer or production artist, you need to know a bit about what happens when you're finished with your part of the job. The more you know, the more you can do to prevent problems—and missed deadlines—later in the life cycle of your job.

NOTE: *See the glossary at the end of this chapter for more detailed explanations of some common printing terms, both modern and historical, used in this chapter and throughout the book. Terms that are italicized in this chapter's text are expanded in the glossary, which also includes additional terms you may find helpful.*

First, a little history.

THE OLDEN DAYS

Twenty-five years ago, the responsibilities in the graphic arts professions were rather clearly defined, and there wasn't much overlap of skills or responsibility. Designers knew a bit about prepress and printing endeavors, but they usually weren't required to perform any work typical of those operations. Design was a more hands-on process involving more hand drawing and pen-and-ink work. Production artists created page layouts by gluing down photo prints with wax or rubber cement to a piece of thick illustration board, creating a *mechanical* (short for mechanical artwork). We did type corrections with X-Acto® knives and rubber cement, sometimes going home at the end of a long day with words glued to our elbows and the occasional consonant stuck in our hair. Who knows—maybe that was the inspiration for refrigerator magnet poetry.

The design and print process moved at a slower pace than it does today, largely out of necessity. It's certainly not that we were more patient in those days—it's just that all that handwork took time. There was more specialization. Dedicated *typesetters* generated text using phototypesetting equipment (after the demise of lead-based *hot type*), *trade shops* employed *cameramen* to create color separations and shoot *line shots* of mechanicals, and *dot etchers* performed color corrections by etching film with acid solutions to change the size of the dots.

Film strippers combined line shots and color separation films from the camera to create final page film. *Page proofs* were created by exposing the final composed page films onto photosensitive materials. *Color Key* proofs consisted of individual color overlays, one for each printing ink. *Matchprint* proofs consisted of color layers laminated to printing stock. And *Cromalin* proofs were made by dusting pigment onto a sticky image. Sounds primitive now, perhaps, but we were high-tech in our day!

Proofs and film were given to the printer, where *imposition* took place (although some trade shops also did imposition and shipped plate-ready films). *Bluelines* (single-color proofs that actually weren't always blue) were exposed from the imposed *flats*, and then folded up to check the mechanics of the page contents and imposition. Plates were burned from the imposed flats, then mounted on the press. Using the page proofs from the trade shop, pressmen adjusted ink coverage on the press during the process of getting the press up to speed and the ink behavior optimal—referred to as *makeready*. Then, when everything was up to speed, the customer might be asked to attend a *press check* to assure that everything looked good. Some of these processes, such as Cromalin proofing, no longer take place. Some have morphed into digital versions. Imposed bluelines, for example, have largely been replaced by output from large-format, inkjet printers. Press makeready has been streamlined by technological advances. But you'll be happy to know that press checks are much the same as they have always been.

In those (relatively) ancient times, the workflow looked something like **Figure 1.1**. There were variations, of course. Some design houses had in-house typesetting and photography, and some trade shops supplied finished plates to printers. Some printers had in-house designers as well as prepress departments to perform trade shop functions. And then, as now, some printers used outside firms to perform specialty finishing such as *embossing, foil stamping,* and *die cutting*.

The introduction of electronic *scanners* and *color electronic prepress systems* (CEPS) revolutionized the art of color separation. What had been a nuanced and specialized undertaking involving masking, tricky exposures, and chemical baths became accessible to a wider range of graphic arts professionals. Old instincts for camera work and dot etching were channeled into scanning and onscreen color correction. It was a wonderful new world. And our hands healed up as a result.

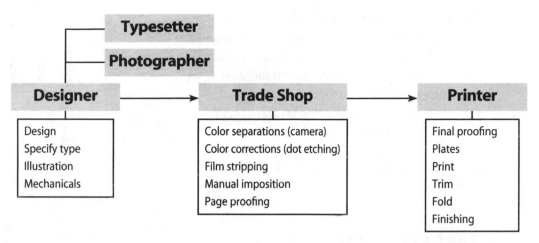

Figure 1.1 Historically, functions were divided between trades and professions that specialized in an individual aspect of graphic arts and printing. Designers designed, trade shops assembled all the pieces, and printers printed and performed finishing. Typesetters were often independent providers, although many design firms had in house typesetting. Photography studios, while usually separate companies, were occasionally part of a design firm or a department within a trade shop providing photography services. The advent of desktop publishing changed this ecosystem radically.

BRAVE NEW WORLD: DESKTOP PUBLISHING

With the appearance of the first Apple® desktop units, computers were no longer quite so foreign and mysterious to the rest of us. In 1985, the advent of page-layout programs such as Ready, Set, Go!® and Aldus PageMaker® made the computer a replacement for X-Acto knives and hot wax applicators.

Adobe's PostScript® page-description language brought laser printers to life and turned them into viable output devices for *camera-ready art*. Soon, what had been the sole province of specialized craftsmen became a public playing field. The good news? Anyone with a computer, a page-layout program, and an Apple LaserWriter® could now do much of the work involved in publishing. Tasks that had traditionally been performed in trade shops were accomplished by desktop computer users. Page-layout applications began to replace the separate jobs of setting type, creating mechanicals, and stripping film. Adobe Photoshop became the most widespread tool for retouching and color correction, seriously eroding the market for the million-dollar, high-end CEPS. New desktop publishers leapfrogged the former apprentice-to-journeyman training of printing craftsmen, and hit the ground running. And while the speed of electronic systems accelerated the pace in the industry and redistributed the tasks, it also redistributed the responsibilities. The distribution of labor began to look more like **Table 1.1**.

For example, in the Old Days, designers might indicate *color break*—what color is used in each element of the page—but it was usually up to the prep workers in the color trade shop to cut masks to accomplish this, in a process called *mechanical color*. But now color break is part of a page layout or illustration. Designers have a finished product ready to print when it leaves their hands rather than a guide for someone else's work.

JOB SUBMISSION

Your method of submitting files will depend on your print service provider's requirements. Chapter Eight, "Job Submission," is devoted to these issues, including some helpful checklists to aid you if your print service provider doesn't provide a similar guide.

SCENIC TOUR OF A TYPICAL PRINTING PLANT

Depending on the size and structure of your print service provider, some of the functions

	Designer	Photographer	Printer	Other
Design	●			
Illustration	○			○
Page layout	●			
Photography	○	○		
Scanning	○	○	○	
Color correction	○	○	○	
Retouching	○	○	○	
Imposition			●	
Page proofing			●	
Final proofing			●	
Burn plates			●	
Print			●	
Trim			●	
Fold			●	
Finishing			○	○

● = Primary vendor

○ = Possible vendors

Table 1.1 Desktop publishing's redistribution of graphic arts tasks. Traditional tradeshop tasks like retouching, for example, might be done by a designer, a photographer, or a printer.

described in this section might be combined. For example, in some companies, job planning might be done by a dedicated planner, by customer service representatives, or by an estimator. And some prepress departments make no distinction between preflight (looking for job errors) and production—they just watch for problems as they prepare a job for later prepress functions. The departments are described below in the approximate order in which they handle your job. **Figure 1.2** provides an overview of a fictional printing company to give you a general idea of job flow.

The flow of a job in a given printing company is governed by the company's capabilities and the type of work they usually perform. For example, a small printing company that specializes in business collateral such as letterheads, business cards, and envelopes is not likely to have binding equipment such as saddle stitchers or custom inline inkjet heads for on-press *personalization*.

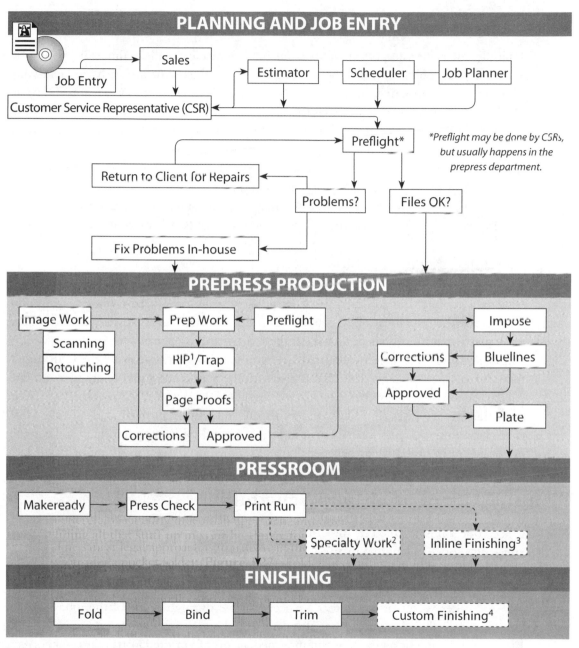

PLANNING AND JOB ENTRY

Job Entry → Sales → Customer Service Representative (CSR)

Estimator → Scheduler → Job Planner

Preflight*

Preflight may be done by CSRs, but usually happens in the prepress department.

Return to Client for Repairs

Problems?   Files OK?

Fix Problems In-house

PREPRESS PRODUCTION

Image Work → Prep Work ← Preflight   Impose

Scanning

Retouching

RIP[1]/Trap   Corrections ← Bluelines

Page Proofs   Approved

Corrections   Approved   Plate

PRESSROOM

Makeready → Press Check → Print Run

Specialty Work[2]   Inline Finishing[3]

FINISHING

Fold → Bind → Trim → Custom Finishing[4]

[1] RIP = Raster Image Processor. See Glossary for full definition.
[2] Specialty press work: includes add-ons such as inline personalization, varnishing, and fragrance application.
[3] Inline finishing includes on-press trimming and folding.
[4] Custom finishing includes die cutting, embossing, foil stamping, and hand assembly.

Figure 1.2 Job flow in a typical printing company. Your mileage may vary. Some printers divide departments differently, and some use external suppliers for operations such as custom finishing. (*Dashed lines indicate functions that may not be performed by all print service providers.*)

Sales

Typically, the print salesperson will be your first contact and will set things in motion by initiating your job's entry into the printing plant's workflow. At this early point in your job's life, it's important to discuss any concerns you may have about the job. Learn as much as you can about the processes that will be used in manufacturing your job. If your job will require any special stock such as vellum or heavy cover stock, discuss this with the salesperson. Also discuss any special finishing treatments that will be used, such as embossing or die cutting. The salesperson will probably be the person who provides you with an estimate of job costs and gives you an idea of the timeline of the job's trip through the printing plant. Initially, the salesperson may be your primary contact, but your job will probably be assigned to a customer service representative (CSR) early in the job.

Customer Service

After you submit your job files, the CSR is likely to become your prime contact point throughout the remainder of the job. If the production staff has any questions about how job issues should be handled, they'll ask the CSR to call or e-mail you for the answer. If you need to send corrected or updated files, you may be asked to contact the CSR rather than the salesperson, since the CSR is closer to the action and more likely to know the current status of your job in the workflow. A skilled, proactive CSR is your best friend and often has the foresight to help you anticipate and prevent problems. Ideally, the CSR is fluent in both design-speak and printing concepts and can act as a translator to keep the lines of communication open between you and production staff for the duration of the job.

Planning, Estimating, and Scheduling

Once your job is accepted by the print service provider, it will be assigned a job number and some sort of identifying name. This information will become part of a printed *job ticket,* which will travel with the job materials. The job ticket will be affixed to a physical *job jacket* containing job materials such as your digital media, your printed hard copy of the job, and other pertinent pieces that are accumulated during the life of the job. In some environments, digital job tickets are also used, based on the Job Definition Format (JDF). Eventually, the job jacket may contain intermediate proofs, printed instructions for correction cycles, and approved final proofs to be used as a reference during the press run. The attached job ticket serves as a job identifier and job information reference as the materials travel through the printing plant. Some printing plants use bar codes on their job tickets to aid in job tracking, but many rely on plant employees to note a job's process by making entries in computer-based tracking systems.

Job ticketing conventions vary between printing companies, but the job ticket will contain vital information about the job's requirements, including such information as:

- Job number (a unique identifier assigned at the print service provider)

- Client contact information

- Internal contacts (salesperson, CSR)

- Intended press

- Inks, including specially mixed inks

- Due dates (final print, as well as intermediate events, such as page proofs)

- Line screen

- Custom handling required, such as special folding or other finishing operations

Planners establish the basic flow of your job, including its timeline. The timeline identifies when each segment of the job will take place and how the print service provider can wedge your job into the ocean of other jobs occurring at the same time. They may also plan how jobs will run on press to take advantage of available time—your job may be combined with another, similar job to run simultaneously and save on the time and materials devoted to makeready.

Like air traffic controllers, *schedulers* track all the jobs running through a printing plant at any given time. They have to ensure that the plant's equipment is kept humming and that deadlines are met. As they juggle all the live jobs in the plant, they have to take into consideration any jobs whose progress hits a snag. They're constantly rearranging indicators on large scheduling boards, which resemble huge bulletin boards or whiteboards with all jobs represented by identifying tickets or labels.

Estimators determine job costs, including labor, paper, ink, and proofing materials, as well as press time and bindery time. In some plants, estimating and planning tasks are combined. Once the estimating and planning groundwork is laid, the job is often subjected to a preflight process. In some printing plants, preflight is performed by CSRs. In most plants, however, preflight is done by prepress operators when the job enters the prepress department.

Preflight

On its way to prepress production, your job will usually be run through a preflight process to check for problems with setup and content. Don't take it personally. It's better to find problems early in the job rather than later when deadlines loom. For application files such as Illustrator or Adobe InDesign® files, many prepress departments use dedicated preflight software such as FlightCheck® Professional from Markzware. Some departments rely on dedicated preflight operators to manually check files for problems, and some combine FlightCheck with manual checks geared toward the printer's particular workflow. To preflight submitted PDF files, many print service providers use PDF-specific software such as Enfocus PitStop, PDF/X Checkup from Apago, or the print production tools in Adobe Acrobat® Professional. However preflight is performed, when problems are found, you may be asked whether you'd like to fix the problems yourself or incur a charge for letting the printer fix them. Common problems include issues such as lack of sufficient bleed, misspelled words, overset text, incorrect or extraneous spot colors, or wrong document size.

Preflight personnel are also often responsible for organizing job files into a standard folder hierarchy used by the printing plant, which may require that they rename some files and reestablish image links in page layouts as a result.

Prepress

These days, many prepress departments refer to themselves as electronic prepress departments, a holdover from earlier days when the computer-based activities were a parallel process, and manual prepress activities such as film stripping still encompassed much of the work. But now you'd be hard-pressed to find extensive stripping capabilities in all but the smallest shops. As long as plates were still being exposed manually from large film flats, strippers would be called upon to make last-minute corrections by taping out or grafting in replacement film pieces. But with the overwhelming move to *computer-to-plate* (CTP), dedicated film strippers and their light tables are increasingly rare.

Production

Many of today's affordable desktop scanners can produce high-quality results, but some designers prefer to do quick-and-dirty FPO (For Position Only) scans to use in their page layouts while color professionals at the print service provider do the final, high-resolution scans. Once the job enters prepress production at the printer, the FPO images will be replaced with the final scans. Any silhouetting (eliminating backgrounds) will have to be performed at this point, which will add to job cost and time. If your printer does the scans and provides you with low-resolution, placeholder images to use in your layouts, replacing those placeholders with the high-resolution images will already be part of the standard job costs. Even if there are no true errors in the way the file is built, it's likely that prepress production operators will still need to tweak your job to get it ready for other parts of the workflow, such as raster image processing (RIPping), trapping, and imposition.

For example, if your job contains large solid areas of black, the prepress production operator may replace the single black ink with a rich-black mix such as C60-M40-Y40-K100 to facilitate a good outcome on the press. Another example: Gradients created in QuarkXPress are routinely replaced with Photoshop gradients to prevent a banded appearance in output. Such alterations are for the printer's convenience and are not usually charged to the customer.

Digital Photography

As digital photography has widely supplanted film photography, it's likely that most of your photographs will be submitted as digital images, whether you have shot the images, have hired a photographer, or are using stock images. Initially, many of these images are supplied as RGB files; many printers prefer that images be in CMYK when they receive your job, unless they are using a color-managed workflow that fully supports RGB images. For more information on converting RGB images to CMYK, see Chapter Four, "Preparing Raster Images."

Scanning

If you've supplied reflective artwork such as drawings, paintings, or photographic prints as artwork to be placed in the layout, the print service provider or an outside vendor will have to scan the artwork. Whether scanning is performed by you, the print service provider, or someone else, you should expect to see random proofs — raw, individual proofs of the artwork before the images are placed into the layout — so that you can determine at an early stage whether color correction or retouching will be necessary. Even the best scan may not be able to initially capture your intent for the image because of the limitations inherent in the scanning process and the inherent difficulty of reproducing some colors in the standard CMYK printing inks. Color correction can compensate for some of these issues, but be prepared for the limitations of CMYK (see Chapter Two, "Ink on Paper," for more on these issues). Early random proofs will prepare you for the appearance of images in the final printed piece.

Image Work

If you're not comfortable with creating clipping paths or performing other image manipulations such as retouching, color correction, or compositing, specialists in the prepress department will do those things. Often, the scanner operator is an accomplished Photoshop user with a good eye for color, and knowledge of what works best in the operator's particular printing environment.

Raster Image Processor (RIP)

Believe it or not, "We RIPped your file" is *good* news. At its most basic, a RIP interprets the incoming page-description (PostScript or PDF) information and converts that data to a literal bitmap image that instructs the marking engine of the output device how to image the film, plates, or, in the case of toner-based printers, the electrostatic drum (**Figure 1.3**). Many RIPs also perform other operations, such as in-RIP trapping or the low-resolution to high-resolution image swap functions of an *OPI* workflow.

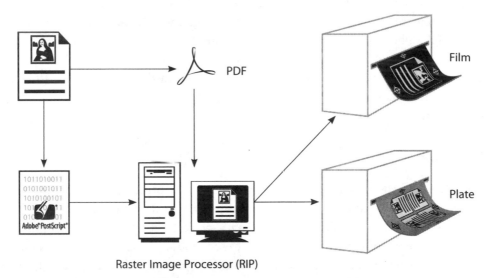

Raster Image Processor (RIP)

Figure 1.3 A RIP is a dedicated computer with specialized software that converts PostScript or PDF information into bitmapped information. This process drives an imagesetter to image film or a platesetter to image plates. Since each manufacturer's RIP consists of a proprietary combination of hardware and software, capabilities differ among brands.

In some workflows, individual pages are processed by the RIP, and then combined in imposition software. In other workflows, EPS, PDF, or PostScript files for individual pages are imposed, and the imposed file is processed by the RIP.

PostScript is actually a programming language that is used to describe and define pages so that output devices know how to image those pages. PDF files contain information that's much like PostScript (and in fact shares many of the concepts of PostScript). But PDFs can also contain information, such as transparency, which goes beyond the capabilities of the PostScript language. Some RIPs take in PDFs, but internally convert them to PostScript for further processing. Whereas RIPs have traditionally feasted on PostScript, some manufacturers' RIPs such as those from Artwork Systems Group and Global Graphics® handle native PDF files. This is the source of some imaging errors when you submit PDF files containing native transparency from applications such as InDesign or Adobe Illustrator. RIPs that maintain PDFs as PDFs throughout the raster imaging processing rather than converting PDFs to PostScript do a better job of imaging PDF content. The announcement of the Adobe PDF Print Engine opens the way for true PDF-based RIPs from even more vendors.

The Adobe PDF Print Engine

PostScript has given us many years of fine imaging service since its initial release in 1984, but it has its limits: For example, it doesn't support live, unflattened transparency. The Adobe PDF Print Engine is not a software product that end users purchase and install: It's used by vendors in their RIP products. The current RIPs from Kodak, Heidelberg, Rampage Systems, AGFA, DALiM, Océ, Xerox, and other manufacturers incorporate the PDF Print Engine. RIPs using the PDF Print Engine haven't dropped support for PostScript; they've added support for the expanded capabilities of PDFs.

Advantages include support for JDF job ticketing schemes and variable data printing (VDP), as well as faster and more streamlined processing of files. What does this mean to you? It translates to faster processing, more reliable output, and no more strange artifacts in jobs with transparency. Isn't technology wonderful?

Trapping

It's necessary to compensate for slight errors in the alignment of the printing inks as they're laid down sequentially on presses. Trapping provides a combination of colors at the edges of abutting color areas to camouflage any slippage. See Chapter Two, "Ink on Paper," for an in-depth description of trapping and why it's necessary. Since trapping can be a complex undertaking and because requirements vary according to printing conditions, this is an arcane art best left to prepress professionals. Aren't you glad? Whereas in the past trapping was accomplished within originating applications such as Illustrator or with dedicated trapping software, the majority of trapping now takes place at the RIP.

Imposition

Using the job information provided by planners, imposition operators combine individual pages in the proper pagination for plating. In some companies, separate groups handle prepress operations (such as preflight) and plating functions (such as imposition). This allows specialized operators to perform plate-related tasks while general prepress operators continue to do preflight and production. For a more detailed description of imposition, see Chapter Three, "Binding and Finishing."

Proofing

Several different rounds — and several different kinds — of proofing may occur in the life of a job:

- Random proofs of images early in the job help determine whether color correction or retouching is needed.

- Desktop printer output may be used for internal checks of the content of pages after preflight and before proceeding to prepress production.

- Color or single-color proofs (often called *bluelines*) after prepress production are used for customer markup or approval before proceeding to imposition and output to plates. This type of proof is intended for checking mechanical content, looking for typos, and finding incorrectly placed images.

- Online soft proofs are onscreen proofs (usually PDF-based). Soft proofs are faster than waiting for a proof to print, but unless your monitor is fully calibrated, it is difficult to judge color. It may also be a challenge to judge pagination issues such as crossovers.

- Color proofs of finished pages are used for color match on press. The proofs may be single page proofs, proofs of reader spreads, or proofs of multiple pages in their final imposed position. These proofs are viewed under controlled conditions in a viewing booth, which is painted a neutral gray and uses special lights for a standardized environment. The color temperature (5000–6500° K) is intended to mimic daylight. (The K stands for Kelvin, a thermodynamic temperature scale. Now, don't you feel better knowing that?) You may be asked to sign these proofs to indicate that you approve of the color and the content of the pages. This is often referred to as a *contract proof*, since it constitutes a contract between you and the printer. Your approval of the proof indicates that you're satisfied with the appearance of the proof. The print service provider is then expected to match the appearance of the contract proof on the press.

- Blueline folded comps, created after imposition, are used on press and in the bindery to check page position and content.

Corrections

Printer alterations are sometimes the result of mistakes that are made during production, but they can also be voluntary changes performed by the printer to ensure satisfactory printing under the required press or bindery conditions. For example, if there are large, solid color areas in a single ink, the printer may elect to print that area with two separate applications of the same ink to achieve a uniform appearance on press. Since this is elective, such an alteration is not chargeable to the customer.

Artist alterations (AAs), also called customer alterations, are alterations requested by the designer or the designer's client. AAs include such changes as type changes, replacing images, or moving content. Charges vary depending on the complexity of the change and the stage in the job at which the change is requested. For example, adding a comma at the preflight stage might be a freebie, whereas adding it after the job is on the press might require stopping the press, correcting the affected page, and resending it through the RIP, retrapping, re-imposing, and burning a new plate (or more if the comma affects multiple colors). The new plate (or plates) must be mounted on press, and the makeready process repeated. The expense of labor, materials, and lost press time could be considerable. Once the job is pulled off press, you've lost your slot in the production cycle and, depending on how busy the presses are, you may wait a day or more for another opportunity to run your job.

Creating Plates

In the earlier days of electronic desktop publishing, film was output for individual pages, and then taped down in flats on large, clear carrier sheets in the proper printing position. (A flat is just that: a flat carrier sheet with one or more pieces of film in final position.) These imposed flats were used to expose printing plates with powerful light sources. Because intermediate films were stripped and combined to create the page films, and then the page films used to expose the plates (or to create huge, composite single films for each plate), some tiny details could be eroded by the multiple generations of exposures. Any errors in aligning the individual pieces would affect the quality on press.

The introduction of computer-to-plate (CTP) revolutionized this process. In a CTP workflow, the imposition is digitally created, and then the printing plate is directly exposed in a large imaging device, using no intermediate film. The photosensitive coating on the imaged plate is chemically developed much like photographic film and baked, if necessary, to harden the image for printing. This usually takes place in an inline unit attached to the exposure unit, so a finished plate emerges ready for mounting on the press. Think of the photosensitive plate coating as being a bit tender while it's still fresh. The plate is heated to stabilize the imaged coating so it will be able to stand up to the rigors of being mounted and used on the printing press.

The elimination of intermediate films reduces opportunities for error and considerably improves the process. There's less chance for loss of detail and, understandably, some cost and time savings.

A variation of this concept is on-press imaging, which is most commonly used on smaller-format presses. Unexposed plates are mounted on the press, and imaging units on the press expose the plates in position. This approach can reduce makeready time because plates are already in position on the press when they're exposed, eliminating handling and possible registration issues.

Pressroom

The printing process that will be used on your job will have some bearing on how your job must be prepared, so the choice of printing process is one more important topic in your initial conversations with a print service provider. *Offset printing* is probably the process that you envision when someone says "printing press," and it's the printing method you will probably encounter most frequently. But there are other printing methods. The choice of printing process is dictated by the end product. *Gravure* is often used for long print runs typical of catalogs and magazines. *Flexography* is used for flexible packaging such as wrappers, foil bags, and labels. *Letterpress printing* is most often used for artistic applications these days, such as invitations or special publications. You may think of *screen printing* as only for clothing, such as t-shirts, but it's also capable of producing fine-art pieces, and often used to print on irregular surfaces such as cans, bottles, and other containers.

Preparation in the pressroom includes adjusting the ink coverage, varying the pressure of the ink-bearing plates and the transfer blankets, and adjusting the paper-feeding mechanisms. Much of this process is facilitated by on-press technology, but the pressmen's instincts are indispensable for fine-tuning the mechanics. The term *makeready* refers to the process of getting the press up to speed and the ink behavior optimal. The press crew will be using approved *contract proofs* to guide them in setup. The color and content of the printed piece should match what the client has approved. Once everything is behaving as it should, you may be asked to attend a *press check* to approve the results, especially if there are special treatments that are difficult to simulate with a contract proof, such as custom-mixed inks or specialty stock.

Other specialty work that may take place in the pressroom includes personalization such as addressing, as well as on-press finishing that might include perforation and scoring. In addition, coatings, such as varnishes, may be applied during the press run. Even fragrances and adhesives may be applied with inline units attached to the press.

Digital Printing

Increasingly, *digital printing* is used for short-run printing jobs such as brochures, product literature, mailings, and small-circulation magazines. The ability to utilize *variable data* with digital printing opens up some interesting possibilities for marketing with printed pieces containing content fully customized for individual recipients. Output from high-end digital presses such as the Xerox iGen and HP Indigo often rivals the quality of conventional offset presses. Please don't think of these presses as giant copiers: They're most certainly not. Their rich color, short runs, quick turnaround, and sophisticated inline finishing solutions can put full color printing within reach of more designers. The setup and makeready are faster on digital presses, and there's no need for drying before finishing. Digital presses are not limited to short runs; they're just more affordable for smaller jobs that would be prohibitively expensive if run on large conventional offset presses.

Finishing

There's some overlap between the pressroom and a dedicated bindery, since some finishing functions, such as scoring or perforation, may take place on press or may be accomplished in the bindery. But traditionally, operations such as trimming, folding, stitching, and die cutting are done in the finishing department or bindery.

Trimming

Large, heavy-duty trimming equipment is used to cut printed sheets to final size or to cut apart *ganged* content such as business cards. In some cases, trimming may take place before binding, although some pieces are bound first. For example, a business-reply card would be trimmed to the correct size before being bound into a publication. But the signatures of a book would be trimmed after being bound together in the final book configuration, ensuring that exterior page edges are cleanly aligned.

Folding

Simple folding may be performed inline as the printed sheet comes off the press, or it may be done in the bindery. More complex folding, such as that required for pocket folders or packaging, uses dedicated folding equipment. More complicated folding operations may require handwork to finish the job, which adds to the cost of the job.

Stitching

When a piece requires stitching, thread may be used to anchor the pages of a *signature* for subsequent binding into a larger, finished book. But wire is often used for stitching smaller page-count projects, such as magazines. In this process, the gathered pages are fed into stitching heads that feed, bend, and cut the wire simultaneously, resulting in a stapled piece. You'll often hear the term *saddle stitching*, which refers to the way a group of pages is held—as if draped over a saddle—while it is stitched.

Die Cutting

A *die* is a shaped metal cutter that is used to trim the edge of a printed piece in a special shape or to punch a shaped hole through the piece. The tabs on the edges of dividers are a simple example of die cutting. Many companies have standing dies for tab creation and can supply you with a template for creating your artwork so that it fits their existing dies. This avoids the cost of creating a custom die.

In a more complex example, a packaging piece may require that the printed sheet be scored and die cut to the final configuration for folding, creating all the interlocking panels that fold up to create the final box. If you're creating artwork for packaging, it's important to work closely with the print service provider and the die creator to ensure that your artwork is correct. Special handling is required at the intersections of panels to avoid artwork falling onto the wrong panel. Many printing companies do not create custom dies in-house, so be prepared for the cost and time involved in creating them. While the design of a custom die can be computerized, the assembly of the die itself still requires the knowledge of skilled craftspeople. For more information on die cutting, see Chapter Three, "Binding and Finishing."

Binding

Many forms of assembly fall under the heading of binding, from stitching to bookbinding. The most common forms of binding are *saddle stitching* (see the previous section on stitching) and *perfect binding*, in which multiple signatures are combined into a bundle, anchored with an adhesive, and then bound with tape or paper binding to hold them together.

Additional binding methods include *coil binding*, *comb binding,* and *wire binding*. The binding method may require that you avoid placing artwork in a specified margin so that it clears the punching or binding area. Consult with the print service provider early in the job to determine what the practical page area will be when binding is taken into consideration. For more information on binding methods, see Chapter Three, "Binding and Finishing."

Gluing

Binding methods such as perfect binding require gluing to keep all the pages together. But gluing is also an integral part of the manufacturing process for pocket folders and packaging that requires folding. Because glue should be applied to a clean, ink-free substrate, artwork for the job needs to provide clean areas for glue application. Consult with the print service provider as you create your files so you'll know where glue needs to be applied. You may also request that they modify your artwork to accommodate gluing.

Fulfillment and Shipping

Some printing companies provide services beyond the production of printed pieces. Many offer mailing and fulfillment services, or they partner with other companies to provide such services. Fulfillment is especially useful for product literature and other pieces with a relatively long life span, such as product manuals, pocket folders, and presentation binders. Rather than requiring the customer to store boxes or stacks of printed materials, the printer keeps the inventory and ships it as needed.

Printers who specialize in mailers such as catalogs often offer mailing as part of the job cost and process. This may include variable data addressing (whether on-press or offline) as well as the actual mailing.

Glossary of Printing Terms

This glossary is by no means a comprehensive record of printing terms. But it may come in handy before and during your conversations with a print service provider.

Aqueous Coating: A water-based coating applied over the entire printed area, usually by the last printing unit on a press. Aqueous coatings protect the printed ink and may enhance the appearance of the piece. For example, a pocket folder may benefit from the ability of aqueous coating to prevent scuffing as the pocket folder is repeatedly handled.

Baseline: An imaginary line at the base of a row of text. All text sits on the baseline, with descenders such as the lowercase *y* and *g* extending below the baseline.

Bindery: Sometimes also called a finishing department, the bindery performs trimming, folding, gluing, and stitching for finished pieces.

Blanket: An intermediate, rubber blanket used in offset printing to transfer the printing ink to the paper surface. The inked printing plate transfers ink to the blanket, which then applies the ink to the paper. The use of the intermediate blanket is the reason the printing process is called offset printing.

Blueline: A single-color proof made by exposing photosensitive paper to a strong light source through film (usually a multipage, imposed layout for plate). Bluelines are used for proofreading, checking for scratches in film, and correct pagination of the flat. In a computer-to-plate (CTP) environment where no plate film is necessary, bluelines are often digitally output on large-format inkjet printers.

Cameraman: In the days before scanners, cameramen used masking and exposure techniques to create film color separations on large cameras. Transparencies, color prints, or original artwork were mounted on a large plate and then photographed through color filters to generate the films for the printing inks.

Camera-ready art: Ink drawings for illustrations, logos, or finished mechanicals ready to be photographed by the cameraman. The line shots of the clean, camera-ready artwork were used as the starting point for film stripping.

CEPS (color electronic prepress system): A specialized computer system for retouching and assembly of images. Marketed by Scitex, Crosfield, Linotype-Hell, and Dainippon Screen, they often cost in excess of a million dollars. Largely rendered obsolete by the advent of Photoshop and the affordability of the Macintosh.

Chase: A frame that contains the metal printing components used in a letterpress printing press.

Coil binding: (Also called *spiral binding*.) Pages are punched (usually at the left or top edge), and then a single coil (spiral) of plastic or wire is threaded through the punched holes to anchor the pages together. Coil binding is useful for presentations and workbooks because pages lie flat when the finished piece is opened. One disadvantage is that there is no printable spine.

Color break: How color should be used in various areas of a page. In the days of physical *mechanicals*, colored markers were used to mark a tissue paper overlay so that *film strippers* would know how to apply color to type, rules, and boxes. Since the underlying mechanical artwork consisted of only black-and-white contents (to facilitate the shooting of *line shots*), an indication of color break was necessary. For example, headlines might be circled and marked to print as M100–Y100, and quick sweeps of a blue marker, accompanied by a written instruction, might be used to indicate that all boxes on the page should print with a mix of C50–Y15. It was sort of like coloring books for adults. The term color break is still used in discussions of page-layout contents.

Color Key™: A product of 3M, the Color Key proofing system used individual photosensitive color overlays to create proofs. Each sheet was exposed to a high-powered light source through the appropriate color separation film (for cyan, magenta, yellow, black, or a spot color). After development in a alcohol-based bath, the unexposed areas of the sheet would wash off, leaving the exposed areas to represent the printing ink. The overlays were aligned, and then taped to a white paper base. (No longer used.)

Color separations: Individual sheets of film for each printing ink to be used in reproducing artwork. In four-color designs, four pieces of film are used: one each for cyan, magenta, yellow, and black. For a duotone image, two films would be generated, one for each ink (usually black plus a spot color, but not always). For tritones, three pieces of film would be generated, and so on. Formerly created by cameramen until the introduction of scanners.

Color temperature: A standardized measure of the value of a light source to control viewing conditions. Think of a piece of iron being heated in a furnace. As its temperature increases, the color given off by the piece of iron goes from dull red to bright red, followed by orange, and so on. The Kelvin temperature scale is used, under which water freezes at 273 degrees K (the abbreviation for *Kelvin*), and all molecular motion stops at 0 degrees K. This is, no doubt, more than you care to know. But, for reference, it may be helpful to know that a household tungsten bulb measures about 2700–2800K, and average sunlight is approximately 5000K. The sun at high noon measures between 6000–6500 degrees K. For many years, the graphic arts industry was standardized on 5000K viewing conditions, often referred to as *D50* lighting. But in recent years there has been a move toward the brighter, 6500K (*D65*) standard.

Comb binding: A binding method in which pages are punched, and then a comb-like piece of curved plastic is inserted (usually at the left or top edge). The teeth of the curved comb (hence the name) curl into the punched holes, and the curvature of the insert draws it closed. Comb binding allows the finished piece to open flat, which makes it suitable for textbooks and workbooks. Since the exterior of the bound piece is solid, the spine can be imprinted, although this isn't frequently done.

Comp: Short for *comprehensive*. A representation of the final printed piece, usually printed on a desktop printer and manually assembled to show a client (or the print service provider) how the finished piece should look. Comps are helpful for checking pagination and for planning complicated pieces such as those involving inserts, tabs, or custom trimming. Also sometimes called *mockup*.

Computer-to-plate (CTP): Direct imaging of a printing plate from digital information. CTP replaces previous methods of generating intermediate film and exposing plates. The imposition is digitally created, and then the printing plate is directly exposed in a large imaging device using no intermediate film.

Continuous tone: A smooth transition from one color to another, such as the variations of color in a color photograph. While the emulsion of a photographic print can replicate continuous tones, printing presses cannot. Instead, the printing process approximates a variety of color by using *halftone* dots (see Chapter Two, "Ink on Paper," for more information on halftones).

Contract proof: A proof intended to represent the appearance of the final printed piece. Contract proofs are used for color and content matching on press. Traditionally, they are made by exposing proofing materials through final film, but now they are usually generated digitally from the same information used to generate plates. Signing a contract proof constitutes an agreement between printer and client. The client's signature indicates that the proof shows correct color and final content. The printer is obliged to match the proof on press.

Cromalin®: A product of DuPont™, the Cromalin proofing offerings include both analog (film-based) and digital proofing options. The film-based Cromalin proofing systems use photosensitive coatings adhered to a heavy carrier sheet. A layer of photosensitive coating is exposed to a high intensity light source through film for one of the printing inks. In the positive-acting version of Cromalin, the exposure hardens areas of the photosensitive coating, leaving the remainder slightly sticky. Very fine, pigmented toning powder is applied to the proof, adhering to the sticky imaged areas. Another layer of the photosensitive material is laid down on the carrier, and exposed through the film for the next color, and so on. When the process is finished, you have a one-piece proof with all colors in place. As the printing industry moves more toward an all-digital workflow, less film is generated, so DuPont now also markets digital proofing solutions under the Cromalin name.

Cure: To dry or harden an ink or other applied material. Heat, pressure, air, or ultraviolet light may be used, depending on the material and the substrate to which it is applied. The purpose of curing is to minimize smearing or scuffing of the printed piece.

Custom-mixed inks: While the variety of ink recipes available from Pantone®, Toyo Ink, and other firms provide a huge rainbow of colors from which to choose, it is sometimes necessary to mix a custom color to get exactly the right shade. There's more involved than "a cup of this and a cup of that," since what's important is the appearance and behavior of the ink on the final printing surface under press conditions. To ensure realistic expectations, the printer should provide an ink draw-down, which is a thin film of the custom ink applied to paper (ideally, the actual printing stock) to simulate the appearance of the ink when printed.

Die cutting: Using pressure and shaped metal dies to cut a printed piece in an interesting shape. Sometimes done by the printer, and sometimes done by outside specialty companies that subcontract with the printer.

Digital camera: Filmless photography, thanks to tiny photosensitive circuitry. Images can be downloaded directly to a computer and used immediately in design. Maybe you should soften those wrinkles first, though.

Digital press: While this term usually refers to plateless, toner-based printing devices, it may also refer to presses that enable on-press imaging of conventional plates. The output of high-end, toner-based presses rivals the appearance of offset printing while enabling functions such as the customization of each piece.

Dot etcher: A skilled craftsperson who performed color corrections by delicately etching color-separation films in mild acid baths. The acid eroded the edges of halftone dots, which would alter the diameter and thus the amount of ink that the resulting printing plate would hold. Etching a positive film would lighten color, and etching a negative film would increase color. To prevent etching in some areas of the film, the dot etcher would paint on a varnish-like protective mask. After etching, the mask would be removed with a solvent. While this may seem primitive compared to the ease with which we now make color corrections in Photoshop, the concepts are the same. In fact, many dot etchers were quick to adopt Photoshop and excel at using the program to perform color corrections. Imagine how relieved they were to go home without acid burns in their clothes! Dot etching, alas, is completely extinct.

Dot gain: The tendency of ink to spread when applied to a substrate, resulting in a perceived darkening of the printed image. Touch a fine-point pen to a paper towel, and you'll get the idea. Dot gain is an unavoidable physical occurrence, but plate imaging and press controls can mitigate it. Contract proofs should approximate the results of dot gain so that the printed piece isn't a surprise.

Embossing/debossing: Using pressure and shaped dies to press paper into a three-dimensional relief. Embossing raises the surface on the finished side; debossing indents the surface on the finished side. When used in an unprinted area, this is referred to as *blind embossing*.

Estimator: A knowledgeable and important part of the printing plant's front line, an estimator is responsible for estimating the time, labor, paper, ink, and other materials that will be required to complete a printing job.

Film stripper: A nearly extinct breed of trained crafts-people who use tape, photographic masks, and dark-room techniques to combine type and images for final film. In some ways, the film stripper was the equivalent of a production artist of today, although the job title made for some very awkward moments during intro-ductions. "You're a *stripper*?!" This would be followed by a brief explanation to your date's parents, during which you attempted to condense the printing process into a few convincing sentences.

Finishing: The manufacturing processes that take place after the job leaves the printing press. Finishing can include such processes as folding, binding, trim-ming, die cutting, embossing, and foil stamping.

Flat: Pieces of film taped to plastic carrier sheets for subsequent exposure. Film strippers taped the compo-nent parts of a page to flats, and then exposed them in a certain order through masks to create a finished film for the individual printing inks. Platemakers taped down films for pages in the correct position as part of very large imposed flats. With the increasing use of computer-to-plate technology, these processes are rarely used. Instead, pages are created in page-layout programs, and imposition software positions the pages in the correct orientation for directly exposing plates.

Flexography: A printing process that uses fast-drying inks and plastic, rubber, or photopolymer plates with raised image areas carrying the ink. Flexographic print-ing transfers the ink directly to the printing surface rather than using an intermediate blanket as in offset printing. Flexo printing, as it is usually called, is often used for printing flexible substrates such as plastic sheeting or thin packaging foils. While flexography may have previously been regarded as inappropri-ate for higher quality work, that's no longer the case. Improvements in inks and plate materials have greatly expanded the capabilities of flexography.

Foil stamping: Using pressure and heat to transfer a special, film-backed sheet of color (often metallic or iridescent) to paper. Foil stamping often uses a die to transfer a shaped design or to accentuate printed type and can be combined with embossing for elegant effects.

Folding dummy: A blank sheet of paper folded in the configuration that will be used in finishing the job. Pages are numbered to indicate the correct imposed page position. A folding dummy may be made by the planning department or by imposition operators and is used to check for correct folding and imposition.

FPO (for position only): Placeholder content (usually an image) used in the early stages of design. FPO images are later replaced by final, high-resolution images.

Ganged: The process of combining images on one mounting to be scanned simultaneously. Business cards or other similar pieces may be ganged together for simultaneous printing, and then separated when the printed sheet is trimmed apart. Ganging saves time and labor.

Gravure printing: A specialized printing method using engraved metal cylinders. Chrome-plated gravure cylinders are capable of extended printing runs, making gravure appropriate for publication and packaging applications. After printing, the chrome plating can be stripped off and replaced, so the cylinder can be reused.

Halftone: Since it's not possible to print millions of colors in a continuous-tone fashion, the predominant printing processes approximate a wide range of colors by using cyan, magenta, yellow, and black inks (usu-ally) printed with halftone dots of varying diameters. (See Chapter Two, "Ink on Paper," for a more detailed description.)

Hot type: A method of creating type with a raised printing surface by injecting molten metal into a shaped form called a matrix. Usually a combination of lead, tin, and other metals, the molten metal filled the mold and cooled to form the printing surface, called a slug. A slug might be just a single word, portions of a page, or an entire page. This process is also the source of the term *leading* (pronounced *ledding*). Thin strips of lead were placed between lines of text as shims to pro-vide space between the lines. The concepts and terms remain, although we no longer have to pour hot lead.

Imagesetter: A digitally driven device for imaging film. A RIP converts incoming PostScript or PDF information to very high-resolution bitmaps that guide the imagesetter's marking engine to expose the film with a laser or light-emitting diodes.

Imposition: Placing individual pages of a multipage document in the correct position for final printing.

Job jacket: A large plastic or cardboard carrier containing materials for a job. Usually open on one side like a big, flapless envelope, the job jacket allows the job materials to travel together throughout a printing plant. A job jacket might contain your original digital media and hard copy, as well as any proofs and necessary paperwork pertaining to the job. Usually an identifying *job ticket* is affixed to the job jacket to identify it and serve as a job information reference.

Job ticket: Usually attached to the *job jacket*, a job ticket contains important information about a printing job, such as the job number, the customer name, contact information for key personnel, the number of inks used, the press to be used, and important dates in the job's timeline.

Knock out: In printing, an area where no ink prints. For example, white text *knocks out* of an area of black ink, leaving unprinted paper. The term is also used to refer to creating a silhouette of a portion of an image, as in *knocking out* an object so that its background disappears.

Laminate: To coat a printed piece with a clear film by using heat, pressure, and adhesive. Laminates are used to protect printed pieces from abrasion and other wear and tear.

Leading: Pronounced *ledding*. The amount of space between the baseline of one line of text and the *baseline* of the following line of text, expressed in *points*.

Letterpress printing: Printing from a raised plate or collection of printing components that are held together in a *chase*. The pressure of letterpress printing creates a slight indentation, especially in heavy stock. It is a slow, mechanical, hand-intensive process, but creates unique pieces. Used by Gutenberg to print his famous Bibles, letterpress was once the standard printing process before offset printing began to replace it in the 1950s. Now it is used mainly for invitations, announcements, and fine-art printing.

Linen tester: A small, rectangular, folding magnifier used to check artwork, proofs, or printed pieces. It's called a linen tester because of its origins in the fabric industry.

Line shots: In the old manual days, a camera shot of black-and-white, hard-edged artwork such as type or line drawings. High-contrast film eliminated shades of gray, thereby producing a sharp image with no soft edges. The digital equivalent would be line-art scans.

Lithography: A printing process based on the mutual repulsion of water and oil. Oil-based ink adheres to areas of a lithographic printing plate that are not moistened by water.

Loupe: A small, folding magnifying glass that is used to examine small details in artwork, on a proof, or on a printed piece. A loupe folds into itself horizontally, whereas a linen tester pops up vertically.

Lowercase: Uncapitalized text such as a, b, c, d, and so on. As compared to uppercase (capitalized) text such as A, B, C, D. Originally, the term referred to the physical location of the wooden case containing the uncapitalized letters that were made of molded lead.

Makeready: The process of getting a printing press up to operating conditions. Makeready includes adjusting ink feed, paper tension, and blanket pressure. Also used to refer to the waste material produced during this process.

Matchprint: Originally a film-based proofing system marketed by 3M, the Matchprint proofing system became a product marketed by 3M's spin-off company, Imation. Ultimately, Kodak Polychrome Graphics purchased Imation, and now Matchprint is a digital system using high-quality inkjet proofing.

Mechanical: In the days of manual artwork creation, a mechanical consisted of hand-inked artwork and black-and-white photo prints that were affixed to heavy artboard with adhesive wax or rubber cement. Line shots of the mechanical were used by film strippers as the starting point for creating film for printing. Now, the term is sometimes used to describe a finished page-layout file.

Mechanical color: The process of cutting complicated, stencil-like masks for *color break*. Since each distinct color mix in a page required a separate mask, the process was exacting and time consuming. Fine knives were used to cut shapes in a red (Rubylith® brand from the Ulano® Corporation) or amber (Amberlith® brand also from Ulano) varnish-like coating on a thick, clear plastic backing. Once the masking shape was cut, sections of the coating were lifted and peeled off to reveal the clear plastic. Since the amber or red mask was opaque to the light used to expose the film, film strippers used these masks in the darkroom to create the final page films.

Offset printing: Offset printing is based on *lithographic* principles, which take advantage of the repellent properties of oil and water. The imaged area attracts oil-based inks, whereas the nonimaged area attracts water. On each revolution of the press, a thin film of water is applied to the plate, followed by a film of ink, which only adheres to areas not coated with water. The ink image is transferred to a *blanket*, which then transfers the ink to the paper. The use of an intermediate blanket is the reason the process is called *offset* printing.

OPI (Open Prepress Interface): A method developed originally by the Aldus Corporation (but also implemented by other vendors) that allows the use of low-resolution (and thus smaller) images in creating a page layout. These low-resolution images represent the original high-resolution images but take up less hard drive (or server) space and print more quickly. They contain PostScript comments that identify their high-resolution replacements. During final imaging, a server- or RIP-based process replaces the low-resolution image with the high-resolution image. OPI is used less often with today's faster networks and larger storage devices, but it is still implemented in workflows that deal with high volumes of images, such as catalog production. Pronounced "oh-pea-eye," not "opey."

Page proof: A proof of an individual page, which is usually created to obtain customer approval of color and content at a fairly early stage in the job.

Perfect binding: Combines multiple signatures into a bundle, anchors them with an adhesive, and then applies a tape or paper binding to hold them together for a flat spine. The paper binding may also be a printed cover that allows a title and other information to be printed on the spine.

Personalization: A data-driven method of inserting a recipient's name or other personal information during printing. In offset print environments, this is usually done via press-mounted inkjet units, although processes such as addressing may be performed during later stages in the bindery. As data-driven processes become more sophisticated, and the inkjet units faster and more refined, it is becoming possible to personalize with more than just a few lines of type — even custom images can be applied.

Pica: A unit of measurement. There are six picas in an inch. A pica is equal to 12 points.

Planner: A printing company specialist who establishes which press will be used to print a job, how the job will be imposed for the press, and what finishing processes should be scheduled to complete the job. Planners may also be involved in job scheduling. In many printing plants, the jobs of estimating and planning may overlap or may even be performed by the same person.

Platesetter: An output device that uses a laser or light-emitting diodes (LEDs) to expose the photo-sensitive surface of a printing plate by using digital information.

Point: A unit of measurement. There are 72 points in an inch. Text size, leading, baseline grids, and the thickness of rules and strokes are almost always specified in points. Some designers specify everything in points and picas, but many are accustomed to specifying page sizes and the dimensions of objects in inches, and they only use points when referring to text size and rule thickness.

PostScript: A programming language used to describe the contents of a page so that an imaging device such as a laser printer, an imagesetter, or a platesetter can produce output. Developed by Adobe Systems, Inc., PostScript was the major driving force in the birth of desktop publishing. Since its advent in 1985, PostScript has gone through several revisions. The current version of PostScript is Level 3.

Preflight: Inspecting job files at an early stage of the job to find content errors that might prevent the file from printing as the customer intends. While there are dedicated software programs such as FlightCheck from Markzware, some print service providers rely on skilled preflight operators to examine files. Designers can also preflight their outgoing jobs as a check before submitting the job for print. This allows problems to be fixed before incurring repair charges from the print service provider.

Prepress: All the preparatory work that takes place before actual printing. Prepress includes preflight, production work to correct or modify files for printing, proofing, trapping, imposition, and plating. It may also include scanning, retouching, and color correction.

Press check: Once makeready is complete and the printing press is in an optimal running state, the client is asked to approve the printed output for content and color. This is often necessary when custom inks or tricky substrates are involved—components that may be difficult to represent faithfully with proofing. Since printing companies often operate 24 hours a day, you may find yourself invited to a press check in the middle of the night.

Press proof: While current proofing methods are adequate for simulating actual printed pieces under most circumstances, special add-ons such as custom inks or applied varnishes may present challenges. For exacting jobs such as complex promotional pieces or annual reports, it may be necessary to perform a small press run to determine if everything looks as expected. While this adds considerably to job cost, it may be worthwhile on a high-profile job to ensure that the finished piece meets expectations.

Printer's spreads: The printing position of pages on the press, determined by the imposition requirements of the job. While pages two and three face each other in a printed eight-page brochure, they don't print together. Instead, page two prints next to page seven, and page three prints next to page six. When the pages are bound together, they are read in the correct order. See Chapter Three, "Binding and Finishing," for more information about imposition.

Proof: A simulation of the final printed piece, used to check the content of the job. Necessary corrections should be marked on the proof, and the marked-up proof should be compared to the next round of proofs to ensure that the requested changes have been made. Signing a proof indicates that you consider everything to be correct in the proof.

Registration: The alignment of all inks printed on a press. Since each color is applied by an individual unit on press, there is some possibility of the successive colors not aligning. While modern presses have sophisticated controls for maintaining proper registration, mechanical or environmental problems may cause slight misregistration, as can stretching or deformation of the paper itself during the printing process. A multi-color fringe at the edge of color areas is a symptom of misregistration.

Raster Image Processor (RIP): A specialized computer that uses a combination of proprietary software and hardware to translate PostScript or PDF input to a very high-resolution bitmap image that drives the marking engine of an output device, such as an imagesetter, platesetter, or desktop printer.

ROOM (RIP Once, Output Many): The practice of processing a page in a RIP, and then using that same information from the RIP to generate proofs, film (if necessary), and plates rather than reprocessing the original digital information through different RIPs for different output. Using the same data for multiple outputs ensures that no processing errors creep in. Using one vendor's RIP for proofing output and a different vendor's RIP for platesetting can result in a proof that does not represent what will be on the plate. This can lead to surprises on press. Surprise is not necessarily a positive thing in printing.

Saddle stitch: Binding multiple pages together with staple-like metal stitches. Often used for magazines and catalogs. See Chapter Three, "Binding and Finishing," for more information about saddle stitching.

Scanner: A device for converting reflective artwork, photographic prints, transparencies, or film negatives to digital information. Early scanners were large, expensive devices with daunting controls that required careful mounting of artwork on large, heavy clear drums. But with advances in optics and software, they have been largely replaced by flatbed scanners, and prices have plummeted accordingly.

Screen printing: A printing method in which a finely woven stretched screen carries a hand-cut or photographically exposed mask. The mask acts as a stencil, and ink is squeezed through the mesh of the screen in open areas of the mask onto the intended substrate. While you may associate screen printing only with apparel printing (such as t-shirts), it's also used for spot application of scratch-off coverings for game pieces, scratch-and-sniff areas, and printing on irregular surfaces such as molded pieces.

Scheduler: A printing-company specialist who determines when each portion of a job occurs (barring errors or other problems). The scheduler must consider how long each process takes and must factor in the effects of other existing jobs, staffing resources, and the required final deadline for the job. In some printing plants, scheduling and planning may overlap, or they may be done by the same persons.

Score: To press a groove into paper or board for easier folding. This ensures a smooth, predictable bend while lessening the chance that the paper or board will tear when folded.

Sheetfed press: An offset press that takes in single sheets of paper from a stack rather than a roll. Typical sheetfed press paper sizes are around 20 by 28 inches or 30 by 40 inches, although there are larger-format (and smaller-format) presses as well.

Signature: A printed sheet folded one or more times to create a single section of a multisection piece. Pages are imposed in the correct position so that when the sheet is folded, trimmed, and bound, the pages will be in the proper reading order. (For more on imposition and signatures, see Chapter Three, "Binding and Finishing.")

Silhouette: To eliminate the background surrounding the important element in an image. This may be done by erasing the background or (more commonly) by creating a mask or path that allows the element to display without the background. Also called *knockout*, *dropout*, *blockout*, *silo*, or *KO*, depending on your locale and your local printer's particular slang.

Spiral binding: see *Coil binding*.

Trade shop: A print service provider that works for other printing providers and performs services such as scanning, retouching, and other prepress services. Some trade shops also provide printing and finishing services.

Transparency: A transparent, positive color image such as a 35 mm slide. Larger formats include 4 by 5 inches and 8 by 10 inches, but the advent of digital photography has made the use of transparencies (and the need to scan them) less common.

Trap: To create overlapping areas of common color in order to minimize gaps during slight misregistration on press. Trapping is usually performed at the RIP stage, although it's also possible to create traps manually in many applications. (See Chapter Two, "Ink on Paper," for a more detailed explanation of trapping issues.)

Typesetter: The definition and responsibilities of a typesetter changed with technological advances. Typesetters no longer handle tiny molded lead characters locked in a chase (container). Currently, *typesetter* usually refers to a specialist who uses page-layout tools to set type with an emphasis on readability and style in long documents.

UPC (universal product code): A machine-readable identifier that consists of two components — a bar code and human-readable numbers. The first six digits identify the product's manufacturer, and the remaining digits identify the product itself and provide a check digit used by the code reader to determine if the code has been read correctly. It's not difficult to generate UPC artwork with special barcode fonts or dedicated software, but you must be mindful of requirements such as minimum size, location, and color of the code itself. It's important that busy backgrounds or dark colors don't interfere with the legibility of the UPC, which is why it's often placed in a white rectangle. You'll have to plan for this when you're creating artwork for publication covers or books, as well as packaging.

Uppercase: Capitalized letters such as A, B, C, D and so on. As compared to lowercase text such as a, b, c, d. Originally, the term referred to the physical location of the wooden case containing the uncapitalized letters, which were made of molded lead. Capitals were kept in an upper case, hence the name.

Variable data printing (VDP): At its most basic, VDP can be the personalization of a printed piece by inserting the recipient's name and address: "Dear [your name here]." While this can be accomplished by using press-mounted inkjet heads with acceptable results, the increased use of fully digital presses opens the way for more extensive customization. Since each impression on a toner-based digital press is unique anyway, a database-driven process can insert custom text — even images — to narrowly target the printed piece to the recipient's demographic or buying history. While variable data printing is more expensive because of the programming and planning involved (as well as the cost of demographic information and mailing lists), the response rate from such targeted mailings is substantially higher than for generic mass mailings.

Viewing booth: A cubicle-like area that provides a controlled viewing environment for judging color. Although a printed piece will be viewed by recipients under a variety of lighting conditions from fluorescent or tungsten to daylight, it's important during production to have standardized lighting and surrounding surfaces so that everyone from designer to retoucher to pressman is viewing proofs and printed materials in a common environment. To prevent any influence from the surroundings, the surfaces of a viewing booth are painted a neutral, medium gray, using matte paint to avoid reflections. To ensure consistent lighting, fluorescent bulbs of a specified color temperature are used. Originally, D50 (5000 K) bulbs were used, but there has been a move in recent years to D65 (6500 K).

Web press: A roll-fed printing press. Trimming to individual sheets may take place at the end of the press on an inline unit called a sheeter, or the printed web may be rolled up onto a takeup reel for offline trimming. The size of the web press dictates the width of the paper roll it accepts.

Wire binding: Similar to comb binding, but wire binding uses wire that is bent into tooth-like prongs.

CHAPTER TWO
Ink on Paper

The craft of printing is a combination of art and science that has been developed and refined over hundreds of years. Because printing is a complicated mechanical undertaking, numerous variables affect the printing process. Such factors include the type of press, the direction of the grain in the paper as it goes through the press, the kind of ink being used, and the prevailing temperature and humidity during the press run. Stand by a thundering press that is running at full speed, watch the paper race through the printing units, and consider the tons of machinery churning out your job. You'll wonder how it ever works at all—it's an impressive feat. A skilled pressman is an artisan who can work miracles, but there are still some physical limitations to what can be achieved with ink on paper. It's a long trip from what you see on your monitor to the printed paper that flies out of the press.

FUNDAMENTALS OF BLACK-AND-WHITE PRINTING

The *black* in black-and-white printing is black ink. The *white* is the paper. When you hear a print job referred to as a *two-color job*, that means that two colors of ink will be required to print it. That may seem obvious, but here's a true story: There once was a poor, befuddled, novice print salesman who priced a black-and-white job as a *two*-color job: *black* and *white*. Understandably, he didn't last long in the trade and is probably selling used cars now. You may have heard the limerick:

> There was a print salesman named Bob
> Who quoted a "two-color job."
> But what did he think?
> There's only black ink
> And the paper. What a doorknob!

Printing a single ink on paper is somewhat simpler than printing a four-color job, but the same rules apply. While a black-and-white photographic print or an image displayed on your monitor is made of a continuous range of thousands of shades of gray, a printing press doesn't print thousands of shades of ink. Instead, a single color of ink is printed in tiny dots called *halftone dots*, which simulate the shades of gray by varying the diameter of the dots (**Figure 2.1**). It's a convincing illusion because, unless your eyesight is *very* good, the individual dots are not apparent. An image printed by this method is commonly called a halftone.

Figure 2.1 A black-and-white image looks smooth on your monitor. But it's actually printed with thousands of tiny halftone dots (right).

Screen ruling (also called *screen frequency*) is the measure of halftone-dot frequency (**Figure 2.2**), usually expressed in *lines per inch* (lpi). Typical screen rulings range from 65–85 lpi (used in newspapers) to 133–150 lpi (often used in magazines and books). Some high-end magazines and art books are printed at even higher line screens—up to 200 or 300 lpi. The higher the screen ruling, the more faithfully images can be rendered, because finer detail can be maintained. So why wouldn't everything be printed at 300 lpi? Because printing conditions impose certain limitations. The coarse stock used for newspapers simply won't support fine line screens. Ink sinks into the absorbent stock and spreads, which is a phenomenon called *dot gain*. Try drawing small dots on a paper towel with a fine permanent marker, and you'll get an idea of the effect. The screen ruling is determined by the print service provider, based on the type of paper being used in the job.

Screen ruling:
Lines per inch (LPI)

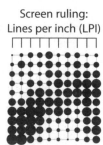

Figure 2.2 Screen ruling is measured in lines per inch (lpi).

To better camouflage the rows of dots, they are printed at time-honored angles. For example, the dots in a black and white halftone image are usually printed at a 45 degree angle (**Figure 2.3**). You don't have to create the halftone dots or figure out the appropriate angle for them. Those attributes are determined by the print service provider. The halftone dots don't come into being until the job is processed by the *raster image processor* (RIP).

Figure 2.3 Screen angle: 45°.

If screen angles and screen frequency are the print service provider's problem, why should designers and production artists even care about such issues? Because it's helpful to have realistic expectations of the printed outcome, and both screen angle and screen ruling have an impact on printed work. Highly patterned image content, such as woven fabric, can result in an unpleasant visual effect when the patterns imposed by image resolution, line screen, and screen angle combine to generate the final product.

Scanning at very high resolutions may help in some instances, but it will also produce large image files. Blurring the troublesome content may help, but is sometimes undesirable ("I thought this was a tweed jacket. It looks like *velveteen*."). Changing the screen ruling or screen angles may reduce moiré in one part of the image, but increase the effect in another area.

DPI, LPI, PPI, TLA

Because the acronyms for various forms of resolution are often used interchangeably, it's easy to get confused.

dpi (dots per inch) Used to describe the resolution of an imaging device such as a desktop printer, an imagesetter, or a platesetter. The typical desktop printer's resolution ranges from 600–1200 dpi, while the resolution of an imagesetter or platesetter is usually 2400 dpi or higher.

lpi (lines per inch) Describes the frequency of halftone dots, measured along a row of dots (see **Figure 2.2**).

ppi (pixels per inch) Describes image resolution. For most printing applications, image resolution should be 250–300 ppi. The rule of thumb is that image resolution should be 1.5 to 2 times the printing screen ruling, but the common convention is to save images at 300 ppi.

tla (three-letter acronym)

FUNDAMENTALS OF COLOR PRINTING

While a printed color image may appear to contain thousands of individual colors, it usually consists of just four inks, referred to as *process colors*: cyan, magenta, yellow, and black (CMYK). The process inks are transparent, so when they are combined on paper, they produce other colors (**Figure 2.4**). Thus, cyan plus yellow makes green. Cyan plus magenta make violet. Yellow and magenta make red, and yellow and magenta combined with cyan makes an unattractive muddy brown. That's still a fairly small box of crayons. How can you make all the colors you need?

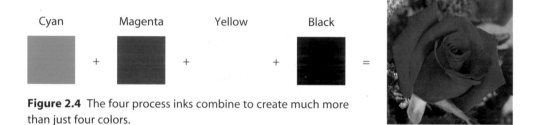

Figure 2.4 The four process inks combine to create much more than just four colors.

In traditional offset printing, the illusion of so many colors is the result of varying sizes of halftone dots, which allow different amounts of the four process colors to interact in a given area. Other printing methods use different ruses to fool the eye into seeing more than four colors, but the concept is the same: Use varying amounts of CMYK to approximate a wide range of colors (**Figure 2.5**).

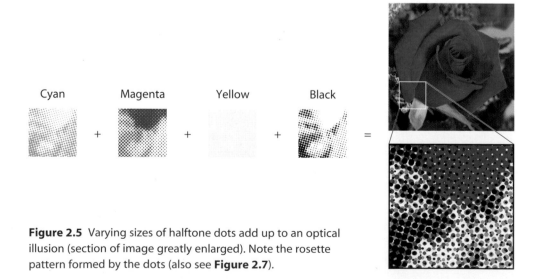

Figure 2.5 Varying sizes of halftone dots add up to an optical illusion (section of image greatly enlarged). Note the rosette pattern formed by the dots (also see **Figure 2.7**).

It's important to avoid unsightly patterns, called *moiré* (**Figure 2.6**). To see the moiré effect, put one piece of window screen on top of another, and then rotate one piece of screen (and be thinking of an excuse for cutting up the kitchen screen). It's a challenge to eliminate an obvious pattern. That's why there are time-honored intervals of 30 degrees between the angles of the inks to create the desired rosette pattern (**Figure 2.7**). Yellow, being the lightest color, falls at a 15-degree angle away from other colors.

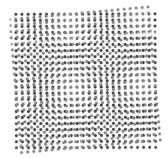

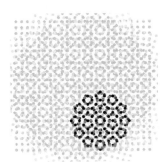

Figure 2.6 Incorrect intervals between screen angles can result in a distracting moiré. This can also be caused by a combination of screen angles and image content such as woven fabric.

Figure 2.7 Optimal screen angles add up to form a rosette pattern. Yes, it's a pattern, but it's usually not noticeable.

Screen angle preferences vary between print service providers and may sometimes be chosen to accommodate job content (**Table 2.1**).

Table 2.1 Screen angle combinations are meant to minimize patterns. Traditionally, they are 30-degrees apart (for example, 45 degrees and 75 degrees). The angle of each color is chosen to minimize interference with the other colors when all inks are combined in the printed piece.

Screen Angle Combinations

C 75°	M 15°	Y 0°	K 45°
C 15°	M 45°	Y 0°	K 75°
C 105°	M 75°	Y 90°	K 15°

Why CMYK Not CMYB?

It's easy to imagine that B might be mistaken for *blue* and thus confused with cyan. But where does the K come from? One theory holds that the K is from *key*, referring to black being printed first, so other colors can be aligned to its registration marks. Another notion is that the K is lifted from the end of the word black. Whatever the true origin of the mysterious K in the acronym, it's here to stay.

Solving the Moiré Problem: Stochastic Screening

One solution for moiré is to eliminate screen angles entirely by using a printing method without the conventional grid of regularly spaced dots. Stochastic screening, also called *FM* (frequency modulation) screening, uses a seemingly random distribution of very small dots (**Figures 2.8** and **2.9**). If you have an inkjet printer, you have a stochastic output device right on your desk. Look at an inkjet print through a magnifying loupe, and you'll see how the scattered arrangement of tiny dots creates an image.

Figure 2.8 Stochastic screening.   **Figure 2.9** Enlarged detail of stochastic screening.

After its first appearance in the 1980s, stochastic screening failed to gain much acceptance due to limitations in plating and proofing systems of the time. But it is experiencing a slight (and cautious) resurgence in the printing industry, thanks to the advent of computer-to-plate (CTP) printing, as well as increased implementation of digital (rather than film-based) proofing systems.

Stochastic screening offers some interesting advantages over conventional halftones:

- Reduced chance of moiré—since there are no angles, there is almost no chance for an interference pattern to be created.
- Ability to use lower resolution images.
- Ability to print images containing more than four ink colors without screen angle issues.
- Retention of smaller details in images.
- Reduced ink usage.
- Misregistration on-press is less obvious.
- Smoother rendition of skin tones.

But stochastic screening has not replaced the old-fashioned halftone dot. In fact, it's used only in a minority of printing. There are some challenges to using FM screening:

- The need for extreme cleanliness in plating: Dust may be bigger than a stochastic dot.
- Modifications to RIPs can be expensive ($15,000–$25,000).
- Slightly increased RIP processing time.
- On-press dot gain is higher than with conventional screening.
- The possibility of visible graininess in large highlight areas.

Consult your print service provider to determine whether stochastic screening is something they offer and whether it might be appropriate for your job. Be prepared for the possibility of increased job cost because of special handling.

Screen Values: Recipes for Color

When you need to describe a combination of cyan, magenta, yellow, and black that will print a particular color, such as the dusky blue in **Figure 2.10**, the recipe is written in this format: C75–M50–Y25–K0. Think of halftone dots as occupying a square grid, each in its own square of the grid. The numbers signify a percentage of the area of that square that will be filled. If the square is full, it's 100 percent. If half the area of the square is filled, it's 50 percent, and so on.

Figure 2.10 Dusty blue is (left to right) 75 percent cyan, 50 percent magenta, and 25 percent yellow.

Limitations of CMYK

While an extensive range of colors can be rendered with various combinations of cyan, magenta, yellow, and black ink, there's still a limit to what CMYK can create. The human eye can see a huge range of colors—larger than even the large gamut of a computer monitor. But the total gamut of the process inks is considerably smaller than the human eye can see, or even the range that the monitor can display. Consequently, images that are quite vibrant on your monitor may print disappointingly dull. It's not because your print service provider is incompetent. It's because of the limitations of the printing-ink spectrum. In **Figure 2.11**, the large, colorful toe is an approximation of the range of colors perceived by the human eye. The solid triangular line corresponds to the range of colors that can be displayed on an RGB (red-green-blue) computer monitor. The much smaller dotted shape indicates the approximate gamut of CMYK inks. Note that the CMYK blob, while rather constricted, does not fall entirely within the RGB gamut. Some colors—bright yellows and cyan shades—fall outside the range that can be displayed faithfully on a monitor. Even a finely tuned and color-managed monitor has its limitations.

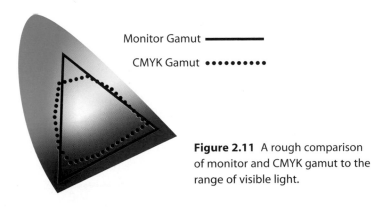

Monitor Gamut ———————

CMYK Gamut • • • • • • • • •

Figure 2.11 A rough comparison of monitor and CMYK gamut to the range of visible light.

This is not intended to plunge you into despondency over the limitations of the printing process. If your expectations are realistic, you can be prepared for the limitations of CMYK. And, equally importantly, you'll know when you need to step *outside* the world of cyan, magenta, yellow, and black to get what you want.

Spot Colors

A spot color is used when it is necessary to print colors that fall outside the range of CMYK inks. While it's obvious that inks such as fluorescent colors and metallics can't be faithfully imitated by process colors, there are also some rather common colors that fall outside the CMYK universe, such as bright orange and navy blue: that's why we need spot colors.

You're probably familiar with the Color Formula Guides from Pantone® Inc. The terms *spot color* and Pantone are often used interchangeably, although that's not strictly correct. The Pantone Matching System is a recipe book for printers, providing ink-mixing formulas for over 1,000 standard colors, many of which cannot be accurately rendered in process colors. While the name Pantone has become synonymous with spot color, there are other spot-color resources, such as the Toyo Color Finder from Toyo Ink, and the DIC guide from Dainippon Ink and Chemicals, Inc., (used predominantly in Japan). And there are Pantone swatchbooks that *don't* depict spot colors, such as the Pantone 4-Color Process Guide, which contains only colors created by combinations of cyan, magenta, yellow, and black, and the Color Bridge guides, which show spot colors next to the nearest CMYK equivalents.

Goe for It

Leafing through the blades in the Pantone Color Formula Guide fan book, you might notice that PMS 181 is not directly followed by PMS 182. In between is the range of intermediate colors numbered PMS 1765–1817. Over the years, this approach to "fill in the blanks" has resulted in a numbering system that's not intuitive.

The new Pantone Goe System arranges 2,058 spot colors in a chromatic scheme and assigns a new numbering convention. The three-part numbering system conveys the color's location within a color family. For example, the Goe-specified color Pantone 98-1-1C belongs to the ninety-eighth color family, is displayed on the first page of that color family, and is the first color on the page, printed on coated stock. There are GoeGuide books for coated and uncoated stock, and a GoeBridge coated book showing Goe spot colors and their closest CMYK equivalents.

The numbering system does not refer to the old familiar numbering scheme, but your years of memorizing the Pantone library are not for naught. You don't have to switch to the new Goe system; the two systems coexist peacefully.

CV, CVC, CVU, M, C, U: Many Acronyms, Just One Ink

It's time to dispel some urban myths about spot-color designations. The terms *Coated* and *Uncoated* refer to *paper*, not ink. Pantone 185C is Pantone 185U is Pantone 185M (apologies to Gertrude Stein). The C represents coated paper, U signifies uncoated stock, and M indicates matte paper, whose surface texture falls between that of coated and uncoated. These designations are primarily intended to keep you oriented as you view color on your computer monitor. For example, you may notice that a U version of a Pantone color looks a bit less saturated compared to the C version. It's just an attempt to mimic ink behavior on different stocks. In the olden days, CVU meant computer video uncoated, and CVC meant computer video coated. But recent DTP software has simplified this to U and C, and added the enlightened M for matte.

While adding a spot color to a four-color job will increase the cost of printing because of the need to purchase additional ink, create another plate, and increase press set-up time, it ensures that important colors will print as desired. If the printer has only a four-color press, the fifth color will necessitate a second run through the press, which will require more clean-up and further makeready time. But using a spot color can also eliminate problems caused by slight misregistration on press. Consider a job containing elements in a burgundy color consisting of a process-color build of C10-M100-Y35-K50. Even the most conscientious pressman can find it challenging to keep fine elements such as small type and narrow rules in register across a large press sheet. It can also be difficult to keep the balance of four inks consistent from one part of the paper to another or from one press sheet to another in a long, multipage job. Any variation will result in color shifts, which would be especially noticeable in facing pages. Replacing the process build with a single ink, such as Pantone 209, simplifies both registration and color-consistency issues. The increase in printing costs (as opposed to a four-color job) might be justified by the improved outcome.

Approximating Spot Colors with Process

It's a widespread practice to pick colors from a swatchbook such as the Pantone Color Formula Guide, even for jobs that are intended to print as process. Just because everyone does it doesn't mean it's right. (Sorry; that sounds like your mother.)

The problem with this approach (as with so many things your mother warned you about), is that it can lead to disappointment. Remember that the purpose of spot colors is to render colors that fall outside the range of CMYK. Understandably, process approximations of spot colors are often unsatisfactory.

For example, a CMYK translation of a dark blue such as Pantone 286 can become a purplish blue. It's unfortunate, but this is as close as a combination of cyan, magenta, yellow, and black can get to the navy blue of the official Brand X logo. As long as you know to expect this color approximation, you aren't shocked by the printed piece (**Figure 2.12**). But the president of Brand X will certainly be disappointed.

Figure 2.12 The Brand X logo is supposed to print in Pantone 286, a navy blue. But approximating that color with CMYK results in an unsightly purple. If you have a Pantone swatch book, compare the real Pantone 286 swatch with the CMYK version at left.

In the interest of realism on process jobs, consider selecting colors from a purely CMYK-based swatchbook instead, such as the TRUMATCH Colorfinder or one of the Pantone process guides. If you want a single-source swatchbook showing Pantone spot-color formulas next to their closest process equivalents, the Pantone Color Bridge™ or the new GoeBridge™ both provide helpful, side-by-side swatches.

PRESS ISSUES

Although it's a highly developed endeavor, the application of ink to paper on a printing press is still a high-speed, physical process. As such, it's subject to the vagaries of temperature, humidity, and craftsmanship. Factor in cantankerous machinery, and it's amazing anything ever gets printed. While you can't run the press, you can anticipate some common problems and build your files to facilitate printing.

Registration

Since printing inks are applied to paper in succession, not simultaneously, accurate alignment of the printed inks (referred to as *registration*) is crucial. While a small amount of misregistration can be easily camouflaged within the natural variation of colors in images, it can be a glaring problem in some special cases. This is most apparent when dissimilar color areas meet with no ink in common. In **Figure 2.13**, the reversed letters of the two-color logo fall apart if it's printed badly out of register. Is it unreasonable to expect the pressman to maintain tight register? Of course not. But keeping such art in very tight register in two dimensions over a large press sheet can be challenging. Even under the best-controlled press conditions, paper is subject to small amounts of stretching due to the physical stress of traveling through the press. Admittedly, the illustration shows a press sheet that is flagrantly out of register, which indicates two important facts: Press conditions are awful, and you need to start looking for a new printing company. However, even under ideal conditions, such art may suffer at least very small shifts, and you should be emotionally prepared. How can you compensate? If you're allowed to do so, print such artwork in shades of a single color. Then, registration isn't an issue (**Figure 2.14**).

Figure 2.13 Even slight misregister in a two-color logo can be fairly ugly. (Here, bad register is exaggerated for dramatic effect.)

Figure 2.14 One solution to registration challenges: Print the logo in a single color.

If you're designing a logo or other art element, you should keep this potential issue in mind. If possible, design to minimize the heartbreak of misregistration by ensuring that color areas share at least one common ink; or, better yet, print in a single ink.

Trapping

As you saw in the Brand X logo, if there is misregistration on-press, the result can be unsightly gaps between color areas that don't share a common ink (**Figure 2.15**).

The remedy for this problem is to use *trapping,* which involves creating a rim of common color between the dissimilar color areas. In **Figure 2.16**, the C100-M100 trap is greatly exaggerated for illustrative purposes. In practice, trap thickness is usually around 0.003 of an inch and fairly unobtrusive. Trap thickness may vary depending on prevailing press conditions and the conventions of the print service provider.

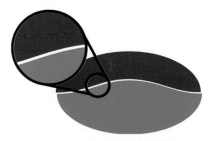

M100

C100

Figure 2.15 Misregistration can cause gaps between color areas that don't have an ink in common.

Figure 2.16 Trapping between two dissimilar colors (here, greatly enlarged).

Here's some great news: *It's not your problem.* Trapping is an arcane pursuit that's best left to the print service provider, who uses specialized trapping software. Many trapping circumstances can be complex to resolve, such as those involving metallic inks or neighboring gradients. And some trapping decisions depend on the order in which inks will be printed. You kids don't know how good you have it; we old folks had to hand-carve traps, in the snow, barefoot.

In trapping, the darker color defines the edge of objects being trapped to each other, and that determines which objects *spread* (expand), which objects *choke* (contract), and which objects remain *sharp* (unchanged). In **Figure 2.17**, you can see that different approaches to trapping are required for different circumstances. The trap line consists of a combination of the adjacent colors, and it is usually not as obvious as it is in the illustration. There's some exaggeration in Figure 2.17, to call attention to the trap itself. However, sometimes it is desirable to subdue the visible trap line, especially when lighter colors combine to create a heavy trap line. In version D, the color in the trap area is reduced from C100-M60 to C50-M30 to make it less noticeable. In version E, trapping is unnecessary because the objects have colors in common, so there's unlikely to be an unsightly gap in printing.

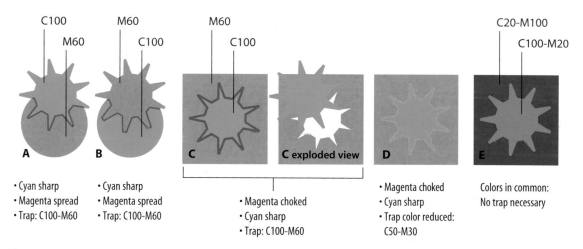

Figure 2.17 Depending on the color, a shape may be *spread* (expanded), *choked* (shrunk inward), or left *sharp* (neither spread nor choked). The darkest color defines the edge, so lighter colors are spread into darker colors.

Even though trapping is the responsibility of the print service provider, you should keep it in mind as you design. If you feel that trap lines will mar the appearance of your artwork, consider creating artwork with common colors, so that trapping is unnecessary. Also, as you examine proofs, you're usually looking for large errors such as missing elements or incorrect color. But, as you can see, it behooves you to also be mindful of the little things such as traps.

Large Ink Coverage Areas

Moving from tiny traps to the opposite end of the size spectrum, you'll discover that large color areas present some problems as well. (You're probably starting to wonder, "Is there *anything* that's easy to print?") Most ink is translucent, not opaque, and its thickness when applied to paper is measured in ten-thousandths of an inch. Consequently, covering a large area with a single spot-color ink can be challenging. Think of painting a wall. It often takes two coats to achieve smooth color coverage. Similarly, one solution is to apply two passes of the ink (called a double hit). But this can increase the cost of the job because it involves an additional unit on the press, as well as extra ink. Depending on the ink color, the first instance of the color might be a screen tint (say, 50 percent) rather than a solid, to avoid an overly heavy final appearance.

If the job already uses a four-color process, a less expensive alternative is to create a process equivalent of the screened underlay described in the previous paragraph, then run a single pass of the spot color on top of it.

Before you take the law into your own hands and start trying to solve these problems on your own, have a conversation with your print service provider about the issues involved. Don't over-engineer the job in an effort to help. Either seek guidance from the print service provider's prepress department, or leave it to the professionals to handle your job appropriately for their printing conditions. While you may incur some additional cost, these special treatments pay off in a better-looking, more professional finished piece.

Rich Black

You don't have to be running spot colors to have large color areas requiring special treatment. Solid black areas bigger than, say, one square inch, usually need to be beefed up or they will appear anemic. The solution is referred to as *rich black*, but the definition of a rich black varies by print service provider. In some cases, just adding a bit of cyan (40 to 60 percent) is considered sufficient, although this can result in a cool black with a bluish tinge. To avoid a color cast to the rich black area, many print service providers add a neutral balance of the three other process colors. This author was raised to believe that C60-M40-Y40-K100 constituted rich black, but your mileage may vary. And your print service provider may fervently disagree with that recipe; such things vary from shop to shop. As always, consult your print service provider for guidance.

If artwork or type knocks out of a rich black area (also called reversing out), it will require special handling to keep edges sharp and avoid color fringes (**Figure 2.18**). Once again, press misregistration is the culprit.

Figure 2.18 Misregistration in a four-color rich black can be ugly. This calls for special handling.

Remember that, in trapping, the darkest color defines the edge. The case of rich blacks might be considered a sort of reverse trap. You want only *one* color to define the edge of the type or other white artwork—the black ink. To accomplish this feat, it's necessary to pull back the other colors so that if there is any misregistration, they don't peek out and create a pink, blue, or yellow halo at the edge of the reversed type.

As you can see in **Figure 2.19**, the white type is knocked out of all four plates of a rich black area. Since the black plate defines the edge of the type, its knockout is sharp (not choked or spread). But the knocked-out type is pulled back in the cyan, magenta, and yellow (hence the bloated appearance). This same approach is used for type or art reversing out of a double-hit spot color.

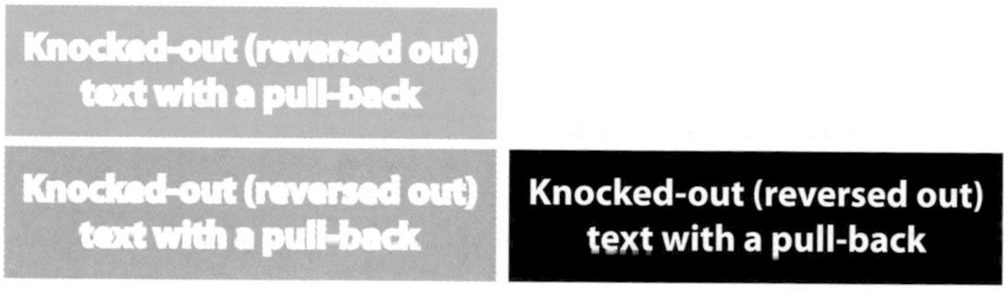

Knocked-out (reversed out) text with a pull-back

Knocked-out (reversed out) text with a pull-back

Knocked-out (reversed out) text with a pull-back

Figure 2.19 Special treatment for text reversed out (knocked out) of a four-color black.

Here comes the familiar, comforting reminder: Setting up this pull-back treatment is the print service provider's responsibility. But it's good for you to be aware of these complexities as you design. All this trapping, knocking out, spreading, and choking (sounds kind of violent, doesn't it?) are part of the daily grind for the print service provider, but you can design in anticipation of these issues. Be mindful of your print service provider's specifications for minimum type size that can be safely reversed out of a multicolor build such as a rich black; even with pull-backs, tiny reversed type can be a challenge to print (and read).

Problem Inks

Inks are a mysterious amalgam of pigment, carriers, solvents, waxes, and extenders. Ink problems can be caused by multiple issues, including inadequate drying time, absorbent stocks, and poor adhesion. But some problems arise from the pigments themselves. Because of its common use and stubborn personality, perhaps the best-known is Reflex

Blue, which is a navy blue. Reflex Blue is notorious for scuffing, smearing, oxidizing, and slow drying times. If you use Reflex Blue in your job, be prepared to tack on an extra day or so for additional post-press drying time. Additives can speed up the drying process. Depending on how heavily the color is used in your job, you can also expect slight surcharges for protective coatings (discussed later in this chapter). An aqueous coating, applied on-press, is a common solution. Clear aqueous coatings usually cover the entire printed area, preventing scuffing without changing the color of the piece.

While Reflex Blue is used in formulating many of the dark blue Pantone colors, it's most troublesome by itself. It may also contribute somewhat to slower drying times and scuffing to some extent in inks mixed with it, but not as aggressively as when used alone. Drying agents can be added to Reflex Blue ink, and aqueous coatings can reduce oxidizing and scuffing.

Specialty Inks

Metallic and fluorescent inks can add visual interest to a printed piece. Metallic inks, while somewhat expensive, are still less costly than using *foil stamping* (a special finishing process involving heat, pressure, and thin sheets of metallic foil. See Chapter Three, "Binding and Finishing," for more information on foil stamping). The problems they pose are once again due to key pigments. Actual aluminum or bronze (zinc/copper) powder provides the basic metallic appearance, while additional pigments introduce other tinges. Metallic inks as accents are not too troublesome but these inks can mottle over large areas. Unlike most inks, metallic inks are almost opaque, which affects trapping and the order in which the ink is printed. Usually, metallic inks are printed first because of their tendency to adhere poorly to previous inks. While metallic ink will never be as shiny as foil stamping, it's most convincing on coated stock and may almost completely lose its metallic appearance on very absorbent uncoated stock. Varnishing metallic ink will not make it shinier (in fact, even gloss varnish will slightly diminish the metallic appearance), although it will subdue metallic ink's tendency to scuff and flake. If you're creating stationery, be very cautious about using metallic inks. The stress of being passed through a laser or inkjet printer can cause metallic flakes to dislodge and find new homes deep inside the printer.

Because of the metallic content, the inks are also subject to oxidation (especially the bronzes). While varnishing (discussed on the next page) may slow down the process, be prepared for some dulling over time. Also be prepared to consider somewhat extended drying times as part of your job timeline. Your printer will tell you what to expect.

Fluorescent inks can add a vibrant punch, but their pigments have a limited life span, especially if exposed to sunlight for extended periods. Printing a double hit of the ink can enhance its vibrancy, since fluorescent inks tend to be transparent. They are also sensitive to heat, so such inks are not the best choice for stationery that will be run through a laser printer or copier because of the heat involved in fusing.

Custom Mixed Inks

If you just can't find a Pantone, Toyo, or DIC ink to match the color you want, your print service provider can custom-mix an ink that's just right for your job. Expect to pay more for this service since it involves extra labor and may consume extra ink (mixed as insurance for the print service provider). If you anticipate reprinting the job at a later date, tell the print service provider up front so they can retain the recipe for future use. It's not practical to "mix enough for later." Unlike wine, ink does not improve with age.

Coatings and Varnishes

Coatings are applied for two reasons: for special visual effects or to protect ink from scuffing or rubbing off. There are three general categories of coatings in print:

- **Aqueous** coatings are water-based coatings. They're applied on-press, and cover the press sheet uniformly with gloss, matte, satin, or dull finishes. They behave best on coated or matte stocks, since the inherent coating on such stocks provides an even surface and consistent absorption. Aqueous coatings can be applied to uncoated stock, but there is the risk of mottling due to the nonuniform surface of uncoated stock. Aqueous coatings actually provide better scuffing protection than varnishes.

- **Ultraviolet** (UV) coatings are cured by UV light for quick drying. Available in matte, dull, satin, and gloss, they can be applied inline on a specially equipped press and can also be applied by silkscreen (which costs more because it's applied by separate equipment after the paper has been printed, but can achieve higher gloss).

- **Varnishes** are also applied on-press (either as the last ink or in a second pass through the press), and are also available in the standard assortment of gloss, dull, satin, and matte. Varnishes are usually applied overall, but special effects can be obtained by using spot varnishes to highlight artwork. Spot-gloss varnishes, for example, can highlight artwork to make it stand out from the page, especially on matte stock. Applying a spot-gloss varnish on a square-cut image is fairly painless, but there's a bit more work involved in spot varnishing silhouetted artwork (**Figure 2.20**). The separate plate used for a spot varnish is handled like a spot color.

Figure 2.20 Adding a spot varnish can accentuate part of an image, but creating the varnish plate requires some work (you'll have to imagine that the palm tree is *very* shiny).

Note that since varnishes and aqueous/UV coatings are sealants, it's necessary to apply the varnish or other coating as the last pass. Pieces requiring gluing (such as pocket folders or packaging) require spot application of such coatings, since gluing and folding take place after varnish or other coatings are applied. Spot application applies the varnish much like an ink, isolating it to certain areas (rather than applying it as an overall coat), so that glued areas are free of ink and varnish. This allows the glue to adhere correctly.

DIGITAL PRINTING

In their earliest iterations, digital printing devices were not much more than glorified laser printers. The toner-based engines were beefed up to print faster and bigger, but they were still prone to have all the characteristics of laser printers. Color consistency between impressions was quite problematic, innocent environmental influences such as humidity were mortal enemies of registration, and halftone reproduction on high-speed, black-and-white machines was, to be charitable, miserable. While digital printing has always offered advantages such as relatively affordable short runs and the ability to print variable data, it was initially deemed appropriate only for basic direct mail or text-only pieces because of the superior quality of offset printing. But all of that has changed.

Digital Printing Advantages

The gap between digital and conventional offset is closing, and the premium digital print offerings from vendors such as Xeikon, Kodak, Xerox, and HP Indigo are beginning to rival the appearance of offset printing while still offering the additional appeal of customization and short runs.

Short Runs

Without the need to image and mount plates, toner-based digital printing offers some advantages here. The minimum run for a digital job can be 200 or less, rather than 10,000. This can lower the cost threshold for color printing for many jobs.

Variable Data

You've received those compelling personal letters: "Dear [Your Name Here]." Such customization is the most basic form of *variable data publishing* (VDP). Since each impression of a document on a toner-based digital press can be different, even images can be customized for very targeted direct-mail pieces. Preparing such a piece requires careful planning, and the VDP software used by the print service provider is rather expensive. However, you may find the added expense and complexity worthwhile, since it's been shown that customized direct mail pieces elicit much higher response than generic mailings. If you have used the mail-merge features available in a word processing program, or the Data Merge features offered in InDesign, you have done basic variable data publishing. The complexities of setting up VDP work are outside the scope of this book.

Digital Printing Issues

Although offset printing benefits from at least 100 years of refinement, digital printing is a relatively recent undertaking. Digital printing solves some problems, such as the need for short runs. But it introduces new challenges, such as the behavior of toner on paper and paper size limitations. Large areas of uniform color can sometimes be problematic on toner-based systems. For example, a brochure cover that is printed with a full-bleed build of C100-Y80 will look mottled compared to the same piece printed on a conventional offset press. For now, it's just one of those things that you have to anticipate. Design around the limitation by using a collage of images or smaller areas of color in which any mottling will not be glaringly apparent (**Figure 2.21**).

Figure 2.21 A screen build that covers large areas uniformly on a conventional offset press (left) may appear mottled when printed on a toner-based digital press (right).

However, you may find it surprising that rich blacks are not necessary on most toner-based presses. Not only is the dense black nature of toner sufficient for complete coverage, adding three other colors can interfere with the toner's adhesion to paper, and will actually make things worse.

Most toner-based printing lacks the inherent shine we're accustomed to seeing in printed pieces, even on coated stock. This is due to the nature of the toners themselves. The HP Indigo presses use a slurry of toner in a carrier (called HP ElectroInk), so their output often more closely resembles traditional offset printing. But all of the toner-based output can be coated, either via extra imaging units, or through coating stations attached to the press. Stand-alone coating equipment can also be used, but this requires that the printed pieces be moved to a separate coating machine and fed through it.

There are other differences between digital, toner-based printing and conventional offset printing. For example, most digital printing processes do not require trapping since toner is usually placed onto a carrier, and all colors are transferred to the paper in one impression, which often eliminates misregistration. Many digital presses use stochastic screening rather than conventional halftone dots and angles. These differences contribute to digital printing being a viable alternative to offset.

Registration

On most toner-based digital presses, toner for all four process colors is accumulated on a carrier that is held by the strange miracle of electrostatic force, then deposited as a single transfer to the paper. As a result, registration is somewhat easier to maintain than on offset presses, which apply each color separately from individual inking units. Sophisticated internal monitoring in these modern presses also ensures consistency. These devices demand tight environmental controls. Slight changes in humidity and temperature can play havoc with output, so toner-based digital presses are usually sequestered in specially constructed rooms that are engineered to maintain a constant environment.

Spot Colors on Toner-Based Digital Presses

Currently, spot-color offerings are limited on toner-based digital presses. Although HP Indigo and Xeikon presses do offer additional units for available spot colors (which include several metallics and fluorescents), not every Pantone color is available for these presses. However, this limitation is not as dire as it sounds. Even though the primary toner colors are called cyan, magenta, yellow, and black on these devices, the pigments are not identical to those used in offset process colors. In some ways, this is actually *good* news. The toners are often more vibrant than standard process inks, so they can simulate a wider range of

Pantone colors without resorting to actual spot colors. At this writing, Pantone provides digital process chip books certified for the HP Indigo and Xerox digital presses.

Paper Requirements and Limitations

Most digital presses are sheet-fed and have much smaller mouths than their offset brethren, which generally limits their output to approximately tabloid sizes. Roll-fed devices such as the Xeikon presses, however, cut the paper only *after* printing. And while the imaging width is about 19 inches, the total length of a piece can be banner-sized.

While there is a wide range of paper certified for toner-based digital presses, stock choice isn't unlimited. Consult your print service provider for samples of supported stock before you get your heart set on a particular paper that is subsequently not deemed appropriate. The complicated paper paths in such devices preclude the use of extremely thin (or extremely heavy) stock. And the high heat of fusing the toner to the substrate can cause curling or waving. In the interior of a digitally printed piece, this may not be so noticeable, but covers may require the extra step of lamination to keep them from curling.

Cracking and Flaking

Toner is fused to the surface of paper rather than being partially absorbed as conventional offset ink is. Consequently, it's sitting on top of the paper like a coat of inflexible paint and is prone to cracking during any folding or creasing processes. Consider this as you design for toner-based digital output, and avoid large instances of crossover art if possible. A rule here and there or the occasional line of headline text shouldn't be a problem. But the more toner encrusting the paper along the fold, the uglier the outcome can be.

Resolution and Screen Ruling

For conventional offset presses, *platesetters* are often used to digitally image plates. Data-driven lasers expose the photosensitive surface of a plate, which is then developed and mounted on a press. *Imagesetters* (which have largely given way to platesetters) are used to expose film, which is then used to create an image on a printing plate (see Chapter One, "Life Cycle of a Print Job," for more information on imagesetters and platesetters). Whereas imagesetters and platesetters achieve resolution of 2400–3600 dpi, most toner-based electrostatic systems fall between 600–1200 dpi. Consequently, while these systems are capable of fairly high line screens (150–200 lpi and higher, depending on the vendor), be cautious about using very fine line weights or type that has extremely fine serifs. It's a good idea to ask your print service provider to provide specifications so you know the limitations of their printing process before you go too far in your design.

YOUR MONITOR IS NOT MADE OF PAPER

Seems hardly worth mentioning: Your monitor uses transmitted light to display a semblance of your design piece, whereas the final printed job consists of ink on physical paper. When you think of things in those terms, you shouldn't be surprised that the two realities don't look the same. Yet, it's easy to forget the fundamental fact that your monitor is not displaying ink on paper, and it can be tempting to make color decisions based on what you view onscreen. Wouldn't it be great if your monitor could more closely match the printed outcome of your job? Your monitor will never be identical to the printed piece, but it is possible to control your software and your monitor for a much closer match.

A Quick Overview of Color Management

It's a challenge to modify your monitor's display to simulate ink on paper. It involves color management, which is the science of profiling one device (such as a monitor) to match another device (such as a press). Profiling is the process of using specialized (and often expensive) equipment to evaluate devices such as scanners, monitors, proofing systems, and presses to determine the color characteristics of each device. Once these characteristics are known, the information can be used by software such as Adobe Photoshop to display an image onscreen in a way that more realistically represents how the image will appear when it is printed. Implementing color management is not cheap, it's not easy, and it's not for the faint of heart. Using color management gets easier as more software incorporates support for it, but it's best left to dedicated color-management consultants to set up a color-managed workflow. Even then, the setup must subsequently be maintained with conscientious calibration of monitors and printers in order to have optimal results.

An in-depth exploration of color management is outside the scope of this book. For an excellent—and very readable—resource on color management, buy a copy of *Real World Color Management, 2nd Edition* by Bruce Fraser, Chris Murphy, and Fred Bunting (Peachpit Press, 2004), and take it to the beach with you.

Feeling a bit intimidated by the concepts of color management? Don't feel bad—that's normal and appropriate. But here's some good news: Even if you fall short of a fully color-managed workflow, you can still benefit by implementing some simple procedures in the interest of consistency between the color on your monitor and the appearance of ink on paper.

Control Your Environment

- **Minimize lighting interference.** Subdue the ambient light in your work space, and avoid glare on your monitor screen. Beware of incidental light reflected from brightly colored painted surfaces. Strive for consistency despite the changing light of day, and if you're like most of us, half the night. The ideal solution is to block windows, have a neutral gray room, and install lights that meet the color temperature of sunlight. (More about lighting in a bit.)

- **Subdue that psychedelic monitor background.** Vivid surrounding colors complicate color judgments when viewing images. And consider the after-effects of constantly staring at a brightly colored desktop. Your eyes' color receptors grow weary, which affects what you view afterward. For example, stare at a bright green square, then shift to a white piece of paper. You'll see a pinkish cast to the paper. So, dull as it may seem, an old-fashioned gray desktop is your best bet. If that makes you cringe, compromise by using a grayscale image, and tell your friends you're going through an Ansel Adams phase.

- **Calibrate and profile your monitor.** For best results, consider using a colorimeter such as the X-Rite i1 Display 2 or ColorMunki. These solutions utilize specialized measuring devices and companion software to build custom color profiles for your monitor.

  However, if you're not ready to invest in such hardware, you can at least use the basics: The Adobe Gamma utility installed with Adobe Photoshop on Windows® (Start > Control Panel > Adobe Gamma) or the built-in Macintosh® color utility (System Preferences > Displays) (**Figure 2.22**). Whichever approach you choose, you should allow your monitor to warm up for at least 30 minutes, and set it to display at least "thousands of colors." It's best if your monitor is set to 24-bit color ("millions of colors"). Each utility guides you through appropriate setup, including which settings to use for the contrast and brightness of your monitor.

  Calibration is not a one-time endeavor. Monitors—whether they are flat-screen LCDs or conventional CRTs—drift over time. Consequently, CRTs should be calibrated every 80–120 hours of use, and LCDs should be calibrated approximately every 200–250 hours. Even so, monitors have a finite life and eventually must be replaced when they can no longer be kept within reasonable values.

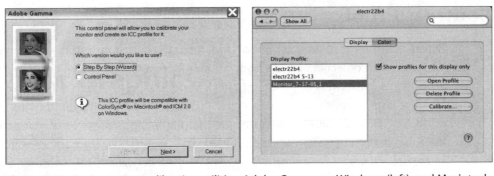

Figure 2.22 Basic monitor-calibration utilities: Adobe Gamma on Windows (left), and Macintosh OS X Displays utility (right).

- **Treat your desktop printer kindly.** Despite the temptation of buying discount paper and inks, you'll find that you get the most predictable printing results by using recommended brand-name paper and ink cartridges. Yes, it's true that printers are cheap because the intention is to get you hooked on ink cartridges. But printer manufacturers put considerable research into creating colorants and substrates that work well together. What you save on off-brand refills and cheap paper will be offset by frustration when your output looks lousy.

- **Invoke printer profiles.** Even if you can't afford custom profiles for your devices, use the aforementioned monitor profiles and the canned printer profiles that are added when you install a printer, so that at least you'll be in the ballpark. Current versions of most graphics software offer color-management controls that make it fairly easy to plug in canned printer profiles when you print.

Realistic Expectations

If your expensive monitor is freshly calibrated, you've profiled all of your printers, painted your room a neutral gray, and you wear nothing but nonreflective black clothing…well, you're very stylish. But even the best monitor and most expensive desktop printer are, at best, an approximation of what will happen when your job goes to press. It's important to have a realistic idea of how your job will look, and everything you can do to improve its appearance on your monitor and your in-house output is beneficial. You don't want any surprises late in the game.

Consequently, your *final* judgment on job appearance should be based on *contract proofs* created by your print service provider.

Contract Proofs

Before a commercial print service provider cranks up a multimillion-dollar press for your job, *proofs* will be generated to check color and content. Internally, print service providers may use various kinds of proofs to check various aspects of a job. For example, desktop inkjet or laser output is used to check for problem fonts or mechanical issues, large-format prints are used to check imposed pages, and film-based proofs or digital proofs are used for color matching. Whereas in the olden days, print service providers generated film to create proofs, we've moved into the age of *computer-to-plate* (CTP) printing, so film output is increasingly rare. But don't feel that a digital proof is somehow less official than a film-based proof. If digital proofs are based on the same data from the *raster image processor* (RIP) that creates plates, they should be reliable for content. However, not all digital proofs show halftones, so you may be unable to check for problems such as moiré. And it may not be possible to generate a digital proof on all paper stocks.

A signed contract proof carries obligations (hence the name *contract*). The designer's signature says "this proof accurately reflects my intended design. Match this on press, and I'll be happy." And the print service provider's responsibility is to match the color and mechanical content of the contract proof onpress.

In addition to portraying the mechanics of the piece, such as type flow, image crop, and page content, contract proofs also represent final color onpress. If you're going to be viewing proofs in your own office or a client's office, it's important that the viewing conditions be as close as possible to those used by the print service provider. This avoids a phenomenon known as metamerism, wherein two colors may appear to match under one light source but don't match under different lighting conditions. For example, a sample paint chip and a piece of fabric might appear very close in color under a store's commercial lighting, but look very different in your living room. There are companies such as X-Rite that specialize in color-viewing solutions, and your printer's viewing booth will give you an idea of industry standards. There are also suppliers who sell lighting (although not specific to the graphic arts industry) that falls in the desired 5000–6500 K color temperature range. For more information on viewing conditions and color temperature, see Chapter One, "Life Cycle of a Print Job."

If the printed piece doesn't match the proof you signed, you have a legitimate gripe with the print service provider. If you miss something important on the proof, but the print service provider faithfully matches it, you're at fault. So it behooves you to very carefully inspect a contract proof before signing off on it.

CHAPTER THREE
Binding and Finishing

Getting ink on paper isn't the end of the story. The printed piece must be trimmed to its final size and subjected to any required folding and gluing. Build it the wrong size in the beginning, and you'll suffer the slings and arrows of irritated prepress operators who have to perform surgery on your file. Layout repairs cost money and time. The mechanical alterations required to mend incorrect page size or configuration can be complex (and expensive). Even if your artwork is perfect, you must keep in mind that trimming, folding, binding, and fancy finishing treatments such as embossing are all physical processes. Environmental influences such as temperature and humidity, coupled with the stresses of moving paper through printing presses, folding equipment, and trimming devices, can result in errors in the final piece. As a designer, you can't control those physical processes. But if you take those possibilities into account as you prepare artwork and create page layouts, you may be able to minimize adverse effects.

ONE SIZE DOES NOT FIT ALL

Even if you don't sew, you can nonetheless anticipate the unfortunate results of using a defective pattern. The old adage "measure twice, cut once" applies to any manufacturing process, whether it's sewing or printing (**Figure 3.1**).

Figure 3.1 Careful planning when creating a pattern can mean the difference between being stylish (left) and facing public humiliation (right).

Building your files without considering the finishing processes (like trimming and binding) can cost you money and delay your job. Consequently, the more you know about folding, trimming, binding, and imposition, the better prepared you'll be to correctly build files. Let's start with two dimensions—width and height—and work our way up to the challenge of designing in three dimensions. Think of it as one of those fun, spatial reasoning games that you loved as a child. (Or maybe you didn't. In that case, you'll hate this part of the book.) And all games have rules….

Rule Number One: Build to the Correct Trim Size

If you're creating an odd-sized piece—say, a 5-by-4 inch invitation—don't put it all alone in the middle of a letter-sized page. Create a custom page size that matches the final trim size of your piece. In Adobe InDesign, specify the trim size as you begin the document, along with bleed, if necessary (**Figure 3.2**).

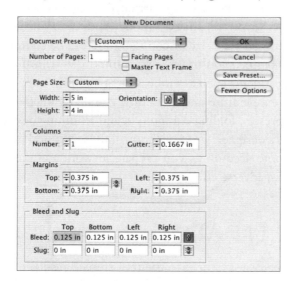

Figure 3.2 To specify a custom page size, enter the correct values in the Width and Height fields as you create a new file in InDesign. Don't forget to specify a bleed setting.

Slang Terms

There's a lot of colorful language in printing, and much of it has to do with the arts of trimming, folding, and binding: creep, dummy, bleed, guillotine, jogging, nipping, perfect, shingle, twist, punch, bust… (I believe some of these were also dance crazes in the 1960s).

If you're using Adobe Illustrator, the Artboard dimensions equal the trim size. For more information on the way Illustrator handles Artboards, see Chapter Ten, "Illustrator CS4 Production Tips."

Why is this important? Take a simple business card as an example. The print service provider doesn't feed little individual 3.5–by–2 inch pieces of paper through a press to create cards one at a time. Nor does your business card float alone in the middle of a press sheet as in **Figure 3.3**. Instead, multiple copies of the card are printed simultaneously—imposed—for a press sheet, which is subsequently trimmed to final size to yield the individual cards. That's why it's important to supply artwork of the correct size (**Figure 3.4**).

Bob Smith
SmithcoMatic Industries, Inc.
1411 Smithfield Road, #345
Smithfield, VA 23431
1-555-555-5432
S

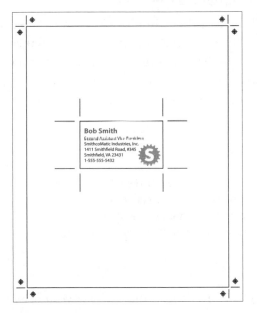

Figure 3.3 Incorrect: A single business card on an oversized page.

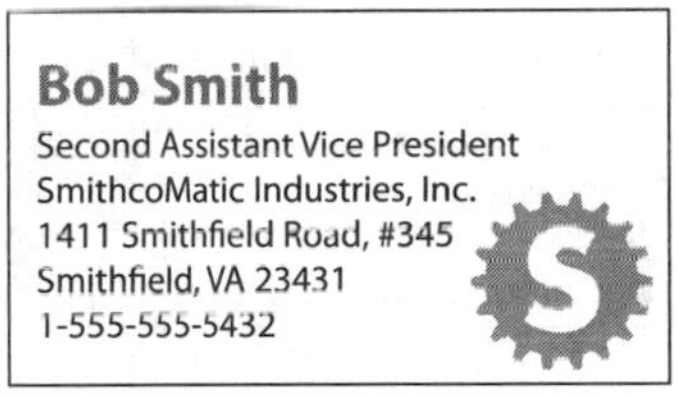

Bob Smith
Second Assistant Vice President
SmithcoMatic Industries, Inc.
1411 Smithfield Road, #345
Smithfield, VA 23431
1-555-555-5432
S

Figure 3.4 Correct: A single business card built to correct size: 3.5 by 2 inches.

If you supply business card art as a lonely card on a letter-sized page, a prepress operator will have to copy the card art into a new page of the correct size (or change the dimensions of the existing file) so it's correct for everything down the line. In addition to requiring an extra, time-consuming step, this also introduces the possibility of error—not copying some little detail or moving something in the process. **Figure 3.13**, later in this chapter, shows one method of imposing business cards. The imposition used by your print service provider might be different, depending on their press and the size of paper used.

Rule Number Two: Provide Bleed

Trimming is the finishing process that chops the printed piece to the final size. Since this is a mechanical process, it helps to have some margin for error in both the printing and trimming processes. Consequently, any time there is artwork intended to extend to the edge of the page, it's necessary to provide bleed—extra image beyond the edge of the true page size. Commonly, bleed extends one-eighth of an inch (.125 inch or 9 points) beyond the trim line, but your print service provider may request a different bleed value, especially on larger pieces such as posters or pocket folders. As with all issues, it behooves you to check the print service provider's specifications as you begin the job.

However, Rule Number Two does not invalidate Rule Number One, which stipulates that you should build to the correct trim size. Start with the correct trim size, and then add the extra image (or flat color) beyond the trim limits by dragging the edges of the appropriate frames. In InDesign or Illustrator, it's a simple matter to pull on the handles of image and tint frames to extend them beyond the page edges for sufficient bleed (**Figure 3.5**).

Figure 3.5 Extending artwork to provide bleed. The document is built to the correct final trim size, and the bleed extends beyond the trim.

In Illustrator, the visible Artboard edge is equivalent to the trim for your artwork. You can specify a bleed zone outside the Artboard and invoke that bleed zone when you print the file or save it as a PDF. Any artwork extending beyond the bleed zone is retained if the file is saved as an EPS (Encapsulated PostScript). Artwork is visually cropped at the bleed edge if the file is saved as a native Illustrator (.AI) file, however. This behavior can be a bit confusing when you're trying to make sure that you're building your artwork to the correct size with appropriate bleed. For specific information about handling this issue, see Chapter Ten, "Illustrator CS4 Production Tips."

Rule Number Three: Stay Away from the Edge

You may have your heart set on that adorable doggie paw-print border, but placing it too close to the edge or fold may result in disappointing results if there's any error in printing, folding, or binding. The closer your artwork is to the trim edge, the smaller the margin (literally) for error, and the more obvious any inaccuracy will be. What to do?

Don't place artwork perilously close to the edges (both internal and external). But, if you just must, make the margin as wide as possible to camouflage any problems. A small trimming error is less obvious against a larger total margin (**Figure 3.6**). Which leads us to Rule Number Four.

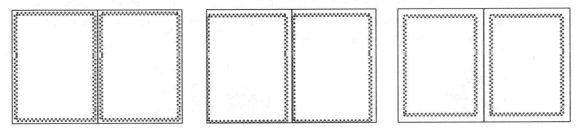

Figure 3.6 In an ideal world, your cute little paw-print border will print and trim perfectly. But a slight misalignment during printing, combined with binding and trimming errors, can produce disappointing results (middle). The effect is exaggerated for dramatic effect, but you get the idea. A larger margin (right) makes it easier to camouflage a binding error.

Rule Number Four: Follow the Print Specifications

Your print service provider should provide folding and trimming specifications to guide you as you create your work, including such information as:

- Minimum distance from edges and folds for artwork
- Minimum amount of bleed (usually $1/8$ of an inch)
- Suggested sizes for panels in folded pieces

FOLDING: HIGH-SPEED ORIGAMI

Consider something as simple as a three-panel, letter-fold brochure. If all panels were the same width, the innermost panel would buckle, and the piece would never fold completely flat—the brochure would spring open or the oversized panel would crinkle when forced (**Figure 3.7**). You can demonstrate this for yourself by folding a sheet of paper into approximate thirds, as if you were going to stuff it in an envelope.

The solution? Make the fold-in panel more narrow (**Figure 3.8**). Sounds simple, but think of the effect on your design: You have to build your design to accommodate the shorter third panel. The sanest way to do this is to build such a piece as a two-page job—one page for the outside and one for the inside. Don't build such a piece as a pair of three-page spreads because this provides no way to create the narrower panel (page layout applications only allow one page size per document).

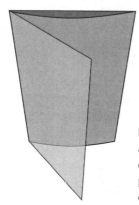

Figure 3.7 Wrong: a three-panel piece with equal-sized panels. The inner panel buckles, so the piece can't fold properly.

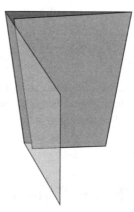

Figure 3.8 Right: three-panel piece folded so the innermost panel is narrower. Now the piece folds flat.

For example, if the finished, open flat width is 11 inches, build the file with two panels that are 3 11/16 inches wide and one panel 3 5/8 inches wide. Keep in mind that the inside and outside of the piece are mirrors of each other: The outside of the brochure will need the short trim panel on the left, and the inside of the brochure will need the short trim panel on the right (**Figure 3.9**).

Before starting, ask your print service provider what panel sizes they suggest, based on the paper stock to be used on the job, and the requirements of their equipment. Some folding configurations, such as the accordion fold (also sometimes called a z-fold), don't require short panels (**Figure 3.10**).

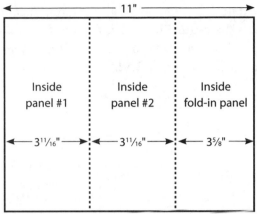

Figure 3.9 Building a trifold brochure with a narrower fold-in panel.

Figure 3.10 Folding configurations such as the accordion fold don't require a short-trim panel.

How can you ensure that you're laying out your panels correctly? Use guidelines to indicate the location of folds, and it will be easier to place artwork so it won't be marred by the trimming and folding process.

InDesign and Illustrator allow you to numerically specify the position of guidelines (**Figure 3.11**). Additionally, both applications provide methods of numerically positioning page elements. Options in the Control panel in InDesign and Illustrator, as well as the Transform panel, allow you to enter values for position and dimensions of selected objects.

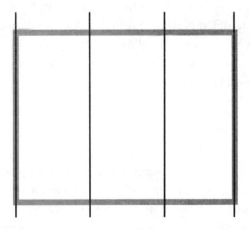

Figure 3.11 Numerically placed guidelines help you position artwork in the layout.

If you're aiming for a particular finished folded size, work backwards from that, following the same rules. For example, to create a three-panel piece that folds to a closed width of 8 1/2 inches, create the outside three panels in one 25 3/8 inch page (not three, letter-sized pages stitched together in a spread), as shown in **Figure 3.12**.

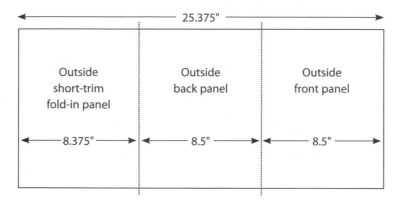

Figure 3.12 This piece will fold to a finished size of 8.5 by 11 inches. (Outside panels are shown here—the inside panels will mirror this configuration.)

As always, check with the print service provider early in the game, to ensure that your artwork meets their requirements. Note that thick paper stock may necessitate even greater short-trim values (that is, even more lopped off that short-trimmed panel) to compensate for the thickness of the folded piece.

In fact, your print service provider may be able to provide you with a standard set of measurements—or even a working template file—to use as the basis for your folding piece.

If you frequently create multipanel pieces, consider taking the easy way out by using the FOLDRite plug-in for InDesign (www.foldfactory.com). Not only does it automatically generate pages of the correct size (with marks and guidelines in place), the FOLDRite plug-in is educational: A side panel discusses the impact of paper weight and grain on folding, as well as the repercussions of postal needs.

IMPOSITION

The process of laying out individual pages or other pieces in final printing position is called *imposition*. The size and configuration of an imposition arrangement is dictated by the dimensions and printing orientation of the paper running through the press. For simple pieces such as business cards or labels, the imposition may consist of the same piece printed repeatedly.

Basic Imposition

As mentioned earlier in this chapter, business cards don't shoot out of the press one by one. Multiple cards are laid out on each sheet, then cut apart. If you've created business cards on a desktop printer, you have some idea of what's involved. It's fun trying to get the edges of those little rascals to line up with the perforations on your desktop printer's output, isn't it? That alone should give you some sympathy for the challenges faced by a commercial print service provider. They're not printing on perforated stock, but it gives you an idea of the difficulty of trimming printed sheets exactly.

Imposing a simple business card with a plain, white background (**Figure 3.13**) is fairly straightforward: Line them up and cut them apart.

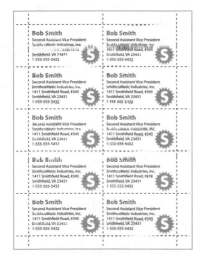

Figure 3.13 Simple, ten-up imposition for homemade business cards. Looks easy enough (dashed lines indicate trim).

However, if there is artwork that needs to bleed off the edge of the card or fall close to the trim edge, the imposition and trimming process must ensure that, if there are small errors in the process, important artwork is not inadvertently trimmed off (**Figure 3.14**).

Figure 3.14 Oops. The heartbreak of poor trim (left). A proper, well-trimmed business card (right).

To avoid messy edges on pieces with artwork that bleeds or is positioned close to the edge, the prepress operator has to be a bit creative with the multicard layout, arranging the art so that similar sides of the cards print adjacent to each other (**Figure 3.15**). Keep this trick in mind the next time you're printing homemade cards—it may save you some aggravation and some paper.

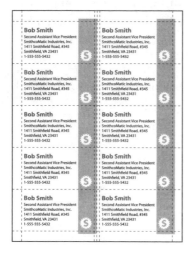
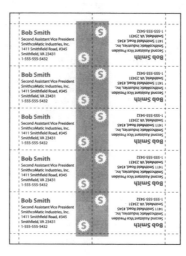

Figure 3.15 Bleeding artwork presents additional challenges during imposition and trimming. Here are two possible solutions to trimming cards with bleed (dashed lines indicate trim).

On the left, a double-trim layout (easy to lay out, but requires an additional cut).

On the right, a more economical layout to accommodate a single cut.

Multipage Imposition

Let the spatial reasoning games begin! As you move beyond single pieces like business cards, you won't be surprised to discover that things get a bit trickier.

When multipage pieces are imposed, the sheet is folded and trimmed to become a group of printed pages, called a *signature*. Depending on the page size, the press capabilities, and the type of binding to be used, a signature could comprise 8, 16, 32, or more pages.

This might be a good time to get a little destructive in the name of science. Buy (or borrow) a weekly news magazine and leaf through it. The pages appear, as you might expect, in reader's spreads: 2–3, 4–5, 6–7, and so on.

But pry out the staples at the center of the magazine and note how the pages were printed. For example, in a saddle-stitched 96-page magazine, you'll find that page 96 is printed across from page 1, page 2 is across from page 95, 94–3, and so on. Thus, the term *printer's spreads* (**Figure 3.16**).

If the spatial reasoning challenge of figuring out which pages should face each other on the final printed sheet frightens you, there is good news: You don't have to build your files in printer's spreads. In fact, you *shouldn't*. It's better to let the print service provider take care of imposition. Build your facing-page document as two-page reader's spreads. Additionally, don't build your spreads as single pages (that is, don't put pages two and three on one big page).

If your print service provider requests that you supply files already in printer's spreads, you have a right to be concerned. Imposition of pages is a very basic printing service, and a printer who lacks that capability is likely to fall short in other areas. Asking you to perform imposition places additional responsibility on you, and the complexity of imposition increases proportionally with the number of pages in your publication, as well as the thickness of the printing stock.

Since facing pages don't actually print next to each other (except for the center spread), a number of errors can creep in. Variations in ink coverage across a press sheet may result in colors not matching, and errors in print, trim, and binding can cause crossover elements to be misaligned or mismatched in the finished piece (**Figure 3.17**).

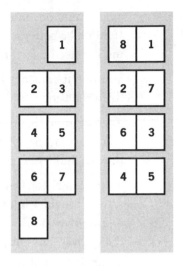

Figure 3.16 Reader's spreads (left) compared to pages imposed in printer's spreads (right). Pages four and five face each other in both examples because they make up the center spread.

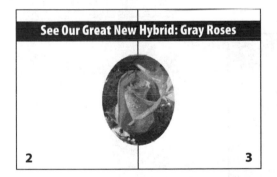 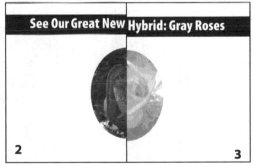

Figure 3.17 Reader spreads as they appear onscreen (left), compared to printer spreads exhibiting printing and binding problems (right). Color and binding errors are exaggerated for dramatic effect.

Usually the results are not as dramatic as shown in Figure 3.17, but you should take the possibilities into consideration as you design. Is there a crucial piece of artwork that needs to span two pages? If so, it will fare best if it's placed on the center spread, where it will print intact. Now that you know that most spreads are not printed together, this may also inspire you to avoid placing photographs so that they extend onto a facing page. Since the pages aren't printed together, even a very slight variation in ink coverage between the pages could become obvious where the two portions of the photograph meet at the center. It might be better to stop the photograph at the inner edge of one page rather than continuing it onto the facing page.

You might consider modifying your design to allow for these issues. Move artwork away from the center fold to avoid crossover issues entirely. That's not cheating; it's *planning*.

Keep in mind that the awful outcome depicted in Figure 3.17 is a dramatic exaggeration of a worst-case scenario. The printing and binding process is not usually this sloppy (if it is, it's time to find a new print service provider). But it gives you an idea of what can go wrong.

To get a feel for how your piece is actually printed, folded, and trimmed, ask your print service provider to give you a *folding dummy* for your job. It's a folded and numbered blank representation of how your pages will be printed, and it's very helpful as you contemplate the realities of your job.

If you're given to origami, you can make your own miniature folding dummy for an eight-page document by following the illustration below. This isn't meant to replace an authentic folding dummy created by your printer. It's just a great way for you to get some sense of what really goes on when your pages are split apart and grafted back together in the finished, imposed piece (**Figure 3.18**). If you want a true representation of how your job will print and fold, consult with the printer's customer service representative who is handling your job. They can help you communicate with the bindery department.

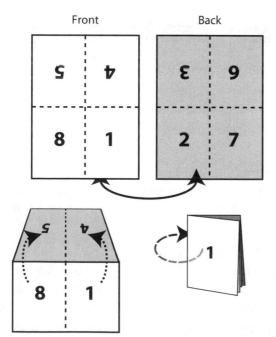

Figure 3.18 A simple folding dummy for an eight-page document. Note how the pages are printed, and the order in which the folds occur.

If you're creating a piece that contains a fold-in panel, remember that the fold-in panel will be short-trimmed, and position your art accordingly, allowing for at least .125 of an inch less page width on those pages. Build the file as shown in **Figure 3.19**, wherein the dashed lines over pages six and seven indicate the short trim.

Note that the page numbers are just for identification. You'll have to decide whether to number pages by position in the document or by viewing order. For example, as this piece is opened and unfolded, the pages would be viewed in this order: 1-2-3-4-7-5-6-8 9-10. Not surprisingly, many designers elect to omit page numbers in such brochures. Feel free to claim that page numbers would just detract from your fresh, clean design.

It's not just the width and height you have to worry about when preparing your piece for print. Paper thickness also contributes to the behavior of a finished printed product. To illustrate, stack several sheets of heavy paper, and then fold the stack in the middle. Notice what happens to the

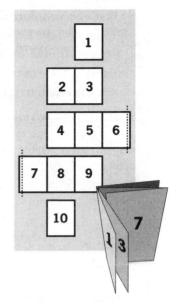

Figure 3.19 Visualizing an eight-page brochure containing a fold-in panel.

edges of the individual pieces of paper—they don't line up, because the cumulative paper thickness at the fold drives the innermost pages out (**Figure 3.20**). This is called page creep. The more pages (and the heavier the stock), the more pronounced the effect.

Figure 3.20 Paper thickness causes edges of pages to creep outward during binding. When the finished pages are trimmed, artwork on the inner pages will be closer to the trim edge.

But look at a publication such as a weekly magazine: All the pages are nice and even because the finished piece is trimmed. Of course, this makes for a more attractive magazine, but consider the side effects. Artwork near the edge of the page would be even *closer* to the trimmed edge of the page on the innermost pages, so the appearance of some elements—such as page numbers—would become inconsistent.

The fix? To maintain a consistent outer margin despite the page creep, the page content must be shifted incrementally to compensate, a process known as shingling. The closer a page is to the center of the magazine, the more content must be moved very slightly inward. While this results in tighter margins at the center, the result is usually less noticeable than margin errors on the outside edges of the pages (**Figure 3.21**).

Figure 3.21 The results of shingling to compensate for page creep during folding. The outermost pages of a signature (left) are fine. But to keep the external margins consistent throughout the bound piece, page content is moved inward, which results in tighter inner margins (right).

The good news is that designers aren't expected to do shingling. It's done by the print service provider as part of the *imposition* process, which positions individual pages correctly for final printing, trimming, and binding. But you should still be mindful of the process as you design your pages so you can minimize problems. It helps if you have generous inside margins so that moving content inward during shingling won't cause any artwork to be crammed into the spine of the printed and bound piece.

Some binding processes incur shingling more frequently (or to a more pronounced degree) than others. As you might expect, binding a relatively large number of pages, such as those in a weekly magazine, will result in the need for more shingling than binding a publication containing only eight pages.

BINDING METHODS

There are many ways of combining multiple pages into a single, finished piece. At home, we use staples, paper clips, or binder clips to consolidate sheets of paper. The methods used in printing plants are rather more elaborate.

Saddle Stitching

Take another look at the magazine that we've been using as an example. The staples that anchor the pages at the spine of the magazine are actually created from a spool of wire. For the binding process, the loose sheets of printed pages that constitute the magazine are draped together over a saddle-like holder (hence the term *saddle stitching*). The wire is fed into position, cut to the correct length for the thickness of the magazine, bent into shape, and then the legs of the staple are driven through the pages. Finally, the legs are bent into the final staple shape (**Figure 3.22**). Of course, this all takes place at high speed, in about the same amount of time it takes you to say the word *magazine*.

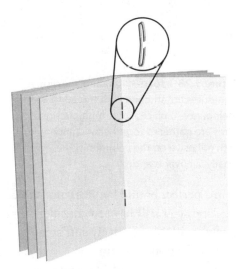

Figure 3.22 In saddle stitching, wire is fed from a roll, and then cut to form staples, which are driven through a sheaf of paper and then crimped.

Perfect Binding and Case Binding

There is another method of binding—perfect binding—that is used for larger publications such as textbooks (and some high-page-count journals). In perfect binding, creep is not as large an issue as it is with other binding methods, although it can still occur. Whereas magazines might combine over 100 pages in a saddle-stitched issue, when perfect binding is used, pages are gathered in much smaller groups—such as 16-page signatures—which are likely to result in less-pronounced creep. Then, multiple signatures are stacked together, trimmed (or ground off), and glued at the spine (**Figure 3.23**). Finally, a cover is added to enclose the pages, which is held in place by glue along the spine. For larger books such as textbooks, the spine is reinforced by adhering a cloth strip to the spine of the gathered signatures before affixing a hard cover. This is called case binding.

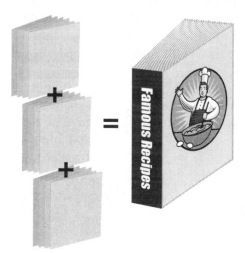

Figure 3.23 In perfect binding, individual signatures are stitched with thread to keep their pages in place. Then, multiple signatures are gathered together and anchored with adhesive on the common spine. Finally, a cover is added.

Although the smaller constituent signatures in a perfect bound book are not subject to the degree of creep that you might see in a magazine, you still have to consider some of the side effects of combining a high number of pages with the relatively stiff spine of a perfect binding. Even in a comparatively slender, perfect bound magazine of 192 pages, there is pronounced pinching of the pages at the center of the finished magazine, making it difficult to read some text near the interior bound edge. You can compensate for this by using wider inside margins when you build your pages (**Figure 3.24**).

Figure 3.24 Anticipate the pinch of perfect binding by setting wider inside margins (right).

Comb Binding

Often used for publications such as cookbooks, textbooks, and workbooks, *comb binding* allows a book to be opened flat. Rectangular holes are punched in the pages of the book, and then the teeth of the plastic comb are pushed through the holes. Because the combs are coil-like and curly, the teeth curve back under a spine-like collar that forms a solid spine for the bound book (**Figure 3.25**). The plastic combs come in a variety of colors and diameters. Comb-bound books usually use heavier stock for the front and back covers, or they use clear plastic sheets as a protective first page.

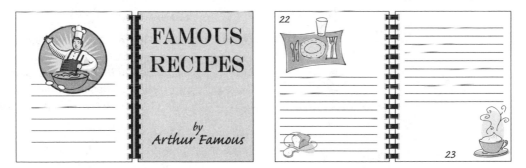

Figure 3.25 Comb binding allows books to be opened flat. It's great for cookbooks and workbooks, but makes it challenging to add a printed spine.

Comb binding has one disadvantage: It's a challenge to put a title or other copy on the spine, although it's possible to apply adhesive labels or even imprint the plastic combs by using silk screening at extra cost.

In preparing artwork for a publication that will be comb bound, you have to provide sufficiently wide inside margins so the punched holes won't impinge on any content. Your print service provider can give you specifications for their punches.

Most print service providers and many office-supply stores can perform comb binding for you. But if you frequently produce short-run books or other small-quantity publications that require comb binding, you might consider purchasing punching and binding equipment of your own.

Coil Binding

In coil binding, a spiral of wire or plastic is threaded through round holes punched in the book (**Figure 3.26**). As with comb binding, coil binding (also called spiral binding) allows a piece to lie flat when open. However, there's no way to imprint a spine, and you must create a wide inner margin as you design the piece so that the printed area of the page will clear the punch holes.

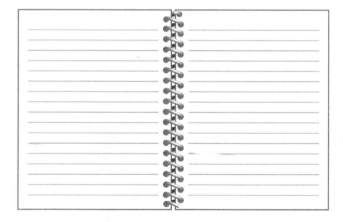

Figure 3.26 Coil binding is suitable for notebooks, cookbooks, and textbooks. While this binding method allows a book to lie flat when open, there's no way to imprint a spine.

Other Binding Methods

If you're creating textbooks or notebook-like workbooks, you'll encounter other punch-and-bind methods that are similar in configuration to comb and coil binding. *Wire binding* uses tooth-like loops of wire similar in appearance to the teeth of comb binding, but it produces a sturdier binding than the plastic combs. By now, you're probably reciting the mantra, "Use wider inner margins to avoid the punch holes." Hold that thought. It applies to most specialty-binding methods.

For heavy-duty books with constantly changing content, such as a wallpaper sample book, *post binding* may be the most appropriate solution. In this binding method, metal posts are pushed through punched holes in the book and anchored with bolts that thread into the post centers. This method has the advantage of allowing you to add or replace pages, and it's possible to have an exterior cover with an imprinted spine.

Special presentations or other artistic publishing concepts may involve custom binding solutions such as handmade covers or cases and decorative binding devices such as screws or ribbons. Such pieces are usually used in very limited print runs and entail a considerable amount of handwork. Consequently, these undertakings require extremely careful planning.

MOVING BEYOND TWO DIMENSIONS

When you start building more complicated pieces it's really helpful to create a dummy of some sort, so you can visualize the finished piece. It's easy to think of how the finished piece will *look*, but you need to consider how the piece will *print* and *fold* so you can create it correctly. An anatomically correct dummy will let you visualize both the *inside* and *outside* and will shed light on the difficulties of positioning tricky artwork. In fact, the challenge of lining all that stuff up in your head may force you to simplify your concept.

Consider a pocket folder (**Figure 3.27**). Folded, its configuration resembles a simple, two-page spread. But take a folder apart so you can see how the pocket and its glue flaps are positioned, and you'll see that the printed piece is rather more complex. Any art falling over the pocket has to be carefully aligned with art on the inside of the piece, and this can present a challenge in design as well as in printing and finishing.

How do you build such a piece? Think of it as having an inside and an outside, and build it as a two-page document. As with all printed pieces, build to trim size. But you also have to think in three dimensions to take into consideration the physical processes of folding and gluing.

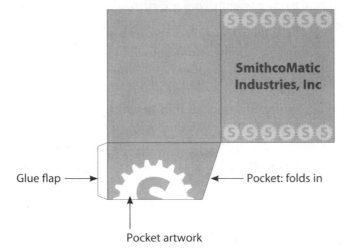

Figure 3.27 The outside of the finished pocket folder looks like this…

…but it should be created like this. Note that the pocket and glue flap affect the dimensions of the piece.

Glue flap

Pocket: folds in

Pocket artwork

The complex trimming for a piece like a pocket folder requires a shaped cutter called a *die*. If possible, obtain artwork for the finished die line to use as the basis of your file, as well as a physical example of the final configuration. A die line is a drawing of the open, flat piece, with all the folds and cuts indicated. This will help you visualize how the artwork must be positioned on the panels of the pocket folder. You'll also learn a lot about how your files must be created if you disassemble a printed example of a finished pocket folder. You'll see how the thickness of the heavy stock affects artwork at the folds, and you'll see how you must accommodate gluing requirements in your design.

Most print service providers who specialize in printing pocket folders can provide vector artwork for standard die lines, which you can use as a guide for building your piece. Since the glue area must be blank because glue will not adhere to unprinted stock, follow the print service provider's guidelines for the size and position of the unprinted area to ensure that no artwork falls within it (**Figure 3.28**).

Figure 3.28 The inside of the finished pocket folder may look like this…

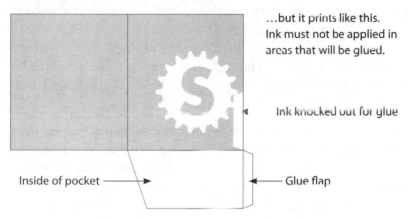

…but it prints like this. Ink must not be applied in areas that will be glued.

Ink knocked out for glue

Inside of pocket ⟶   ⟵ Glue flap

In addition to considering the unfolded size of the folder, you must include the glue flap in the overall size of the piece. In **Figure 3.29**, the *folded* size would be 9 by 12 inches, but the *actual* size of the artwork is 19 by 16 inches to accommodate the one-inch glue flap and the four-inch height of the pocket.

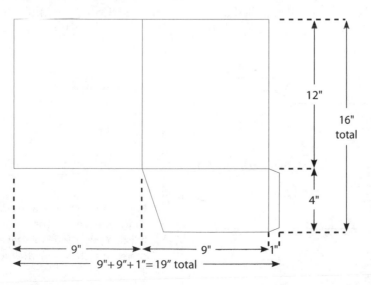

12"

16" total

4"

9"   9"   1"

9"+9"+1"=19" total

Figure 3.29 The dimensions of pocket-folder artwork must include the glue flap and the pocket area. It's helpful to take apart a blank or printed example that is made from the cutting die that will be used on your job. This helps you visualize how the artwork should be created.

Die Cutting

When your design requires specially shaped edges or complicated folding and assembly, special *dies* must be created to score and cut the printed piece. Scoring is the act of pressing an indentation into the stock to facilitate folding the final piece. Die cutting is the process of cutting the printed piece into a custom shape. Packaging and pocket folders are examples of pieces that require both scoring and die cutting. Scoring ensures predictable folding, and die cutting creates the shape necessary for the printed piece to become a pocket folder or package. The die consists of sharp steel cutting edges anchored in a sturdy wooden base. Although much of the design of cutting dies is now assisted with computer-driven manufacturing, there is still considerable handwork and skill involved in making a successful cutting die. Provisions must be made to ensure that cuts are clean and complete, scoring is correct, and excess material is safely removed without clogging or damaging the cutting edges.

The cutting die is mounted on a specialized, die-cutting press, which uses pressure to score and cut the stock. Most die-cutting devices are platen-based, meaning that the die is a flat surface. But there are also rotary die-cutting presses, which require that the die be affixed to a cylinder. Not all printing companies perform their own die cutting. Some opt instead to contract with companies that specialize in such custom finishing.

If you intend to create a specialized piece for which the printer has no existing die, work closely with their finishing department (or the outside finisher, if that part of the job is being outsourced) to ensure that your artwork is built correctly. They can help you understand finishing issues affecting your job, and their advice can steer you away from problematic designs. It's important that you obtain a die line before you finalize your artwork (**Figure 3.30**). It may be supplied as an EPS or imaged on clear film. Carefully follow the dimensions of the die line as you plan your design, and you'll minimize problems during the finishing process.

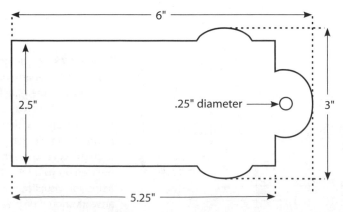

Figure 3.30 Die-line artwork shows the dimensions of the finished piece and indicates any scores, punches, or perforations.

Creating correct artwork for a die-cut piece can sometimes require that you create custom bleed areas that consider the irregular trim of the finished piece. Bleed on a die-cut piece is more than just a concentric rind around the trim. A beveled approach is required where colors meet some trim points to minimize the chances of color falling in the wrong place on the finished piece (**Figure 3.31**). Die creation is a combination of art and engineering. Don't embark on creating the art for a piece that will be elaborately die cut without first consulting with your printer's finishing department or finishing supplier. They may have an existing die line that you can use as a basis for designing your piece, which would reduce job cost.

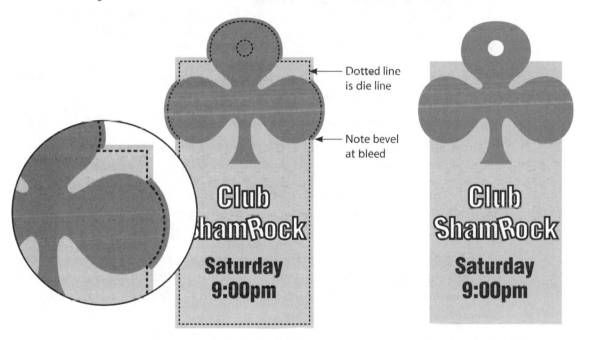

Dotted line is die line

Note bevel at bleed

Figure 3.31 Die-cut pieces like this hang tag may require complicated bleed construction. Note beveled treatment where two colors meet (left). Finished piece (right).

Embossing

Embossing adds dimension to paper by pressing the paper stock between shaped metal pieces, resulting in a raised surface on the top (reading side) of the paper. Heat and pressure help push the paper into the shape of the embossing dies (**Figure 3.32**).

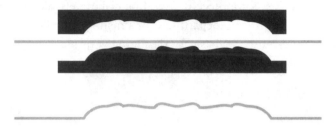

Figure 3.32 Heat and pressure combined with a pair of shaped dies (top) are necessary to produce an embossed effect on paper (bottom, shown in cross section).

Debossing is the same concept, but the shape of the dies creates a convex shape, pushing the surface of the paper *down* rather than raising it.

There are several variations on the concept of embossing:

- *Blind* embossing is an embossed effect in an unprinted area of the paper, thus creating artwork solely from the shape of the embossing.

- *Registered* embossing is aligned with a printed area already on the paper. While registered embossing heightens the dimensional effect, it requires more precision than blind embossing.

- *Glazed* embossing describes the shine that may appear as part of the embossed effect, especially on dark stock. Sometimes glazing is induced intentionally, although the higher heat often used to produce the effect can lead to scorching, and thus must be cautiously applied.

If you plan to use embossing to enhance your printed piece, consult with the print service provider and any participating outside finishing supplier to ensure that the effect you visualize is possible with the stock you intend to use. Understandably, the stock must have sufficient weight to withstand the embossing process. The pressure and heat used to shape the paper can weaken the paper, especially when attempting to force it into extreme or highly detailed embossing dies. The paper must be flexible enough to accomplish the effect, but strong enough to hold up to the deformation. Any texture inherent in the paper must also be taken into consideration, as well as any other finishing effects (such as folding or perforation) occurring close to the embossed area.

The embossing dies are based on artwork such as an EPS file or raster artwork. As you prepare artwork to be used as the basis for embossing, consult with the finishing experts to ensure that you provide artwork in the appropriate format. It's likely that skilled artists will modify your artwork to create the dies and perform handwork on the metal dies to ensure that the final embossed piece matches expectations. Plan for the extra time and cost involved in creating and refining embossing dies. Something this elaborate can't be hurried, but the results can be stunning.

Foil Stamping

Often used as an accent for book covers and packaging, *foil stamping* uses a heated, raised metal die to transfer decorative foil from a roll of carrier material onto the underlying paper. The foil may be metallic, colored, or iridescent. Some foils are holographic in nature, creating a rainbow or three-dimensional effect when applied. The best results are achieved on smooth, coated papers, since pronounced texture may prevent the foil from adhering uniformly. In addition, foil may not adhere to some coatings such as some waxy varnishes, so you should use aqueous coatings or nonwaxy varnishes before foil stamping.

As with embossing, artwork must be created to serve as the basis for the foil stamping die, and it's important to consult with knowledgeable specialists as you begin the process. Foil stamping is most effective in reasonably small areas such as type or patterns. It can be difficult to cover large areas successfully with foil stamping. But if you want a realistic metallic effect, foil stamping can accomplish what could never be equaled with metallic inks. And combined with embossing, foil stamping can create some beautiful effects.

CHAPTER FOUR

Preparing Raster Images

Whether you acquire an image from a scanner, a digital camera, a royalty-free CD with 1,000,000 images, or a stock photography vendor, it's made out of pixels. Pixel is shorthand for picture element, the smallest unit of information in a digitized image. Even though pictures on your monitor look like smooth transitions of color, zoom in sufficiently and you'll see all the little square pixels that actually make up the image (**Figure 4.1**).

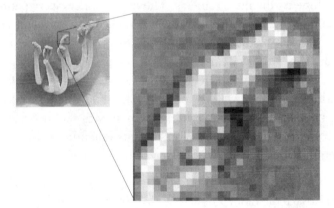

Figure 4.1 Images are made of pixels. Think of them as little-bitty mosaic tiles.

ANCIENT TIMES: B.P. (BEFORE PIXELS)

In the olden days of graphic arts, enormous cameras were used to capture artwork such as drawings, reflective photographic prints, transparencies, or painted illustrations. Highly skilled specialists commandeered these monstrosities, some of which occupied entire rooms. The use of colored filters, masking, and exposure methods to produce color separations (a separate piece of film for each printing ink) was rather arcane and required years of apprenticeship and study to perfect. And since every step required the use of specialized film, there were a lot of trips to a darkroom to develop the results in chemical baths. It all seemed very high-tech at the time (well, compared to cave paintings), but the process was quite time-consuming.

NOW: A.P. (ALL PIXELS, ALL THE TIME)

Film has given way to pixels, and we are now beginning to keep our family photos as shoeboxes full of CDs rather than dog-eared color photographic prints. What was once the province of the darkroom became a daylight venture, and the tools of the craftsmen have become available to anyone brave enough to wade in.

Scanners

While early scanners still required highly skilled graphic arts professionals to operate them, they greatly speeded up the process of capturing artwork for color separations. Early analog models used photomultiplier tubes and a daunting array of knobs and buttons to perform the same job that had been done by the huge cameras. The first scanners were petite only by comparison to their gigantic camera ancestors: Many could easily dwarf a Volkswagen. It was necessary to mount artwork on a heavy, clear plastic drum, and then painstakingly ensure that there was no dust or a trapped air bubble to mar the scan. Scanner operators came from the ranks of color-separation cameramen, and their years of finely honed instincts for camera separations translated well to the newer methods. The first scanners still produced film output, not pixels. But the next development was the move to digital capture and storage of image information, resulting in the introduction of the pixel and the advent of digital retouching.

In the mid-1990s, improvements in the capabilities and simplicity of flatbed scanners, coupled with the widespread usage of Adobe Photoshop, led to a major change in the way color separations were performed. It was no longer necessary to mount artwork on cylindrical drums, and the numerous knobs were replaced with onscreen buttons and dialog boxes. The digital imaging revolution was underway. Suddenly, people who weren't sure what *color separation* meant were *making* color separations.

As flatbed scanners have become more automated and less expensive, it's relatively easy even for novices to make a decent scan. But the more you know about what constitutes a *good* image, the better the chance you can create a *great* image from the pixels generated by your scanner.

Digital Cameras

Today's scanners capture transparencies, reflective images, or illustrations and express them as pixels. But now we're undergoing another revolution. High-end digital cameras now rival—or exceed—the ability of film-based cameras to capture photographic detail. The image captured by the camera is a digital original, so there's no need to scan a print. Of course, the better the camera and the photographer, the better the image. Your mobile phone isn't up to the job.

While conventional camera film—such as 35mm transparencies—must be scanned to be used on your computer, digital camera images can be downloaded directly to the computer and used immediately. Digital photography also cuts out the middleman. Unlike film images, digital images don't have any grain, but an image photographed at low light may tax the resolving capabilities of a digital camera and thus exhibit digital noise.

Consumer point-and-shoot cameras deliver captured images as JPEG, a compressed format. There are degrees of compression, from gentle to aggressive, and you may never notice any visible artifacts betraying the compression. But higher level "prosumer" cameras and professional digital cameras can deliver images in the Camera RAW format, which is subjected to minimal (or no) compression by the camera. While you cannot place a RAW file directly into Illustrator or InDesign, RAW images can be opened directly in Photoshop and saved in another format, such as Photoshop PSD.

In addition to benefiting from minimal compression, RAW files can be color corrected in the Photoshop Camera RAW environment without losing additional information. For example, an image shot under daylight conditions but with the camera's white balance set to fluorescent lighting, can be corrected with one click in the Camera RAW environment without the loss of information that would occur in a Levels or Curves correction.

Camera RAW is a powerful and flexible format; RAW images also take up more space on the camera's memory card, but the advantages are worth the extra heft.

Imaging Software

Once you have captured pixels, it's likely that you'll want (or need) to *do* something with them. The industry standard imaging application is Photoshop, and for good reason. Photoshop provides controls for color correction that enable a knowledgeable user to achieve results equal to those of a knob-twisting scanner operator. And its retouching tools surpass the capabilities of the original, million-dollar dedicated systems. If you're just beginning to learn Photoshop, you won't lack for educational resources. You could probably build an addition to your house from the books and magazines devoted to exploring Photoshop. You can add Chapter Nine, "Photoshop CS4 Production Tips," to the pile.

Photoshop is arguably the most versatile and widely accepted application for image manipulation, but there are other applications that perform useful imaging functions as well.

Adobe Photoshop Elements (Mac/PC) might be regarded as "Photoshop Lite," but it still packs a hefty arsenal of retouching and color-correction tools. The product is geared toward enthusiasts rather than professional photographers and lacks support for CMYK images.

Adobe Lightroom™ (Mac/PC) is engineered for use by photographers working with raw digital images. It provides sophisticated tools for organizing and color correcting images.

Photoshop.com (Mac/PC) is an online image storage service, offering some image editing features (for more information, see www.photoshop.com).

Apple iPhoto® (Mac only) offers features similar to those in Photoshop Album. Geared toward hobbyists, iPhoto has organizational tools and limited color-correction capabilities, but no support for CMYK. As you might expect, iPhoto is available only for the Macintosh operating system.

Apple Aperture (Mac only) is targeted to photographers working with raw digital files. It provides organizational tools as well as color-correction controls.

These are not the only solutions that exist for manipulating images. There are painting programs, such as Painter™ and Paint Shop Pro® (both from Corel®), which let you easily make images resemble watercolors or oil paintings. There are countless plug-ins that enhance the Photoshop toolset. Imaging tools for consumer and hobbyist photographers increase on a daily basis. However, most of these programs don't offer support for CMYK images, so they're not the best tools if you're preparing images for print.

RESOLUTION AND IMAGE FIDELITY

The resolution of an image is generally measured in pixels per inch (ppi) unless you speak metric, in which case it's expressed in pixels per millimeter. Determining the proper resolution for Web images is simple: 72 ppi at final size. But there are strongly held (and hotly debated) beliefs regarding the appropriate image resolution for printing. Some hold that 150 percent of the final screen ruling value is sufficient, and some believe twice the final ruling is preferable, largely because it's easier to calculate the resolution. For example, an image that will be printed at 150 line screen should have a resolution of 300 ppi. When typical hard drives held 80 MB, networks were glacially slow, and RIPs choked on 15 MB PostScript files, it was important to trim off every little bit of fat, so we agonized over resolution. But now, with hard drives measured in hundreds of gigabytes, and RIPs with much more robust digestive tracts, we can afford the luxury of a few extra pixels. That said, there's rarely an advantage to exceeding 300 ppi, except in some cases for higher line screens such as 175 lpi printing. So put away the calculator. For most circumstances, 300 ppi at final size is adequate and provides a bit of elbow room if you have to slightly reduce or enlarge an image.

But you do have some leeway, depending on the nature of the image and how it will be used. For example, a gauzy, soft-focus shot of a sunset that will be used as a ghosted background accent in a magazine can be used at 200 ppi with no problem. A highly detailed close-up image of an important piece of antique jewelry in a 175 lpi art book should be at 300–350 ppi. At the other end of the spectrum, an image for use in an 85 lpi newspaper can be 130–170 ppi, because much of the information in a 300 ppi image would be lost when printed in the coarse newspaper screen ruling. So you might consider the determination of appropriate resolution to be an equation based on image content and the final printing line screen rather than an absolute number.

Bitmap Images

Sometimes called "line art images," bitmap images contain only black and white pixels with no shades of gray. If you need to scan a signature to add to an editorial page or scan a pen and ink sketch, a bitmap scan can provide a sharp, clean image at very high resolution. Because of the compact nature of bitmap scans, they can be very high resolution (usually 600–1200 ppi) but still produce small file sizes (**Figure 4.2**).

Figure 4.2 This 1200 ppi bitmap scan prints nearly as sharply as vector art. It weighs in at less than 1 MB; a grayscale image of this size and resolution would be nearly 10 MB. Magnified to 400 percent , it may look a bit rough, but at 100 percent it's crisp and clean.

Scaling Up

When enlarging or reducing an image, don't be afraid to *slightly* reduce or enlarge an image. When an image is scanned or captured by a digital camera, the number of pixels contained in that image is fixed. As long as the original digitizing process netted sufficient pixels for your intended use, fine. But when you enlarge an image in an image-editing application such as Photoshop, you're attempting to generate missing information, a process called interpolation. This interpolation process works reasonably well (considering that you're asking it to make something out of nothing), but the result is never as good as a proper-sized original scan. And the more drastic the transformation, the less satisfying the outcome (**Figure 4.3**).

A: Original 300 ppi scan   **B:** Original 72 ppi scan   **C:** Results of increasing resolution of B to 300 ppi   **D:** Results of increasing resolution of B to 300 ppi by using a specialized fractal-based scaling plug-in to enhance the result

Figure 4.3 You can't truly make something from nothing. Notice the loss of detail in the scaled-up versions.

Because of the limitations imposed by resolution, it behooves you to anticipate how the image will be used and to set your scan percentage accordingly. For typical image content, you can probably scale up to 120–125 percent. If the image is background content without much detail, such as a soft-focus landscape, you have more leeway and you can probably get away with scaling up to 150–200 percent. Conversely, if you need to maintain very small details, you may be limited to a maximum of 120 percent.

Scaling Down

Remember that scaling *down* also requires interpolation. While the loss of data may not be quite so obvious when you reduce the size of an image, there *will* be some softening of detail (as shown in **Figure 4.4**), so it's still best to plan ahead, and make your initial scan as close as possible to the dimensions at which you intend to use it in a page-layout program. Generally, if you find it necessary to scale an image down below 50–75 percent in your page layout, consider rescanning. And, as with enlargements, try to use an even scaling factor, such as 120 percent rather than 119.6954 percent.

Figure 4.4 Surprise! Even scaling *down* an image can slightly soften detail, because so much information is discarded. The image at the lower left was reduced to 25 percent using Photoshop's Bicubic method. The image at the lower right was reduced using the Bicubic Sharper method. Then it was sharpened with default settings (Filter > Sharpen > Unsharp Mask), giving the illusion that there is more detail.

Planning Ahead

Now that you're terrified to scale an image up *or* down, what is the safe path? If you do your own high-resolution scans, and you anticipate doing a lot of experimentation with image size as the design develops, you might consider just doing quick-and-dirty FPO (for position only) scans to start. Since such images are meant to be used only as placeholders, they can be low resolution (72–100 ppi). Build and tweak the design, scaling images as you wish. Then, when the layout is finalized, note the image scale factors, do the final scans to size, and replace the FPO images with the real scans. (Digital photographs are discussed shortly.)

Alternatively, if you want to do all your scanning at one time, but still would like some flexibility in scaling, scan one large and one small version of each image at the outset and work with those.

If you rely on the print service provider to perform scanning, the responsibility may be on their scanner operator's shoulders, not yours, depending on the workflow. Previously, when desktop scanners produced considerably lower-quality scans than those of service providers, there were two common approaches to placing scans.

In one approach, the printer was given transparencies and an indication of scan size, usually via markings on the transparency sleeve (since there still had to be some notion of final size, however sketchy). The printer then provided low-resolution FPO scans to be used in designing. When the job was submitted, the printer substituted the high-resolution images for the FPOs. This approach is still used frequently in catalog production, since it's saner for the print service provider to color correct and manage the large repositories of images that are used in multiple publications. This low-resolution/high-resolution swap is usually referred to as *OPI* (Open Prepress Interface), Automatic Picture Replacement (APR, a Scitex solution), or just plain image swap. It's a bit more complicated than simply reducing the resolution of the images used as FPO scans. In these image-replacement workflows, the low-resolution images contain internal PostScript comments that identify them as low-resolution versions of particular images. Special server-based processes are required to perform the high-resolution substitution when the job is imaged. Because the high-resolution scans have already been done, it's advisable to avoid scaling images outside the standard 75–125 percent range in your page layout. If your design demands scaling beyond those limitations, let the print service provider know. They may need to rescan the image, and then supply you with a new low-resolution placeholder image for best results.

> **NOTE:** There is a significant issue to be considered when using OPI/APR workflows for work incorporating transparency, such as that available in Adobe InDesign, Illustrator, and later versions of QuarkXPress. The short story is that high-resolution final images need to be in place in layouts when the job is imaged or exported to PDF. If your printer is supplying OPI-based, low-resolution images to you, ask them to advise you of the best way to approach this issue. It doesn't mean you can't use transparency. It just means some special handling may be required. For an extensive discussion of transparency in InDesign, see Chapter Eleven, "InDesign CS4 Production Tips."

The second approach is to do your own FPO scans, resizing to your heart's content in a page-layout application. Supply the transparencies and other art (such as reflective prints or original artwork) to the print service provider with 100-percent-sized printouts of your job, and let them do the scans and image replacement.

In both of these scenarios, it's important to note that you can't do anything useful to the low-resolution FPO images. Any retouching, color correction, compositing, or silhouetting would have to be re-created on the high-resolution scans, thus wasting any work performed on their low-resolution representations.

Digital Photographs

Although digital photography has rapidly replaced film-based images, the basic rules for handling images are still the same. Photographers who formerly supplied transparencies now provide digital images, which eliminates the scanning step. While direct digital images lack the visible grain that would be apparent in extreme enlargements of transparencies, some digital images may still exhibit pixelation when greatly enlarged (depending on the nature of the subject).

Since there is no film original to rescan, and it's rarely feasible to reshoot, you may occasionally be forced to enlarge digital images. Fractal enlargement plug-ins such as Genuine Fractals from onOne Software (www.ononesoftware.com) may give you better results with extreme enlargements.

Cropping and Transforming Images

It would be great if you could anticipate the exact size, crop, and angle at which you'll want to use an image in your page layout. But it's difficult to see that far down the line at the moment you're slipping a print under the lid of your flatbed scanner. Oh, and watch out for that little gust of wind that comes along just as you're putting the lid down…

Cropping

Should you crop your images during scanning or when you're saving a digital photograph? Maybe. If you're certain about future image use, feel free to crop. Leave a reasonable rind around the image area you intend to use to provide some elbow room when you place the image in the final page. However, if you think there's even a remote chance that you'll want to crop the image more generously in the near future — maybe you're not sure if you might want to show a row of four buildings instead of just the one in the middle — then it's worth keeping the whole shebang. While you may be reluctant to store an entire image just to keep the two-inch golf ball that you're sure you will silhouette, give yourself a safety net and at least keep an uncropped backup copy of the image. Hard drive space is plentiful and you can always crop it later.

Rotating Images

Almost any transformation, whether resizing or rotating, will require interpolation of pixel information. The only safe rotations are 90-degree increments—anything else will result in softening of detail (see **Figure 4.5**). Think of those rows and columns of pixels, much like the grid of a needlepoint pattern. Imagine what a challenge it would be to redraw that pattern at a 42-degree angle. It should give you a little sympathy for the math Photoshop has to do.

 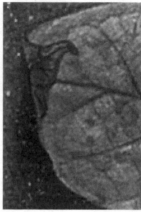

Figure 4.5 Rotation at anything other than 90-degree increments degrades detail. An image scanned at the correct angle (left) is sharper than an image rotated 42 degrees after scanning (right).

All these cautions about transformations such as scaling and rotating are not intended to strike terror in your heart. Don't be afraid to enlarge, reduce, or rotate if you need to. Just be prepared for the slight but unavoidable loss of detail and the degradation of the image's appearance. Try to resize in even increments, and beware of oddball rotations such as 1.25 degrees in the interest of maintaining as much information as possible.

Successive transformations—scaling and then rotating, for example—are particularly destructive. Let your conscience be your guide. How important is the detail in the image? If it's a key product shot, it's worth rescanning (if possible). If it's a less important image, such as a ghosted background or a decorative bit, you needn't feel quite so guilty about the transformation.

Where to Transform: Image Editor versus Page-Layout Application

If you *are* going to transform images, does it matter where the transformation takes place? If you use Photoshop to scale an image, is the result superior to the outcome of scaling within your page-layout application?

The answer is an unqualified, "It depends."

If you perform your scaling and rotation in Photoshop or another image-editing application, and then place the resulting image in a page layout at 100 percent with no rotation, you will have a pretty good idea of how the finished piece will look.

If, however, you induce the scaling or rotation in a page layout, you've only *requested* those transformations. They don't really take place until the job is processed by the RIP. This adds a bit to the processing time and job complexity at the RIP, and it also puts you at the mercy of that RIP's implementation of scaling and rotation algorithms. If you generate and submit PDFs, scaling will be performed as the PDF is created (if you choose an option that performs resampling, such as PDF/X-1a), but the rotations or distortions within that PDF are still pending, and they are implemented only when the PDF is processed by a RIP.

Be comforted by the fact that late-model RIPs can chew a lot more information in a shorter time than they used to. Rotating a few images here and there won't prevent the processing of your job. However, despite the improvements in RIP technology, it is still possible (though rare) to build a job that can't be processed by a RIP. (Please don't take that remark as a personal challenge.)

Keep in mind, too, that if you've rotated an image in Photoshop, and then subsequently applied additional scaling or rotation in a page layout, you've transformed it twice. It's not the end of the world, but you may see some slight softening of detail in the finished piece.

APPROPRIATE IMAGE FORMATS FOR PRINT

How you should save your raster images is governed largely by how you intend to use them. Often, you will be placing images in a page-layout or illustration program, so you're limited to the formats supported by those applications. The application may be willing to let you import a wide variety of file formats, but the most commonly used image formats have traditionally been TIFF and EPS. However, native Photoshop files (PSD) and Photoshop PDF files are much more flexible, and both formats are supported by InDesign and Illustrator. (We'll discuss vector artwork formats in the next chapter.)

TIFF

TIFF (tagged image file format) is perhaps the most widely supported image file format. It's happy being imported into Illustrator, InDesign, QuarkXPress, Microsoft Word, and some text editors—almost any application that accepts images. The TIFF image format supports multiple layers as well as RGB and CMYK color spaces, and even allows an image to contain spot-color channels (although some applications, such as Word, do not support such nontraditional contents in a TIFF).

Photoshop EPS

While many people equate the term EPS (encapsulated PostScript) with vector art, the *encapsulated* part of the format's name gives a hint about the flexibility of the format. It's a *container* for artwork. An EPS can contain vector art, raster images, or a combination of raster and vector content. As its name implies, EPS is PostScript in a bag (see the sidebar, "EPS: Raster or Vector?"). The historic reasons for saving an image as a Photoshop EPS were to preserve the special function of a PostScript-based vector clipping path used to silhouette an image or to preserve an image set up to image as a duotone.

As applications and RIPs have progressed, it's no longer strictly required to save such images as Photoshop EPS. Pixel for pixel, a Photoshop native PSD is a smaller file than an equivalent EPS and offers support for clipping paths as well as duotone definitions.

This doesn't mean you need to hunt down your legacy Photoshop EPS files and resave them as PSD (unless you're terribly bored). Just know that unless you need to accommodate someone else's requirements, there's no advantage to saving as Photoshop EPS.

EPS: Raster or Vector?

It may be a bit confusing that there are raster-based EPSs (saved from an image-editing program such as Photoshop) and vector-based EPSs (saved from a vector drawing program such as Adobe Illustrator or Adobe [formerly Macromedia] FreeHand). The uninitiated sometimes think that saving an image as an EPS magically vectorizes it. Not so. Think of the EPS format as a type of container. The pixels within an EPS are no different from those in their TIFF brethren. They're just contained and presented in a different way.

Photoshop Native (PSD)

Historically, the native PSD (Photoshop document) format has been used solely for working files in Photoshop. Copies of those working files were flattened and saved in TIFF or EPS formats for placement in a page-layout program. While PageMaker allowed placement of native Photoshop files (yes, really—although it did not honor transparency), QuarkXPress required TIFF or EPS instead. Old habits die hard, and thus TIFF and EPS have long been the standard of the industry.

However, Illustrator, InDesign, and QuarkXPress 7 and 8 can take advantage of the layers and transparency in Photoshop native files, eliminating the need to go back through two generations of an image to make corrections to an original file. The working image and the finished file are the same file. QuarkXPress 6.5 allows the placement of native PSDs but does not recognize transparency. QuarkXPress 7.0 and 8, however, honor transparency in layered, native Photoshop files.

> **TRANSPARENCY TIP:** *Although Illustrator, InDesign, and QuarkXPress (version 7 and above) accept and correctly handle opacity settings in a placed Photoshop native file, they do not correctly handle blending modes in a Photoshop file. The most common example is a drop shadow created in Photoshop. While the shadow will correctly darken image content beneath it in Photoshop, it will knock out of content beneath it in InDesign or Illustrator. The result is an anemic and unrealistic gray shadow—not what you want. There are some workarounds for InDesign detailed in Chapter Eleven, "InDesign CS4 Production Tips," but a simple solution is to omit the shadow in Photoshop, and generate it instead in InDesign or Illustrator, whose shadows behave correctly, darkening content beneath the shadows as you intended.*

Photoshop PDF

A Photoshop PDF (Portable Document Format) contains the same pixels as a garden-variety PSD, but those pixels are encased in a PDF wrapper. There's usually no reason to use a Photoshop PDF when a PSD will suffice, but a Photoshop PDF has special features. It can contain vector and type elements without converting the vector content to pixels, a process called rasterizing. And a Photoshop PDF allows round-trip editing in Photoshop. While a Photoshop EPS can contain vectors and text, the vector content will be converted to pixels if the file is reopened in Photoshop, thus losing the crisp vector edge. As a result, you lose the ability to edit text or vector content, since it's been converted to pixels. A native Photoshop PSD can contain vector components, but page-layout programs rasterize the content. However, Photoshop PDFs maintain vector content when placed in other applications. For vector content, Photoshop PDF is the solution, because it is able to hold both transparency and vector components (see **Table 4.1** for a feature comparison of common image formats).

Table 4.1 Image format features

Supported Feature	TIFF	EPS	PSD	PDF
RGB color space	X	X	X	X
CMYK color space	X	X	X	X
Grayscale	X	X	X	X
ICC profiles	X	X	X	X
Clipping paths	X	X	X	X
Layers	X	—	X	X
Alpha channels	X	—	X	X
Spot color channels	X	1	X	X
Duotones	—	X	X	X
Bitmap (bi-level content)	X	X	X	X
Vector data	2	3	2	X
Transparency	X	—	X	X

1 Must save as DCS2 (a variant of the EPS format)
2 Page-layout applications rasterize vector content in TIFFs and PSDs
3 EPSs cannot be re-opened in Photoshop with vector content intact

Moving to Native PSD and PDF

As the major page-layout applications increasingly support native PSDs and PDFs, is there any compelling reason to continue using old-fashioned TIFFs and EPSs? It may seem adventurous to use such new-fangled files, but workflow is changing. The demarcation between photo-compositing and page layout is blurring, and designers demand more power and flexibility from software. RIPs are more robust than ever, networks are faster, and hard drives are huge. It's still important to know the imaging challenges posed by using native files (such as transparency), and wise to communicate with your print service provider before you embark on the all-native path. You're still at the mercy of their equipment and processes, and if they're lagging a bit behind the latest software developments, you'll have to be governed by their capabilities.

Special Case: Screen Captures

If you're creating software documentation for print, or you want to show an image of a Web page in your project, you may need to include screen captures in your page layouts. Screen captures are easy to make using a system utility or special screen-capture software, but they require some special handling to print clearly. Especially when they're part of software documentation or instructional materials, it's important that the details are as sharply rendered as possible.

Funny thing about screen captures: Whether you take them by using your system's built-in screen-capture functionality or a third-party screen-capture application, you are merely intercepting information that eventually becomes pixels on your monitor. Whatever your current monitor resolution, there is a one-to-one relationship between the fixed *number* of pixels that the system generates and the number of pixels you see on your screen. The *size* of the image you see is just a function of your current monitor resolution (**Figure 4.6**)

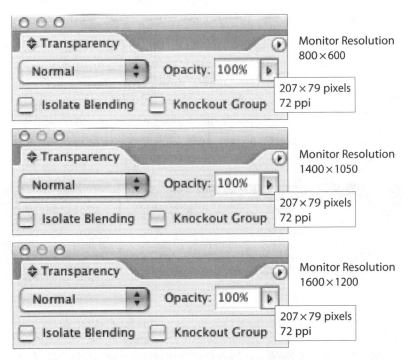

Figure 4.6 The resolution setting of your monitor has no effect on the number of pixels captured in a screen capture. Although this panel was captured at three different monitor resolutions, the three captures are identical, each consisting of exactly the same number of pixels.

An application panel that measures 208 pixels by 80 pixels may appear larger when your screen resolution is set to 800 by 600, and it appears almost unreadably small when your monitor is set to 1600 by 1200. However, the panel is made of exactly the same *number* of pixels in both instances. So it doesn't matter at what resolution your monitor is set or how large the panels may appear on screen. You'll capture the same image regardless of monitor setting, and the resulting image will be 72 ppi.

Since it's been drilled into you that 300 ppi is the Holy Grail of image resolution, it's tempting to try to improve screen captures by increasing the resolution. Unfortunately, this usually makes them look *worse* by softening small details during interpolation.

If you plan to use a screen capture at 100-percent enlargement, just leave it at 72 ppi. Yes, the print service provider's prepress department will raise a flag, but the examples below show why screen captures are not improved by increasing their resolution.

As you can see in **Figure 4.7A**, the original 72-ppi screen capture seems a bit coarse, but it's readable. Increasing the resolution to 300 ppi in Photoshop may sound like a good idea, but as shown in **Figure 4.7B**, the interpolation will soften detail in the image.

If you do feel compelled to increase the resolution of a screen capture, there is an approach that may yield better results than resampling up to 300 ppi. In Photoshop, choose Image > Image Size, and then set the resolution to an even multiple of 72, such as 288 ppi. In that same dialog, set the Resample Image option to Nearest Neighbor (**Figure 4.7C**). This avoids interpolation by simply *repeating* pixels rather than attempting to *create* pixels. It's not an appropriate approach when scaling images of a photographic nature, but it's a helpful solution for screen captures, because of their special nature.

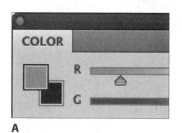 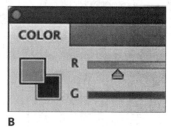 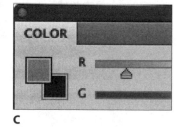

A   B   C

Figure 4.7 Image A is the original 72 ppi screen shot. Image B is the result of increasing the resolution to 300 ppi, using the default Bicubic method: Note the blurry text and softened edges. Image C was created by increasing the resolution to 288 ppi by using the Nearest Neighbor method. If you must scale or resample a screen shot, you'll achieve the best results by increasing the resolution in even multiples of its original resolution and using the Nearest Neighbor method. A Windows screen shot, for example, may be 96 ppi: Increase its resolution to 192.

Converting Screen Captures to CMYK

Since screen captures are generated as RGB images, they must be converted to CMYK for print. When performing that conversion, a special approach is recommended to maintain the best rendering of black type. The default conversion of RGB to CMYK in Photoshop will render black as a four-color mix (**Figure 4.8**), with the possibility that slight misregistration on press will turn tiny details to mush.

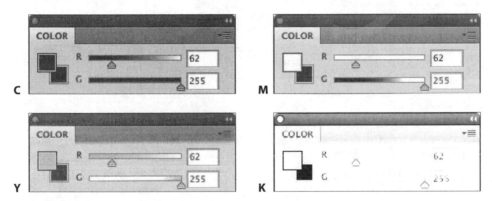

Figure 4.8 A conventional conversion from RGB to CMYK produces four-color equivalents of the gray and black parts of a screen capture. Press misregistration will turn text and other black or gray elements to an out-of-focus rainbow. Festive, but hard to read

To simplify printing of screen captures, use a color-separation recipe that ensures that all neutral black or gray areas of the image will print only in black ink during the RGB-to-CMYK conversion. Neutral areas in an RGB image are those areas in which the RGB values are equal; for example, R128–G128–B128 would constitute a midtone gray.

To create this custom, screen-capture conversion recipe in Photoshop, choose Edit > Color Settings to access the color-separation controls. Under Working Spaces, choose Custom for the CMYK setting. In the Custom CMYK dialog box, select Maximum Black Generation (**Figure 4.9**). The curve you see may seem odd, but it merely indicates that all equivalent RGB values are being replaced with black. The appearance of color elements won't be compromised.

Color elements will be composed of four colors in the final CMYK image. But black and gray elements will be rendered only in black (**Figure 4.10**). While this may look odd, it results in cleaner printing of the screen capture, since there aren't four colors gumming up the works in most of the image.

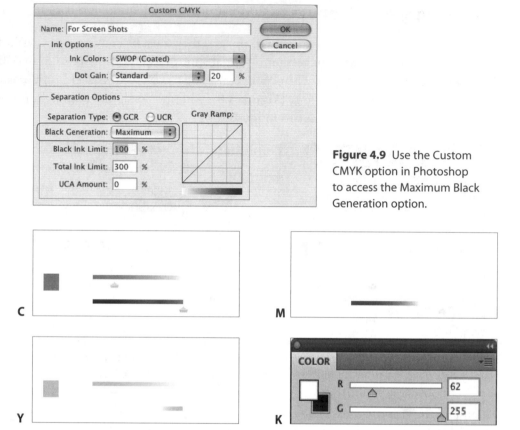

Figure 4.9 Use the Custom CMYK option in Photoshop to access the Maximum Black Generation option.

Figure 4.10 By setting the Black Generation option (on the Custom CMYK dialog) to Maximum, all gray and black content images only on the black plate.

RGB versus CMYK

Since the dawn of desktop publishing, it's been unquestioned that Thou Shalt Convert to CMYK. Those who submitted RGB files were considered uninformed, even uncivilized. But here's a secret: Scanners and digital cameras see in RGB. High-end production scanners such as those from Fujifilm/Enovation and Kodak produce CMYK files only because they utilize software to perform the conversion from RGB to CMYK on the fly.

As shown in Chapter Two, "Ink on Paper," the RGB gamut is larger than that of CMYK. Consequently, it's often preferable to perform color corrections and compositing with RGB files, converting to CMYK as late in the process as possible. If you are participating in a fully color-managed workflow, you will keep your images as RGB with ICC profiles. The International Color Consortium (ICC) was formed by a group of graphic arts industry vendors, with the goal of promoting the use and standardization of color management tools. ICC profiles are methods of describing the characteristics of devices such as scanners, presses, and printers for optimal results. Conversion will not take place until the job is imaged. Much of today's software offers sophisticated support of color management. For example, when exporting a PDF or printing, InDesign will perform the same conversion of RGB to CMYK that Photoshop would (assuming consistent and correct profiles).

Some print service providers and their customers have fully adopted color managed workflows as part of their regular operation. But many print service providers (especially in North America) expect CMYK when you submit your job, believing that it's what Nature intended. Consult with your printer to see what they prefer. If you're using digital photography or scanning your own artwork, they should be able to provide you with their preferred settings, so you can make appropriate conversions to CMYK.

INAPPROPRIATE IMAGE FORMATS FOR PRINT

Some image formats are intended primarily for onscreen and Web use. **Portable Network Graphics** (PNG) images can contain RGB and indexed color, as well as transparency. While PNG can be high resolution, it has no support for CMYK color space.

The Windows format **BMP** (an abbreviation for bitmap) supports color depths from one-bit (black and white, with no shades of gray) to 32-bit (millions of colors), but lacks support for CMYK. BMP is not appropriate for print.

Graphics Interchange Format (GIF) is appropriate only for Web use because of its inherently low resolution and an indexed color palette limited to a maximum of 256 colors. Don't use GIF for print.

JPEG (Joint Photographic Experts Group), named after the committee that created it, has an unsavory reputation in graphic arts. Just whisper "jay-peg," and watch prepress operators cringe. It is a lossy compression scheme, meaning that it discards information to make a smaller digital file.

Assuming an image has adequate resolution, a very slight amount of initial JPEG compression doesn't noticeably impair image quality, but aggressive compression introduces ugly rectangular artifacts, especially in detailed areas (**Figure 4.11**).

Figure 4.11 Overly aggressive JPEG compression produces unattractive rectangular artifacts. A slight amount of JPEG compression, however, is not noticeable. So don't fear JPEG compression. Just don't overdo it.

Each time you re*save* an image as a JPEG, you re*compress* it. Prepress paranoids will shriek that you're ruining your image, and there's some truth to that. While it's true that repeatedly resaving an image with low-quality compression settings would eventually erode detail, the mere fact that an image has been saved as a JPEG does not render it unusable, especially if you use a minimal level of compression. Despite the reputation, JPEGs aren't inherently evil. They *can* be decent graphic citizens, even capable of containing high-resolution CMYK image data. That said, when you acquire a JPEG image from your digital camera or a stock photo service, it's still advisable to immediately resave the image as a TIFF or PSD file to prevent further compression. However, JPEGs intended for Web use are low-resolution RGB files, inappropriate for print. If your customer provides a low-resolution or aggressively compressed JPEG, there's nothing you can do to improve it.

CHAPTER FIVE

Vector Graphics

While raster images are made up of pixels, vector graphics are refreshingly pixel free. As such, vector graphics are not subject to the scaling restrictions that plague raster images (**Figure 5.1**). The smooth shapes of a purely vector drawing have no inherent resolution, so it can be enlarged and reduced with no penalty.

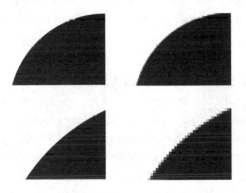

Figure 5.1 Vector drawings (top left) are mathematically generated smooth lines, whereas raster images (top right) are composed of pixels.

Vector art can be scaled up with no limit (bottom left). Raster images, however, don't fare well at extreme enlargements (bottom right).

VECTOR FILE FORMATS

Since the File > Save and File > Export dialogs of popular drawing programs offer a dizzying list of prospective file types, it's important to know what's acceptable for print and what's not.

Encapsulated PostScript (EPS)

The most common file format for containing vector artwork used to be EPS. In fact, the acronym EPS is so deeply associated with vector graphics that new entrants to the mysteries of graphic arts sometimes believe that merely saving an image in the EPS format magically converts it to vectors. They're subsequently disappointed when they discover that they must instead use the dreaded Pen tool to create vector art. See Chapter Four, "Preparing Raster Images," for an explanation of the difference between raster EPS files and vector EPS files.

Encapsulated PostScript is, as the name implies, a container for PostScript information that allows it to be understood by other applications. An EPS file contains drawing information, of course, but it may also contain font information as well as embedded raster images. A preview image is also usually included to provide an appearance for the file when it's placed in a page-layout program. However, if you travel off the beaten path and attempt to use EPS artwork in word-processing or presentation programs, you may find that the artwork does not appear correctly because the program can't correctly read the preview image that represents the contents of the EPS. And some programs can't correctly interpret the PostScript information itself, resulting in poor output. It isn't the fault of the EPS—it's the application's inability to utilize the PostScript contents.

EPS files can be placed in a wide range of applications such as the dedicated page-layout applications QuarkXPress and Adobe InDesign, which understand how to display and print EPS content. However, page-layout programs can't directly interact with the contents of an EPS, so any editing must be performed in the originating application, such as Adobe Illustrator.

EPS files are usually used for placed artwork, but are also used as files for output. (Some print workflows are based on EPS files rather than application files.) Since PostScript is a published specification and thus available to any software developer, *any* application can potentially generate EPS files. However, not all applications create EPS files that are intended to be opened by drawing applications. It is generally *not* advisable to open an EPS in Illustrator that wasn't originally generated from Illustrator. Yes, it's an EPS, but it is intended only for *placement*, not for *editing*. You *may* successfully edit such an EPS, but don't count on it. You may damage font embedding or inadvertently make changes that won't be apparent until the job images. As they always say in B-rated science fiction films, "We were never meant to go in there."

There are cautions, even when opening up EPS files generated by the most popular drawing programs. FreeHand can safely open up EPS files created by FreeHand. Illustrator can successfully open its own Illustrator EPS files. This may not seem surprising, but it only works because each application adds extra information to create an editable EPS, which allows it to be reopened in the originating application.

If you attempt to use Illustrator to edit EPS files created by other applications (such as page-layout programs), the translations are not always successful. Text may become point text (little isolated clumps of editable text), and some special features such as shadows may not translate correctly. Some elements may completely disappear or become rasterized. It's best to keep such files in their own species to avoid problems.

Why is this? PostScript is a programming language that provides instructions for imaging. Thus, an EPS is more than a drawing in some sort of container. In essence, it's a tiny computer program. So, just as one programmer might not understand another's style of coding, one application may not correctly interpret an EPS produced by another program. Man was never meant to reopen EPS files, but you know what always happens in sci-fi movies. They just *have* to pry open that EPS. They just *have* to go into that darkened room. With a flashlight. In a nightgown. Thus, some real-world advice: Make edits in the originating application.

TIP: *When saving an EPS from Illustrator, choose TIFF 8-bit for the preview option. In addition to providing better cross-platform support, it also prevents a known problem in InDesign versions through Creative Suite 1 (CS). If you place an EPS with a Macintosh preview in InDesign and then add a drop shadow, the shadow will follow the edge of the graphic frame rather than the edge of the graphic. If, however, you save the EPS with a TIFF 8-bit preview, the shadow will correctly follow the shape of the vector graphic. It's just one of life's little mysteries. If you use native Illustrator files or you're placing EPS files in InDesign CS2 or later, this isn't an issue.*

Native File Formats

Welcome to the future: Unless you are submitting a vector file for use in a workflow that doesn't support native Illustrator files (such as a word-processing program or some sign-cutting workflows), there's no reason to save an Illustrator file as EPS in the current environment, and a number of reasons in favor of using the native Illustrator (.AI) format.

If you're planning to place the artwork into an InDesign page, there is some motivation to go native. InDesign honors transparency and blending modes in a native Illustrator file. This means that a placed Illustrator file can interact with other artwork in InDesign, allowing you to create some interesting opacity and blending effects that would not be possible with an EPS, whose internal contents are opaque to other applications. In addition, InDesign allows you to control the visibility of layers within a placed Illustrator native file without having to modify the file in Illustrator, but doesn't provide that nifty flexibility for placed EPS files.

Adobe PDF

If you are creating vector artwork for placement in another application such as a page-layout file, there's usually not much reason to save your file as a PDF. However, if the vector art is not destined for placement in a page layout, but will be submitted as finished art, saving it as PDF allows you to protect your artwork from unwanted editing. And under most circumstances, saving as PDF eliminates the need to supply fonts with your job (assuming you're using fonts that don't forbid embedding).

In all cases, before you send your job as PDF, ask the print service provider to provide detailed specifications for PDF creation.

Vector Formats Not Appropriate for Print

Not all vector formats are created equal. While page-layout programs may allow you to import them, some vector file formats do not print satisfactorily.

Microsoft Windows Metafile Format (WMF)

WMF is intended for placement in applications such as Microsoft Word or PowerPoint. While WMF can contain both vector and raster content, it offers no support for CMYK content. Curved shapes are rendered as choppy, chiseled sections (**Figure 5.2**). WMF is a very limited format and simply isn't appropriate for print.

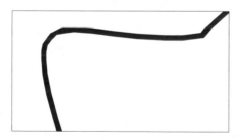

Figure 5.2 WMF renders curved shapes as choppy approximations. While it may be acceptable in a Microsoft Word or PowerPoint file, WMF should not be used for print.

Enhanced Metafile Format (EMF)

EMF, like WMF, is intended for use in applications such as Word and PowerPoint. While curves are smoother than those in a WMF, strokes become concentric shapes. EMF offers no support for CMYK, and some vector artwork may be rasterized. And, like WMF, EMF is not appropriate for print production.

Raster Formats

Illustrator offers options for exporting to raster formats such as TIFF, JPEG, PNG, and BMP. Of course, a vector format provides more flexibility and sharper output. But if you do need to rasterize the content of a vector artwork file (say, for Web use), choose File > Export and select the appropriate format and settings. The Illustrator file is unchanged; a new file is created during export.

HANDLING TEXT

When you include text in your vector artwork, you have to take steps to ensure that it will print as expected. Of course, you can use the same approach that's recommended for page-layout applications: Gather up the fonts and support artwork (such as placed images) and include them when you submit your vector artwork to the print service provider. While Illustrator doesn't naturally do this, the Scoop plug-in from Worker 72a (www.worker72a.com) adds the functionality for Illustrator 8.0 through CS4. (As of this writing, the Scoop plug-in is available for Macintosh only.)

The more common methods for dealing with needed fonts in vector graphics, however, are embedding and outlining.

Embedding Fonts

Provided that the font creator has not forbidden embedding, Illustrator can embed fonts in an EPS or AI file *for placement in other programs*. This means that font information should be available for display and printing, but this does *not* make the font available for editing text in the EPS or AI. To edit text, you'll still need the appropriate fonts active on your system; embedding does not deliver the fonts to you.

Not all applications can embed fonts in the EPSs they generate. QuarkXPress, for example, does not embed fonts in an exported EPS. However, a number of XTensions provide this functionality, including XPert Print from ALAP (a lowly apprentice production, inc.), the assets and products of which have been acquired by Quark. (By the way, marketing materials from ALAP consistently displayed the company name in all lowercase letters. We were torn: Should we capitalize, as we were itching to do, or should we follow their example?)

It may come as a surprise to you that not all fonts *can* be embedded. Some font vendors prevent embedding by placing a "don't embed" flag in their fonts. This won't prevent you from using these fonts to create artwork, nor will it prevent printing. But you will be unable to embed the font in any AI, EPS, or PDF file that you create. This means you have to ensure that the print service provider also has the necessary fonts to print your job (more about this thorny issue in Chapter Six, "Fonts").

Even if you *can* embed fonts, there is no guarantee that the embedding will survive what the print service provider might do to your poor, innocent EPS or AI file. If there is a problem that requires editing the file, they'll need to open the file. Opening the file without the necessary fonts loaded will result in the font embedding being destroyed. As long as the file is left unopened, it will image as expected when placed into a page-layout program such as InDesign.

Some smaller printers do informal imposition by positioning EPS files in a page-layout application. Trapping, imposition, and RIP software all must correctly interpret font information. Each step has the potential to corrupt font information. Don't freak out, these are worst-case scenarios. But the prospects are worth considering.

Now that you fear for the safety of your fonts, what can you do to ensure successful imaging? Your best bet is to create a PDF. But some printers or publications may insist that you convert your text to outlines. Of course, save a second version of the file without outlined text to use as a working file in anticipation of possible corrections or the sobering discovery of a misspelled word.

Outlining Text

Fonts contain information, called *hinting*, which refines the display and printing of text. Consequently, some purists hold that those who outline text should be tarred and feathered. It's true that converting text to outlines eliminates hinting, so text may display onscreen as if slightly bloated and will print slightly heavier on desktop printers because of the lower resolution of those devices. You should avoid outlining text if the job will be printed on a digital press such as a Xerox iGen or an HP Indigo: The 600–1200 dpi resolution of digital presses can result in obvious thickening of small text. However, the fattening is *not* usually apparent when outlined text is imaged on higher-resolution devices such as imagesetters and platesetters. It's worth mentioning that very small text or type with delicate serifs may lose definition when outlined, regardless of the output device or printing process.

> **NOTE:** *Please read the section on font licensing in Chapter Six, "Fonts." Not all font vendors allow you to outline text. This is probably a surprise to you, but it's an issue that you must consider.*

Converting text to outlines eliminates the worry that font embedding might be undone by incautious editing or a process that fails to honor the embedded fonts. If you are submitting PDF files, it's unnecessary to outline fonts, because of the limited editability of PDF files.

INCORPORATING IMAGES INTO VECTOR FILES

It's possible to place images in vector drawings in much the same way they're placed in page layouts. It's accepted practice in page layout to *link* the images rather than *embed* them, and this same approach is an option when incorporating images in vector artwork. However, linking images rather than embedding them can cause some problems when the finished artwork is placed into another document, such as a page-layout file. If, in the heat of battle, you neglect to send the linked images along with the parent vector file, things will understandably fall apart.

The alternative is to embed the image in your vector drawing as you create the EPS or AI, so that it can't fall by the wayside. Embedding, as you might expect, increases the size of the resulting file. It's pretty easy math. If you've embedded a 2 MB image, you'll be adding 2 MB to your final size. But you have to remember to choose the option to embed images rather than link them.

Fortunately for us, we live in civilized times. Whereas earlier versions of Illustrator didn't do so, the current version provides the option to embed images as you save an EPS or AI file. You can then fearlessly send your file out into the world, fully outfitted with its outlined text and embedded images, with all your eggs in one digital basket.

What if it's subsequently necessary to color correct an image embedded in an EPS or drawing file? If you created the file and still have the image, just do the corrections and replace the image in the drawing. But if there's no access to the original image—for example, if someone else created the illustration—what do you do?

Illustrator doesn't offer such a straightforward method for image extraction, but you can cheat. Select the embedded image in the Illustrator file, and then copy it to the clipboard. Launch Photoshop and choose File > New. A new, blank document is created that's the same size as the clipboard contents. Select Edit > Paste, and voilà, there's the image.

While effects such as feathered edges, blurs, and soft shadows look like pixels, they're only *potentially* pixels. They don't become *literal* pixels until you export or print the Illustrator file. Within Illustrator, you may feel free to transform the object because the effects are regenerated anew during each transform. However, if you transform a placed Illustrator file in InDesign, its effects become subject to the same restrictions that would apply to a raster image. If you find it necessary to drastically scale up a placed Illustrator file with effects, consider returning to Illustrator to do the scaling, then update the file in InDesign.

> **NOTE:** For more details on issues pertaining to creating and imaging these special effects, see Chapter Ten, "Illustrator CS4 Production Tips."

AVOIDING UNNECESSARY COMPLEXITY

RIPs are more robust than ever, but there are still reasons to simplify vector artwork. Simpler drawings usually result in a smoother appearance, and they're easier to edit later. If you've used the drawing tools in Illustrator, you know that vector art is made of straight and curved lines called Bézier shapes. The anchor points and direction handles that allow you to modify such shapes are fairly confusing when you first use them. So, in our timid early experiments in drawing programs, we tend to tiptoe around shapes, using a bazillion clicks to create a drawing. Eventually, we become more comfortable with the tools and learn to do more with less.

Simplify Your Paths

Stop clicking. Really. Right now. More points do not equal a better drawing. In fact, *fewer* points—if they're the *right* points—result in a smoother drawing, as you can see in **Figure 5.3**. Of course, in the early stages of learning vector drawing tools, it's difficult to draw so elegantly. But even if your drawing is a bit lumpy, there are tools in Illustrator that smooth and simplify paths.

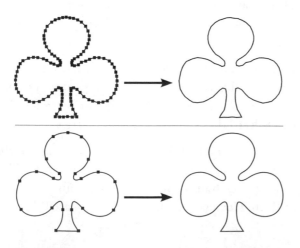

Figure 5.3 Too many points (top row) result in a choppy drawing. Correct Pen tool technique produces fewer points and a smoother finished drawing (bottom row).

In the early days of desktop drawing, it was crucial to minimize the number of points in a drawing to ensure successful imaging. The overly busy shamrock on the top row of Figure 5.3 might have been called a RIP-buster in those ancient days, resulting in glacially slow print times and the possibility that it would produce the dreaded limitcheck error and fail to be processed by the RIP. Modern RIPs are much more robust and computers are exponentially faster, but smoothness is still a strong motivation to master the Zen of fewer clicks while drawing. And your mouse will last longer.

Recommended Approaches to Document Construction

The original purpose of vector drawing programs was to create logos and other geometric shapes. With each release, these programs add features that delight artists and frighten print service providers. Illustrator 9.0 was the first version to offer the ability to go far beyond simple logos, with painterly effects, soft edges, shadows, glows, and complicated patterns. As the distinctions between *paint* and *draw* are blurred, you must decide where best to create your artwork. Sometimes it's preferable to use an image-editing application such as Photoshop to create a piece, in the interest of predictable output. And sometimes it's more sensible to wade into page layout rather than trying to strain the capabilities of your drawing program.

It's a Drawing Program

Well, *duh*, you're thinking. Of course it is! And that's the point; Illustrator is a *drawing* program, not a *page-layout* program.

If you are creating a single-page piece such as a magazine ad and you're more comfortable working in a drawing program, it's acceptable to use Illustrator, provided you correctly build in any necessary bleed.

But if you're contemplating creating something like an annual report, it's time to consider learning a dedicated page-layout application. As you will see in Chapter Ten, "Illustrator CS4 Production Tips," it is possible to have multiple Artboards in Illustrator CS4, so it may seem that the distinctions are becoming blurred between InDesign and Illustrator. However, Illustrator is still intended for illustration, and it lacks the dedicated page-layout features that InDesign boasts, such as automatic page numbering, cross-references, and the ability to generate a table of contents or index.

CHAPTER SIX
Fonts

We have a love-hate relationship with fonts. We love their chiseled serifs, we swoon over their graceful swashes, we kern them to the verge of claustrophobia. We painstakingly track text to perfection, and agonize over minuscule leading values. Wait a minute. This is starting to sound like a romance novel. That would be the *love* part of the equation. Alas, this chapter is more about the *hate* part.

FONT FLAVORS

Fonts come in several formats: PostScript (often also referred to as Type 1), TrueType, and OpenType. Within those major species, there are subspecies, but it's sufficient to know the major species. We'll ignore ancient Mac system fonts, which were just bitmap information.

PostScript (Type 1) Fonts

We were all raised to believe that PostScript fonts were the Only Right Way, convinced that any other font format was evil (pronounced as in old horror movies—*eve-yil*). In the earlier days of desktop publishing, this was a well-founded belief, because early RIPs couldn't handle TrueType. (However, that's no longer the case.)

PostScript fonts consist of two files: A bitmap "screen font" component for onscreen display and a printer component that contains PostScript instructions for actually printing the character. Since it's made of pixels, the bitmap component alone can't provide acceptable resolution for output, so if you misplace the printer font, you're out of luck. Don't discard the screen font either: It contains additional resources required by the system.

Whereas the screen font was once necessary for onscreen display of a PostScript font, current Macintosh and Windows operating systems can rasterize a printer font for onscreen display once it's activated without needing a companion screen font to do so. Font activation applications, such as Extensis™ Suitcase or Suitcase Fusion, or FontAgent Pro from Insider Software won't activate a lone printer font without its companion screen font, but some applications such as Adobe InDesign activate printer fonts placed in their own private fonts folders. Placing a PostScript printer font in InDesign's fonts folder makes it available to InDesign on both Windows and Macintosh. In either case, the operating system handles the onscreen display without having a screen font.

InDesign's dedicated fonts folder can be found here:

- **Windows:** Program Files\Adobe\Adobe InDesign CS4\Fonts

- **Macintosh:** Applications/Adobe InDesign CS4/Fonts

TrueType Fonts

The TrueType format was the result of a collaboration between Apple Computer and Microsoft and consists of a single file (that is, no separate screen and printer font component). Thus there is no need to keep track of two separate components for screen and print. However, in more primitive times—say, 1993—just mentioning TrueType could strike terror in the heart of a prepress operator. Earlier PostScript RIPs could not interpret TrueType fonts, so it was routine to use a font-conversion utility to change the flavor of the font to PostScript. While such conversions enabled the job to be processed by a RIP, they often resulted in slight translation errors and some compromise of the hinting stored in the TrueType version of the font. Consequently, text appearance was altered, however slightly, from the designer's expectations. But we were desperate people in those times, and we accepted the slight differences in the interest of actually getting the job to print.

Fast-forward to current times. It's no longer necessary to jump through these treacherous hoops. RIPs can now process TrueType just as easily as PostScript fonts. Really. There is no longer any need to sneer at TrueType fonts as being somehow inferior. Admittedly, if you buy TrueType fonts in a $9.95 font collection called Larry's Boatload o'Fonts, there's a chance that they won't be well behaved. But that isn't because they're TrueType fonts. It's because Larry builds lousy fonts.

OpenType Fonts

OpenType fonts are single-file fonts and do not have separate screen and printer fonts to keep track of. But here's where the real font fun begins. OpenType fonts are cross platform. This doesn't mean that Adobe Garamond Pro comes in a Macintosh version and an identical Windows version. Instead, the *same* font file can be used on a Mac or on a PC with no special handling.

But, as the late night TV ads say: Wait, there's more. Whereas PostScript fonts are limited to a paltry 256 characters (isn't that *enough*?), OpenType fonts can contain more than 65,000 *glyphs*. A glyph is any distinct letterform, such as a number, a lowercase *p*, or an ampersand. This allows a font designer to include swashes, contextual ligatures, titling alternates—even fractions—all in one font. The entirety of a font family that previously required separate expert and titling sets can now be contained in one font. See **Figure 6.1** for a glimpse of just a few of OpenType's possibilities.

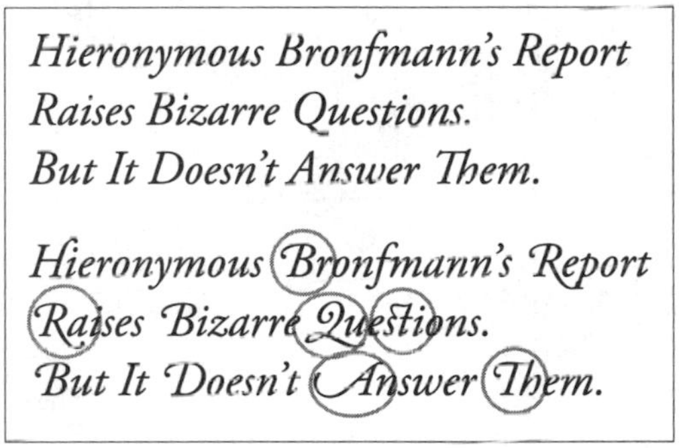

Hieronymous Bronfmann's Report
Raises Bizarre Questions.
But It Doesn't Answer Them.

Hieronymous Bronfmann's Report
Raises Bizarre Questions.
But It Doesn't Answer Them.

Figure 6.1 Adobe Garamond Pro is a lovely font even without invoking its special OpenType features (top). But look what happens when Swashes and Discretionary Ligatures are turned on (bottom).

Not all OpenType fonts contain glyphs in every one of those 65,000 available character positions. For example, one font may have swashes, but another may not. However, the adherence to Unicode mapping ensures that a character exists in the same position from font to font. Unicode is a standard that provides a unique universal identifier for every character, regardless of language, application, or platform. For more information, visit the Unicode Web site (www.unicode.org). If you set text using some of the special diacritical characters in Caslon Pro, for example, and then change the font used to Garamond Pro, the diacriticals (special language characters, such as á, ä, and ç) are intact because they exist in both fonts.

You can use OpenType fonts without fear of imaging problems. They are compatible with all recent RIPs, and all current font-management software supports OpenType. Not using font-management software? OpenType fonts can be activated by the built-in Font Book application on the Macintosh and by the Windows Fonts control panel. Or you can drop them in the Macintosh system fonts folders to make them available to all applications (although it's preferable to use font-management software). And having OpenType fonts doesn't mean you have to stop using the PostScript and TrueType fonts you already have.

The benefits of OpenType extend far beyond typographic beauty. One of the motivations for the OpenType format was to provide multilingual support. In **Figure 6.2**, you can see the extensive character set in just one font, Myriad Pro from Adobe Systems.

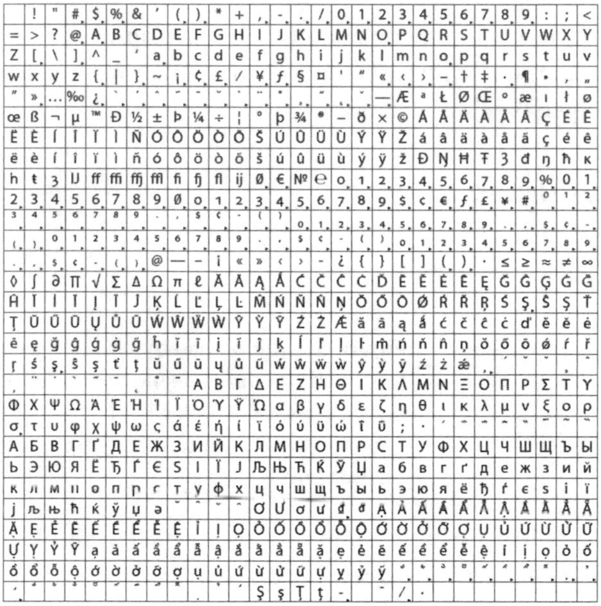

Figure 6.2 Multilingual support available within the OpenType font Myriad Pro, viewed in the InDesign Glyphs panel.

You won't be able to use all 65,000 glyphs unless you're using software that recognizes the additional features. Adobe InDesign, Illustrator, and Photoshop can see and use the entire contents of an OpenType font, whereas QuarkXPress through version 6.5 has blinders on, and it can only utilize the same old 256 characters. QuarkXPress 7.0 introduces support for the complete range of OpenType features.

Adobe has converted its entire font library to OpenType and will no longer be offering PostScript Type 1 fonts. It's easy to spot OpenType fonts from Adobe: They have *Std* or *Pro* as part of their names. Adobe is not the only font vendor marketing OpenType fonts. Most major font vendors now offer OpenType. Given the linguistic support and the enhanced typographic features offered by OpenType fonts, it's easy to see that it's the font format of the future. And it's here today, unlike those flying automobiles we've been waiting for.

NOTE: *The* Std *is short for Standard, indicating an Adobe OpenType version of a previously available PostScript Type 1 font. Adobe OpenType fonts with the* Pro *indicator have more expanded glyph sets and are often the result of combining what once were expert font sets and their base companions.*

Glyphs and Characters

It's easy to confuse the terms *character* and *glyph*, but they describe different concepts. A *character* corresponds to a single position in the Unicode standard, which is a uniform, agreed-upon mapping system for the contents of a font. A *glyph*, however, is a distinct letterform. Multiple glyphs may exist for a single character position in an OpenType font, such as Q and $\mathcal{Q}$ for the uppercase Q in Adobe Garamond Pro Italic.

Macintosh OS X System Fonts

Macintosh system fonts such as Geneva, Monaco, Chicago, and Charcoal had traditionally been easy to spot because of their distinctive names. But with the introduction of OS X, Apple threw a monkey wrench into the font wars by including system fonts named Helvetica, Helvetica Neue, and Times Roman, just like their PostScript cousins. Under the hood, these are TrueType fonts, but you'll see them described as *dfonts*, a moniker derived from the fact that the fonts are data-only, and not a two-headed file consisting of a data fork and a resource fork. (If this doesn't mean much to you, don't worry.)

Macintosh dfonts aren't inherently evil, but they are problematic because their names are indistinguishable from their PostScript counterparts. If the job is created by multiple people who are using different versions of a font, this may result in font substitution and consequent reflow. Since they're system fonts, they're active by default. To use the PostScript fonts of the same names, you have to sneak up on the dfonts to control their activation or deactivation by using dedicated font-management software as described in the earlier section, "PostScript (Type 1) Fonts."

With the advent of the Leopard (10.5) operating system on the Mac, this became more of an issue: Leopard insists on having certain fonts available to it. Try to disable them, and, like zombies in bad B-movies, they keep coming back. If you're a fan of Helvetica or Helvetica Neue, your PostScript fonts will conflict with the insistent system fonts. Solution? Purchase the OpenType versions of those fonts, and ignore the aggressive versions forced on you by the operating system.

Additionally, dfonts don't work under OS 9 because they're not recognized as fonts by the OS 9 operating system or its font-management schemes. If you're still jumping back to OS 9 to use earlier versions of software such as QuarkXPress 4.x or 5.x, this can complicate your font usage. Imagine that you have used a dfont in a QuarkXPress 6.0 file created in

Macintosh OS X, and then saved the page-layout file down for QuarkXPress version 5.0. A user of QuarkXPress 5.0 will open the file under OS 9, and the dfont will not be available. The users will be forced to substitute a similar font, possibly leading to text reflow. One solution is to use the dfontifier utility from Mark Douma (http://homepage.mac.com/mdouma46/dfont/dfont.html) to convert dfonts to a font format that is recognized under OS 9. The utility is not supported under Leopard (Mac OS 10.5), however.

OpenType fonts are innocent bystanders in this battle. Their names distinguish them from TrueType, PostScript, and dfont files. As you can see in **Figure 6.3**, the OpenType version of Times is named TimesLTStd, making it much easier to pick it out of the pack.

Times   TimesRom   TimesLTStd Roman.otf   Times Roman.dfont

Figure 6.3 Sign of the Times. On the left, Macintosh OS X icons for PostScript screen font (left) and printer font (second from left). The OpenType icon is in the center, and Macintosh dfont is on the right. While they look the same at a casual glance, look closer and note the identifiers: FFIL, LWFN, OTF, DFONT.

Windows System Fonts

PC users may now revel in the fact that, starting with Windows 2000, their system fonts are OpenType fonts. In fact, the birth of OpenType is the result of a collaboration between Adobe Systems and Microsoft. The Arial system font has the ability to display an extensive character set, including Greek, Hebrew, and Arabic characters.

Multiple Master Fonts

The term Multiple Master probably elicits as much fear in a prepress department as yelling "TrueType," and for much the same reason—fear of the unknown. Adobe's Multiple Master fonts were a great idea: Start with a PostScript font, and then give users the ability to create multiple weights, angles, and widths (such as condensed or extended) of a single font. It was an enlightened idea. The problems arose from a lack of education. It wasn't obvious how to make all the cool variants, how to collect the variants necessary for your job, or how to ensure that the print service provider knew how to use them. So the Multiple Master concept sort of died on the vine. Its creative promise was never fully realized, and it's been phased out as an available font product. However, Multiple Master technology is still used for display and printing when fonts are missing in a PDF and for displaying text when fonts are unavailable for an InDesign or Illustrator file.

Substituting One Font Species for Another

A variation on the old joke:

PATIENT: I didn't have the necessary PostScript font, so I used my TrueType version. The type reflowed and the line breaks are all wrong now.

DOCTOR: Don't do that.

When you collaborate on designs, try to avoid substituting a TrueType version of a font for a PostScript version, or vice versa. Don't use an OpenType font instead of the file creator's original font choice, despite your conviction that it's somehow better. You may get lucky, but you're still risking type reflow.

This is particularly treacherous if you move a job between platforms. A Windows font and its Macintosh namesake may both be PostScript, but that's still no guarantee that they were created by the same foundry with the same nuances. The solution to this dilemma, of course, is to use OpenType fonts because of their cross-platform usability. The Creative Suite ships with a generous helping of OpenType fonts to get you started.

ACTIVATING FONTS IN THE OPERATING SYSTEM

Just having a font somewhere on your hard drive isn't enough. You must activate it to make it available to all the applications on your computer. Both Windows and the Macintosh provide built-in font activation. If you tend to use the same fonts, and don't need to frequently add fonts, the built-in font activation schemes may be sufficient for your needs.

Apple Font Book

Apple's free Font Book utility ships as part of OS X. If you're using a limited selection of fonts for the majority of your work and don't need the control afforded by creating font sets, Font Book is probably adequate. It may appear to be a font manager, but earlier versions of Font Book did some ugly things. Fonts were moved into the system library, and then deleted from their original location. (There goes your job folder!) And it never deactivated a font that was removed from Font Book's collections. Fonts remained in the system, eternally activated.

Mercifully, this uncivilized behavior is somewhat improved under OS 10.4 (Tiger). Font Book now copies rather than moves font files. And it actually deactivates fonts when Font Book's collections are disabled or removed. However, it still leaves a duplicate of the font files in the your Library/Fonts folder.

Windows Control Panel

Windows users can activate fonts by placing them in the Fonts folder of the Control Panel. Much like Apple's Font Book, the Fonts control panel provides a common system location so that fonts are available to applications. Deleting a font from Windows' Fonts control panel puts it in the Recycle Bin. There is no provision for creating sets of fonts. Activated fonts are stored together in a single folder, and they're all awake, all the time.

FONT-MANAGEMENT PROGRAMS

It's important to note that the font activation methods provided by your operating system are just that—font *activation*, not font *management*. As an application launches, it takes note of all the activated fonts. Do you really need to have 500 fonts awake all the time? If you have hundreds of fonts active, you're adding to system overhead and slowing down all your applications. If you're tired of taking ten minutes to get from *A* to *H* in your overly long font listings, it's a sign that it's time to adopt some sort of font management.

Font-management programs allow you to selectively activate and deactivate fonts as necessary to reduce system overhead. These programs also allow you to create custom sets of fonts, so you can easily activate all the fonts needed for a job or a particular customer with just one click.

Some of the commonly used font-management applications include Extensis Suitcase Fusion 2 (Mac-only as of this writing) and Suitcase for Windows, FontAgent Pro from Insider Software (Mac and Windows), Linotype Font Explorer X (Mac only), and Alsoft MasterJuggler® (Mac only). Which solution should you choose? There's no easy answer: It depends on your own tastes. These products provide approximately the same functionality, so your choice will likely depend on your fondness for a particular interface. Download a trial version of the software, give it a spin, and see if it fits with your workflow and requirements.

Automatic Font Activation

In addition to allowing you to create and activate font sets, some font-management solutions install plug-ins or XTensions that provide the ability to automatically activate fonts as needed when document files are launched. Occasionally, an auto-activation plug-in can conflict with other plug-ins in some applications. Symptoms may include minor effects such as display glitches or pauses while fonts are activated. Such glitches are rarely dangerous, but be prepared for them.

Font Conflicts

It is possible to have multiple font files with the same name: For example, over the years you may have bought a PostScript Type 1 version of Helvetica and a TrueType version, and then found that those legacy fonts now conflict with the Macintosh system font also named Helvetica. How do you know which font is the "right" font?

That's how your font-management software feels when it encounters PostScript, TrueType, and Macintosh system fonts—all with the same name. If one flavor is active, and you attempt to activate another, things get exciting, as shown in **Figure 6.4**.

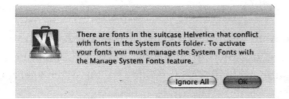

Figure 6.4 Attempting to activate a PostScript version of Helvetica prompts an alert because the OS already has its own version of Helvetica. Fortunately, font-management software (Extensis Suitcase shown here) allows you to sneak around and fix this.

As mentioned earlier, this can happen when the desired font has the same name as an operating system font; take advantage of your font management applications's ability to manage system fonts to resolve the conflict, if possible. It also pays to perform some font housecleaning. Use a utility such as Morrison SoftDesign's FontDoctor™ (available for both Mac and Windows) to check for damaged and duplicate fonts. FontDoctor also organizes fonts into a sensible library to make your font life easier. You might consider discarding TrueType versions of fonts in favor of the PostScript duplicates.

And, once again, OpenType can come to the rescue. The unique names of OpenType fonts preclude such conflicts. It may seem that I'm shilling for OpenType, but the format truly is the solution to so many issues, and it offers so many other advantages. It's like a wonder drug with no bad side effects!

FONT LICENSING ISSUES

You probably don't think of fonts as software, but that's how fonts are distributed and licensed. They're not just little drawings of letters. Fonts also contain instructions for font appearance and imaging. Consider the prodigious amount of work that goes into creating a font, and perhaps you'll understand why you shouldn't just freely distribute fonts. Each character must be painstakingly drawn. The designer must take into consideration how characters fit together, how they will look at various sizes, create hinting information, and much more. Professional font-creation software is expensive and complex because designing fonts is not a simple undertaking. Consider that a copy of the FontLab font editing application costs $650—that should give you an idea of the nontrivial nature of font creation and font editing!

End User License Agreements (EULAs)

Yes, you'll find EULAs with fonts that you purchase (you did *purchase* them, didn't you?), although there's a good chance you've never read them. Most font foundries allow use of a purchased font on several workstations and one or two printing devices, so if you've bought a font for a three-person workgroup that shares one networked printer, you're probably abiding by the EULA (commonly pronounced *yoo-la*).

But the licensing situation is more complex than you may have realized. When you send your job to a print service provider, you gather up all the necessary files, including fonts. Surprise—you're probably in violation of the EULA for doing so. Here's an excerpt from a major font foundry's EULA.

> You may send a copy of any font along with your documents to a commercial printer or other service bureau to enable the editing or printing of your document, *provided that such party has informed you that it owns a valid license to use that particular font software.* [Italics added]

In other words, to be in compliance with the EULA, both you and the print service provider must have purchased licenses for the font. You may have never read the fine print, but this is indeed the letter of the law when it comes to font licensing. In other words, your inclusion of the font in a collection of job files submitted to the printer is not legal if the printer doesn't also own the font. And what are the chances that your printer owns every font on Earth?

Embedding Fonts in PDFs

You may think that no font vendor would object to an end user embedding a licensed font in a PDF. Well, some do. (The surprises just keep coming, don't they?) While we're not aware of any method for extracting a font from a PDF, apparently some font vendors fear that it is (or may become) possible. To forestall such thievery, some have included clauses in their EULAs that prescribe that fonts must be subset, which is a good idea, font licensing issues aside. Subsetting embeds only the characters needed to image the PDF file rather than the entire font. (Illustrator and InDesign automatically subset any embedded fonts.) They further stipulate that only one copy of the PDF must be supplied to the recipient. But beyond these two fairly harmless requirements, there's a rather sinister stipulation: They insist that the PDF must contain security settings to allow only viewing and printing.

These strictures don't sound unreasonable until you consider an important aspect of securing PDFs. To make security settings stick in a PDF, you must use at least a permissions password to protect the security settings. Otherwise, the recipient could just remove the security limitations. However, to place a secured PDF into a page, or to use it in an imposition process, the recipient will have to know the password to allow the file to be used. This defeats the purpose of imposing security, and seems to put both the creator of the PDF and the print service provider in the position of violating the EULA. So, once again, the legally acceptable solution is for the print service provider to purchase a license for the font. Note that some font vendors sell what is called a *service bureau license* at a reduced price, which is considered an extension of your license and may be exercised by the print service provider only for output of your jobs. Yes, it's a complex subject. But the proprieties of font licensing are widely overlooked.

Several EULAs suggest submitting PostScript files to the print service provider. While this would certainly force a designer to painstakingly check files before setting them in digital concrete, it's a fairly draconian approach, and offers no provision for corrections.

The sanest legal approach is to truly read the EULAs for fonts you own, and take the measures necessary to be in compliance with their stipulations, even if it means purchasing additional licenses for your print service provider. It's a small addition to job cost in the interest of unquestionable legality. Going forward, it would be wise to pore over the EULA for any fonts you're thinking of buying, keeping these issues in mind.

There are also some fonts that contain a "don't embed" flag which prevents these fonts from being embedded in a PDF. Such fonts are rare, and you will be warned that you have used a non-embeddable font if you attempt to create a PDF in InDesign or Illustrator. If the EULA for the font does not allow converting text to outlines, you will have to substitute a font that does allow embedding.

Converting Text To Outlines

By now you're probably thinking, "Surely I can just convert my text to outlines and completely avoid the Font Police." Surprisingly (or perhaps not, at this point), converting text to outlines does not sidestep the provisions of the font vendor's EULA. In fact, while some font vendors' licensing allows conversion of text to outlines, many expressly forbid it.

Additionally, you must consider that, even if a font vendor's EULA permits outlining fonts, you may see some slight loss of quality when printing to low-resolution devices such as in-house printers if you convert to outlines, especially with small, serif text.

What's a concerned citizen to do? First and foremost, read the license before you purchase fonts. If you're purchasing fonts online, the vendor should make the EULA available to you before you commit to purchasing a font. You'll find that some font foundries are less restrictive than others on issues such as font embedding and outlining. Either patronize those with less stringent EULAs, purchase fonts for your print service provider...or learn how to create your own fonts. *That* will give you some sympathy for font designers!

And don't name your firstborn child Eula, or she won't be able to go *anywhere* or do *anything*.

Sending Fonts to the Print Service Provider

If you have studied the fine print in the licensing agreements for all the fonts you're using in a project, and you've determined that you and your print service provider are in full compliance with any applicable licenses, remember to gather up all the necessary fonts when you submit your files for printing. See Chapter Eleven, "InDesign CS4 Production Tips" for specific information on preparing page-layout files (including fonts) for the print service provider.

If you submit PDF files, make sure you've correctly embedded the fonts. See Chapter Twelve, "Acrobat Production Tips," for general information about font handling in PDF files. For detailed information about creating PDF files from an individual application, see the appropriate chapter:

- Chapter Ten, "Illustrator CS4 Production Tips"

- Chapter Eleven, "InDesign CS4 Production Tips"

- Chapter Twelve, "Acrobat Production Tips"

CHAPTER SEVEN

Cross-Platform Issues

Allegiance to an operating system can be a tribal issue, rivaling politics as a trigger for heated discussions, innuendo, condescension, and insults regarding parentage and one's fitness for procreation. It's part of the fun of using computers.

In the early 1990s, this chapter would not have been necessary. In fact, it would have been fairly pointless. (Depending on your platform preference, you may feel that it's pointless *now*.) In those days, if you were involved in graphic arts, you were using a Macintosh. Period. End of story. Windows users were treated like second-class citizens when they dared take their jobs to a print service provider. If you wanted to clear out a prepress department in 1992, all you had to do was yell "PC job!" It was much like yelling "Fire!" in a crowded theater.

Fast-forward to the present day: It's not a Macintosh-only world. The major graphics applications such as InDesign, Illustrator, Photoshop, Acrobat, and QuarkXPress are almost indistinguishable across platforms. But while the applications themselves are generally compatible, operating system issues still must be addressed if we're all to get along peacefully. Now, put down that wooden stake.

CROSSING THE GREAT DIVIDE

Gone are the days when we needed special translation software to even read files from The Other Side. Whereas network connections once required arcane geek incantations and burnt offerings, mere mortals can now point, click, and magically access a networked PC from their Mac. We live in wonderful times.

But that doesn't mean things are perfect or painless. Windows users have to accept that many Macintosh users don't consider file extensions important (even though the current Mac OS uses them). Macintosh users must learn to avoid florid naming conventions. And everybody *still* needs to gather up the fonts before they send a job out the door.

While setting up a network is outside the scope of this book, the assumption is that you've figured out some way to get your stuff to wherever it needs to be. We've come a long way from floppies (Grandma, what are floppies?) and SyQuest drives. It was very chic to have huge whopping 44 MB SyQuest cartridges ten years ago, and blank CDs cost nearly 20 dollars apiece. Now, we have large-capacity CDs, DVDs, and memory sticks, and none of the current methods is platform-specific. Pardon the flashback. The author suddenly feels very, ah, mature.

NAMING FILES

It's great to be creative while you're designing an annual report or sales brochure. But when it's time to name and save files, control your imagination. Both Windows and Macintosh computers, as well as popular server platforms, are more forgiving than in the days of old eight-dot-three naming conventions (eight-character filename, followed by a three-letter file extension). In those days, a Macintosh user wanting to share with a PC user had to be fairly creative to come up with filenames. AnRepCov.eps, AnRepCv2.eps. You get the idea.

Let's Have a Lot of Brevity

The ancient eight-dot-three limitation has long been lifted. Given expanded freedom in naming files, some of us get a little carried away. Here's a file from one of the author's clients, slightly altered to protect the innocent: **SSGC holiday wreath photos and logos -- Publisher (10-19-05).pub**. Because spaces, periods, and parentheses also count, that's a 64-character filename. Windows and Macintosh platforms currently allow a total of 255 characters, which is perhaps overly generous. That's an entire paragraph.

While Windows allows filenames of 255 *characters*, it limits a total *path designation* to 260 characters. Path designation is the literal pathway to the file's location. For example, a file named Test.doc stored at the root level of a PC's C drive would have a path designation of **C:\Test.doc**, a total of 11 characters. File extensions like .doc or .pdf are included in the total character count for a filename.

If you're a Mac OS X user, you may not think of Mac OS 9 as another platform, but in many ways it is. Users of Mac OS 9 are limited to 31 character filenames, so if you're sharing files with colleagues who are still languishing under Mac OS 9, you'll have to take that into consideration, and keep your filenames appropriately brief. Think of filenaming as a game: What's the shortest name you can think of but still find useful?

Filenames Don't Need Punctuation. Period.

Length is not the only issue affecting proper naming of files. There are certain characters—even certain *names*—that should be avoided. A good rule of thumb is this: Don't include any characters traditionally used in comic strips to indicate profanity, such as !@#$*% (pardon my language). Stick to solely alphanumeric contents—uppercase and lowercase letters, coupled with numerals, spaces, underscores, and hyphens. There's an urban myth that spaces are forbidden in filenames, but this doesn't usually matter in a graphics/print environment. In Web work, however, it's best to omit spaces from file names, because some server platforms don't correctly handle spaces: A space will be replaced with the characters "%20."

Avoid colons and slashes, since those characters are reserved to mark directory breaks. Although the Mac OS won't prevent you from naming a file with forward or backward slashes, you won't be able to copy it to a Windows drive. PCs prevent the problem by stopping you in your tracks when you press either slash key, displaying an alert listing forbidden characters. And even Macintosh CD burning applications will convert slashes to underscores during the creation of a data CD.

If you're creating your job on the Mac and sending it to a print service provider who will be handling it on a Mac, why should you care about slashes? Because they'll probably copy your job to a server for storage. If it's a Windows server, they'll have to rename your files to even allow copying, which will then munge all your image links, forcing them to update your images. Ouch. Since you have no control over where your files may land, forestall such problems by getting in the habit of using safe filenames.

Both Windows and Mac OS X prevent you from typing colons in filenames, and neither operating system allows you to begin a file or folder name with a period. An initial period renders a file invisible under UNIX.

Although current operating systems prevent much of this filenaming misbehavior, beware of legacy files created before the Macintosh adopted UNIX under the hood. While files whose naming began with a period were not problematic under Mac OS 9, they'll cause problems when you attempt to use them under Mac OS X. They'll disappear.

While some filenaming purists object to using multiple periods as visual separators in filenames, such as *Smith.Brochure.new.pdf*, newer Windows and Mac OS computers don't care, although this practice may cause problems with some persnickety applications. Some older server processes may modify the name by substituting underscores for extra periods, or by truncating the filename. Rather than risk this reaction, consider using underscores (*Smith_Brochure_new.pdf*) or capitalization (*SmithBrochureNew.pdf*).

Watch Your Language

Although Mac OS has no objection to using them in filenames, some combinations of letters and numbers are reserved by Windows. Names such as com1, com2, all the way through com9 are reserved for communication ports on the PC. If you were to create a Word file named com1.doc on the Mac, you might successfully copy it to a Windows drive, but you'd be unable to open it under Windows. Other forbidden names include lpt1 through lpt9 (reserved for printer ports), as well as prn, con, and nul.

Include File Extensions

Like two-button mice, file extensions (for example, .txt and .doc) have long been considered by some Macintosh users as symptoms of consorting with the Dark Side. Under previous Macintosh operating systems, file extensions were not required. In those days, files consisted of two forks, a data fork and a resource fork. The data fork held the true guts of the file, while the resource fork told the system which icon to use and how to open the file. Under UNIX-based OS X, the Macintosh does not yet require file extensions to determine which application should be used to open a file, and which icon should represent the file—that can be accomplished with the Get Info palette. But file extensions are still helpful for human identification of files, and crucial for cross-platform compatibility. On both Macs and PCs, you can choose to hide those extensions, but they are there nonetheless.

Most file extensions consist of three letters (for example, .rtf, .pdf, .tif), but some applications create files with longer extensions such as .html (Web page), .indd (InDesign), or .joboptions (Acrobat). A period always separates the filename from its extension, as in Image.tif or Brochure.indd.

Failure to append the correct file extension on the Macintosh can prevent a Windows user from opening the file by double-clicking it. In addition, lack of a file extension may prevent accessing such a file in other ways, such as attempting to import or place the file in another document. Of course, it's easy to add the extension if you encounter this problem, but it's better to just develop the habit of adding the extensions when you save the file. All Windows applications and most Mac OS X applications are smart enough to do this for you.

Whereas even the most ancient Windows file will be sporting a file extension, Macintosh files saved under Mac OS 9 (or earlier) may be extension-free. So as you dig up old files for new jobs you're creating under Mac OS X, either manually add the appropriate extension or open the file in the appropriate application by choosing File > Open from within the program. Then resave the file with a shiny new extension.

FONTS

Macintosh-specific fonts don't function on PCs, and Windows PostScript or TrueType fonts don't automatically work on a Mac (they can be forced: see the "Font Trick" note below). That's why there are a number of utilities to convert PC fonts to Macintosh fonts, and vice versa.

The most common motivation for such gyrations is to submit a Windows-based job to a Mac-based print service provider. There is only one correct way for the print service provider to treat the job, but unfortunately it's not what usually happens. The solutions range from bad to bearable to acceptable.

- **Bad idea.** Copy the job to a Mac and use the closest available fonts. "Hmmm… Helvetica is pretty much the same as Arial, isn't it?"

- **Painful compromise.** If the font vendor's licensing agreement allows it, convert the PC fonts to Macintosh versions with a high-end font-editing program such as FontLab or Fontographer (both now owned by FontLab). Check the converted file carefully against hard copy; or, better yet, a PDF supplied by the creator of the file.

- **Better approach.** The printer should keep the files in their native habitat. It's not that hard to just bite the bullet and learn the basics of Windows, and avoid any conversion. PCs are really not as scary or neurotic as they used to be. If you're designing on Windows computers, have a heart-to-heart conversation with the print service provider before submitting your job. Elicit some assurance that they will not use either of the first two approaches above. If that assurance is not forthcoming, consider submitting print-ready PDFs to avoid font issues.

- **Best approach.** Switch to OpenType fonts. They're completely cross-platform and full of tempting typographical features. If you use OpenType fonts exclusively, you don't have to worry about the platform fate of your document. If the printer goes against the grain and opens your Windows file on a Mac, nothing will reflow, nothing will fall off. Life is good.

FONT TRICK: Windows TrueType fonts can be used under OS X if placed in Macintosh HD/Library/Fonts. To use both Windows TrueType and PostScript fonts in Adobe applications on the Mac, place them in Macintosh HD/Library/Application Support/Adobe/Fonts. You can place the font in an individual Adobe applications Fonts folder, but it will then be available only to that single application. You have to be pretty bored or fontless to do this, and you must check the font vendor's licensing agreement to see if this is legal.

GRAPHICS FORMATS

All current graphics formats—including TIFF, PSD, EPS, AI, JPEG, and PDF—are perfectly happy jumping platforms. Just don't forget the file extensions. That was easy, wasn't it?

CHAPTER EIGHT
Job Submission

The planning that goes into your job should begin long before you hand your job files to the print service provider. As you've seen in the preceding chapters, it behooves you to anticipate the challenges presented by the physical processes of printing. It's less traumatic to prevent problems early in the game than to frantically fix something as the deadline looms. And it's not just the big stuff that bites you. It's no fun to be leaning blearily over a printed sheet on a 3:00 a.m. press check and have a pressman remark, "Hey, didja notice that this guy's name is spelled three different ways in this brochure—is that right?"

In the heat of battle, it's easy to overlook the basics while you're focused on the tricky parts of the job. And tunnel vision can cause you to lose sight of the big picture. But if you break the process into several smaller chunks, it's easier to catch problems at each stage.

This chapter serves as a reminder of some of the issues you've read about in earlier chapters and provides a number of checklists to review while you're preparing to send your job to the print service provider. You'll find expanded information on many of these topics in other chapters. This chapter is meant to provide a starting point, and to call your attention to key issues.

PREPARATIONS DURING THE DESIGN PROCESS

It's exciting to get started on a new project, and there's no such thing as too much time to do a job. However, before you wade right into the project, take a breath. Take two.

Lean back and consider the end product. Try to isolate the most challenging aspects of manufacturing the printed piece. Does it involve spot colors or varnishes? Does it require special finishing treatments such as die cutting or embossing? Is it an odd size? Does it involve multiple, collateral pieces that have to fit together, such as a pocket folder with inserted literature and a business reply card?

As you sketch out the prospects in your mind, start having conversations with the printer. In the very earliest stage of the job, you may not always have the luxury of knowing who the print service provider will be. But as soon as you do, start paving the way for a successful print project by opening up the lines of communication. Their staff can help you build your project successfully, and you will have prepared them for the incoming job. In printing, as in any kind of manufacturing, *surprise* is rarely a good word.

Talking with the Printer

Your first contact at the printing company will probably be with a salesperson. The ideal salesperson asks questions about your expectations for the job, advises you of any potential problems if your job contains some challenging aspects such as special stock or fancy finishing requirements, and gives you a realistic idea of the outcome. The salesperson will gather your initial information and will provide you with an estimate of job costs and a proposed timeline for the steps along the way. Those steps will include such events as when your files must be submitted, when you can expect the first proofs, when the press run will take place, and when the final job will be delivered. Finally, the salesperson will hand you and your job off to a customer service representative (CSR).

If you're fortunate, your CSR will be an experienced print professional who can give you some insight into your job's special needs. If you find yourself dealing with someone who seems to know less about the print process than you do, you might try diplomatically to expand your list of contacts at the printing company. A few print service providers frown on allowing customers to talk to production personnel, but it really does make life easier for everyone if you can deal with knowledgeable operators. Your salesman may be able to smooth the way if necessary. But speaking as a production person, I'll volunteer that most production personnel welcome a customer who's interested in providing a job that's not a nightmare. There's a fine line between being a conscientious client and being a pest, but you, of course, would never cross that line. You shouldn't call the prepress department unnecessarily (they'll start hiding from you), and it's important that you keep the CSR in the loop if you are allowed to contact production staff directly. The CSR is the common contact point for jobs, and is expected to know everything about a job, so don't forget to inform the CSR immediately if anything about the job needs to be changed.

In your initial conversations with the CSR, make sure they're aware of any special issues with your job. Here are a few topics you may need to discuss:

- **Unusual stock.** Substrates such as metallic stock or paper with pronounced texture or of unusually thick (or thin) weight may require additional time to order, and may also dictate which press will be used for the job.

- **Special mixed inks.** If you need something beyond what's available in the Pantone, Toyo, or other swatch libraries, you can request a special, custom-mixed ink. Since this ink is not picked from an existing swatch book, you may want to see ink draw-down samples on the final stock before the job is printed. A draw-down sample is created by spreading a thin coating of the desired ink on the intended stock to present a realistic preview of how the ink will look on press.

- **Varnishes or other coatings.** Special add-ons such as spot varnishes, aqueous coatings, or scratch-off spots require planning, since their use may dictate which press will be used to print the job.

- **Custom finishing.** Operations such as perforation, die cutting, embossing, foil stamping, or unusual folds require advance planning and equipment setup. Since custom finishing can take extra time, adequate time must be included in the schedule for the job. Complicated folding may also require modifications to the standard configurations of the folding equipment to ensure that the folds occur in the proper manner. See Chapter Three, "Binding and Finishing," for more information on finishing processes.

- **Unusual content.** If you require special print add-ons such as customized content for variable data printing (VDP) or custom addressing, it may be necessary to add time for programming and acquisition of data such as mailing list files.

For your sanity—and theirs—make sure you obtain the following crucial information:

- A detailed schedule that includes dates for intermediate events such as random proofs, page proofs, bluelines, and any press checks. Yes, the final delivery date is important, but unless you're aware of all the intermediate dates, you'll jeopardize the final goal.

- Contact information for all the people who are (or should be) familiar with your job, including the salesman, the CSR, and any prepress staff you've been told you can call with questions. Make sure that they know how to contact *you* if questions arise. And keep in mind that printing plants often operate 24 hours a day. You may not be accustomed to phone calls after midnight, but if your job is on a tight schedule and there's a problem during night shift, your phone may ring. This prospect alone may be a strong incentive to check your job thoroughly before you submit it.

PLANNING FOR PRINT

As your files take shape, it's important to build from the ground up. It's not much fun to deconstruct a complex file and then reassemble it because it was built one-half inch too big or all the artwork uses the wrong six spot colors. Before you choose File > New, make sure you've established the following important specifications:

- **External document size.** If you're printing letterheads, that's easy. But if you're creating a piece that folds, such as a trifold brochure or a pocket folder, whip out the ruler and make sure you know the correct external dimensions before you go too far.

- **Adequate bleed.** While one-eighth of an inch is standard bleed, some print service providers may request a larger value, especially on packaging or large-format output.

- **Internal panel sizes.** In folding pieces such as trifold brochures, remember that you have to allow for shorter panels that fold in (see Chapter Three, "Binding and Finishing"). In your page-layout program, set up guidelines to help you position content. Your print service provider may be able to provide a template to use if you're building to a common size.

- **Artwork interactions with folds, perforations, or die cut trims.** If artwork stops at a fold, special handling may be required to ensure that it doesn't dribble over onto the next panel, especially on packaging. Your print service provider can provide some guidance for preparing artwork, especially if you're printing on heavy stock whose thickness has a bearing on how wide the folded edge will be.

- **Correct number of pages.** In a common-format, multipage document (facing pages), the number of pages should be divisible by four. If you were inspired to pull the staples out of a magazine while you were reading Chapter Three, look at the loose pages and note that each loose sheet consists of four pages—two front, two back. In a longer document, such as a textbook, you (or the printer) can take up the slack by providing blank pages for notes.

- **Correct inks.** If it's not a 27-color job, there shouldn't be 27 spot colors in your application's color palette. Delete unnecessary colors, or convert them to CMYK if they're not intended to print as spot colors.

Checking Raster Images

As you've seen in Chapter Four, "Preparing Raster Images," it's important that your images are of sufficient resolution at final size, and that you've saved the images in an appropriate format and in the correct color space.

If the images you're creating are your final art (that is, they're not being placed into an illustration or page-layout application), check them in Photoshop or the application in which you created them. Consult your print service provider to make sure you know their requirements, but here are some general guidelines:

- **Resolution.** Raster images should usually be at least 300 ppi (pixels per inch) at their final imaging size. However, there are exceptions—for example, large-format output such as posters, store signage, and billboards. Since readers will probably be at least several feet away from the finished poster or large sign, the net effect is the same as viewing a smaller image at a shorter distance. In other words, a 150 ppi image viewed from a distance of several feet is the equivalent of a smaller, 300 ppi image viewed up close.

  It may be necessary to create images of higher resolution for high line-screen work (200 lpi or higher). If you are creating images for special printed pieces such as art prints or art books, you may be asked to supply images at higher than 300 ppi. Keep in mind that it's best if the original scan or digital photograph is of adequate size and resolution. Scaling up or increasing resolution through interpolation never produces results equivalent to healthy original images.

- **Color space.** Images usually come in one of five major flavors for printing purposes: CMYK, RGB, grayscale, monochrome (bitmap black and white, with no shades of gray), and duotone. Unless you're working in a color-managed environment, you'll be asked to provide CMYK images for color images. If your print service provider utilizes color management, ensure that you've tagged your RGB images with the appropriate color profile. Make sure that grayscale images are truly black-only files, not gray-appearing RGB or CMYK images.

- **Retouching.** If you're not comfortable performing retouching work beyond simple blemish removal, let the print service provider know that you'd like them to perform the work instead. It's helpful if you print the images in question, and then indicate the problems you'd like them to fix. It's likely that you'll incur additional job charges for this service.

- **Rotations and scaling.** You'll achieve the best results if your scans or digital photographs are created at the proper size and rotation for final use. But let's be realistic. You can't always anticipate how you'll use an image. If you've simply flipped an image horizontally or vertically in a page layout, don't worry about it. If you've rotated an image by increments of 90 degrees, don't worry about that. But, if you rotate an image in a page layout by anything other than 90-degree increments, or if you scale—or both—you'll see some slight softening of detail in the final output. For more information on performing transformations on images, see Chapter Four, "Preparing Raster Images."

- **Filenames.** Avoid using periods, asterisks, and other characters to flag filenames (see Chapter Seven, "Cross-Platform Issues"). Even if you and your print service provider are both using Macintosh computers, remember that your files will probably be copied to a server that may be based on another platform such as Unix or Windows.

Checking Vector Artwork

Since illustration programs such as Illustrator and FreeHand allow you to place raster images as content, you have to consider some of the same issues that you encounter in page-layout applications. Don't forget to check the following:

- **Correct colors.** If you'll be placing vector art into a page-layout program, try to avoid multiple instances of what should be a single spot color. If the job uses Pantone 384, for example, make sure that the color isn't Pantone 384C in your illustration program and PMS 384CVC in the final page-layout document. Ensure that color naming is consistent across all constituent files.

- **Images.** Most illustration programs offer the choice of embedding or linking placed images. Embedding increases the file size and it ensures that all the pieces are in place. However, it may limit editing if the print service provider needs to modify the image. If you anticipate the need to color correct or retouch images placed in illustrations, send the image along just to be safe.

- **Fonts.** Embed fonts or outline text (the font EULA permitting). Note that while Illustrator enables the embedding of fonts with proper permissions, this only facilitates correct imaging. The fonts are not available for text editing unless the user (in this case, the printer) also has the fonts active on their system. If you're tempted to convert text to outlines, be advised that some text effects such as underlining or strikethrough may be lost when you outline the text. Another consequence of outlining text to consider: Fonts contain special information called *hinting*, which is lost when text is converted to outlines. As a result, outlined text will not be as crisp as the original text when printed on a desktop printer. However, on a high-resolution output device such as an imagesetter or platesetter, outlined text should be satisfactory. But if your job will be printed on a digital press, such as a Xerox iGen or HP Indigo press, avoid outlining text if possible: While these presses provide very high-quality output, they print at 600–800 dpi. Consequently, outlined text—especially small serif text—may be visibly coarser than true text.

- **Text.** Spell-check content, and check for pesky little empty remnants of text where you unintentionally clicked with the Type tool (it happens to all of us sooner or later). Those empty instances may result in preflight reports of a font being needed, resulting in time wasted troubleshooting something that isn't truly a problem if the font isn't used anywhere else.

- **Bleed.** If the vector artwork file is your final artwork (that is, you're not going to place it in a page layout file for further assembly), ensure that you've included adequate bleed. Even though you create bleed artwork correctly, the export format that you choose in Illustrator determines whether that artwork is correctly retained during file export. Refer to Chapter Ten, "Illustrator CS4 Production Tips," for some clarification of how Illustrator handles bleed, depending on the export format.

Checking Page Layout Files

Once you've determined that your raster images and vector artwork pieces are healthy, you still need to examine any page-layout file that combines that content to make sure that additional errors are not introduced. Don't forget to do the following:

- **Spell check.** It's important to weed out typing errors, but be particularly careful with product names and proper names. You also need to check for mistakes that spellcheckers don't catch, such as grammatical errors and words that are spelled correctly but aren't what you intend. You don't want to go to press with a headline that reads "The Clam Before the Storm."

- **Delete extra junk.** Clean off the pasteboard, and eliminate empty elements.

- **Avoid styled text.** Rather than clicking the *B* or *I* button, choose the genuine bold or italic font. Fortunately, InDesign and Illustrator do not allow you to stylize text.

- **Delete double spaces.** If you were still setting type with a typewriter, double spaces would be fine. But you're not. Double spaces in computer typesetting are large, airy gaps. Perform a find-and-replace to replace double spaces with single spaces. And quit hitting that spacebar.

- **Check for scaling and rotation.** While a few rotations here and there aren't a problem, and it's permissible to scale within a reasonable range (70–125 percent), an image-heavy document with lots of such transformations can be slow to RIP. Especially if you are greatly reducing large images, consider doing those transformations in Photoshop, and then updating the images in the page layout so they can be handled without rotation.

- **Provide printouts of your job.** They're really helpful to CSRs, planners, estimators, and prepress operators at the print service provider for quick visual aids. It's best if printouts are actual size, but if the piece is too large to print at final size (or you don't feel like tiling output and taping pieces of paper together), mark the printout prominently with the scale factor. This is especially important if the print service provider will be scanning transparencies or other artwork for you. The scanner operator will need to measure your transparencies, measure your printouts, and then determine the proper scale factor for each image. If you indicate the scale factor used in your printout, you reduce the chance for error by alerting the scanner operator and by providing an important factor in his scaling equation.

- **Preflight your job.** The term preflight comes from the aviation industry. If you are about to become airborne in a 150,000-pound metal tube, you check all the operating systems before you pull back on the stick. If you want to minimize problems in a print job, you check all the contents. The preceding sections have provided some guidance for manually checking your job, but you'd do well to consider using dedicated preflight software to do the job for you. The FlightCheck family of products from Markzware—FlightCheck Designer and FlightCheck Professional—can automate the process of preflighting by allowing you to set up test parameters for checking documents.

Have realistic expectations. Your monitor and your desktop printer's approximation of the final printed piece may be fairly good if you calibrate your monitor and you're using a high-end printer with careful color management. Otherwise, you have to wait for contract proofs from the print service provider to have a good idea of the appearance of the final output.

SENDING JOB FILES

The print service provider should give you some guidelines for submitting job files. Some prefer PDF files, while some would rather have application files such as QuarkXPress, InDesign, or Illustrator. Usually, you'll be asked to provide multipage documents in *reader's spreads*, which is how you normally build such documents: page two facing page three, and so on. If you're asked to provide *printer's spreads*—imposed for plating—you should be suspicious that the printer doesn't have dedicated software to perform imposition. This may be a sign that the printer lacks other important capabilities.

Submitting PDF Files

If the print service provider requests that you submit PDF files, they should give you specifications for creating PDF files. While PDF creation has been discussed in other chapters, be sure to address these crucial issues:

- **Preflight PDFs before submitting.** Even if you have performed a preflight on the application files that generated the PDF files, it's a good idea to preflight the PDF files themselves. Markzware's FlightCheck Designer and FlightCheck Professional products can preflight PDF files. The print production tools in Acrobat Professional offer extensive preflighting features as well.

- **Follow print service provider specifications.** Faithfully replicate the specifications that are provided for creating PDF files. Restrict your PDF to the version your printer requests. That is, don't send them an Acrobat 9.0 file if they've asked for an Acrobat 4.0 file. Ask the print service provider to send you PDF job options files (.joboptions) so you can easily create the correct type of PDF for their workflow. CS4 applications share a common repository of PDF-creation settings, and importing the options into any one of the applications makes those settings available to other CS4 applications.

- **Embed fonts.** By default, Illustrator and InDesign correctly embed fonts in generated PDFs. If you've used fonts whose vendor forbids embedding or supplying the fonts separately, you must either request that the print service provider purchase the same fonts, or you'll have to substitute fonts that *can* be embedded. Consult the end user licensing agreement (EULA) for your fonts to be sur that you're in compliance.

- **Ensure safe transit.** Even though it's easy to think of PDF files as being hermetically sealed, they can sometimes be corrupted when sent as e-mail attachments unless they're first compressed with a utility like StuffIt on the Macintosh or WinZip on Windows. Encasing the PDF files in a compressed archive protects them in transit. If you are submitting the job on digital media, this isn't an issue, and you don't need to compress the PDF files.

Submitting Application Files

It isn't sufficient to send only your finished page-layout file to the print service provider. The page-layout file is like a recipe for the printed piece. And a recipe is not much good without all the necessary ingredients. The fonts and images used in your page layout are the ingredients, and you must supply all those constituent parts for the print service provider to complete your job. While you're working on your project, you may be using graphics stored in multiple locations on your hard drive or on a server. Graphics are simply linked to your page-layout file and *referenced* by the page-layout file, as are the fonts you've used. By default, graphics are not embedded in the page-layout file, so the graphics and fonts must be gathered up to constitute a complete kit for your project. (While it's possible to embed graphics, this adds to the file size of a page-layout file.) Fortunately, your page-layout programs provide methods for rounding up all the necessary images, vector artwork files, and fonts.

When you're sure all your work is in good shape, the *Package* function in InDesign and the *Collect for Output* feature in QuarkXPress make it easy to gather up all the pieces necessary for printing a page-layout file, including support art and necessary fonts. In InDesign, choose File > Package. In QuarkXPress, choose File > Collect for Output.

Before you exercise your layout program's collection feature, make sure that all necessary fonts are active, and that support art links are current. Make sure that no graphics are missing or in need of updating. The final package for a page-layout file should contain the following components:

- The layout file.

- All support art, including all raster images and all vector artwork. Also include any raster images that have been placed in vector drawings from Illustrator (unless you embedded the images).

- All necessary fonts, including those needed by support art such as Illustrator or Photoshop files. Be mindful of the end-user licensing agreements (EULAs) for the fonts you've used—some forbid supplying fonts to print service providers (see Chapter Six, "Fonts"). Carefully examine the collected job.

If you have created any elaborate compositions with multilayered Photoshop files, and you choose to use a flattened, simplified version of the image in your page-layout file, include the layered working file with the job. The flattened image may be your final file, but if the print service provider needs to make any corrections to the image, it is easier to modify your working, layered Photoshop file than to work with the flattened image. Keep in mind that, unless the Photoshop file is enormous or if you want to thwart easy editing, there's no need to flatten it before placing it in InDesign or Illustrator.

Since software is constantly being updated, make sure the print service provider knows which version of the page-layout application you are using. If you like to upgrade the minute new software is released, don't assume that your printer is quite so avid. You might think that print service providers would be the first to buy new software, but they're just like many of the rest of us—they don't buy new software until they have to.

This leads to another important thought. If you are using an *earlier* version of software than the print service provider, this may present problems if the printer needs to perform any corrections to your files, and then return them to you for future use. Most print service providers maintain earlier versions of software so they can keep client files in their original version. But not all printers are so conscientious, so it's worthwhile to mention that you're using an earlier version than the current release in the marketplace. If you're one version behind them in InDesign or Illustrator, they can usually save your files to your earlier version. Don't forget that, while it's possible to save an InDesign CS4 file to InDesign CS3, there's no provision for saving back from InDesign CS4 to InDesign CS2. That highway doesn't exist. If you have no intentions of upgrading, this may become an issue for you. Discuss this with your print service provider. You may have to perform any corrections on your own files using your own, earlier version of the software, and then submit new, corrected files.

Platform Issues

Generally speaking, it's preferable to keep a job on one platform throughout its lifespan. While sending files across platforms is not the major undertaking it once was, fonts remain an issue. If you're using all OpenType fonts, there's no need to worry. But if you are using PostScript or TrueType fonts on Windows, and your print service provider is Macintosh-only, you should insist on submitting your job in PDF format. While there may be Macintosh fonts with the same names as your Windows fonts, they aren't necessarily identical in terms of font metrics, and there may be text reflow as a result of opening the job on a Mac (see Chapter Seven, "Cross-Platform Issues"). Most print service providers sensibly keep Windows files in their native habitat for this reason, but if you're using Windows, it's worth mentioning this concern early in your discussions with the CSR.

Sending Files

Ask the print service provider about their preferred method of file submission. If they provide a way of submitting files online via FTP (File Transfer Protocol), they'll give you directions for accessing the correct target directory. Use a file-compression program such as StuffIt (Macintosh and Windows), ZipMagic (Windows), or WinZip (Windows) to consolidate the job into a single archive and to reduce the amount of data you're uploading. Additionally, both the Macintosh OS X operating system and Windows XP and later have built-in file compression utilities. On the Mac, select a file or folder, and then Control-click it (or right-click with a two-button mouse) to select Create Archive from the context menu that appears. In Mac OS 10.5 (Leopard), choose Compress [file or folder name]. In Windows, select a folder, and then right-click and select Send To > Compressed (zipped) Folder. Windows will then create a compressed archive of the folder and its contents.

While CDs and DVDs are probably the most commonly used physical methods of transporting files, some extremely large jobs may be submitted on large-capacity portable external drives that connect via FireWire or USB connections.

In addition to the files themselves, it's helpful if you provide these collateral materials to the print service provider:

- Contact information for you, along with any alternate contacts such as other members of your design team, or appropriate contacts at your client if you're acting as an intermediary.

- Comprehensive assembled printouts of the job (*comps*) if there's anything tricky about the final piece, such as inserts or foldout panels.

PREPARING FOR PROOFING CYCLES

Depending on the workflow of your print service provider and the nature of the job you are submitting, you may be asked to check proofs at several points during the life of the job. You've probably been looking at the same content for so long that it all starts to look alike, and it's easy to develop blind spots when you're in a hurry to approve a proof. Here are some checklists to help you remember key issues at each stage.

Checking Image Proofs

Image proofs are sometimes referred to as *random proofs* or *scatter proofs*, since they are proofs of just the images without any page-layout context. If you're unsure of how your own scans or digital photos will reproduce, or if the print service provider has performed scans of supplied artwork or transparencies, you may want to proof images before going ahead with the remaining print production steps. Check these issues:

- **Size.** Are images the correct size? If some images are used multiple times at different sizes within the project, are there separate images for wide variations in scale factor?

- **Crop.** Is there sufficient image to fill the intended area when you place it in the page layout? Make sure nothing important has been cropped out. Also, if you need only a small portion of a large image, it's OK to crop out unused image area to save storage space and processing time.

- **Orientation.** Does the image need to be flipped vertically or horizontally for use in the final layout?

- **Angle.** Is the image at the same angle at which it will be used in the final piece?

- **Matching the original artwork.** Is the proof a fair rendering of the transparency, reflective art, or digital photo? Matching the art is sometimes a subjective evaluation but, given the limitations of CMYK pigments, is it a reasonable match to the original?

- **Color.** Is it too dark? Too light? Does it lack contrast? Are neutral areas such as whites, grays, and blacks free of any tinge of unwanted color? For example, check gray areas such as concrete or paved road and make sure there's no reddish, bluish, or greenish tinge (called a color cast).

- **Detail.** Is there discernible detail in the highlight and shadow areas? If the original image or original artwork lacks detail, it can't be manufactured, but any existing detail should be maintained.

- **Moiré.** Especially when photographing or scanning patterned originals such as woven fabric or geometric patterns, it may be necessary to give special treatment to all or part of an image. Sometimes slight blurring may be used in Photoshop to subdue the moiré. You may have to decide which is more objectionable—the unwanted pattern or the loss of detail due to blurring.

- **Silhouettes.** This is a good opportunity to check the edges of any silhouettes, whether you've created them or asked the print service provider to create them. An edge that looks acceptable onscreen may need some cleanup once you see a proof of it.

- **Retouching.** If you've requested retouching, does the proof show that it's been done? Does it need additional work to accomplish what you wish? Are there problems that weren't apparent before, that now should be retouched?

Checking Page Proofs

Not every print service provider creates proofs of individual pages. Some may show you imposed proofs, which serve a dual purpose: You can check page content and color, and you and the print service provider can check for correct pagination (page position as a result of imposition). When viewing page proofs, you should check for the following:

- **Correct size.** Make sure the page dimensions are correct.

- **Bleed.** Make sure there is adequate bleed. If images must bleed, make sure they don't fall short.

- **Image area.** Make sure no artwork or text falls too close to the trim edge or interior spine. Such artwork will be at risk of trimming out or disappearing into a fold.

- **Correct fonts.** Check to make sure text intended to be bold or italic really is bold or italic. Look for the Courier font being used instead of your intended font (some RIPs use Courier to call attention to font substitution).

- **Overset text.** Check the end of text flows to make sure the last line is intact. It's helpful if you hold your own printout over the proof and flip it up to check for disparities between your prints and the service provider's proof.

- **Text reflow.** Using the same technique as above, flip between your printout and the service provider's proof to check for changes in line breaks. Reflow could be caused by font substitution or incorrect hyphenation settings.

- **Correct images.** Make sure incorrect images have not been used, especially if intermediate retouching or color corrections have been performed.

- **Crop.** Make sure images fill their frames, and that they are cropped as you intended.

- **Special effects.** If you are using drop shadows or transparency effects created in InDesign, Illustrator, or QuarkXPress, make sure the effects are correctly rendered, especially where they interact with spot-color content. Look for missing shadows, portions of objects printing as white shapes, or discoloration around transparent elements.

- **Rules and other strokes.** Make sure rules are unbroken and uniform in weight.

- **Trapping.** While there should be no misregistration on proofs, look for any unattractive dark lines where trapping has been performed. Some darkening may be unavoidable, but it's possible to mitigate the effect by changing trap settings, especially where light colors interact with each other.

- **Overprint.** Make sure black text and art don't knock out of underlying areas if they're not intended to do so.

- **Rich blacks.** Check that rich blacks have been created for large black coverage areas, or ask the print service provider to assure you that such areas will not be anemic or mottled when printed. The same cautions apply to large single-color areas other than black, such as spot color areas. If the job will be printed on a toner-based digital press such as the Xerox iGen, rich blacks are unnecessary; the black toner is sufficiently dense.

- **Moiré in screen tints or images.** While patterns and woven pieces are prone to moiré, the effect can also occur in some combinations of flat-color screen tints, such as combinations of yellow and black. Moiré in an image can occur when a patterned original, such as fabric, is scanned, but it may not be apparent when you view the scanned image on your monitor. When such an image is rendered as a halftone, the combination of fabric pattern and the halftone pattern can produce an unattractive moiré. If you notice the effect at the proofing stage, don't ignore it. Consult with the print service provider to determine if additional work such as rescanning, softening the pattern, or perhaps even changing the screen angles might improve the outcome.

- **Crossover art.** Check the alignment and color match for artwork that crosses from one page to another. Make sure that crossover text isn't awkwardly divided and that any art that should stop at the spine *does* stop at the spine without falling over onto the facing page.

- **Spot colors.** Make sure there are no unnecessary spot colors.

Checking Corrections

By now, you're probably tired of looking at this job. It's particularly hard to focus on corrections because they tend to consist of small details such as typographical errors. It's helpful to place a marked-up intermediate proof on top of a later proof, and then flip it back and forth to look for the corrected areas.

Checking Imposed Bluelines

- **Crossover art.** Make sure that no text or artwork is incorrectly cropped at the spine where pages meet. Make sure that nothing falls short of the spine if it's intended to go all the way to the center of the spread.

- **Correct pagination.** Refer to the folding dummy created by the print service provider's planner or imposition department, and check the imposed blueline against the pagination in the original folding dummy.

- **Changes from page proof stage.** Make sure nothing has moved or disappeared, especially if corrections have been made since an earlier stage.

Signing Off on Proofs

When you sign off on a proof, you're indicating that you are satisfied with the work. This places responsibility on both you and the print service provider. If the print service provider fails to match the signed proof in subsequent steps, those mistakes should be fixed at no cost to you. However, if you fail to notice problems before you sign off on the proof, you will incur costs when you ask the print service provider to make changes.

ATTENDING A PRESS CHECK

Not all jobs warrant a press check. If all the intermediate proofs have been satisfactory, and the job doesn't involve exotic stock or ink effects, there's no need for the printer to invite a customer to sign off on a live press run. However, there are numerous reasons for holding a press check: There may be concerns about printing on challenging stock, or there may be the need to ensure the successful outcome of a high-profile job such as an annual report. Don't be intimidated by the atmosphere of a press check. The roar and bustle of a pressroom can be overwhelming, but just take a deep breath—a good whiff of all those solvents may have a calming effect.

Note that since printing plants often run around the clock, a press check may be held at any hour of the day or night. The print service provider will attempt to give you an idea of the time, but problems with other jobs may change the schedule for your job. You may find yourself camping out at the printer or waiting for a call.

During a press check, these are the things you should watch for:

- **Accuracy.** Make sure the press sheet matches the approved intermediate proofs (page proofs and bluelines). Check images, text, content, and color.

- **Ink on paper.** Watch for flaws in registration, color, and ink coverage. Look for smearing, and watch small details for distortion. Small text (especially white text reversed out of multiple colors) may close up. Check color consistency in elements that repeat on separate pages. Check that crossover art matches from page to page — you may need to fold up printed sheets to lay the pages side by side to check the match.

    Minor adjustments can be made on press, but major problems — such as the need for a second hit of a solid color or the creation of a rich black — will require pulling the job off press, reworking the job, replating, and going through makeready again.

- **Stock behavior.** Watch for flaking or *picking* (small fibers of paper breaking off after printing, leaving unprinted areas), especially with heavily textured stock. Watch for wrinkling in thin stock. Check for showthrough from the other side of the sheet. To some extent, the pressman can compensate for stock behavior, but if the stock proves unwieldy, you may have to reconsider your choice of paper. Such a drastic change will result in the job being pulled off press. New stock will have to be located (or ordered), and your job will have to be rescheduled. An ink draw-down sample might have established that the inks would look satisfactory when applied to the stock manually, but the combined effects of multiple ink impressions over large areas of the paper and the mechanical actions of paper being pulled through the press may result in unexpected results when the job is actually printed.

- **Debris and scratches.** Keep an eye out for hickeys — small white halos in solid color areas that are caused by a foreign particle stuck to the plate or blanket. Hickeys are fairly easily fixed by wiping the particle away. Watch for scratches in text or large areas of color coverage.

While the prospect of stopping a press and juggling the complexities of corrections and rescheduling may seem distasteful, the costs incurred at this stage may still pale in comparison to the expense of completely reprinting a job if the printed outcome is not satisfactory to your own customer.

At each step of the process, through your design stages and the successive proofing stages at the print service provider, there are multiple opportunities for things to go awry. While you're focused on kerning an important headline on the cover, it's easy to overlook a typographical error on the last page of the publication. While a harried prepress operator at the printer is replacing an image with a color-corrected version, he might err in positioning the new image.

Tiny errors can lead to expensive problems. Tunnel vision is unavoidable, especially in complex projects. That's why proofing is so important. It's also helpful to solicit input from someone who hasn't been staring at the job as long as you have. An innocent bystander can often spot errors you've missed: "Hey, this looks great, but shouldn't there be a picture in this big empty white box?"

This is no time to make trivial changes: Stopping a job because you want to move a photo a fraction of an inch will incur thousands of dollars in press time and alteration charges, not to mention driving the pressman crazy. Your job deadline may suffer a considerable impact, so it's wise to consider the huge ramifications before suggesting any changes so late in the game.

CHAPTER NINE

Photoshop CS4 Production Tips

There are numerous books and Web sites devoted to using Adobe Photoshop for the entire spectrum of skill levels from beginner to Master of the Pixel-Based Universe. (See the Appendix for a selection of Photoshop resources.) We're assuming you know how to handle the basics of Photoshop, so you won't find any basic how-to instructions here. Nor is this a Hot Tips & Tricks compendium. What you *will* find are tips to help you create print-ready files and some heads-up warnings regarding tricks that the software can play on you. Because Photoshop is used for a wide variety of purposes, from Web to print and video, it provides multiple methods for accomplishing what you want to do to an image. The method that might be ideal for Web is not necessarily appropriate in an image intended for print.

NOTE: *Everything in this chapter is appropriate for both Photoshop CS4 and Photoshop CS4 Extended.*

OFF TO A GOOD START

Before you start slinging pixels around, do a bit of planning. You may just be stuck with a supplied image, with no control over how it began life. In that case, you may have to make some compromises for print. But if you have some control over the birth of an image, you can better prepare for a better outcome. You might glance at Chapter Four, "Preparing Raster Images," for some general image guidelines.

Know the Fate of the Image

Before you scan an image, or photograph a subject with a digital camera, it's helpful to know how the image will ultimately be used. Consider some important issues:

- **At what scale factor will the image will be used?** Scan the image to that size rather than scaling the image in Photoshop or a page-layout application.

- **Will the image be used at multiple sizes?** If the scale factors are fairly close—the image is used at 150 percent and at 140 percent, for example—scan for the larger size and just use scaling tools in the page layout for the smaller size. But if there is a substantial difference in scale factors—an image used at 150 percent and 25 percent, for example—it's worth making a separate scan for each use. Alternatively, scan the image for the larger scale factor, and then scale it down in Photoshop (Image > Image Size), using the *Bicubic Sharper* resampling option (**Figure 9.1**). Why have two images, when you could just place the same image twice in your page layout and scale it there? You have a bit more control over the resampling and scaling if you perform the scaling yourself in Photoshop. And you slightly reduce the processing burden on the raster image processor (RIP) that ultimately handles your job by using images that are already the correct size.

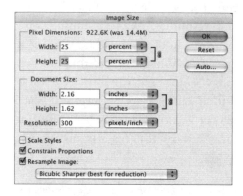

Figure 9.1 When reducing the size of an image in Photoshop, you'll achieve better results by using the Bicubic Sharper resampling method.

- **Will the image be rotated in its final use?** Scan the image at the correct angle. Photographing a subject at an angle, however, may be more challenging ("Can you stand on your head just a little bit longer?"). As with scaling, you'll achieve better results by performing the rotation in Photoshop rather than in a page-layout program. Since multiple rotations may slightly erode image detail, it's best if you determine the correct final angle and perform a single rotation. If you anticipate doing a lot of experimentation with the angle of the image, consider using Smart Objects to minimize any data loss (see the section on Smart Objects later in this chapter).

- **What are the important elements in the image?** If the image is a product shot, concentrate your efforts on maintaining the best detail and most faithful color rendition in the product, even if that means slightly hurting the incidental contents of the image. Worry about the red in the product package rather than agonizing over the color of the two partial tulips accenting the upper-right corner of the shot.

- **Will the image be used on the Web, as well as for print?** Consider keeping the image in RGB as you perform color corrections and retouching work. Then save an RGB version of the image to be used as the source file for Web work. Save another copy of the image as CMYK. You should also keep your RGB working file in case you need to do additional work, so that you can regenerate the Web and print images from a new parent image if necessary.

Image Resolution

The rules for image resolution are the same as for image size, because the concepts are intertwined. Start with as much image information as you can. You can always *discard* information, but you can't convincingly *create* it out of nothing. Once you've determined the correct final dimensions for your image, scan the artwork or transparency to those dimensions at the appropriate resolution. What's the appropriate resolution? Generally speaking, 300 ppi at final size is sufficient for printing at 133–150 line screen (see Chapter Four, "Preparing Raster Images," for a discussion of resolution, and Chapter Two, "Ink on Paper," for information about line screen). If your project will be printed at a very high line screen (175 lpi or above), and it is important to maintain a high level of detail in the content—images of jewelry, fine art, or antiques, for example—it may be beneficial to scan at a resolution greater than 300 ppi. If you are doing your own scans for such a projects, consult with the print service provider to determine the proper resolution to use. If the print service provider is doing the scanning, they will take care of the resolution issue.

Color Space

Our eyes see in RGB, yet we print (usually) with CMYK. As mentioned in Chapter Four, "Preparing Raster Images," RGB is the native tongue for scanners and digital cameras as well. Even though an image may be fated to printing in CMYK, there are advantages to keeping the image in RGB as you perform color correction, retouching, and compositing. The wider color gamut of RGB gives you more to work with as you make color corrections, and some interesting Photoshop effects, such as the Vanishing Point, Texturizer, and Artistic filters, are not available in CMYK images.

Once you convert an image to CMYK for a given printing condition, you lose some flexibility. Keeping the image in RGB allows you to defer the conversion until later in the workflow, rather than locking you in to a particular print condition early in the life of the job.

Converting RGB to CMYK

Unless you and your print service provider are working in a color-managed workflow, you'll be expected to provide CMYK images (except, of course, those images intended to print as grayscale or duotone). Ideally, you'll be given conversion settings customized for their presses, as well as instructions on applying those settings. Lacking that, you should find that Photoshop's built-in conversion settings are serviceable. Choose Edit > Color Settings and then select North America Prepress 2, or use the custom settings provided by your print service provider.

Photoshop invokes these settings when you select Image > Mode > CMYK Color or Image > Mode > Grayscale. Keep this in mind if your print service provider gives you high-resolution scans to incorporate in your design. If you convert those images to RGB to perform a color correction, or apply a filter that's only available in RGB mode, your conversion back to CMYK will result in color values that differ from the original image supplied to you, although the change may not be apparent in your onscreen display. As long as your color settings are not extreme, this will probably not result in a drastic alteration of the printed piece, but it's something you should consider before you begin jumping between color spaces.

WORKING IN LAYERS

While the intricacies of creating and editing Photoshop layers are beyond the scope of this chapter, it's worth mentioning some of the benefits of working with layered files. Layers can keep the individual components of a complicated composition from being glued together prematurely, giving you a safety net in case you change your mind. Multiple undo capabilities are great during a working session, but they don't help if you've saved a file and realize—days later—that you've inadvertently cropped out something crucial, or performed a color correction that doesn't look so great.

Layers offer the advantage of providing nondestructive methods for combining images, for creating silhouette and soft-edged effects, and for doing color corrections without permanently altering pixels.

Don't Erase that Pixel!

When you need to eliminate part of an image, it's tempting to just choose the Eraser tool from the Tools panel in Photoshop, and get rid of it. When you permanently delete pixels, they're gone forever (**Figure 9.2**). If you accidentally erased the CEO's left ear in his portrait for the prestigious annual report, I hope you remember where you backed up the original image. I'll wait while you frantically search through that pile of CDs.

Figure 9.2 Nice seashore! Well, it *was*. Too bad you accidentally erased the ocean and some of the scenic rocks (right). But you still have the original image somewhere. Don't you?

There's a safer and more flexible way to eliminate pixels. Use the Layer Mask feature in Photoshop to selectively *hide* pixels without *destroying* them. If you can create a silhouette, you can create a layer mask.

1. Create a selection by using your favorite method, and make sure it's still an active selection. An active selection appears as a black-and-white dashed shape, often referred to by the highly technical term "marching ants."

2. The layer must be a floating layer to use a layer mask. If the layer is named *Background* (and its name is italicized), it needs to first be converted to a floating layer. To do this, double-click the layer name. In the dialog box that follows, you can enter a new name for the layer or accept Photoshop's default name for the newly floating layer.

3. Make sure your ants are still marching, and then select Layer > Layer Mask > Reveal Selection, or just click the Add Layer Mask button (⬚) on the bottom edge of the Layers panel. You should see the selected part of the image floating on a transparent background, and a mask icon will be added to the layer in the Layers panel (**Figure 9.3**).

Figure 9.3 A layer mask reveals content rather than erasing pixels. You can always modify the layer mask later, to reveal or hide image contents in a non-destructive way.

Color Corrections with a Safety Net

Some of the color-correction options in Photoshop, including Shadow/Highlight, Match Color, and Replace Color, can only be applied directly to pixels in the image, which alters them permanently. But some of the most commonly used color corrections can be stored in Adjustment layers, which are nondestructive. No pixels are harmed in this type of color correction, and you can always change your mind later. The Adjustments panel in Photoshop CS4 provides quick access to the 15 adjustments that can be performed nondestructively. You can choose from a wide assortment of color-correction options, including Curves, Levels, Color Balance, Brightness/Contrast, and more. When you select an adjustment, the Adjustments panel changes to display the options for that adjustment (**Figure 9.4**). Controls on the bottom of the panel allow you to preview, reset, cancel, or commit to the adjustment. Click the arrow icon at the bottom left of the panel to return the panel to its original display mode and commit to the adjustment.

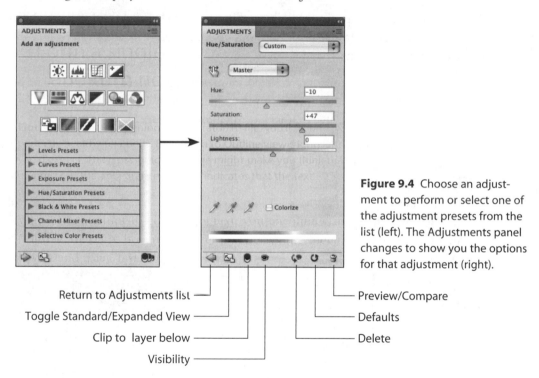

Figure 9.4 Choose an adjustment to perform or select one of the adjustment presets from the list (left). The Adjustments panel changes to show you the options for that adjustment (right).

Return to Adjustments list
Toggle Standard/Expanded View
Clip to layer below
Visibility

Preview/Compare
Defaults
Delete

After performing an adjustment, you'll see a new entry in the Layers panel (**Figure 9.5**). You can control the visibility and opacity of an adjustment layer as you would any layer.

Note that the adjustment layer automatically creates a layer mask for itself. Initially, it's all open (that is, it isn't hiding anything). But if you'd like to prevent the color correction from affecting some areas of the underlying image, use the Paintbrush tool to paint those areas of the mask with black. If you want to rework the color correction, double-click the leftmost icon in the adjustment layer to display a dialog box. To disable the correction, click the eye icon to turn off the visibility of the adjustment layer. To permanently delete the adjustment layer, select the layer in the Layers panel, and then choose Delete Layer from the Layers panel menu, or drag the layer to the trash can at the bottom of the Layers panel.

Figure 9.5 An adjustment layer performs a color correction without actually altering pixels. Don't like it? Delete it or click the eye icon next to the layer to hide the correction.

Smart Objects

To minimize the loss of data that results from transformations such as scaling or rotation, use Smart Objects when possible. Smart Objects store the original information for raster or vector content within the Photoshop file, allowing the program to perform cumulative transformations without multiple interpolations of data. Usually, if you scale, then rotate, then scale again, Photoshop performs three separate sets of interpolation, and you lose a bit of data (and, therefore, detail) in each transformation. With a Smart Object, however, Photoshop starts afresh with the original data (whether it's vector or pixel), and calculates the total effects of the transformations together, resulting in only one step of interpolation.

There are two methods for creating a Smart Object. Choose File > Place and select a Photoshop image of any format, an Illustrator AI or EPS file, or a PDF. Position and scale the artwork as necessary, and then press the Return or Enter key to finish the operation; a Smart Object is automatically created (**Figure 9.6**). Alternatively, you can paste or move pixels from another open Photoshop file, then choose Convert to Smart Object from the Layers panel menu. If you paste from an open Illustrator file, you have the option to paste as a Smart Object.

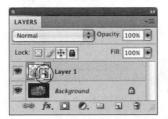

Figure 9.6 A special icon identifies a layer designated as a Smart Object, whether the artwork is vector or pixel-based.

There are important differences between a vector Smart Object and a pixel-based Smart Object. As you might expect, a vector Smart Object can be scaled up endlessly, whereas a pixel-based Smart Object can be scaled down without penalty, but should not be scaled up much beyond its original size (despite the temptation to do so).

Smart Objects embed a copy of the original vector or pixel-based art in the Photoshop file; there is no link to the original file. While this results in increased file size, the flexibility and portability far outweighs the file size increase. To edit a Smart Object, double-click it in the Layers panel. You can also choose Edit Contents from the Layers panel menu, or right-click in the image and choose Edit Contents to edit the Smart Object. Raster image content will be opened in Photoshop, and PDF or vector content will be opened in Illustrator. Perform any edits, and then save the edited file. The edited information is sent back to Photoshop, and the parent Photoshop file is automatically updated.

Vector Smart Objects do have one limitation: While other vector content, such as Shape Layers, vector masks, or vector text, can be rendered as true vector art if the file is saved as a Photoshop PDF, Smart Objects will always render at the resolution of the containing image. If this presents a problem, consider performing a bit of surgery on the Photoshop file to separate the vector and raster components. Double-click vector content to open it in Illustrator, and then choose Save As to create a stand-alone Illustrator file. Delete or hide the vector Smart Object in the Photoshop image, and recombine the vector and raster components in Illustrator or InDesign.

Clipping Masks

A layer mask controls the visibility of the contents of a single layer, but a Clipping Mask controls the visibility of the contents of multiple layers. If you need to establish a common edge for multiple layers, this is the easiest way to do so. Using a Clipping Mask requires a bit of upside-down thinking, though. We're accustomed to a mask controlling what's underneath it, based on real-world examples such as the mat around a framed painting. But a Clipping Masks falls *below* the content it masks (**Figure 9.7**). The color of the painted area of the mask layer isn't important; the transparency or opacity of each pixel in the mask layer governs the transparency and opacity of the layers above it in the group.

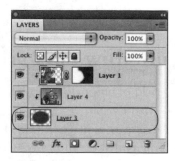

Figure 9.7 The bottom layer is a Clipping Mask, modifying the grouped layers above it and creating a common edge.

To create a Clipping Mask group, make sure that the bottom (mask) layer is a floating layer (i.e., not a glued-down Background layer). Select the layers above the mask layer that you want to mask (but *don't* select the mask layer), and choose Create Clipping Mask from the Layers panel menu. The indented appearance of upper layers and the downward-pointing arrows next to the layer icons indicate that the layers are being affected by the mask. To prevent one of the masked layers from being affected by the mask, select the affected layer (*not* the mask layer) and choose Release from Clipping Mask from the Layers panel menu.

Should You Flatten a Layered File?

Native Photoshop files offer the benefits of layers and transparency—what's not to love? Since current versions of Illustrator and InDesign support unflattened native Photoshop files, there's no need to flatten for compatibility. Admittedly, if a Photoshop file has grown to hundreds of megabytes, it might be more efficient to use a flattened file for placement into a page layout. In some cases, you may wish to flatten a file to prevent unwanted editing by others. But you'd be wise to keep a copy of the original, layered, working Photoshop file in case you need to do additional edits. To flatten a layered file, choose Flatten Image from the Layers panel menu. You can also merge several layers by selecting the layers and choosing Merge Layers from the Layers panel menu.

TRANSPARENCY

Adding effects such as ghosted areas or drop shadows is an easy way to add visual interest to images. Such effects are no longer limited to Photoshop, but as you step outside Photoshop to incorporate those effects, you'll encounter some challenges. Since you can incorporate Photoshop files into Illustrator drawings and Adobe InDesign pages, it's important to realize that you're governed by the limitations of those programs. Just because Photoshop can handle an effect doesn't mean that other programs can interpret that content correctly.

For example, Illustrator and InDesign both honor *transparency* in placed Photoshop files, but neither program correctly handles Photoshop *blending modes*. Transparency and blending may sound like interchangeable terms, but they're not.

Transparency is expressed in percentage opacity. For example, a white square with 20-percent opacity allows what's underneath to show through at 80-percent strength. Opacity settings in a Photoshop file are honored by InDesign and Illustrator, which enables you to create organic soft-edged mask effects and composite images together in InDesign or Illustrator files without having to combine the content in Photoshop.

However, blending modes involve much more complicated math. For example, drop shadows created in Photoshop by selecting Layer > Layer Style > Drop Shadow are set to use the Multiply blend mode with anything they encounter in Photoshop. This results in a realistic darkening of underlying image areas, but only within Photoshop.

Unfortunately, neither Illustrator, QuarkXPress, nor InDesign can understand blending modes within a Photoshop file. So drop shadows created in Photoshop do not interact correctly with elements underneath when they're placed in Illustrator or InDesign (**Figure 9.8**). Instead of darkening underlying elements, Photoshop shadows knock out the shadow area.

Figure 9.8 A Photoshop shadow behaves correctly within Photoshop (left). But when the image is placed in another application, its shadow incorrectly knocks out underlying color rather than darkening it (shown on the right without the black plate).

One solution is to do what we've done for years—combine the elements by placing them on various layers in a Photoshop file. After combining the objects, shadows, and underlying elements in Photoshop, save a layered working file for editing, and then place a flattened image in your final document. Although any changes will require you to go back two generations to the working file (and will require keeping track of both the working file and its descendant), this workflow has been used for years.

If an element requires a simple, soft-edged drop shadow, the solution is simple: Don't create the shadow in Photoshop. Instead, wait until the image is placed in Illustrator or InDesign and create the shadow there, since both applications handle their own shadows correctly. If you're doing your final layout in QuarkXPress up through version 6.5, you can use a third-party XTension to create the shadow, such as ShadowCaster from Quark, Inc. In QuarkXPress 7.0, use the built-in Drop Shadow feature (Item > Drop Shadow).

SILHOUETTES AND MASKING

The traditional method of silhouetting an object to knock out its background involves using the dreaded Pen tool to create a path, earmarking that path as an official clipping path, and then saving the file as an EPS. However, since few people have any actual fondness for the Pen tool in Photoshop, they have instead become adept at avoiding the issue in several ways:

Figure 9.9 You could silhouette this strawberry with the Pen tool. (Or perhaps you could persuade someone else to do it.)

- Deciding that a square-cut image is much more tasteful

- Bribing someone else to draw the path

- Making a selection with the Magic Wand tool, and then converting the selection to a path

The first two options are adequate, but using the Magic Wand will result in a lousy path. The Magic Wand is not truly magic (sorry). It's acceptable for creating some selections to be used in Photoshop or as a starting point for a mask, but it's not the way to make a suitable path. Let's use the strawberry in **Figure 9.9** to explore the path-making options.

Creating a Path: Right and Wrong

Photoshop's attempts to convert an active selection ("marching ants") to a clipping path are valiant, but the results are usually less than stellar. Because a Magic Wand selection follows the rectangular edges of pixels, it's not a very good basis for a smooth clipping path.

In some instances, noodling with the Make Work Path tolerance setting on the Paths panel (Window > Paths) can soften the granularity of the generated path (**Figure 9.10**), but you'll have to keep reloading the selection and experimenting with the tolerance settings, since this function doesn't offer any preview of the outcome.

Figure 9.11 shows the unsavory result of taking the easy way out by converting a selection to a path with the tightest tolerance setting, 0.5 pixels.

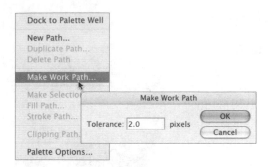

Figure 9.10 The Make Work Path tolerance setting smooths a path that's generated from an active selection.

Figure 9.11 The result of converting a selection to a path by using a 0.5 pixel tolerance. The Wand doesn't seem so magic now, does it?

Using a 10-pixel tolerance setting (**Figure 9.12**) cures the granular look of the path, but note that the smoothness results in a looser clipping path, which lops off some of the strawberry and shows some background.

Figure 9.12 Selection converted to a path, using a 10-pixel tolerance. Smoother than Figure 9.8, but at the expense of fidelity.

It's far better to bite the bullet and draw the path with the Pen tool (**Figure 9.13**). There's no need to obsessively follow every annoying little wiggle. Your goal is a reasonably faithful but smooth rendition of the object's edge, and it's perfectly legal to take a bit of artistic license to improve the edge of the silhouetted image.

Figure 9.13 Clipping path drawn the way nature intended — with the Pen tool.

A dedicated tutorial on using the Pen tool is outside the scope of this book, but check the Appendix for some excellent references and tutorial resources.

Path Flatness Settings

In the olden days of anemic RIPs, users were encouraged to set a high *flatness* value for paths to ease the burden on the RIP. Think of the RIP as constructing curved lines as a series of tiny straight segments. The fewer of those segments the RIP had to chisel—the flatter it could render curves—the faster the job would process. **Figure 9.14** shows a circle imaged with a high flatness setting. It might be easy on the RIP, but it's not easy on the eye.

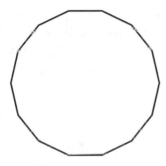

Figure 9.14 A high flatness setting makes things easier for the RIP, but it results in a chiseled appearance for what should be curved lines.

In reaction to seeing such clunky output, some people adopted the unfortunate habit of specifying very *low* flatness values in the Clipping Path dialog (Window > Paths > Clipping Path), such as 0.2 device pixels, in the hopes that this would encourage the RIP to carve more petite segments. Forcing the RIP to chew this finely had the unpleasant side effect of slowing job processing and in some cases, completely preventing the job from being processed by a RIP. When you choose Clipping Path from the Paths panel menu, you have the option to select the correct path and to enter a Flatness value. While RIPs are more robust now, it's actually best to leave the Flatness field *blank* (**Figure 9.15**), which allows the RIP to use its optimal flatness setting without additional calculations. So stop agonizing over what to put in the Flatness field. Just leave it empty, and the RIP will do what it knows is best.

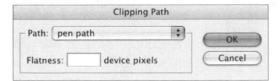

Figure 9.15 When specifying a clipping path, resist the urge to put a microscopic value in the Flatness field. Leaving it blank allows the imaging device to handle curves with its own optimal setting.

Paths that Aren't Clipping Paths

Besides being challenging to draw, clipping paths are bullies. When placed in a page-layout application, an image with an official clipping path can only display what's within the area of the clipping path—that's the whole point of a clipping path. But paths aren't *official* clipping paths until you designate them as such via the Paths panel menu.

Consider an image that contains several elements that you'd like to use selectively in a page layout. If you're planning to use the clipping path approach to silhouetting those elements, you'd have to save multiple versions of the image, resulting in a separate image for each element you plan to use.

But there's a more flexible approach available to you. InDesign recognizes *any* paths in JPEG, EPS, and TIFF files, providing the option of choosing which path you'd like to use to silhouette the image (**Figure 9.16**). The paths don't have to be official clipping paths—they just have to be named paths. Select the image, choose Object > Clipping Path > Options, and select the name of the path to be used to silhouette the image.

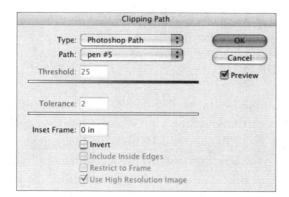

Figure 9.16 Choose a path in InDesign; it doesn't have to be an official clipping path to silhouette the image. It only needs to be named and saved in Photoshop.

Taking this approach allows you to use the same image in multiple ways without saving multiple versions. In **Figure 9.17**, the same image provides seven uses—a square-cut version and the six, individual silhouetted pens. There is no limit to the number of named paths you can have in an image. Note, however, that an unsaved work path isn't recognized by InDesign.

Figure 9.17 Six pens, six paths, one single image used in multiple ways.

Alternative Silhouetting Methods

Here's some good news for those who loathe the Pen tool. Since version 2.0, InDesign has honored transparency in Photoshop images. In addition to providing liberation from the dreaded Pen tool, this means that you can perform the equivalent of photocomposition within a page layout (**Figure 9.18**), if you know how to create realistic masks.

Figure 9.18 The dandelion (left) can be extracted from its background by using a density-based mask (center). Since InDesign honors transparency, the dandelion can then be composited with other elements in a page layout (right).

If the subject is a simple one, you can use the Lasso or Magnetic Lasso tool to start a mask, and then view the mask in Quick Mask mode (Select > Edit in Quick Mask Mode, or press the Q key on the keyboard). Use painting tools to refine the edge of the mask.

If the subject was photographed on a fairly consistent background (by which we don't mean *plaid*), you can create a density-based mask similar to that of the dandelion by starting with one of the channels of the image. Open the Channels panel in Photoshop (Window > Channels) to inspect the channels. Click the name of each channel, one by one, until you find the channel with the most contrast between the subject and the background. It doesn't have to be perfect. It just has to provide a good start. In the case of the dandelion, the cyan channel is the most promising. The black channel is a close second choice, but the cyan has finer detail, so it's the winner (**Figure 9.19**).

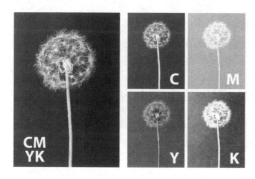

Figure 9.19 Shopping for a channel to provide a starting point for a mask. Either the cyan or black channel might work, but the cyan has more detail.

Once you've decided on the channel that provides the best start for a mask, duplicate it. Select the channel in the Channels panel and, from the Channels panel menu, choose Duplicate Channel. You can name it something memorable in the dialog that follows, or just accept the default name—in this case, *Cyan copy*.

The next step is to manipulate the contrast in the Cyan copy channel so that it becomes solid black and white. Since you want to affect only the mask channel, rather than performing a color correction on the color image, you won't use the Adjustments panel. Choose Levels (Image > Adjustments > Levels) or Curves (Image > Adjustments > Curves) to exaggerate the contrast in the mask channel (**Figure 9.20**). The goal in our dandelion image is a white dandelion-shaped hole in a black background. Since each image is different, you'll have to experiment with the values in your images.

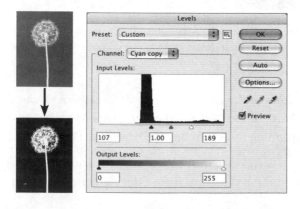

Figure 9.20 Using Levels to increase the contrast of the mask channel. Your values will depend on your image.

You'll probably have to use your paintbrush to edit the mask to your satisfaction. Paint with white to open up areas of the mask (which will reveal those parts of the image when you're finished). Paint with black to fill in the mask where you want to hide areas of the image. The mask is stored in an alpha channel (**Figure 9.21**). It doesn't act as a mask until you load it as an active selection. For the rest of the steps of loading a selection, refer to Figure 9.2, and the instructions in the section, "Don't Erase that Pixel!" earlier in this chapter.

Figure 9.21 When you create and save a mask, it's stored in an alpha channel. But it's just waiting there. It isn't an active mask until you load it as an active selection.

Since the mask is derived from image contents, it creates a much more natural silhouette without the hard-edged cutout appearance that results from using a clipping path.

Non-Destructive Mask Edits

While a selection is still loaded and active—you still see "marching ants" onscreen—you can use the Refine Edge option in the Control panel to contract, expand, or even feather the selection before saving it as a static mask in an alpha channel. Photoshop CS4 adds the ability to perform such modifications to a *saved* mask with the options available in the new Masks panel (Window > Masks). See **Figure 9.22**.

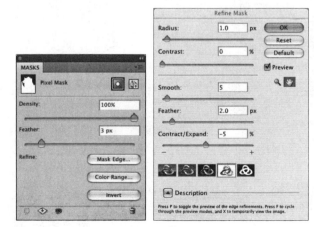

Figure 9.22 The Masks panel (far left) offers options for Density and Feathering, as well as the Mask Edge feature (right), which allows you to Smooth, Expand and Contract the mask nondestructively.

You can contract, expand, feather, and smooth the edge of an alpha channel or layer mask without permanently altering it. Save and close the file, reopen it, and cancel the modifications, and the mask returns to its original edge.

BEYOND CMYK

You're not limited to just cyan, magenta, yellow, and black inks when you print a color image. You can create images that consist of combinations of CMYK and spot color, or even images that print only in spot colors.

Creating Duotones

A *duotone* image is composed of two colors, usually black and a spot color. Such images are a great way to add visual interest to a job with a limited color palette. There are variations on this theme, such as *tritones* (three colors), *quadtones* (four colors), and so on. Since these images usually contain spot-color components, it's important to create them correctly to ensure that they print as intended. Note that these images may be composed of all spot colors or a combination of spot colors and process colors. Start with a grayscale image, and then choose Image > Mode > Duotone (which is the starting point, even if you intend to create a tritone or quadtone image).

In creating a basic spot-plus-black duotone image, designers may make the understandable mistake of thinking that the Black ink listed in the Duotone Options dialog is a spot color (**Figure 9.23**). Don't worry: It's really just the plain, old-fashioned process black of CMYK fame, and there's no need to change it.

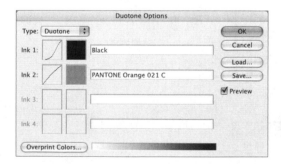

Figure 9.23 The Black ink chosen by Photoshop in the Duotone Options dialog is plain old process black. Don't alter it.

In fact, if you get ambitious and change the name of Black in the Duotone Options dialog to, say, Pantone Process Black C, for example, you actually *cause* what you're trying to *prevent*: You create an extraneous spot color when you import the image into a page layout, as shown in the InDesign Swatches panel (**Figure 9.24**). So just leave the default name of the black plate alone, and Photoshop will do the right thing. Of course, if you are using two separate black inks on the job—process black plus a Pantone black for some special effect—you may be intending to use a special Pantone black in your duotones. In that case, just be sure to use a consistent name for the ink in Photoshop, Illustrator, and InDesign, so that you don't accidentally create extraneous inks in the final job file.

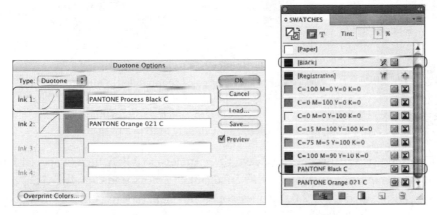

Figure 9.24 Changing the definition of Black in Photoshop's Duotone Options creates an extra black ink when you place the image in a page-layout program such as InDesign (right). Not what you had in mind.

Adding Spot Color to a CMYK Image

Occasionally, special handling is needed to accentuate portions of an image or to ensure faithful rendering of a color that falls outside the CMYK gamut. Adding spot ink on top of an image of flowers might allow the printed piece to better render the true color of the actual flowers, if process color falls short of doing so. In this approach—variously called *bump plate*, *touch plate,* or *kiss plate*—the image contains additional colors beyond the standard cyan, magenta, yellow, and black. Bump plates are often used in high-end printing projects such as fine art reproductions, to ensure a closer rendition of the original artwork.

To add a spot color to a CMYK image, choose New Spot Channel from the Channels panel menu. Click on the Color block to select an ink color, and then click on the Color Libraries button to access the standard color books (**Figure 9.25**). Choose the correct ink from the color list, and then click OK. In the New Spot Channel dialog, leave the name as it appears. The Solidity option controls visual opacity of the spot ink plate as it is displayed in Photoshop; it has nothing to do with how the plate will print. Varying the Solidity setting may make it easier for you to work on the spot channel, but the actual contents of the channel will not be affected by the Solidity setting.

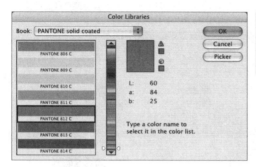

Figure 9.25 Choosing the ink for a spot color channel (left). Don't change the name of the ink (above), unless you need to match a color-naming convention already used in a project.

In the olden days, it was necessary to save these images as DCS files (a special flavor of EPS). The most common format for this amalgam of colors traditionally has been a special flavor of EPS called DCS 2.0, for Desktop Color Separations. Under the hood, these special images consist of all the individual color plates plus a low-resolution representation image for display. But DCS files present challenges when placed into some other applications, or into some older workflows.

It's no longer necessary to save images containing spot color channels in the old-fashioned DCS format; Photoshop native PSD files do the job. If the file contains vector content such as type or shape layers which should image as crisp, vector edges, save the file as Photoshop PDF.

Creating a Spot Varnish Plate

Even though it isn't usually colored, a spot varnish plate is handled just like a spot color ink. Remember, a spot varnish is a shaped application of varnish, commonly used to highlight an object, as opposed to an allover flood varnish (for more information see "Coatings and Varnishes" in Chapter Two, "Ink on Paper").

To create a spot varnish plate, start as you would when creating a spot color: Choose New Spot Channel from the Channels panel menu. If varnish components have already been created, name your varnish plate consistent with the existing files, and then click the Color block in the Spot Channel dialog and create a color mix in keeping with existing files. If you're starting fresh, we'd suggest naming the channel Spot Varnish, and coloring it something obvious, such as a bright green, so it will be easy to identify when placed into other applications. Create the varnish area in the spot channel by painting or pasting content: Solid areas in the varnish channel represent the areas where the solid varnish will be printed (**Figure 9.26**).

Figure 9.26 The spot varnish plate (right) will result in a gloss varnish printed to highlight parts of the antique motorcycle.

When you place an image with a spot color or spot varnish plate into an Illustrator or InDesign document, the spot color is automatically added to the Swatches list.

The color you assign to the varnish plate just serves to identify it when you view the file in Photoshop or place it into another application. The color does not affect the color appearance of the image when the file is output. The varnish plate that is generated during output will be used to print the varnish on press.

BEYOND PIXELS

Pixels and vectors can live together in graphic harmony, enabling you to combine smooth, sharp text with images for interesting results. But it's important to save such constructions correctly so that other programs produce expected output.

Vector Elements

While Photoshop is primarily devoted to pixels, it is possible to add text and other vector elements to a Photoshop image. It's not appropriate to create body text in Photoshop, and most text should be created in an illustration or page-layout application. But if you want to bevel and emboss text (**Figure 9.27**), or give a special treatment to a vector logo, you may be compelled to handle it in Photoshop.

Figure 9.27 Vector or text elements are an interesting (although not necessarily tasteful) addition to an image.

Vector elements in Photoshop do not have any inherent resolution, although any shading applied through effects such as embossing must be accomplished with pixels. Those pixels are just part of the effect, and they don't become literal pixels until the file is printed. Consequently, you can scale vector elements within the Photoshop image and the effects will be recalculated, growing new pixels of the appropriate resolution. Since the edges of vector elements are vector, not pixels, they remain crisp.

It's important to save such hybrid files in a way that ensures that the vector edges print sharply, and this is where we encounter an alphabet soup of acronyms.

The ideal file format for cohabiting pixels and vectors is one that retains the crisp edges of vectors when the file is placed in an illustration or page-layout file, and allows round-tripping back to Photoshop for any needed editing. There are several file-format options for this type of image, of which only one is truly satisfactory (**Figure 9.28**).

Figure 9.28 A Photoshop file containing vector elements can be saved in several formats. The sharp vector edges in a native PSD file become rasterized when placed in a page-layout program (left). An EPS retains the desired crisp edges when placed in a page layout (middle), but will lose the vector content if reopened in Photoshop for editing. Only a Photoshop PDF (right) retains vector information for placement in a page layout *and* allows round-tripping back into Photoshop.

A native Photoshop file (PSD) keeps the text and vector elements live in Photoshop and allows round-tripping. You can reopen the file at any time to correct misspelled text or edit anchor points on vector shapes. When PSD files containing text or vector content are placed in an illustration or page-layout file, the vector edges are rendered as pixels during output, taking on the resolution of the underlying image. Consequently, PSDs containing vector elements may serve as working files, but be aware that the vector edges are rasterized when placed into other applications. (There may be occasions when you prefer the rasterization to keeping the crisp vector edge.)

Saving such an image as an EPS preserves sharp vector edges, even when placed in an illustration or page-layout file. However, while the EPS format ensures good output, it prevents the file from being safely reopened in Photoshop. Photoshop can open it, but the vector content will be rasterized in the process, thus ruining the integrity of the image.

For this special type of image, only a Photoshop PDF provides full functionality. A Photoshop PDF can be reopened by Photoshop without rasterizing, and the vector content is correctly displayed and imaged when a Photoshop PDF is placed into documents created by Illustrator, InDesign, and QuarkXPress. Think of it as two files in one: Photoshop sees the original PSD, with its editable text and vector content; and other applications see the public face of the PDF file, with its nice, crisp edges.

Saving as a Photoshop PDF

To save a PDF that can be reopened by Photoshop, choose File > Save As, and then in the Format list, select Photoshop PDF. When the Save Adobe PDF dialog is displayed, make sure that the Preserve Photoshop Editing Capabilities check box is selected (**Figure 9.29**). This is the default setting for Photoshop PDF files.

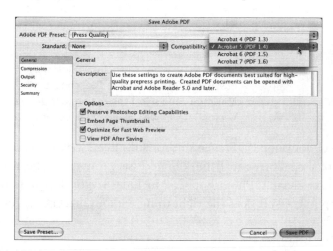

Figure 9.29 To ensure that you can reopen a Photoshop PDF, select the Preserve Photoshop Editing Capabilities check box. For maximum portability, choose Acrobat 4 (PDF 1.3). To maintain transparency, choose Acrobat 5 (PDF 1.4).

If you want to maintain transparency in the image when it is placed into Illustrator or InDesign, you must save with Acrobat 5.0 or above compatibility. If you plan to place the Photoshop PDF into QuarkXPress, choose the PDF/X-1a preset from the list at the top of the dialog. You'll lose the transparency, but the file will print more predictably. For more information on Acrobat and PDF files, see Chapter Twelve, "Acrobat Production Tips."

Older Photoshop versions (prior to CS2) require you to be mindful of vector settings in the PDF Options dialog that is displayed when you choose File > Save As and choose the Photoshop PDF format (**Figure 9.30**). If you don't select Include Vector Data, the edges of vector and text content will appear rasterized in other applications and will be output as raster content. For maximum portability, also select Use Outlines for Text in the PDF Options dialog so that there are no embedded fonts that might be mishandled by subsequent processes that affect the PDF file. The Use Outlines for Text option has *no* effect on content when the PDF is reopened in Photoshop. The PDF part of the file is perceived by other applications, which will see only the outlined text.

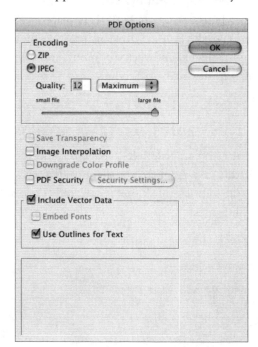

Figure 9.30 When saving as a Photoshop PDF in Photoshop prior to CS2, choose JPEG Maximum, and select the option to Include Vector Data, as well as Use Outlines for Text.

In the PSD part of the saved Photoshop PDF, everything is still "live," so when you reopen the file in Photoshop, the text is still true text, and the necessary fonts must be active on your system to edit the text. By default, Photoshop CS2 includes vector data and outlines the text for use in other applications. It does the right thing without presenting you with confusing options.

SAVING FOR OTHER APPLICATIONS

The old recommendations to save as TIFF or EPS were solid in their day, and you still can't go wrong by adhering to the old ways. However, native, layered Photoshop files (PSD) offer appealing features such as transparency, editable vector elements, and nondestructive color corrections. InDesign allows you to control the visibility of placed, layered, native Photoshop files (but not TIFFs). TIFF files can contain layers, but offer no support for vector elements, so Photoshop PSDs and PDFs trump TIFF files for flexibility.

It's now acceptable to loosen up a bit. InDesign and Illustrator accept layered Photoshop files in all their glory, including transparency effects. QuarkXPress 6.5 allows placement of native PSDs, although it doesn't recognize transparency. QuarkXPress 7.0 and 8.0 offer expanded support for native Photoshop features, recognizing transparency and even allowing you to use alpha channels as soft-edged masks. There's no need to squeeze the fun out of your images before you place them into a page layout. But it's still worthwhile to do some housecleaning before you save and close your Photoshop file.

- Delete unused layers. Select an unwanted layer (or Shift-click to select multiple layers), and then choose Delete Layer from the Layers panel menu.

- Delete unused alpha channels. Select an unwanted channel (or Shift-click to select multiple channels), and then choose Delete Channel from the Channels panel menu.

- Delete unused paths. Select the unwanted path and then choose Delete Path from the Paths panel menu. You'll have to delete paths one by one—Shift-clicking doesn't work when selecting paths.

- Make sure the image is in the correct color space for its final use.

- If you're certain about the final use of the image, crop out any unnecessary image content. But leave a rind of extra image around the outside, just in case you need a bit of elbow room when the image is placed in a page layout.

- If you've created multiple, experimental files on your way to the final image, name the final image in a way that makes it clear It's The One, and put the older, obsolete files in a quarantine folder. Don't send a job to the print service provider with a folder full of images with names like *Final.tif*, *Final2.tif*, *NewFinal.tif*, *Newfinal2.tif*, *NewerFinal3.tif*, *NewestFinal.tif*, *FinalButDon'tUse.tif*, and so on. If *you're* confused, think how *they'll* feel.

CHAPTER TEN

Illustrator CS4 Production Tips

As Adobe Illustrator has evolved over the years, it has morphed from a relatively simple vector drawing program into a full-featured graphic arts tool. The addition of live effects has blurred the line between drawing and painting, and the introduction of multiple artboards in Illustrator CS4 extends the concept of the drawing board beyond a single size of digital "paper." Substantial enhancements to key tools such as the Appearance panel and gradient controller will also make you much more productive.

DOCUMENT PROFILE AND COLOR MODE

As you begin a new Illustrator file, you're prompted to choose a New Document Profile as a starting point (**Figure 10.1**). You can choose from Print, Web, Mobile and Devices, Video and Film, Basic CMYK, and Basic RGB. Each profile has presets for such attributes as dimensions, color mode, measurement units, and Raster Effects resolution. You can also base a new document on one of Illustrator's supplied templates, which contain more "furniture" (such as swatches, artboards, brushes, and artwork) than a simple document profile.

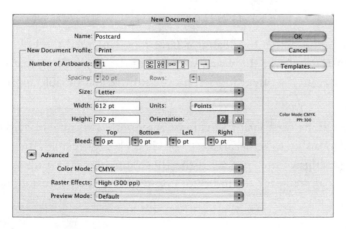

Figure 10.1 Document profiles give you a head start on the settings for a new document. Click the triangle next to Advanced to reveal options for Color Mode, Raster Effects Resolution, and default Preview Mode.

While these settings are in effect when the document is first created, all of the attributes can be changed over the life of the document if necessary. Understandably, the Print document profile is set up as CMYK color, as is the generic CMYK profile. But what does this do to non-CMYK content?

Within a CMYK Illustrator file, you are allowed to specify colors as CMYK, RGB, or HSB (Hue-Saturation-Brightness), but, whatever color mode you might use to mix a color, it takes on the color mode governing the document. For example, in a document with a CMYK color mode, an object set to an RGB value of R200-G40-B30 is converted to C2-M98-Y100-K0 in the final file if your color management options are set to North America Prepress 2. The CMYK value that's created depends on the current color management settings, so your mileage (and CMYK values) may vary.

While this may initially be confusing, the net effect is that it keeps you out of trouble as you choose colors for objects, as long as you establish the correct color mode to begin with, and pay attention to the color space of linked images. If you didn't make the correct choice as you began the document, you can rectify that by choosing File > Document Color Mode. All content created within Illustrator changes to the new color mode. However, the color space of a placed image depends on whether an image is linked or embedded: An embedded image will take on the color space of the Illustrator file, but a linked image retains its original color space.

If you save the Illustrator file as a PDF, the color space of all content in the PDF depends on the PDF settings used. For example, an Illustrator file set up in the RGB document color mode containing all RGB linked images will yield a CMYK PDF when the PDF/X-1a PDF creation setting is used. For more information on the PDF/X-1a standard, see Chapter Twelve, "Acrobat Production Tips."

ARTBOARDS

FreeHand users who made the switch to Illustrator have long lamented the lack of multiple page support in Illustrator. Over the years, we've used the Page Tiling feature as a kludgy solution, but Illustrator CS4 offers an even more intuitive and flexible approach—multiple artboards.

The single artboard in previous versions of Illustrator represented an imaginary piece of drawing paper, and its relationship to actual artwork could be a bit confusing. After all, you could draw far beyond the edge of the "paper." If the Illustrator file was set up as an odd size (say, 3 by 3 inches), the dotted page tile indicator compounded the confusion; novices couldn't figure out where the true edge of Illustrator reality fell. Add the fact that AI files and EPS files represent the "true edge" differently to other applications, and it's no wonder we might get confused. You may be pleasantly surprised to discover that the new concept of multiple artboards actually makes things less confusing. And if you're familiar with the Crop Area tool in Illustrator CS3, the artboard concept will make sense immediately. In fact, if you created crop areas in an Illustrator CS3 file, the crop areas will be automatically converted to artboards when you open the file in Illustrator CS4.

Here's an aerial view of the CS4 environment to help you get oriented (**Figure 10.2**).

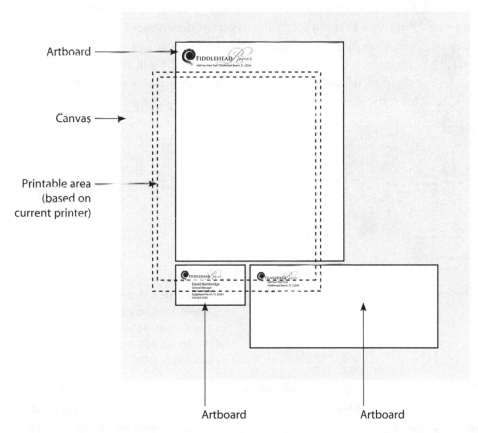

Figure 10.2 Think of the gray *canvas* area as a large drawing table (227 by 227 inches), and the *artboards* as pieces of drawing paper arranged on the drawing table. The *printable area* indicator (displayed when you choose View > Show Print Tiling) is based on the capabilities of the currently chosen printer, but don't consider that a firm limitation for artwork creation.

Creating Artboards

When you create a new Illustrator document, one artboard is automatically created. Its dimensions are dictated by a preset in the document profile on which the new file is based. However, you have the option to change both the dimensions and number of artboards in the New Document dialog.

You can also create up to a total of 100 artboards manually in an existing document by clicking and dragging with the Artboard tool (⬚). The width and height of the new artboard is displayed next to your cursor as you drag, but it's almost impossible to create an exact size. Don't fret; to specify the dimensions of the artboard exactly, create the artboard at any size, and then press the Enter key on the keyboard or click the Artboard Options icon (▦) in the Control panel to display the Artboard Options dialog (**Figure 10.3**). You can also use the dimension fields in the Control panel to view and modify the dimensions of the selected artboard.

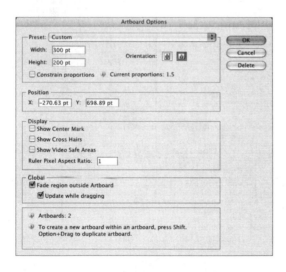

Figure 10.3 Artboard options include dimensions, position, and orientation. The default global option to fade the region outside artboards makes it easier to identify artboard areas.

You can choose from the extensive list of preset artboard sizes, including common print sizes such as letter and A4, and video sizes such as NTSC DV. You can also create a custom size up to the maximum 227.54 inches square (the dimensions of the Illustrator canvas environment). Artboards can be in any position within the overall canvas, and can even overlap. Artboards are numbered according to the order in which they were created; there is no option to change the numbering. All artboards share the same color space.

You can also create an artboard by clicking on an existing object with the Artboard tool. If the object is rectangular, the artboard coincides with the dimensions of the rectangle. If the object is not a rectangle, the artboard corresponds to the object's bounding box (**Figure 10.4**).

Figure 10.4 When you click an irregular object with the Artboard tool (left), a new artboard is created, corresponding to the bounding box of the object (right).

To create an artboard on top of another artboard, hold down the Shift key as you click and begin dragging the new artboard. Release the Shift key before you release the mouse button if you don't want the artboard to be square — the Shift key is also a constrainer.

To hide artboards, choose View > Hide Artboards. If that option isn't available, it's because you have an Artboard selected.

To focus on a single artboard, select it with the Artboard tool and choose View > Fit Artboard in Window, or choose the artboard number from the status area at the lower-left corner of the application window. You can also select artboards by choosing the Artboard tool, and then using the arrow keys and the Option (Mac) or Alt (Windows) key. The down and right arrows cycle through artboards in *ascending* numerical order (artboard 1, artboard 2, artboard 3, and so on). The left and up arrows cycle through the artboards in *descending* order; not exactly intuitive, is it?

Modifying Artboards

Select an artboard by clicking inside it with the Artboard tool. To change the dimensions of an artboard, drag the handles of the artboard, or press the Enter key to open the Artboard Options dialog to specify the new dimensions numerically. To delete a selected artboard, press the Delete key on the keyboard, or click the "X" icon in the upper-right corner of the artboard. You can delete all but one artboard. As you delete artboards, the artboard identification numbers reset themselves. Artwork inside the artboard is not deleted (it remains in place on the canvas), but the artwork will be printed or exported only if Ignore Artboards is chosen in the output dialog; then, all content is regarded as one large illustration, as in previous versions of Illustrator.

To reposition an artboard, select it with the Artboard tool and then drag to the new position. But what happens to artwork within the artboard area? It depends on the status of an easily overlooked option in the Control panel — the Move/Copy Artwork with Artboard tool (🖼). If this option is chosen, the icon has a dark background, and any artwork that falls partially or completely within the area of an artboard will move with the artboard. If the Move/Copy option is deselected, the icon background is light gray like the rest of the Control panel, and a selected artboard moves independently of the artwork within it.

Since artboards can overlap, and larger artwork might fall within several artboards even if the artboards do not overlap, be mindful of the Move/Copy setting before you move any artboard or artwork. If you want to duplicate an artboard and its artwork, select the Move/Copy option by clicking the icon in the Control panel, choose the Artboard tool, and then hold down the Option (Mac) or Alt (Windows) key as you drag the artboard.

Bleed Settings

When you create a new Illustrator document, you are given the option to specify a bleed value. You can also specify bleed in an existing document by choosing File > Document Setup. Bleeds can be asymmetrical, and can be up to one inch in depth. The specified bleed value is applied to all artboards within an Illustrator file; there is no option to create a unique bleed setting for an individual artboard. How bleed is handled in exported PDFs, AI, or EPS files depends both on the settings used during export and the import options chosen when the file is placed into another application, such as InDesign. For more on this topic, see "Saving for Other Applications," later in this chapter.

Please Don't Call Artboards "Pages"

The artboard concept is best suited for projects such as collateral pieces that share swatches and common bits of artwork, or projects with multiple versions. While it's tempting (and easy) to refer to artboards as pages, please don't think of them as pages: Think of them as sheets of drawing paper. Perhaps that will help you resist being lured into building a 16-page brochure as an Illustrator file with 16 artboards (this will cause the prepress guys to refer to you in unflattering terms once you are out of earshot). It's a case of "just because you *can*, doesn't mean you *should*." Artboards don't provide basic page-layout features such as master pages, margin guides, and automatic page numbers. Consider those omissions to be nature's way of saying "Use InDesign."

Is there a sound technical reason why you couldn't build the 16-page job in Illustrator? The grudging answer is that there isn't, but your print service provider will probably be a little aggravated at you, especially if you forget to send the support images and fonts. If you use the Scoop plug-in from Worker 72a (*www.worker72a.com*) to gather up fonts and images, at least you will have sent all the pieces. But better yet, *learn InDesign*!

USING SYMBOLS

What if you needed to create a school of 100 fish in Illustrator? You could draw 100 individual fish, which would be exhausting (but great for billing). Or you could draw one fish, and then copy and paste 99 duplicates; that's much faster, but still tedious. And what do you do when your customer says the fish should be *sharks* rather than the 100 flounders you've just finished creating? You scream a lot, and then you start over—unless you were clever enough to use Illustrator's Symbols tools.

A symbol is a special species of artwork that solves the need-a-lot-of-fish-in-a-hurry problem and makes it painless to change all those fish simultaneously. (The alliteration is intentional: It will prepare you for the stunning selection of Symbol tools, all with names starting with *S*, including the Symbol Sprayer, Symbol Shifter, Symbol Scruncher, and so on—you get the idea. See **Figure 10.5**.)

Figure 10.5 The Symbol tools. From left to right: the Sprayer, Shifter, Scruncher, Sizer, Spinner, Stainer, Screener, and Styler.

Artwork saved as a symbol can be reused multiple times in a document, and all the *instances* of the symbol retain a relationship to the original, ancestral symbol. This offers several advantages:

- **Efficiency:** It's easy to populate the document with lots of instances of a symbol (think: school of fish, gaggle of geese, flock of sheep, etc.).

- **Quick corrections:** You can edit the original artwork in the ancestral symbol and all instances are automatically updated.

- **Smaller file size:** Using symbols can greatly reduce file size if you save in the native Illustrator AI format, because you're just hauling around one copy of the artwork, not 100 copies. If you save as an EPS, the file can be considerably larger because each instance of the symbol takes up space in the EPS format.

To create a symbol, draw an object (or multiple objects), and then drag the selected artwork to the open Symbols panel, or select New Symbol from the Symbols panel menu (Window > Symbols). Name the symbol and then click OK. A thumbnail of the new symbol is added to the Symbols panel. In the Symbol Options dialog, choose Movie Clip if you are planning to export the file to Flash for use in an animation. Either Movie Clip or Graphic will work just fine if the file is to be used for print (**Figure 10.6**).

Figure 10.6 Save as a Movie Clip if you are planning to export the Illustrator to Flash. If the file will be used for print, it doesn't matter which option you choose.

The symbol is stored in the current Illustrator file, not as a universally available symbol. However, you can import symbols from another file by choosing Open Symbol Library > Other Library from the Symbols panel menu. Navigate to the donor Illustrator file, and click Open. Click on symbols you would like to add to the internal Symbol library in the currently open document. You can also save symbols in a freestanding Symbol library by choosing Save Symbol Library from the Symbols panel menu (a Symbol library is actually just an Illustrator AI file containing the symbols).

> *NOTE: If you use a CMYK symbol in an Illustrator file whose document color mode is RGB, the symbol artwork, like placed images and other artwork, will also take on the RGB color space.*

To add a symbol to a drawing, either drag it from the Symbols panel onto the Illustrator document window to create a single instance of the symbol, or (and this is much more fun) use the Symbol Sprayer to quickly populate the drawing with multiple instances. Tweak the distribution, size, and color of the symbols with the Symbol tools.

Once you've sprayed a bunch of symbols onto your Illustrator drawing, switch to Outline view (View > Outline). Notice that there are no outlines of any of the symbol instances. That's because symbols are *live effects*. Live effects can be continually added, removed, edited, and changed, because they are not yet literal vector artwork. The underlying object is not altered by live effects. If you want to edit individual points on the artwork, you can expand the symbols to editable objects (**Figure 10.7**). Click in the area occupied by the symbols, and then choose Object > Expand. If the original symbol used any effects, you may have to expand again or choose Object > Expand Appearance to fully release all objects for editing. You may also have to perform several rounds of ungrouping (Object > Ungroup) to completely dismantle aggregations of objects, depending on the internal complexity of the artwork. Some content, such as shadows and glows, will be converted to embedded image content.

Once you've expanded symbol instances, there's no link between the original symbol and the expanded artwork based on it. If you edit the parent symbol, any changes will not be reflected in the expanded objects. As a result, you lose one of the big advantages of symbols. File size will increase as well, sometimes enormously, because of the complexity of the expanded artwork. Unless you need to edit individual pieces of symbol instances, there's no reason to expand symbols. The content is treated the same by InDesign and imaging devices, whether it's expanded or not.

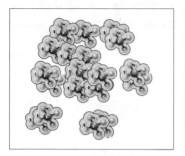  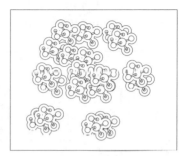

Figure 10.7 A spray of symbols (left) represents multiple instances of the single-symbol artwork. View the document in Outline mode (center) and you'll see that the vectors are not yet literal content, just an area containing a live effect. To convert the symbol instances to literal, editable vectors, select the symbol area and then choose Object > Expand (right).

SIMPLIFYING COMPLEX ARTWORK

Even though today's computers and current RIPs are significantly faster than their ancestors, there are still some benefits to eliminating complexity where possible. Pen paths with too many points can be lumpy and rough. And extraneous, empty points can result in incorrect boundaries for artwork, since the bounding box of an Illustrator file can be determined by the outermost points in the artwork (depending on how the file is saved, as well as how it's imported into another application).

Fortunately, Illustrator offers some tools for polishing your drawing. Choose Object > Path > Clean Up to delete those little stray points that you might create with inadvertent pen clicks, objects with no fill and stroke, and those pesky empty text paths that spring up when you *swear* you didn't really click anywhere with the Type tool (**Figure 10.8**). Clean Up makes intelligent decisions: While masks don't have a fill and stroke, the Clean Up function is clever enough to recognize and preserve them.

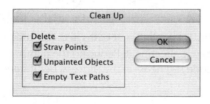

Figure 10.8 Illustrator's Clean Up dialog provides controls for eliminating extraneous paths and points, for a much cleaner drawing.

Given their names, it's easy to confuse Clean Up with another function, Simplify. Clean Up *deletes* unnecessary objects in the drawing, and it performs that task on a global basis. By contrast, Simplify (Object > Path > Simplify) *modifies* selected objects by reducing the number of points in those objects (**Figure 10.9**). You can control the fidelity to the initial path by using the Curve Precision slider: The higher the precision, the more points are retained.

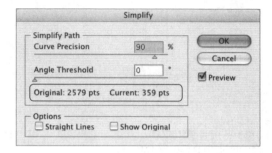

Figure 10.9 Simplify, indeed. Note the striking reduction in number of points from 2579 to 359!

When using Simplify, select the Preview check box so you can immediately see the effect of your settings before you commit to the change. In general, keeping the Curve Precision value around 90–95 percent will achieve a satisfactory smoothing and a beneficial reduction in the number of points without significantly degrading detail (**Figure 10.10**).

Figure 10.10 Using Object > Path > Simplify reduces the total number of paths in the document. Used judiciously, it can smooth a drawing without adversely affecting it. Reducing the number of points from 2579 (left) to 359 (right) does alter some subtle segments in the process, but it does not substantially degrade the overall look of the drawing.

However, it's possible to overdo things with the Simplify function. Dipping much below 95 percent for the Curve Precision value will quickly erode detail in the drawing by deleting too many points (**Figure 10.11**).

LIVE EFFECTS

Illustrator offers a number of imaginative live effects that allow you to transform a simple object into something much more interesting with just a few clicks. Effects are "live," which means that you can modify how an object looks by editing effects in the Appearance panel, without permanently altering the object itself. You can also hide or remove an effect to return an object to its original appearance.

Figure 10.11 Going too far: The result of using a Curve Precision value of 70 percent.

Why Filters Are Gone

In previous versions of Illustrator, users were given the choice of adding shadows, glows, feathers, and other visual adornments to objects with Filters or Effects. Because of the redundancy—for example, both features offered a Drop Shadow option—users were understandably confused: Which was the best method?

Filters created literal content: For example, the Drop Shadow filter generated the shadow as an embedded image. The Zig Zag filter repositioned points on the object and added new points, permanently altering the shape of the object.

By contrast, *effects* are live *appearances*, not literal content: No pixels are generated by the Drop Shadow effect until the Illustrator file is printed (that is, when a print stream is generated by choosing File > Print) or exported to a PDF. The true underlying shape of an object using the Zig Zag effect is not changed in the Illustrator file (**Figure 10.12**).

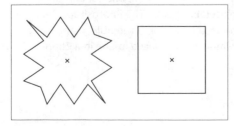

Figure 10.12 The object on the left was distorted with the Zig Zag effect. But under the hood, it's still the same old rectangle (right). This allows you to experiment more freely, or return to the original shape with no penalty. If you want to tweak individual points of the Zig Zag effect, use Expand to convert the object to editable vectors.

Filters were a vestige of the olden days, when Illustrator was governed by the limitations of the PostScript imaging model. Illustrator 9 was the first version of Illustrator to go beyond PostScript limitations by adopting the expanded Adobe Graphics Model (shared by Acrobat 5 and InDesign 2.0) with support for transparency and live effects.

Both filters and effects were offered in versions of Illustrator up through CS3, but Illustrator CS4 no longer includes filters. Since effects can be expanded to become literal pixel and vector content, filters have actually been redundant for several versions, so they've now been laid to rest.

Using Effects

The Effects menu is divided into two sections—Illustrator Effects and Photoshop Effects. The Illustrator Effects are applied to the interiors and the edges of vector objects, including objects being used as Clipping Masks for placed images. The SVG filters generate raster content for the interior of an object without modifying the edge of the object. Photoshop Effects are applied only to the interior of vector objects, including those used as Clipping Masks (**Figure 10.13**).

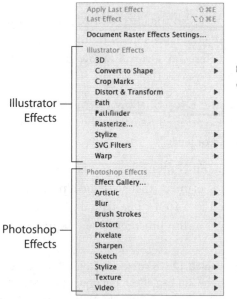

Illustrator Effects:
Stylize > Scribble

Photoshop Effects:
Artistic > Rough Pastels

Figure 10.13 With the exception of the SVG filters, effects listed in the Illustrator Effects section of the Effects menu affect the interior *and* the edge of the object (above, left). The Photoshop Effects are applied only to the interior of the object (above, right). This example uses a placed image in a Clipping Mask.

Some effects, such as glows or shadows, can only be accomplished with pixels. But since such effects are *potential* pixels, not literal pixels, Illustrator generates *potential* pixels. If you switch to Outline view, you don't see the outline of an image placed for an effect such as a shadow. That's because there *isn't* a shadow image (**Figure 10.14**). The shadow doesn't turn into literal pixels until the file is exported or imaged.

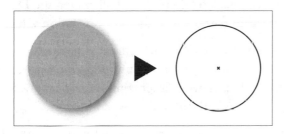

Figure 10.14 Effect > Stylize > Drop Shadow uses imaginary pixels to display a shadow. Those pixels don't become literal pixels until the file is exported or imaged.

Document Raster Effects Settings

You might notice that dialogs for pixel-based effects don't offer an option to specify the resolution of these effects. The control for effects resolution is hiding in plain sight: Choose Effect > Document Raster Effects Settings (**Figure 10.15**).

The resolution setting in the Document Raster Effects dialog governs all pixel-based effects, including drop shadows, feathering, the shading on 3D extrusions, and some Graphic Styles confections.

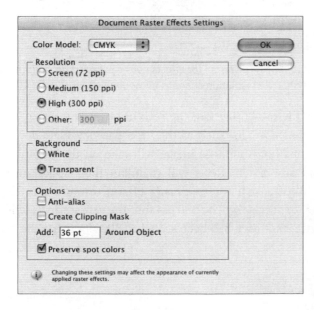

Figure 10.15 The default Document Raster Effects value is 300 ppi, which is appropriate for artwork created to print at 100 percent size. If the artwork will be greatly scaled up (for example, if you are working at half size), you may want to increase the ppi accordingly. Note that the default behavior is to preserve spot colors.

Consider the computational overhead involved in generating these pixels on the fly. In a complex drawing, rendering such effects at full resolution can cause your computer to slow to a crawl. Want to speed things up? You can work on your drawing with the Document Raster Effects value set to 72 ppi (or lower, if you like) and achieve pretty zippy performance. Then, when you're ready to finalize the drawing, change the setting to your final intended resolution. Since effects such as shadows aren't literal, changing the Document Raster Effects setting causes these effects to regenerate at the new resolution value.

If the document uses lots of effects, be prepared for a slow redraw as the screen refreshes at the new resolution. Look on the bright side—you might use this as an opportunity to convince your boss that you really do need that newer, faster computer: "See how long this takes? You can't expect me to meet deadlines with this old, slow computer…"

There is no penalty (other than the time required for redraw) for repeatedly altering the Raster Effects setting; any effects will redraw at the new resolution immediately (**Figure 10.16**). Since the pixels are generated on the fly, there is no resampling.

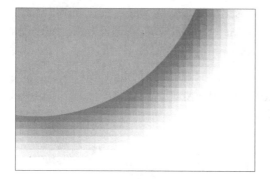 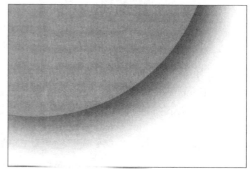

Figure 10.16 Using a Document Raster Effects of 72 ppi for effects (left) can speed up performance. Change the value to 300 ppi, and the shadow resolution changes immediately (right).

If you place a native Illustrator file into InDesign, the resolution of any raster effects is not influenced by any settings in InDesign (such as the Transparency Flattener Preset). If you open the Illustrator file in Photoshop, the image will take on the resolution you assign in the Open dialog, but any raster effects will maintain their appearance from Illustrator. For example, if an Illustrator file whose raster effects resolution is 72 ppi is opened in Photoshop at 300 ppi, the image will be 300 ppi, but the raster effects will retain their coarse, pixelated appearance, as if they had been scaled to 300 ppi using the Nearest Neighbor setting.

Getting a Head Start

A custom document template or profile can be populated with custom Swatches, Symbols, Graphic Styles, and default stroke widths. You can even set the rulers to display automatically (a common request).

Templates: To create a template, create a new document, make the desired modifications, and then choose Illustrator Template (.ait) as the format in the Save dialog. Illustrator takes you to the default template folder, but you can save it anywhere. To use the template, click the Templates button in the New Document dialog and navigate to the template file. Illustrator opens a copy of the file as a new document.

New Document Profiles: Create and modify a new document and then save the file in the New Document Profiles folder (if you are using a non-English version of Illustrator, the "en_US" folder will be named differently):

- **Windows:** Documents and Settings\[username]\Application Data\Adobe\Adobe Illustrator CS4 Settings\en_US\New Document Profiles
- **Mac:** [username]/Library/Application Support/Adobe/Adobe Illustrator CS4/en_US/New Document Profiles

Choose your custom document profile from the New Document Profile drop-down menu as you create a new document. Both custom document profiles and templates are available even if you reset Illustrator preferences.

When you create a new Illustrator document, the document profile or template you choose as a starting point dictates the raster effects resolution for the document. However, you can click the Advanced arrow to show more options, and choose from 72, 150, or 300 ppi instead. Once you have begun working in the document, you can specify any raster effects resolution you want.

USING THE APPEARANCE PANEL

Once you've applied an effect to an object, use the Appearance panel to modify the effect rather than returning to the Effect menu to make the change. If you attempt to modify an effect by choosing the effect again from the Effects menu, an alert appears warning that if you continue, you'll apply another instance of the effect.

To edit an effect, select the object and then open the Appearance panel (Window > Appearance). Click on the name of the effect to open the options dialog for that effect, and modify the settings (**Figure 10.17**).

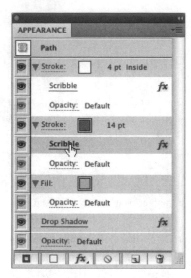

Figure 10.17 To edit an effect, click its name in the Appearance panel.

The Appearance panel is one of the handiest panels in Illustrator: It's actually one-stop shopping for choosing fill and stroke colors, stroke widths, opacity settings, blending modes, and effects options. You can add new effects by clicking the **fx** icon at the bottom of the panel, and control the visibility of fills, strokes, and effects by clicking the eye icons next to those attributes. You can even add multiple strokes and fills to an object by choosing Add New Stroke, Add New Fill, or Duplicate Item from the Appearance panel menu.

To modify a stroke, click on that row in the Appearance panel list to target the stroke. You don't have to visit the Swatches panel to change the stroke color: Click on the color block in the stroke's row, and it becomes a drop-down menu that expands to display a remote version of the Swatches panel (**Figure 10.18**). Press the Enter key to dismiss the Swatches display.

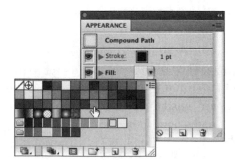

Figure 10.18 There's no need to travel to the Swatches panel to change a fill color; just click on the fill color block in the Appearance panel to view swatches.

Click on the stroke weight value in the stroke row, and it becomes a combination drop-down menu and type-in field (**Figure 10.19**): Choose from the preset widths in the drop-down menu, or type your own value in the field. Press Enter when you're finished.

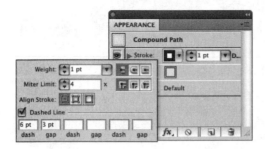

Figure 10.19 When you select the Stroke attribute, the Appearance panel offers the same options as the Stroke panel.

You may also be surprised that you can change the order in which attributes are applied by dragging a fill, stroke, or effect up and down in the Appearance panel list. Even though strokes and fills are attributes of a single object, they can be treated as separate entities.

CREATING 3D ARTWORK

If you need an excuse to buy a faster computer, you may find your excuse in the 3D effects that made their debut in Illustrator CS. Similar to the old Adobe application Dimensions,® the 3D effects in Illustrator don't rival genuine 3D programs, but they do allow you to add dimensionality to shapes through revolving or extruding operations. Such effects can generate very complex files. Since the illusion of dimensionality depends on realistic shading, 3D effects rely on the Document Raster Effects Settings dialog to determine the resolution of that shading. To speed up processing and display, use the default setting of 72 ppi while you're working on the file.

If you perform a 3D operation on a spot-color object, the default setting converts the object to process color; Illustrator subtly warns you in the 3D options dialog ("Spot colors will be converted to process") in tiny text, but doesn't mention that you have the power to change things. If you click the More Options button, you will discover lighting options, and an easy-to-miss check box: Preserve Spot Colors (**Figure 10.20**).

After you click the Preserve Spot Colors check box, Illustrator provides another subtle warning, but this time it adds some guidance: "Spot colors will be shaded with black overprint. Turn on Overprint Preview to view." Illustrator renders the 3D spot object as a combination of black and the spot color, and uses overprint to image the 3D effect correctly. At first, it seems that your object has become grayscale, but if you follow Illustrator's advice and turn on Overprint Preview (View > Overprint Preview), you'll see that all is well (**Figure 10.21**).

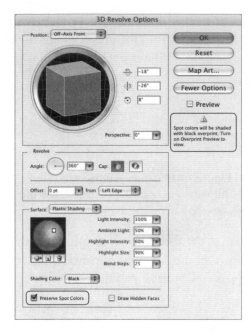

Figure 10.20 By default, Illustrator's 3D operations will convert spot colors to process. However, you can preserve spot colors by clicking on the More Options button to reveal the Preserve Spot Colors option. Note the warning (and advice) under the Preview checkbox.

Figure 10.21 The initial view of a 3D spot-color object is disturbing (left); it appears mostly grayscale, with some spot color segments showing through. Turn on Overprint Preview to see the artwork as it will print (right).

TRANSPARENCY

The opacity and blending mode options in Illustrator allow you to create interesting visual interactions between objects, but some operations may result in undesirable results when spot colors are involved. For example, the blending modes Difference and Exclusion will cause overlapping spot color areas to be converted to CMYK (or RGB if that's the document's working color mode). You may also have undesirable results if you create spot-color objects, apply blending modes to them in Illustrator, and then place the files into another application such as InDesign and output as CMYK. If you convert spot colors to CMYK in InDesign by using the Ink Manager, the output may not show the same color interactions as the original Illustrator file. Illustrator provides a warning as you save the file (**Figure 10.22**).

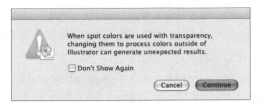

Figure 10.22 Spot-color objects using transparency may not fare well when other applications render the Illustrator file as CMYK. At least Illustrator warns you. Don't check the Don't Show Again option — it's good to keep this warning in mind.

Even if you don't intend to convert spot colors to CMYK, Illustrator's display can mislead you about the final outcome. For example, the most you can have of any given single ink is 100 percent—solid ink coverage. You can't fill an object with 200 percent of Pantone 285 unless you're printing a double hit of the color. But if you fill two objects with a solid ink, and then apply a blending mode of Multiply, Illustrator will darken the overlapping area (**Figure 10.23**). It's an unfortunate display error. However, if you turn on Overprint Preview (View > Overprint Preview), the display is correct. Overprint Preview is a great forensic tool to help you diagnose numerous problems, but it does slow down performance. Use it when you need it, and then deactivate it.

Figure 10.23 The word and the rectangle are both filled with 100–percent Pantone 415. The word uses the Multiply blend mode. The Illustrator display (top) falsely implies that there will be 200–percent coverage of Pantone 415 in the overlap area, which is impossible without a second ink. However, if you turn on Overprint Preview (View > Overprint Preview), you'll see the true story (bottom).

FLATTENING TRANSPARENCY

Transparency in Illustrator is a wonderful feature first bestowed on designers with the release of Illustrator 9.0. This was followed by several years of printers screaming and hiding under desks because of early imaging difficulties. Some printers are still traumatized by their initial experiences and may not realize that transparency is really not that scary these days, as long as everyone plays by some simple rules.

If your print service provider is using very old equipment that has not been upgraded in years, they may have difficulty outputting files containing transparency. If this is the case, consider sending your work to a more modern print service provider with better capabilities. If you have the option to shop around for your printer, consult the Adobe Partner Web site to find Adobe-authorized printers who possess the equipment and know-how to handle your files correctly. Visit the Partner site (*www.claudiamccue.com/go/PHSa*) and enter your file type, platform, and location to narrow your search. Adobe authorized printers have access to educational resources and technical support channels that ensure that they are well equipped to handle your job.

Effects like transparency and blending modes enhance the design flexibility of Illustrator, but those effects go beyond the imaging model of Adobe PostScript, which has long been the native language of imagesetters (devices that output film for printing plates), platesetters (which directly output printing plates), and many desktop printers. While major RIP vendors are now marketing imaging devices that use the Adobe PDF Print Engine, which supports live, unflattened transparency, you will still encounter printers and publications that use older workflows based on PostScript. You should be aware of the limitations this imposes. (For more information on the PDF Print Engine, see Chapter One, "Life Cycle of a Print Job.")

Illustrator, InDesign, and Acrobat all support live, unflattened transparency. If you're creating artwork in Illustrator with the intention of later placing it as a native AI file in InDesign, you don't have to worry about any special handling for transparent objects while you're working in Illustrator; any transparency flattening is deferred until the output from InDesign.

But if your Illustrator file is going to land somewhere else in a file format such as EPS or PDF/X-1a (a subset of PDF that doesn't support live transparency), then you must face the mysteries of *transparency flattening*. Don't worry—the Illustrator file won't be flattened. Your layers are untouched, your shadows are intact, and everything remains editable. The flattening process affects only output and export and takes place on the fly during export or printing. The purpose is to replace transparent elements with opaque elements, mimicking the colors created in transparent overlaps by creating new colors and invoking PostScript overprint. If images interact with text, flattening may even create letter-shaped clipping paths to contain image material. The result resembles a very complex puzzle, but it's a purely PostScript puzzle that is easily digested by PostScript imaging devices (**Figure 10.24**). It's a fairly impressive engineering feat. And the results are much more sophisticated and well behaved than when they made their debut in Illustrator 9.0.

If you must downsave for a much earlier version that doesn't support transparency (such as Illustrator 8 or earlier), you will have to specify a transparency flattener preset. If the recipient of your file gives you any guidance, follow that person's lead. Lacking that, you should create a widely applicable recipe for flattening. Choose Edit > Transparency Flattener Presets. Select High Resolution and then click New. In the Custom Transparency Flattener Options dialog (**Figure 10.25**), set Line Art and Text Resolution to the resolution of the final imaging device. If you don't know that, use 2400 ppi. And 300 ppi is a safe bet for the Gradient and Mesh Resolution.

Figure 10.24 Native transparency (left) involves opacity settings and blending modes. For output or export to PostScript-based formats, all the fun stuff is replaced with opaque jigsaw puzzle pieces (right); hence the term *flattening*.

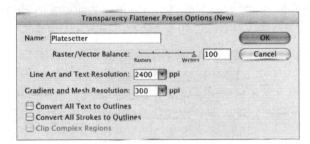

Figure 10.25 Creating a custom transparency flattener preset. Select High Resolution and then click New. Ideally, the Line Art and Text Resolution setting should be in keeping with the ultimate device resolution. The Gradient and Mesh Resolution can usually remain at 300 ppi.

LINKED AND EMBEDDED IMAGES

When you place raster images in an Illustrator file, you can choose to link or embed those images. Each method has its advantages and disadvantages.

Linking an image results in a smaller Illustrator file than embedding. Additionally, since images are externally stored, they are easily color corrected or retouched. To open an image linked in an Illustrator file, hold down the Option (Mac) or Alt (Windows) key and then double-click the image. The image opens in Photoshop, where you can make your edits and save the file. When you return to Illustrator, you'll receive an alert asking if you'd like to update modified images. Click Yes to update the image.

As you might expect, *embedding* an image increases the Illustrator file size, since the size of the image is added to the file. While embedding makes it easier to keep track of all components of a file, it complicates image editing. If the original image is still available, you can choose Relink from the Links panel menu, and then navigate to the external image. Edit the newly linked image as necessary, update the link, and then embed the image if you wish.

However, if you've inherited an Illustrator file containing an embedded image and have no access to the original image, Illustrator doesn't provide a straightforward way to extract it for editing. Don't panic. If you can't obtain the original image from the content creator, you can still cheat your way out of this predicament. Select the embedded image in Illustrator with the Selection tool (black arrow), and then copy it to the clipboard. Start Photoshop and choose File > New. A new, blank document is created that's the same size as the clipboard contents. Note that you will need to set the color mode of the new image to the correct setting (CMYK or RGB), in keeping with the image you're extracting. Paste the image, and you're in business.

Saving an Illustrator file in EPS format automatically embeds images and fonts in the EPS. While this makes the file easily portable, you'll be wise to save the external images as insurance against future editing needs, along with the original AI file. The fonts are embedded for display in other applications, and for output from those applications, not for editing.

If you'd like to gather up all the fonts and graphics required by an Illustrator file for submission to a printer (or to archive the job), you can do that manually, which will strengthen your character (and organizational skills). Or you can take the easy way out: Use the Scoop plug-in from Worker 72a (*www.worker72a.com*). Not only does Scoop assemble all the necessary fonts and images for an Illustrator file, it can even unembed embedded images.

Image resolution rules and restrictions still apply to images placed in Illustrator, of course. That is, scaling up or down beyond reasonable limits (roughly 75 to 125 percent) has repercussions in terms of degradation of detail and increased processing time. As in page-layout applications, it's best if the image is the correct final size to begin with and is placed at 100 percent into Illustrator.

BLENDED OBJECTS

Illustrator allows you to select two different objects and then use the Blend tool (⊞) to create transitional shapes between them. It's an interesting effect, but if the starting objects are filled with spot colors, the intermediate shapes are generated as CMYK objects (**Figure 10.26**).

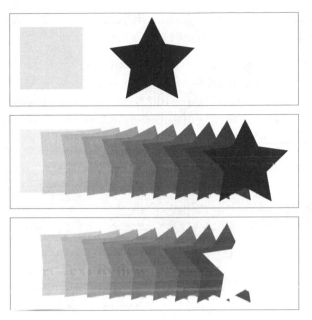

Figure 10.26 Start with two spot-color objects (top). The Blend tool allows you to create discrete intermediate shapes (middle) or a smooth gradient-like transition between the objects. But there's bad news: All the intermediate shapes (bottom) are rendered as CMYK, which is probably not what you want.

If the blend effect is crucial to your design, and the job must be printed in spot colors, you might create each starting shape as a single process color, but let the process color represent a spot color. For example, use cyan in lieu of Pantone 294 and magenta instead of Pantone 128. Then inform the print service provider that the cyan plate should be used to print Pantone 294 and the magenta plate for Pantone 128. If you also have four-color images in the job, this approach won't work for you. Of course, as long as the start and end objects are CMYK, the final effect will be perfectly fine.

SPOT COLORS

In 2000, Pantone revised the recipes for process simulations of the Pantone spot inks. This was done in response to the industry improvements in plating and press controls, which made it possible to more closely approximate spot colors with CMYK simulations. The spot-to-process recipes in desktop publishing programs followed suit. This all sounds wonderful, but there is a little kink in the plumbing as a result. Files created in earlier versions of Illustrator, QuarkXPress, InDesign, and Photoshop use the older recipes. The newer recipes start with Illustrator 10, QuarkXPress 5.0, InDesign 2.0, and Photoshop 7.0. If your goal is to come closer to Pantone colors with CMYK approximations, great. But if you're using old artwork that uses the old recipes, output may differ from what you expect. For example, consider an Illustrator 8.0 EPS with spot elements that is placed into an InDesign CS4 page and output as CMYK. Since the Pantone-to-CMYK conversion is performed with the new recipe, the output may not match a previously printed piece that was generated by placing the same EPS into a QuarkXPress 4.11 page.

If it's important to replicate the old appearance of ancient artwork, open the file in the original version of Illustrator and then convert the spot-color swatches to CMYK so they won't be reinterpreted by other applications (**Figure 10.27**). If you don't have the original version of Illustrator, the conversion to CMYK will be based on the newer spot-to-process recipe, so you may have to tweak the CMYK build values to more closely resemble the original printed job.

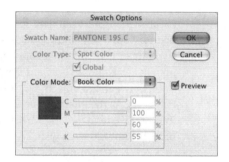 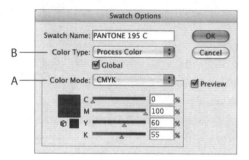

Figure 10.27 In Illustrator CS4, the Swatch Options dialog initially displays Book Color for the Color Mode of a spot-color swatch (left). To convert the swatch to process (right), first change the color mode to CMYK (A). Then you'll be allowed to change the Color Type to Process Color (B).

Going through this might convince you of the wisdom of picking from an all-CMYK color source such as the Pantone four-color process guide or the Pantone Color Bridge guide on future jobs that will print in four-color process. For more on the spot-versus-process issue, see Chapter Two, "Ink on Paper."

If you attempt to use the Overprint Preview feature (View > Output Preview) in an Illustrator file with more than 27 spot colors, you will receive an error (**Figure 10.28**). You'll also see this warning if you try to use the Separations Preview feature (Window > Separations Preview), because Overprint Preview is required to correctly display separations. You are also warned if you attempt to print separated output from a file containing more than 27 spot colors, which is Illustrator's way of saving paper (and embarrassment).

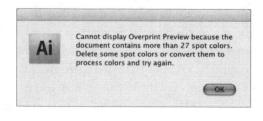

Figure 10.28 Illustrator will not launch Overprint Preview in a document containing more than 27 spot colors. Can you blame it?

Pantone Goe System

As the number of colors in the Pantone spot color guide books has increased over the years, the numbering system has been forced to expand from three digits to four. But the four-digit colors weren't added at the end of the existing colors—they were slipped in between existing colors to label intermediate colors that fell in between the older colors. Thus, Pantone 3252 is just a bit lighter than Pantone 325, with just a wee bit more yellow.

To resolve the numbering anomalies, Pantone started from scratch to create the Pantone Goe system, which is intended to provide a more intuitive arrangement of colors. The Goe system (the letters don't stand for anything; it's just a branding identification) is based on 165 full-strength colors and families of colors derived from them. The colors are identified by three numbers describing the color's position within the overall system, plus the familiar substrate identifier such as *C* (coated) or *U* (uncoated). For example, the color name "Pantone 104-2-5 C" indicates that the color—a lovely blue-green—is in the 104th color family, is on the 2nd page of the family, is the 5th color on that page, and represents how the color would look on coated stock. Whew. That's a lot of information from three numbers.

The Pantone Goe swatch libraries do not ship as part of Creative Suite 4, but you can download the digital color libraries from the Pantone site and import them. Go to *www.claudiamccue.com/go/QpNn* and select the installer for your platform. Follow the instructions in the accompanying user guide to make the swatch libraries available to your applications.

The installer will install the following swatch libraries:

*   Pantone Goe™ coated
*   Pantone Goe™ uncoated
*   Pantone GoeBridge™ coated

What About My Old Pantone Guides?

Your existing Pantone fanbooks and digital libraries are not obsolete: You can continue to use them as references to specify color unless your fanbooks are twenty years old, in which case they're faded and unreliable. New fanbooks for the "old" system are still available from Pantone. The digital libraries can coexist without conflict, because each has its own unique naming convention.

Separations Preview

Viewing individual inks allows you to check an Illustrator file for extraneous spot colors. Choose Window > Separations Preview to open the Separations Preview panel, and then check the Overprint Preview option so you can view all separations (**Figure 10.29**). You can control the visibility of individual printing inks by clicking the eye icons next to ink names. This is much easier (and faster) than printing separated lasers. Think of the trees you'll save.

Figure 10.29 Selectively view individual separations by using the eye icon visibility controls. Note that Overprint Preview must be checked to activate Separations Preview.

WHY VERSIONS MATTER

For many years, a new version of Illustrator just meant the addition of new drawing toys. The file architecture and text composition engine remained fairly static, so there was little danger of adversely affecting a file by bouncing it between users with different versions of the program. Saving to an earlier Illustrator format for someone using an earlier version of the application didn't threaten the integrity of a logo.

However, there can be disappointing results when you attempt to go too far back in time with content produced by using features such as transparency, envelope distortion, 3D effects, or multiple artboards. Illustrator does a valiant job of digesting newer content so that older versions can handle it, but this process is often a one-way street. For example, a dimensional effect created in Illustrator CS4 will display and print correctly in Illustrator 10, which did not have the 3D features, but the dimensional controls will be gone when the file is reopened in Illustrator CS4. If you're working in a mixed environment with users who have multiple vintages of Illustrator, be mindful of these speed bumps. The ideal solution is to move all members of a workgroup to the same version, but that isn't always feasible and is virtually impossible if you are dealing with external suppliers or recipients. In self-defense, keep a current working version of your Illustrator document when it's necessary to save nostalgic versions for collaborators in case something's munged by saving to an earlier version.

Purely vector components survive backsaving and round-tripping, but text is a cause for concern. Illustrator CS and later versions provide support for the extended character sets in OpenType fonts. They also share typographic niceties such as optical kerning, which was borrowed from InDesign in a bit of cross-pollination between applications.

These enhancements to Illustrator opened the door for fine typographic controls and elegant composition. But because the text composition engine was revamped in Illustrator CS to allow these improvements, text in older files from previous versions undergoes conversion when those files are opened in Illustrator CS or later. The change in the composition engine may cause some aggravation when you upgrade from earlier versions, but the long-term typographic benefits far outweigh the hiccups.

Text conversion is unavoidable, but at least you're warned when you open a file from Illustrator 10 or earlier (**Figure 10.30**). The yellow triangle of terror is looming behind the Illustrator icon, and you're presented with three confusing options, none of which seems like a safe choice.

- **Update** will revamp the text according to the newer text composition rules, but you won't be watching while it happens. If there's text reflow, you may not catch it. One could argue that this shouldn't even be an option. Don't choose this.

- **Cancel** prevents the file from opening. You'll have to face this file eventually, so don't chicken out now.

- **OK** opens the file without modifying the text. If you're not planning to edit text in the file, this is the correct choice because it leaves the text untouched. And if you are planning to edit text, this ensures that you'll be watching when the text is translated, so you can make the necessary adjustments. It's understandable that this is the default choice. If you press the Enter key out of habit, you've accidentally done the right thing.

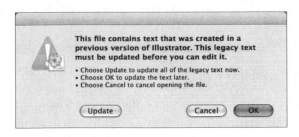

Figure 10.30 When you open a file created by Illustrator 10 or earlier, you're faced with this alert. Don't panic. And don't choose Update! The correct option is to choose OK.

When you choose OK in the opening alert box, you postpone the recomposing of text. As long as the correct fonts are active when you open the file, no harm is done to text by just opening and resaving the file, although resaving does label the file as having been created by the newer version of Illustrator. Performing edits to other elements of the file won't adversely affect the text. Text is protected until you attempt to edit it (**Figure 10.31**).

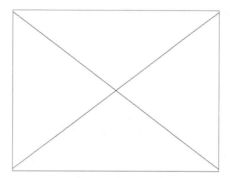

Figure 10.31 After opening an Illustrator 10 file, you'll wonder what all the fuss is about. It looks like perfectly healthy text (left). But switch to Outline view (right), and you'll see that the text isn't quite as you'd expect. The cross-hatched frame might make you think that the text is behaving like a placed graphic, but the appearance actually indicates that the text is protected from editing until you select it with the Type tool.

When you attempt to edit legacy text, you encounter another alert and another decision (**Figure 10.32**). Choosing Cancel just delays the inevitable. The real choice is between *Update* and *Copy Text Object*.

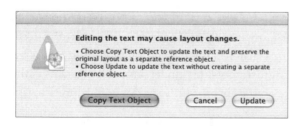

Figure 10.32 When you begin to edit text in a file from Illustrator 10 or earlier, you face yet another alert. Lucky you! The default choice is the correct one: Copy Text Object.

- As in the opening alert, **Update** will recompose the text by the newer rules of Illustrator CS4. Unless you have hard copy or a photographic memory as reference, this option may result in unpleasant text reflow that you might not notice.

- **Copy Text Object** preserves an unchanged copy of the text as it appeared in the original file, while creating a duplicate block of text that plays by the new rules. Most importantly, you now can compare the two versions, see what really happened, and repair as necessary. Once again this default choice is the safe choice.

When you choose Copy Text Object, Illustrator creates a ghosted replica of the text as it appeared in the original file (**Figure 10.33**). Use the reference text as a guide as you make any edits necessary to match the appearance of the text in the original Illustrator file. If you opened files containing legacy text in Illustrator CS or CS2, you will be pleasantly surprised at the results in CS4: You'll rarely see text reflow when opening old Illustrator files in CS4. You may see a very slight change in the vertical position of a text block, or a slight change in line spacing, but these problems are easy to fix.

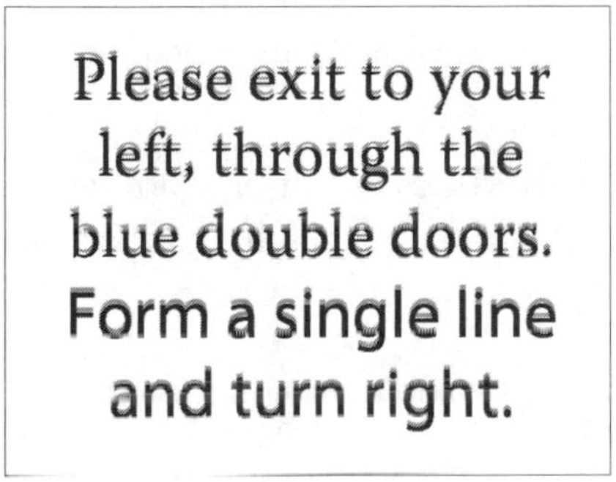

Please exit to your
left, through the
blue double doors.
Form a single line
and turn right.

Figure 10.33 The black text is live text being composed by the newer composition rules of Illustrator CS4. In this instance, leading may have to be tweaked to match the old line spacing seen in the ghosted reference text.

After completing the edits, delete the reference text sublayer so that it doesn't ruin output (**Figure 10.34**). You could just hide the layer, but you run the risk that some well-meaning but misguided person might reawaken it.

Layers
Layer 1
This is text crea...
<Legacy Text C...
1 Layer

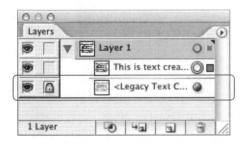

Figure 10.34 After correcting the converted text, delete the reference layer (indicated by a padlock) to ensure correct output.

What about backsaving? You'll find that Illustrator CS4 does a much better job than CS, CS2, or CS3 in its handling of text in a file saved for earlier versions. You'll no longer encounter the conversion to point text or outlines when you save for older versions. If you save for Illustrator 10 or earlier, you may find that multiline text blocks have become separate lines of text rather than a continuous flow of text, but the appearance of the text should be maintained. If you reopen the file in CS4, the text will still be in separate lines. While this slightly complicates the editing of long flows of text, it's far better than dealing with point text (small clumps of unconnected text) or outlines.

SAVING FOR OTHER APPLICATIONS

Whereas the undisputed choice of file format once was EPS, that's no longer the case: There are significant advantages to saving Illustrator files in the native AI format. InDesign fully supports the blending modes and transparency effects in AI files, allowing such attributes to interact with other elements in an InDesign page. The Object Layer Options feature in InDesign allows you to selectively reveal or hide layers of placed Illustrator AI files (this option is not available for EPS files). And even though we now have enormous hard drives and tons of RAM, it's nice to know that an AI file is usually quite a bit smaller than an EPS.

If your file's ultimate fate is placement in a QuarkXPress layout or Word document, the right answer is still the EPS format. But you don't have to reach back in time to export a legacy EPS. Even the venerable QuarkXPress 4.11 can handle a CS4-flavored EPS that was generated by an Illustrator file.

When you save as EPS, you are given the choice of a range of flavors of EPS: Illustrator CS, CS2, CS3, and CS4, as well as Illustrator 10, 9, 8, 3, and Japanese Illustrator 3 (no, we don't know what makes Japanese Illustrator 3 EPS files different from "regular" Illustrator 3 EPS files). If you save an Illustrator file as an EPS earmarked for versions CS through CS4, the resulting EPS is completely editable in Illustrator and still behaves predictably in other applications. Think of the file as an Illustrator native file with an EPS disguise for the benefit of placement into other applications that don't recognize the native Illustrator format.

However, if you save as an Illustrator 10 or earlier version EPS, the contents of the file may be permanently altered: Shadows become embedded images, effects such as Scribble are expanded to literal vectors, and editing becomes much more complex as a result. This is necessary because file formats have changed substantially since these earlier versions. Reopening such a file in Illustrator CS4 will not restore effects to full, live editability, so you should keep a CS4 version of the file as an AI file for full future editability.

Saving Files with Multiple Artboards

If you're planning to place an Illustrator file containing multiple artboards into InDesign, just save the file as a native Illustrator AI file. When you choose File > Place in InDesign, check the Show Import Options check box in the dialog: A second dialog appears that allows you pick which artboard (or range of artboards) you want to place (**Figure 10.35**). You can also specify how the content is cropped: Choose from Bounding Box, Art, Crop, Trim, Bleed, or Media.

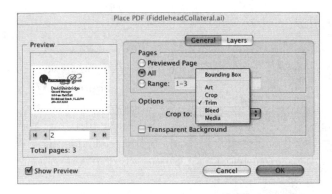

Figure 10.35 Place an Illustrator file with multiple artboards into InDesign, and choose which pages to place. Notice the title bar: "Place PDF..." even though the file is an Illustrator AI file.

Glance at the title bar of the second dialog, and you'll realize that InDesign perceives the artboards as individual pages of a multipage PDF. Why is this? Is InDesign confused? No—this is because, under the hood, Illustrator has a bit of PDF-ish flavor. Illustrator files use the Progressive Graphics Format (PGF) to contain and display transparency (such as blending modes and shadows), and PDF provides the wrapper so the file is accepted by other applications such as InDesign and Photoshop.

For this reason, you should always check the Create PDF Compatible File option when saving an Illustrator AI file. This is the default option. If you uncheck the option, you'll see nothing but a tiled pattern of warning text when you place the file in InDesign, or attempt to open it in Photoshop (**Figure 10.36**).

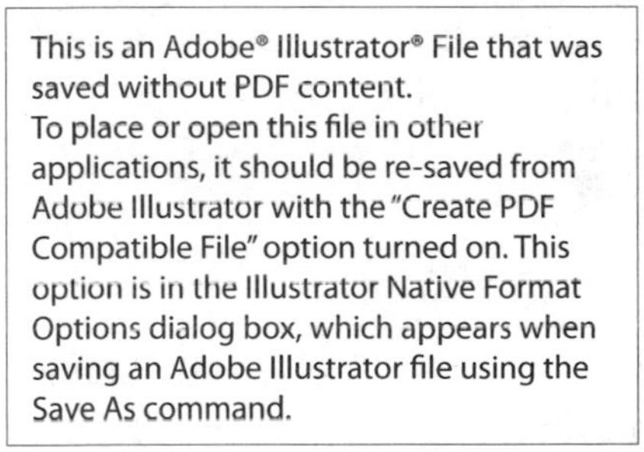

This is an Adobe® Illustrator® File that was saved without PDF content.
To place or open this file in other applications, it should be re-saved from Adobe Illustrator with the "Create PDF Compatible File" option turned on. This option is in the Illustrator Native Format Options dialog box, which appears when saving an Adobe Illustrator file using the Save As command.

Figure 10.36 If you uncheck the Create PDF Compatible File option, this is what you'll see when you place the file in InDesign or open it in Photoshop. At least it tells you what to do.

Saving Artboards to Older Versions

If you save an Illustrator file containing multiple artboards to an earlier version of Illustrator, you can choose between saving each artboard as a separate Illustrator file or saving all the artwork on the canvas as a single file. While all artwork will be retained, the artboard definitions are lost, and are not restored if you reopen the file in Illustrator CS4.

Saving as EPS

Since the EPS format does not support multiple artboards, Illustrator gives you the option of saving each artboard as a separate EPS or saving the entirety of the artwork as a single EPS. If you choose the Use Artboards option in the Save dialog (**Figure 10.37**), a separate EPS will be created for each artboard. The default filenames are based on the name of the Illustrator file with -01.eps, -02.eps, and so on appended to the filename. You can also specify a new base filename, which will receive the same numbered addenda.

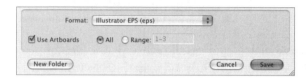

Figure 10.37 Saving as EPS yields a separate EPS from each artboard.

Including Bleed in Export

If the Illustrator file has been set up with a defined document bleed (File > Document Setup), the bleed is included automatically and is recognized by Photoshop and InDesign, whether the file is saved as an AI or EPS. Both applications give you the option to crop the incoming file according to the trim, bleed, or bounding box. Photoshop displays a preview window with these options. When you choose File > Place in InDesign, hold down Shift as you click OK in the Place dialog to display the Import Options dialog, which provides the same crop options for an AI file. However, you will not see those options when you place an EPS with bleed—the bleed is included by default.

CREATING PDF FILES

Even though most print service providers should have no problem outputting a native Illustrator file, there are some advantages to submitting your Illustrator job as a PDF. Doing so eliminates the need to gather up images and fonts, since everything is included in the PDF. It prevents casual editing (and the resultant errors).

Since Illustrator speaks fluent PDF, creating a PDF is a Save As function, not an export operation. There is rarely a legitimate reason to go the long way around, generating PostScript and cranking up Distiller to create a PDF. Don't feel guilty—do it the easy way.

Saving to PDF

As always, consult your print service provider or publication for the correct specifications before you submit a PDF file. Make sure you know the version of PDF they will accept and whether they allow live transparency in a PDF, or whether it must be flattened.

If your printer or publication has provided specifications or settings, of course you should use them. But you'll find that some printers and publications still leave it up to you — "just send us a nice PDF" — and then you're on your own.

Choose File > Save As, and select Adobe PDF as the format. Notice that Use Artboards is checked by default, and cannot be unchecked (**Figure 10.38**). If you want to save all the artwork on a single page of a PDF, ignoring the boundaries of artboards, this would be one of the rare circumstances that would require you to either print to the Adobe PDF printer, or generate PostScript and use Distiller. Choose a range of artboards if necessary, select the appropriate bleed value (if applicable), choose a directory, provide a filename for the PDF, and then click Save.

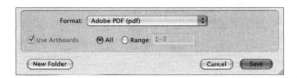

Figure 10.38 When you save as PDF, regardless of the settings used, multiple artboards become multiple pages in the PDF.

You'll then see the same PDF creation settings (.joboptions) in Illustrator as you would see in InDesign and Distiller (with the exception of a few extras in Distiller). If you have created or imported custom settings, those will also appear.

The default setting is Illustrator Default: The PDF that is generated is essentially a fully editable Illustrator file in a PDF wrapper. The option to Preserve PDF Editing Capabilities ensures that you can safely reopen the PDF in Illustrator. But this option can create very large files, and some prepress workflow software, such as imposition applications, may have difficulty handling such a new-fangled PDF, so this is usually not ideal for job submission.

If the printer or publication has not provided specifications, you can't go wrong by saving as PDF/X-1a:2001. The default PDF/X-1a settings are fine, but you will have to set the bleed value. If you created bleed in the document setup, just check the option to Use Document Bleed Settings under the Marks and Bleed topic.

Opening PDF Files in Illustrator

With the exception of PDFs created from Illustrator with the Preserve PDF Editing Capabilities option selected, it's rarely a good idea to open and edit PDF files in Illustrator. Even though Illustrator is willing to give it a try, you run the risk of causing damage to the file integrity, especially when the PDF has been generated by non-Adobe applications.

If a PDF contains very simple content—say, just a vector logo—you may be successful editing the file in Illustrator. But if you attempt to edit a file containing a font not available on your system, you won't be able to edit any text, and the file will not image correctly since font substitution will be take place.

If you are frequently required to edit PDFs created by others, consider purchasing a dedicated PDF editor, such as PitStop from Enfocus (*www.enfocus.com*).

CHAPTER ELEVEN

InDesign CS4 Production Tips

InDesign offers wonderful creative tools and splendid typographical controls. Thanks to its integration with other Adobe applications, it's part of a nearly seamless graphic ecosystem. But like any application, it has some little quirks that can surprise you if you don't know the workarounds.

GRAPHICS

InDesign accepts a wide variety of graphics formats, but that doesn't mean that all those formats are equally well behaved. In addition, while InDesign offers some interesting methods of placing graphics, not all of those methods will yield satisfactory results.

Placing Graphics

If you were raised on QuarkXPress, you're accustomed to making a box before importing graphics. PageMaker users making a switch to QuarkXPress were irked by the need to create a box, and QuarkXPress users regarded it as unnatural that PageMaker allowed you to just plop an image in the page. InDesign gives you the best of both worlds: Both PageMaker and QuarkXPress users can work the way they wish. QuarkXPress users are usually most comfortable making a frame first. It's helpful to know that both the Rectangle Frame tool ([⊠]) and the plain old Rectangle tool ([▢]) can create shapes that accept graphics as content. (Notice that the Rectangle Frame tool looks suspiciously like the Picture Box tool in QuarkXPress.) In fact, any enclosed shape—even one drawn by the Pen tool—will accept graphic content.

It's worth noting some differences in the behavior of the two tools. This would be so much easier to explain if the tools had noticeably different names. How about—just between us—we refer to the Rectangle Frame tool and its friends as Graphic Frame tools for this short conversation? And we'll call the other, more annoying tools the Plain Old Shape tools. Adobe doesn't have to know.

The "Graphic Frame" tools creates shapes with a fill and stroke of None, which is sort of like clear plastic: You can select these shapes by clicking anywhere inside them. This makes it easy to determine where objects are in the stacking order—just click and see what wakes up.

By contrast, the Plain Old Shape tools create objects that are basically disembodied, floating strokes with no innards. InDesign defines these objects as Unassigned (Object > Content > Unassigned). You can't select the shape by clicking inside (since it's utterly empty). You must click on the stroke instead. Until you discover that, you click everywhere, muttering. And until it has content (either a graphic, text, or a fill color), a plain old shape can really get in the way: If you accidentally click in such a frame with a loaded text or graphics cursor (usually intending to target what's behind it), the plain old shape will intercept and take the content.

A common use of a plain old shape is to generate a keyline outside the main artwork on a page, such as a decorative border at the edge of an ad. As long as the plain old shape is at the bottom of stacking order, it's not as treacherous. But, since it's hollow, it's easy to think of the keyline as "outside everything," even if it's actually at the top of the stacking order. As you try to click with a loaded text or graphics cursor in other frames behind the plain old shape, you won't be able to click in them: The plain old shape gets in the way. However, you can select the frames lying behind the plain old shape beforehand to target them, and then imported content will be placed in the targeted frame.

You get a lot of visual feedback in InDesign, so keep your eye on the cursor's appearance. If your loaded-graphics cursor (⟋) develops parentheses ⟋, you're about to place your graphic in an existing frame. You've been warned. But even if you slip up, you're not stuck. Just undo once, and you're back to a loaded graphics cursor, so you can place the graphic in the correct frame. Changed your mind completely? Click the Selection tool (black arrow) or press the Escape key, and you're relieved of the graphic burden, and you can start over again.

In the Place dialog (File > Place), you can select multiple graphics and text files in a directory by Shift-clicking, Command-clicking (Mac) or Control-clicking (Windows) on multiple filenames; however, you're limited to shopping in a single directory at a time. Once you've filled up your platter, so to speak, return to the InDesign document and start clicking to deposit the graphics or text files. InDesign generates small thumbnails of the graphics so you know what you're about to place by clicking. You can cycle through the files you're carrying by using keyboard arrows, and you can press Escape to discard a file you've decided not to place.

Part of the fun of InDesign is that you don't have to select—or even create—a frame before placing a graphic. Just choose File > Place, select a graphic, and then click anywhere in an empty area of the page. InDesign creates a frame on the fly, positioned at the limits of the image. It's a tremendous time-saver.

There's *Good* Drag and Drop...

There are several methods to bring graphics into a layout besides File > Place—some reliable, some not so much.

One method allows you to drag directly from a folder. Position your InDesign application window and a directory window (the Finder on the Macintosh or Windows Explorer on the PC) side by side, and you'll be able to drag images directly in from folder contents. This is the equivalent of File > Place, and it results in legitimate links. It's a little clunky: Once you've gathered up the files to deposit, you have to click in the InDesign document to become active in the program, and that first click will deposit a graphic or text file where you click (it's that "loaded weapon" thing again). Subsequent clicks place the remaining files.

You can also drag and drop from Adobe Bridge (**Figure 11.1**). Use Bridge to navigate to the appropriate folder, then select multiple files and drag them on top of the InDesign page. This offers a couple of advantages over just dragging from a folder in the operating system. The Bridge window can more easily be positioned over the InDesign page than directory windows. And Bridge provides high-quality thumbnails of graphics to make it easier to find the correct files.

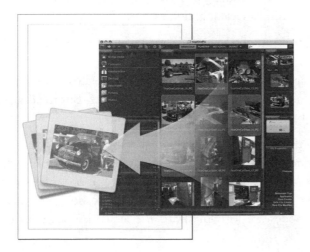

Figure 11.1 Dragging and dropping from Adobe Bridge into an InDesign page. You get a little stack of the same number of slides as the number of images you're dragging into the file. And the topmost slide depicts one of the dragged images. Cute, huh?

... and There's *Bad* Drag and Drop

Once you discover drag and drop, it's tempting to try it with everything. However, not all dragging and dropping (or copying and pasting) will produce usable results. For example, it's (unfortunately) possible to drag and drop directly from Adobe Photoshop into InDesign. Neither application prevents you from doing so, and you're given no warning that you might be dissatisfied with the results. But if you drag and drop directly from an open Photoshop file into an InDesign page (or copy image content in Photoshop and paste it into InDesign), there are unpleasant repercussions:

- The size of the image is added to the heft of the InDesign file. If you drag the contents of a 10 MB Photoshop file into an InDesign page, you've added 10 MB to the file size of the InDesign file.

- The dragged or pasted image content becomes RGB in InDesign, even if the original Photoshop file is CMYK.

- There is no information about the resolution or color space of the image in the InDesign Info panel.

- A dragged or pasted image has no connection to its Photoshop source. There's no entry in the InDesign Links panel, and no direct editability with the Edit Original options. Basically, it's an orphan. If the image later requires retouching or color correction, the image is not available to work with unless you still have the original somewhere. (In desperation, you can export the page to PDF with no compression or resampling, and then use the TouchUp Object tool in Acrobat to extract the image into Photoshop, but this is no way to live.)

So the time you think you're saving by dragging or pasting directly from Photoshop into InDesign isn't really time saved. Bluntly speaking, don't do it.

As for drag and drop or pasting from Adobe Illustrator, results are more reliable (although not perfect). CMYK content is not converted to RGB, and even spot-color content is maintained. The addition of dragged vector content doesn't cause a substantial increase in the size of an InDesign file, because of the svelte nature of vector art. But the dragged file is also an orphan, with no link back to the original Illustrator file.

It's important to note that if the Illustrator file contains transparency effects such as opacity settings or blending modes, those effects are *not* honored when artwork is dragged or pasted into InDesign. Shadows are converted to an assemblage of opaque images with no entry in the Links panel (like image content dragged from Photoshop), and any transparency effects and blending modes are lost. In short, the artwork does not faithfully represent the original.

Special circumstances, however, might motivate you to drag and drop from Illustrator into InDesign. If you want to create a complex shape to use as a container in InDesign for text or an image, you may find Illustrator's drawing tools more flexible than those in InDesign. When you drag content from Illustrator to InDesign, the vector content is fully editable with InDesign's vector tools; you may have to ungroup complex artwork to edit all components.

The File Handling & Clipboard preference in Illustrator governs how dragged or copied Illustrator content behaves in other applications. The default setting in Illustrator CS2 and later ensures that Illustrator passes content through the clipboard correctly (**Figure 11.2**).

As long as you think of this as just allowing you to draw in Illustrator for ultimate use in InDesign, you won't be too disappointed by the loss of transparency and other attributes.

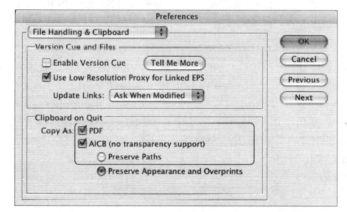

Figure 11.2 To fully utilize dragged or copy-and-pasted Illustrator content in InDesign, make sure Illustrator's File Handling & Clipboard preferences are set to the default options (as shown at left).

Embedding and Unembedding Graphics

While QuarkXPress does not support embedding of graphics in a layout file, InDesign will allow you to cram graphics right into the page-layout file so that they do not need to be externally stored. However, this is *not* the default behavior. By default, InDesign links to external files and only stores a proxy representation of the graphic in the page.

Perhaps it's a vestige of PageMaker-think that InDesign even allows it, but there's usually no reason to embed graphics. Embedding slows down performance by increasing the size of the InDesign file, and embedded images must be extracted for any color correction or retouching. A change to the original graphic file will have no effect on the embedded version, since it no longer has any relationship with the original. A high wind is not going to blow through your hard drive, peeling graphics out of your InDesign file. So there's rarely justification for embedding, and some pretty good reasons *not* to. So if that's your habit, perhaps after years of using PageMaker, maybe you should break it now. There is one circumstance that might inspire you to embed graphics, however: If you are collaborating by using InDesign Snippets, embedding graphics will ensure that the image content is also part of an exported Snippet. Otherwise, the Snippet contains only a reference to a graphic. If your collaborators don't already have the graphic, they'll be faced with a missing link.

To unembed an image for editing, select its name in the Links panel and then choose Unembed File from the Links panel menu. InDesign will ask how you want to handle the unembedding (**Figure 11.3**).

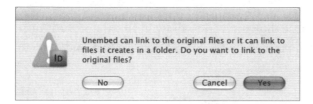

Figure 11.3 In the Unembed Files dialog, selecting Yes allows you to replace the embedded file with a link to an external file. Selecting No gives InDesign permission to extract the embedded images and save them as external files on disk.

The choices might not seem quite clear upon first (or second) reading. If you have a copy of the original graphics file, and you wish to link to it rather than use the embedded version of the graphic, select Yes (meaning, "Yes, I have a copy of the graphic, and I want to link to it rather than embedding it."). If you don't have the file, and you want InDesign to extract the embedded image and put the extracted image in a folder so you can link to it, select No (meaning, "No, I don't want to link to the original file. Well, I *want* to, but I can't. So please extract it.").

Updating Missing or Modified Graphics

The Links panel (**Figure 11.4**) allows you to see which graphics are up to date, which are modified (marked by a yellow triangle), and which are missing (indicated by a red stop sign). If your document is part of an InCopy workflow, assigned stories will be listed in the Links panel. If you have opted to link to placed text or spreadsheet files, they will be listed here, too. The Links panel was completely revamped for CS4, and provides detailed information about linked files.

The Links panel now has two compartments: The top compartment lists the linked files, each followed by the page number where the graphic appears. The page number is blue and underlined, indicating that it's a hyperlink. Click the page number to jump directly to the page where the graphic is used.

If a graphic is used multiple times in the InDesign document, a triangle appears to the left of the name in the Links list, followed by a number in parentheses indicating how many times the graphic is used. Click the triangle to display the individual instances of the graphic.

The bottom compartment of the Links panel is the Link Info area, which displays extensive information about a selected file, including color space, actual PPI, creation and modification dates, and even the date the file was placed into the InDesign document. The only thing missing is the astrological sign (the selected link in Figure 11.4 is an Aquarius).

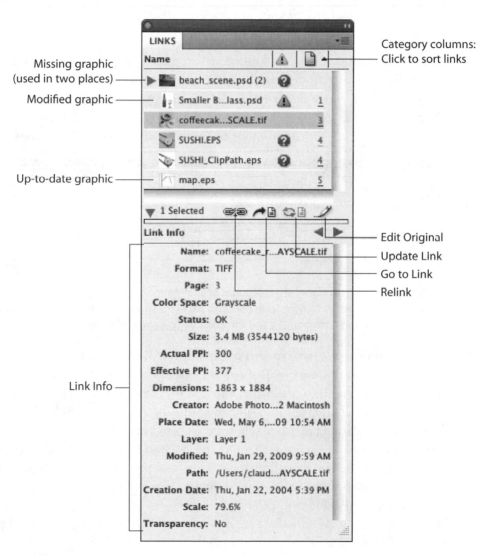

Figure 11.4 Click on an entry in the top part of the Links panel, and the Link Info area below displays everything you'd want to know about that graphic. You can completely customize the information shown in both compartments of the Links panel.

You can sort the list by clicking on a category column head, and you can toggle the display in ascending or descending order by clicking on a column head again. This can be helpful when you'd like to quickly highlight problems, such as low-resolution images. (Note, however, that InDesign still cannot report on the resolution of EPS images, images embedded in or linked to a placed Illustrator file, or placed PDFs.) You can also hide the Link Info compartment by clicking on the small triangle just above the compartment. By the way, the correct name for this kind of control is "disclosure triangle." You can win points at a geek party by knowing obscure facts like that (or maybe you should go to better parties).

Choose Panel Options from the Links panel menu to customize the behavior of the Links panel. You can choose from Small, Regular, or Large row sizes, and you can select which types of information are displayed in each compartment of the Links panel. By default, only Name, Status, and Page are displayed in the top compartment, but you can expand this into Too Much Information mode by selecting additional options (**Figure 11.5**).

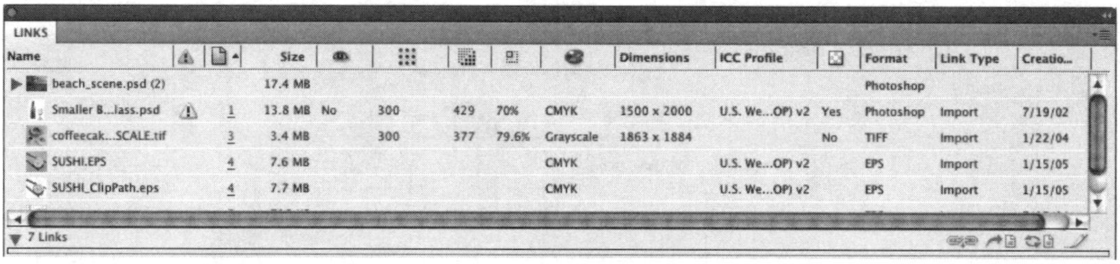

Figure 11.5 You can control which categories of information appear in the Links panel. Customize the display by choosing Panel Options from the Links panel menu and selecting the categories to be displayed in both the top compartment and the Link Info compartment below.

If linked graphics have been moved or renamed, InDesign can't find them, and displays a red stop sign icon by the link name in the Links panel list. If a graphic has been modified and resaved with the same name, a yellow alert triangle is displayed by the link name. When you open an InDesign file containing missing or modified links, an alert gives you the option of updating links then (click the Update Links button in the alert window), or deferring that until later (click the Don't Update Links button). If you've performed all the work and know the status of all the linked files feel free to update all links automatically. But if you're collaborating on a file in a workgroup and you aren't familiar with all the bits and pieces, it's a good idea to defer updating so you can watch as graphics are updated. That way, you can make sure there are no surprises, such as a recropped image or incorrect graphic with the same name.

Finding Missing Graphics

To find a missing graphic, select the link name in the Links panel list, and then choose Relink from the Links panel menu, or click the Relink button under the list (⊜). Navigate to the correct directory and select the graphic. Can't remember the filename? Just look up in the title bar of the Locate window as you search; it lists the complete directory path InDesign remembers, with the filename at the end of the string.

There's an important difference in the relinking behavior in CS4 compared to earlier versions of InDesign. In CS4, if you update a missing link, and other missing links are in the same directory, InDesign by default automatically updates all remaining links it finds in that directory (clearly, trying to be helpful). If you want to update one link at a time, glance down at the lower-left corner of the Locate dialog, and uncheck the Search for Missing Links in This Folder option (**Figure 11.6**). The choice you make is sticky, so if you want to return InDesign to runaway train mode, remember to select the option the next time you update missing links.

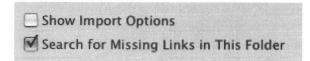

Figure 11.6 By default, InDesign automatically updates all links in the same folder. To derail this behavior, uncheck the option.

Updating Modified Graphics

The method for updating modified graphics has been refined in CS4. If you want to update a single modified link, click its entry in the Links panel list, and then select Update Link from the Links panel or click the Update Link icon below the list (⟳🖹) to kick off the hunt. Only that link will be updated. If you want to update all modified links, Option-click (Mac) or Alt-click (Windows) the Update Link icon.

Replacing Current Graphics

The Relink button is good for more than just finding missing graphics. It's also an easy way to replace an existing graphic with a new one (as opposed to starting over with File > Place). For example, if you've applied a special effect to an image in Photoshop and saved the enhanced image as an alternate version, you don't have to hide the previous image to convince InDesign to take the new one. Just click the Relink button and navigate to the replacement image. By default, InDesign will update the image while retaining any transformations (such as cropping, scaling, or rotation) that had been applied to the original image.

Editing Graphics

InDesign offers several quick methods for opening graphics in their originating applications for editing. You can select the graphic in the Links panel, and then click the Edit Original button ( ) at the bottom of the panel. Or you can select the graphic on the page and right-click (Control-click on the Mac) to display the context menu. The easiest route is to press the Alt key (PC) or the Option key (Mac) while double-clicking the graphic in the page. Regardless of the method you choose, InDesign awakens the original application and opens the graphic.

If you'd like to manually select the application to edit the graphic, right-click (Control-click on the Mac) on the graphic in the page and then choose Edit With from the context menu, and select the application from the Edit With menu. You can also select the link name in the Links panel and choose Edit With from the Links panel menu.

Make the necessary changes to the file in the original application, and then choose File > Save. Return to InDesign and the edited graphic is automatically updated, without so much as a click of a button. If you had manually opened the artwork, edited, and then saved it, you'd also have to manually update the graphic through InDesign's Links panel. The Edit Original approach is a great time-saver.

Why Is My Image Opened by Mac OS X Preview?

Macintosh OS X File Associations

The first time you try the Edit Original trick on the Macintosh, you may be disappointed that a Photoshop image is opened in Apple's Preview application, which doesn't do you any good at all. This is because the default file associations under OS X are incorrect.

The fix? You'll have to educate the operating system. Select a Photoshop native file (PSD) in any directory, then choose File > Get Info. From the Open with list (initially set to Preview), select Adobe Photoshop instead (**Figure 11.7**). If you have several versions of Photoshop installed, go for the newest version.

Very important: You must click the Change All button for this to take hold. And there's more. You'll have to do this for all the popular graphics formats that you wish to open with Photoshop, including TIFF, raster EPS, and JPEG. Find a vector EPS file and hook it up to Illustrator. And don't forget to fix your PDF files so they'll be opened by Acrobat rather than by Preview.

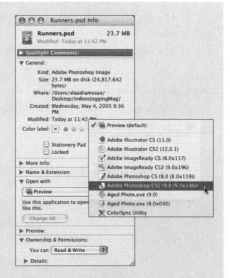

Figure 11.7 To take advantage of the Edit Original feature in InDesign, you may have to straighten out the file associations in OS X on the Macintosh.

Transforming Graphics

There are several ways to scale frames containing graphics in InDesign. Select the frame with the Selection tool (). Then you can use the Scale tool () or the Free Transform tool () to scale the frame and its contents. Or you can enter percentage values in the X/Y scale fields in the Control panel (**Figure 11.8**). You can also scale interactively by pressing Command+Shift (Control+Shift on the PC) and then dragging on a corner of the frame. You may be surprised to learn that, if you'd like to scale a graphic frame to a dimension and don't care to do the math, you can just enter the desired dimension in the Scale field. Really. For example, if you'd like to resize a 6.125-inch wide frame to 4 inches wide, just enter "4 in" in the Horizontal Percentage field. Since the Horizontal and Vertical fields are, by default, linked together (unless you've unlinked them), press the Return (Mac) or Enter (PC) key, and the height of the frame will also be scaled in proportion. It's much more fun than doing math.

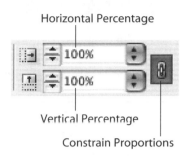

Horizontal Percentage

Vertical Percentage

Constrain Proportions

Figure 11.8 The Horizontal and Vertical Scale fields in the Control panel are linked. Type a value in the top field, press the Return or Enter key, and the bottom field is automatically populated with the proportional value.

 But whichever method you employ to scale a graphic frame, you'll be stunned to see that the X/Y scale fields cheerily insist that the scale factor is still 100 percent. However, if you select the graphic itself with the Direct Selection tool (), the lying-dog fields suddenly tell the truth (**Figure 11.9**). What's going on?

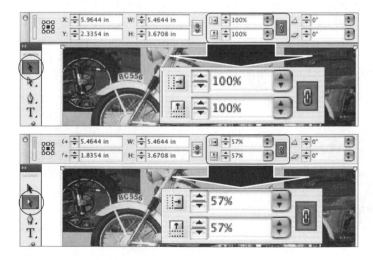

Figure 11.9 Select a graphic frame with the *Selection* tool (top), and the Scale fields in the Control panel tell blatant lies.

Select the image with the *Direct Selection* tool (bottom), and you'll get the true story. This image has been scaled to 57 percent of its original scanned size.

It's important to realize that the two InDesign selection tools perform very different functions. InDesign perceives a graphic and its frame as two distinct entities. When you select a frame with the Selection tool, you're addressing the whole shebang—frame and graphic together. When you select a graphic with the Direct Selection tool, you're speaking directly to the graphic itself. This is the only way to find the true scale factor of a graphic in the Control panel. But if you scale the whole shebang, why don't the X/Y scale fields reflect the new size? Why do they bounce back to 100 percent? That's an unexplained mystery. You'll just have to laugh it off, and ignore the X/Y scale fields unless you're using the Direct Selection tool.

If this drives you nuts (and it will), modify the Links panel options so that the Scale info appears in the Links panel, and just look there instead, while muttering under your breath.

USING NATIVE FILES

One of the joys of InDesign is its ability to use native Photoshop, Illustrator, and PDF files. There's certainly nothing wrong with using old-fashioned TIFF and EPS files, but there are advantages to using native files, including the ability to maintain live transparency and to keep layers aloft.

Photoshop Native Files (PSD)

It's not necessary to flatten Photoshop layered files before placing them in an InDesign page. In fact, unless a Photoshop file has reached an unwieldy size, there are compelling reasons *not* to flatten it because of the flexibility and editability you sacrifice when you flatten. Maintaining live layers means simplified housekeeping because there's no need to keep a separate working image file. But there are some situations that present challenges.

> **TIP:** Be sure to save Photoshop .PSD files with Maximum Compatibility turned **on**, both for compatibility with older (and future) versions of Photoshop, and for better performance in InDesign.

Drop That Shadow

Photoshop, Illustrator, and InDesign make it easy to add drop shadows to objects, which is why you see shadows under *everything* these days. Tastefulness aside, InDesign and Illustrator create perfectly nice drop shadows that interact correctly with other elements in an InDesign page (**Figure 11.10**). As long as you want a simple, concentric drop shadow, it's just one click away.

However, in some cases you may want to create a custom shadow in Photoshop, for a more realistic cast shadow effect. The one-click built-in shadow effects in Photoshop essentially repeat the shape of the parent object. But if you want to create the illusion of a shadow cast on another surface, you'll have to create a new layer, paint a shadow, and then set that layer to Mmultiply. As long as the shadow is interacting with other layers in Photoshop, this works just fine.

Figure 11.10 If you just need a simple drop shadow, InDesign and Illustrator create perfectly good ones.

But there's a limitation in the way InDesign handles shadows from Photoshop. As mentioned in Chapter 9, "Photoshop CS4 Production Tips," Photoshop's blending modes are ignored by InDesign. If the shadow falls on empty space, this doesn't matter. However, if the shadow needs to realistically darken other content beneath it in InDesign, it will require some special handling.

To place a Photoshop image containing a custom shadow on top of other content already in InDesign (**Figure 11.11**), you'll have to perform some surgery to allow the shadow to interact correctly with underlying elements. Since the Multiply blend mode applied to the shadow in Photoshop is not honored by InDesign, the Photoshop shadow is opaque, and it hides (rather than darkens) underlying elements in the page.

Figure 11.11 Custom shadows created in Photoshop (left) need special handling when placed in an InDesign file, or they will not interact correctly with underlying elements in the page (right).

Fortunately, InDesign provides a nifty workaround for this shadow shortfall: Object Layer Options. In the next section, you'll see how to solve this dilemma.

Object Layer Options

The Object Layer Options dialog (Object > Object Layer Options) allows you to selectively hide or display layers within a placed Photoshop file, native Illustrator file, placed InDesign file, or layered PDF. Think of the possibilities for versioning and design flexibility. A single, layered file can be placed multiple times in an InDesign document, displaying a different combination of layers in each instance. And it just so happens that Object Layer Options are a splendid solution to the Photoshop custom shadow dilemma.

You can choose to invoke Object Layer Options either when you import an graphic or after it's placed in the page. To invoke Object Layer Options on a placed graphic, select the object in the page, and then choose Object > Object Layer Options. In the dialog, you'll see a list of all the layers in the graphic, and you can select which layers you want to display (**Figure 11.12**). If you've used Layer Comps in Photoshop, you can also select a Layer Comp state to display. (Layer Comps control the display of multiple layers in Photoshop, and they're a great way to manage complex compositions.)

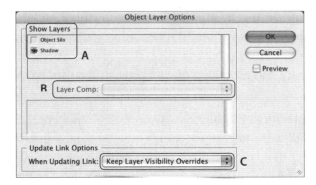

Figure 11.12 Invoked during image import or after an image is placed, Object Layer Options allow you to selectively show or hide layers within a Photoshop or PDF file (A). Extra credit: If you use Layer Comps in Photoshop, InDesign allows you to select them by name (B). The Update Link Options (C) determine what happens if you edit the image in Photoshop after placement.

To correctly handle a manually created shadow like the example in **Figure 11.13**, you'll still have to place the image twice (or duplicate the frame)—once for the shadow and once for the silhouetted object. But at least you only have to keep track of one image on disk with this method. Here's the recipe:

1. Place the image, select the image frame with the Selection tool, and then copy it to the Clipboard (you'll need it later).

2. With the frame still selected, choose Object > Object Layer Options. This frame will serve as the shadow. Turn off the visibility of all layers except the shadow layer. Set the blending mode of this frame to Multiply.

3. Paste the Clipboard copy of the frame, using Edit > Paste in Place to ensure that the copy lines up with the original.

4. With the newly pasted frame still selected, open Object Layer Options. This time, hide the shadow layer. You may find it easier to deal with these two frames by dragging the sides of the topmost frame in a bit, so it's clear when you've selected either the top or bottom object. It's also a good idea to group the two related frames.

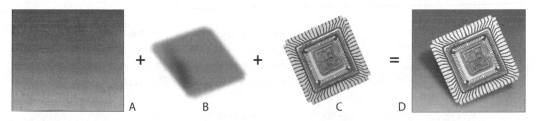

Figure 11.13 Think of this process as creating a shadow sandwich. Start with a background (A). Then place the shadow image (B), and set its frame to Multiply in InDesign. Top it off with the silhouetted object (C), and you have the finished assembly (D).

If you selectively reveal layers, what happens if you edit the image in the originating application, and then update it? You can choose whether to keep InDesign's layer visibility overrides or start over when updating. The default is to retain the overrides you've applied in InDesign, which is what you'd usually want.

Caution: You will lose what you've accomplished with Object Layer Options if you add, delete, or rename layers in the originating application. When you update, InDesign insists on starting over, resetting your custom layer visibility settings to reflect the incoming, updated file's visibility; this is truly annoying. At least you receive an alert (**Figure 11.14**), but you have to relaunch Object Layer Options to restore the custom visibility you'd previously established. This behavior affects any Photoshop, Illustrator, InDesign, or PDF files governed by Object Layer Options.

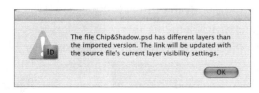

The file Chip&Shadow.psd has different layers than the imported version. The link will be updated with the source file's current layer visibility settings.

OK

Figure 11.14 If you add or delete layers in a placed file affected by Object Layer Options (whether it's a Photoshop, Illustrator, InDesign or PDF file), InDesign insists on resetting layer options after an update. Very annoying.

By default, InDesign does not provide hints in the Links panel that Object Layer Options have been used on a graphic. However, you can use the Links panel options to turn on the Layer Overrides category (**Figure 11.15**). InDesign displays "Yes" in that category for objects affected by Object Layer Options, followed by a number indicating how many layers are involved.

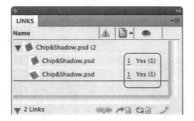

Figure 11.15 If you've turned on the optional Layer Overrides category in the Links panel options, you'll be able to quickly determine which graphics are affected by Object Layer Options.

To take advantage of InDesign's Object Layer Options feature, you have to save graphics files appropriately from other applications:

- Photoshop files must be saved as PSD files. Layers in TIFF files or Photoshop PDF files aren't recognized by InDesign.

- Illustrator files must be saved as native AI files; EPS files can't play.

- InDesign files are fine just as they are.

- PDF files must be saved with Acrobat 6 or later compatibility to contain layers. The layers are created from layers in the originating application, such as InDesign or Illustrator.

Illustrator Native Files (AI)

Illustrator native files offer several advantages over the traditional EPS files when placed in InDesign. Transparency and blending modes in Illustrator AI files are fully honored by InDesign. Drop shadows created in Illustrator with the Effect > Stylize > Drop Shadow method will interact correctly with underlying elements in an InDesign page—unlike Photoshop's drop shadows. Illustrator objects with blending modes such as Multiply, Screen, or Darken will affect InDesign elements as expected: InDesign and Illustrator speak the same dialect when it comes to blending modes. You can also invoke Object Layer Options for an AI file. A native file can also be considerably smaller on disk than an EPS version of the same file with no loss of data. Remember to leave the default Create PDF Compatible File option checked so the Illustrator file can be placed in InDesign (for more information, see Chapter 10, "Illustrator CS4 Production Tips").

While it's unnecessary to open your vast store of Illustrator EPS files and resave them as native AI files, there is one circumstance that may inspire you to change the format of a really old EPS. If you are adding a drop shadow to a truly ancient EPS (say, Illustrator 8 or earlier), you will encounter a quirk in the way the shadow is displayed (**Figure 11.16**). The fix is to either resave the art as an AI file or as an EPS file with a TIFF preview.

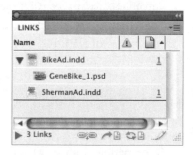

Figure 11.16 Drop shadows created for old EPS files have an unfortunate bug. If you add a drop shadow, it will *print* correctly (top), but will *display* as if the shadow is following the containing frame (bottom). The answer? Save the artwork as a native AI file—then the shadow displays and prints correctly.

InDesign Files as Artwork

You can place one InDesign file into another as artwork, which opens up some interesting possibilities. For example, ads submitted as InDesign files can be placed in the same way you'd traditionally place AI or EPS files, but with greater editability. Just choose File > Place and import the InDesign file. Move it, scale it, and crop it as you would any artwork. The Links panel lists the InDesign file, along with any artwork linked to it (**Figure 11.17**). The artwork names are indented under the placed InDesign file name to highlight their dependent relationship.

Figure 11.17 The Links panel lists any support art linked to a placed InDesign file. It's sort of like those Russian nesting dolls.

If you need to make changes, just right-click (Control-click on the Mac) on the placed InDesign file and choose Edit Original. The original InDesign file is opened, you can make your edits and resave, and the placed file will be updated. If you need to edit artwork linked to the placed InDesign file, it takes an extra step; you can't Edit Original for artwork in a placed file. Instead, open the placed InDesign file via Edit Original, and then select the artwork within *that* file for editing. Save the modified artwork, update *that* InDesign file, and save. Return to the "parent" InDesign file and update the placed file. It sounds more complicated than it is in practice. Just think of it as double bagging.

When you package the job, all the bits and pieces will be gathered up, including the parent InDesign file and all its artwork and fonts, as well as the placed InDesign files and all their fonts and artwork; there's no need to package the placed files separately.

There's one limitation to the file-within-a-file feature: You can't place an InDesign file into itself. Think about it: If you changed the file, you'd invalidate the placed version, which would in turn invalidate the parent file, and so on. Well, you've seen enough science fiction to know this just wouldn't work.

PDF Files as Artwork

In general, you'll use PSD, AI, EPS, and TIFF files as graphic content, but there are times when a PDF is appropriate. For example, Photoshop PDFs contain transparency and true vector art (including text), whereas vector components in a PSD are rasterized when placed in InDesign.

Multipage PDFs can be placed one page at a time. Select the Show Import Options when placing a PDF, and you can page through a preview thumbnail to choose a single page, a range of pages, or the entire, multipage PDF. If you choose multiple pages, your placement cursor changes appearance (⟨🗗⟩), and each mouse click deposits a separate page of the PDF. To stop placing pages at any time, just click the Selection tool.

As an alternative, you can use the PlaceMultipagePDF script (Window > Automation > Scripts; the script is inside the Samples group), which automatically places each page of a PDF on a separate InDesign page. While you can't control which pages are placed or their position, it's still a time-saver if you need to pour in all the pages of a PDF.

SWATCHES

It may seem redundant that InDesign has a Color panel as well as a Swatches panel, but they serve slightly different functions. Think of the Color panel as an informal mixing bowl for creating a color you'll apply only to a selected object. Colors created in the Color panel are not automatically stored in the Swatches panel—they evaporate. In addition, you can only specify CMYK, RGB, or Lab colors with the Colors panel. However, if you select an existing object colored with a spot color, the Colors panel does offer a quick method of creating a tint of the spot color.

In practice, it's best to create swatches rather than informal colors. In addition to allowing you to select from Pantone, Toyo, and TRUMATCH swatchbooks, the Swatches panel ensures that you have global control. Change the recipe for a swatch, and you change every object filled or stroked with the swatch. For information on the new Pantone Goe System, see Chapter Two, "Ink on Paper," and Chapter Ten, "Illustrator CS4 Production Tips."

If you've applied colors with the Color panel, you can easily turn those colors into official swatches without even hunting for the objects to which those colors have been applied. In the Swatches panel menu, choose Add Unnamed Colors, and InDesign hunts them all down and adds them to the Swatches panel.

The Swatches panel can be a bit confusing (**Figure 11.18**). The colorful semaphore flags in its rightmost column do *not* indicate whether a swatch is spot or process. Instead, those icons merely indicate the color mode used to generate the onscreen appearance of the swatch. It's the column with the dull gray icons that answers the question "spot or not?" A gray square indicates a process color (a swatch that will image in CMYK), regardless of the swatch name or the color mode indicated in the far-right column. A white square containing a gray circle—a spot—indicates a spot color.

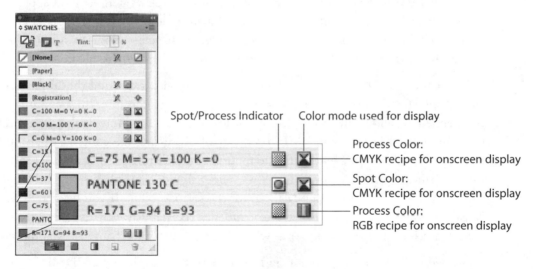

Figure 11.18 The indicators in the Swatches panel can be confusing. Here's a decoder ring.

RGB colors may drastically change appearance when converted to CMYK. If you're in a color-managed workflow, you may wish to retain your RGB swatches, but preview their conversion to CMYK. To do this, first choose the appropriate color profiles in InDesign by choosing Edit > Color Settings, or use the great Synchronize Color Settings function in Adobe Bridge. Then, choose View > Proof Colors to display content using the color profiles in effect.

If you're not in a color-managed workflow, and the print service provider requests that there be no RGB content, double-click the name or an RGB swatch, and then change its color mode to CMYK. Keep in mind that this conversion is governed by your current color settings, so use a color setting provided by your printer. Lacking that, use North America Prepress 2 and hope for the best.

Stubborn Swatches

When you import artwork such as an Illustrator file or a Photoshop duotone containing a spot color, InDesign adds the color to the Swatches panel. As long as that artwork is in the document, you can't delete the spot swatch, nor can you merge it with another swatch—it's protected. If the swatch is used by a paragraph, character, or object style, it will also resist deletion. However, if you delete all artwork and styles related to the swatch, InDesign will allow you to delete the swatch. At least, it *should*.

Occasionally, InDesign develops a fondness for a swatch and will not allow you to delete it or convert it to process, even if you've deleted the artwork or eliminated the styles that inspired it. It's a petty annoyance. If there's truly nothing using the swatch, it won't appear during output or export. If you want to assure yourself that the color is a phantom, use Separations Preview (Window > Output > Separations Preview) to selectively view inks (more about that in the next section). If nothing appears when you display that ink alone, you're safe.

If it just bugs you to see that insolent swatch in the list, exporting the file to InDesign Interchange (.INX) or InDesign Markup (.IDML) may be the cure. InDesign Interchange is intended to allow InDesign CS4 users to save files for individuals using InDesign CS3. InDesign Markup is an XML-based way of expressing the contents of an InDesign document for developers who intend to repurpose content. Exporting to either format can often repair a neurotic document. Choose File > Export, and then select InDesign CS3 Interchange (INX) or InDesign Markup for the format. Note: If you have used Multiple Master format fonts, you will have to manually re-establish font usage for those fonts using Find Font (Type > Find Font) when you open the Interchange or Markup file.

Close the misbehaving document, and then open the Interchange or IDML file by using File > Open. You should now be able to edit or delete the offending swatch. This procedure is helpful for all sorts of file misbehavior or corruption, not just errant swatches. It's especially handy if you encounter residual gunk from a plug-in that you don't have; the export to Interchange or IDML "purifies" the file of plug-in residue.

You'll also find the export to Interchange feature in InDesign CS through CS3. Note that if you're using the INX method for its original intended purpose, it allows backsaving only for users of the previous version—you can't jump two versions.

What to Do About All Those Extra Swatches

Does this sound familiar? You're working on a job that should consist of CMYK plus one spot color, Pantone 130. After importing duotone images created by your team's retouchers and placing the vector art provided by another designer, you realize that there are three spot colors in the Swatches panel—Pantone 130 C, PMS 130 CVC, and something named Harvest Gold. Although we easily recognize that PMS 130 CVC and Pantone 130 C refer to the same color (and we suspect that *Harvest Gold* does too), a RIP sees the different names as indicating different inks and faithfully outputs them separately. Consequently, you need to take measures to ensure that only spot-color plate—Pantone 130—is output. And you'll have to perform some detective work to find the culprits responsible for the extra spot colors.

To determine which artwork uses each spot color, you could print out separated prints if your desktop printer supports that feature (some non-PostScript devices don't). But this would require you to endure the printing process, waste half a tree, and get out of your chair and walk over to the printer. You could export to PDF, and then use the Output Preview feature in Acrobat 9 Professional, but that's an extra step. There's a much more efficient way to determine where the spot colors are being used. You can use the Separations Preview feature in InDesign. Choose Window > Output Preview > Separations Preview.

Initially, the Separations Preview panel (**Figure 11.19**) doesn't do anything special, until you choose Separations from its View menu. When you do, InDesign assumes you want to know as much as possible about your document, so it activates Overprint Preview, which in turn displays all graphics at high resolution. Consequently, in a document containing extensive graphics, you may experience slower performance.

Visibility Controls

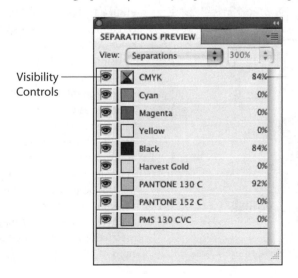

Color Percentages

Figure 11.19 The Separations Preview panel lets you selectively display individual or multiple printing plates. As you move your mouse over areas of the page, the percentage value of each ink color is displayed in the right column. There's bad news here: It's a five-color job, so somebody's going to have to fix those two extra spot colors.

Using the visibility controls in the leftmost column of the Separations Preview panel, you can hide and display individual plates or combinations of plates. As you move your mouse over the document, the right column displays the percentage values of each ink. You can also view areas in excess of a total ink limit value by choosing the Ink Limit option from the Separations Preview panel drop-down menu. Enter the appropriate value (ask your print service provider), and InDesign highlights areas in violation of the specified value.

> **NOTE:** If you close the Separations Preview panel while it's set to Separations view or Ink Limit display, Overprint Preview and High Resolution Display remain in effect, which slows things down a bit. Before closing the Separations Preview panel, choose Off from the View menu. This turns off Overprint Preview and returns display performance to the setting in effect before you activated Separations Preview.

The Separations Preview feature may show you where most color problems are (although it doesn't make it easy to see objects with 0 percent of a spot color), but it can't *fix* the problems. To correct the problem, you could open all the images and vector artwork containing the incorrect color components and change them to use the correct inks. If you're under a tight deadline, you could instruct the print service provider to resolve the problem during output. Or you could be a hero and fix it in seconds by using the Ink Manager.

Ink Manager

The primary purpose of the Ink Manager (**Figure 11.20**) is to fix spot-color errors by remapping extraneous colors to correct inks. In this example, the job should only have one spot color, Pantone 130 C. So the Ink Manager is used to remap the two problematic colors—PMS 130 CVC and Harvest Gold—to the correct Pantone 130 C plate for output.

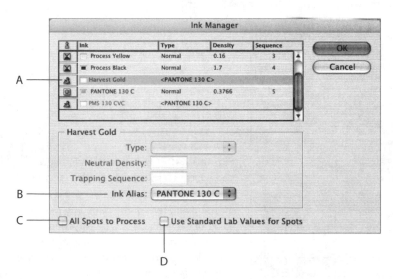

Figure 11.20 The Ink Manager can remap an incorrect spot color (A) to the correct ink (B) by using what InDesign calls Ink Aliasing. With one click, you can designate all spot colors to image as CMYK builds (C). Selecting the Lab option (D) may provide more accurate onscreen approximation of spot colors. In a color-managed workflow, this option may provide more accurate rendering of spot colors in CMYK. However, this may not match output from previous versions of InDesign.

TIP: *For consistent spot-color definitions (and conversion to consistent CMYK values), set InDesign and Illustrator to use Lab Values to display and handle spot colors. In InDesign, open Ink Manager and check the option to Use Standard Lab Values for Spots, and then re-create the spot color. In Illustrator, choose Spot Colors from the Swatches panel menu, and check the option to Use Lab values specified by the book manufacturer, and then re-import the spot color. If no document is open, all future documents will be affected. Otherwise, only the current document is affected. If you want to match files from earlier versions of InDesign and Illustrator, use the default CMYK equivalents instead.*

You can launch the Ink Manager in several ways (**Figure 11.21**). The Separations Preview panel menu offers one route. The Swatches panel menu provides another. You will also find the Ink Manager in the Print dialog (under Output) and in the Export dialogs for both EPS (under Advanced) and Adobe PDF (under Output).

Figure 11.21 The Ink Manager is available from the Separations Preview panel (A), the Swatches panel (B), the Export EPS dialog (C), the Output section of the Print dialog (D), and the Export Adobe PDF dialog (E).

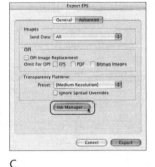

A

B

C

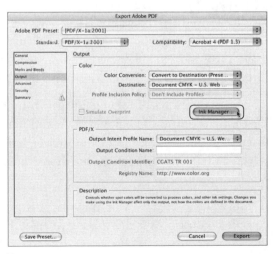

D

E

To map one spot color to another spot color (or to a process color) with the Ink Manager, select the spot color you wish to remap. The dialog comes to life, offering you the Ink Alias list. Choose the correct color in the Ink Alias list and you're done. You can even remap a spot color to a single process plate—output the Harvest Gold on the magenta plate, for example. You cannot, however, map a process color to a spot color. But you can convert all spot colors to process with one click, by selecting the All Spots to Process check box in the Ink Manager dialog.

The remapping function is nondestructive—the remapping takes place in the output stream, as the file is printed or exported to another format such as EPS or PDF. It doesn't actually change placed artwork or any content created in the InDesign file, so it's easy to undo at any time if you make the wrong choices. Just turn off the Ink Alias for an ink, or deselect the Spots to Process option in the Ink Manager dialog.

Changes made in the Ink Manager are not reflected in the Swatches panel, which may unnerve you. But there's a certain logic to this. Since you haven't actually *changed* content, the Swatches panel doesn't feel compelled to change its display. But rest assured that any output—export to EPS or PDF, or File > Print—will contain only the correct inks. You can confirm this by reopening the Separations Preview panel for a correct view of all process and spot-color usage.

If you're sending native InDesign files to the print service provider rather than submitting PDF files, it's a good idea to inform them that you have already rectified the spot-color issues with the Ink Manager, lest they freak out unnecessarily. ("There are 15 spot colors in the Swatches panel!")

Colorizing Images

InDesign allows you to colorize grayscale and bilevel (black and white, with no shades of gray) TIFF and PSD files to create simplistic monotone effects. Colorizing is a quick-and-dirty way to apply color to images with the ability to change your mind late in the game.

There are two ways to colorize images in InDesign. Select the image by clicking with the Direct Selection tool (white arrow), and then choose the swatch. Alternatively, you can just drag a swatch on top of the image (but, counterintuitively, the frame must not be selected first), and then release the mouse button. The swatch is then applied to the image, not the frame.

If you want to create a true duotone, it's preferable to use Photoshop, where you have complete control over the mixing of inks. But if you're in a hurry or don't care about the refined controls in Photoshop, InDesign allows you to create what's often called a *fake duotone*. First, colorize the image using one of the methods above, and then apply another swatch to the frame itself. The frame color will show through the lighter areas of the image in the frame. (Warning—this has the potential to be truly ugly.) For a somewhat more duotone-like result, select the image with the Direct Selection tool (white arrow) and then, using the controls in the Transparency panel, apply the Multiply blend mode to the image itself. This offers the advantage of allowing you to change the applied color quickly without having to rework the image in Photoshop and update.

Note that grayscale TIFF and PSD files with transparency on the bottom layer cannot be colorized by InDesign. All other layers can contain transparency, but the bottom layer cannot. InDesign does not give you any warning or explanation when you attempt to colorize such an image—it just doesn't do anything.

CONVERTING LEGACY QUARKXPRESS AND PAGEMAKER FILES

InDesign can directly open QuarkXPress 3.x and 4.x files, as well as files created by PageMaker 6.0 and later, thereby converting those files to InDesign documents. InDesign CS2 and later can also open and convert QuarkXPress Passport files. On its own, InDesign cannot open and convert QuarkXPress 5.x or later files, because the later QuarkXPress file format was encrypted. However, the Q2ID utility from Markzware can open and convert QuarkXPress 3.x through 8.0 files, and it does a commendable job of translation.

Preparing for Conversion

When you convert a QuarkXPress or PageMaker file to InDesign, it's important to realize that this is a *translation* process—you're not simply opening a file. There are some precautions you can take to minimize problems in conversion, but you should be prepared to massage the resulting InDesign file. You'll achieve the best results if you first ensure the health of the original file you're going to convert.

- Make sure that all the required fonts are active on your system.

- Open the file in the originating application and update all graphics. Skipping this step won't prevent conversion, but it may save you some time hunting for links in the converted file.

- If there are any unnecessary elements in the document, such as extra elements in the pasteboard or unused colors and styles, delete those. It's best to start with a file that's as clean as possible.

- If you're starting with a QuarkXPress 5.x file and don't have the Markzware Q2ID plug-in, save it as a 4.0 file so that InDesign can open it.

- Before closing a PageMaker document, perform a Save As (rather than a File > Save) to streamline the file. The PageMaker Save command is a *fast save*, and there may be vestigial hidden data. Make it easy on InDesign.

- If the document is quite large, consider breaking it into smaller chunks for easier digestion.

- Convert embedded graphics to linked graphics in PageMaker if possible.

- Close the file before you attempt to open it in InDesign.

All of the preceding bits of advice presume that you have access to the original applications, and, understandably, you won't always have that luxury. Just take advantage if you have access in the interest of doing the best conversion.

What to Expect

It's wise to check the results of conversion. You could laboriously compare hard copy to what's displayed onscreen, but here's a suggestion. After you've prepared the file in QuarkXPress or PageMaker, create a PDF from that file. Then, once you've opened the QuarkXPress or PageMaker file in InDesign, create a new topmost layer in the new InDesign file, and then place the pages of the PDF in that layer. Turn on and off the visibility of that layer by using the Layers panel visibility controls, or noodle with the opacity of the placed PDF, and watch for problems.

Expect reflowed or overset text, and keep an eye out for shifting graphics. Watch for subtle changes as you toggle the visibility of the proof PDF.

Tell yourself: It's a conversion process, and it's amazing that it works at all. Here's what happens during the process:

- Styles are converted to InDesign styles.

- Swatches survive the trip.

- Master pages are retained, as are master elements in document pages.

- Graphics links are retained.

- Strokes and lines—even paragraph rules—are preserved.

- Groups are preserved (except for nonprinting items within a group).

- Multi-ink colors in QuarkXPress become mixed inks in InDesign. If the multi-ink color does not contain at least one spot color, a process swatch is created instead.

Frankly, you should expect text reflow—then you can be pleasantly surprised if it doesn't happen. InDesign's text composition engine differs from those of QuarkXPress and PageMaker. If line breaks are not crucial, the good news is that text will look smoother in InDesign because of the default composition method, which is called *Adobe Paragraph Composer*. In the Paragraph Composer approach, InDesign considers the entire content of a paragraph as it determines how to break lines. If you switch to the Single-Line Composer, InDesign behaves like other page-layout applications and makes composition choices on a line-by-line basis. Open the Paragraph panel (Window > Type & Tables > Paragraph), and choose Single-Line Composer from the panel menu if you'd prefer to mimic the composition approach used by QuarkXPress or PageMaker. Text may not be as smooth—you'll see more white rivers, as well as tight and loose lines, especially in justified text—but you may find that line breaks more closely resemble those in the original document. (Note that the choice of Single-Line or Paragraph Composer applies to text on a paragraph-by-paragraph basis.)

PageMaker Conversion Issues

Choosing File > Open to convert a PageMaker file to an InDesign file is a translation process. Here are some of the issues to consider when you perform the conversion:

- PageMaker's pasteboard contents are stored on the first spread's pasteboard, because an InDesign pasteboard is specific to the spread it accompanies, whereas PageMaker has one universal pasteboard that appears around every spread in a document.

- Two layers are created—Master Default (containing all master elements) and Default (containing everything else).

- Hyphenation in InDesign differs from PageMaker's, which may result in reflow.

- PageMaker's Top of Caps and Proportional leading styles become baseline-based leading in InDesign, which contributes to text reflow and occasional overset text.

- InDesign provides no support for OLE (object linking and embedding). Any OLE graphics will be missing.

- PageMaker's Image Control effects are not retained.

- Shadow text becomes plain text.

- Inline graphics may shift vertically.

QuarkXPress Conversion Issues

While InDesign does a remarkable job of opening and converting QuarkXPress files, there are some issues you may encounter:

- InDesign does not have a Superior text style, so text styled as such in QuarkXPress becomes superscript text with a positive (upward) baseline shift (**Figure 11.22**). The Superior style might be described as a version of superscript, and is often used in QuarkXPress for currency symbols such as dollar signs. One of the advantages of the Markzware Q2ID plug-in is that it reworks text using the Superior style so that its appearance is correct in the converted file.

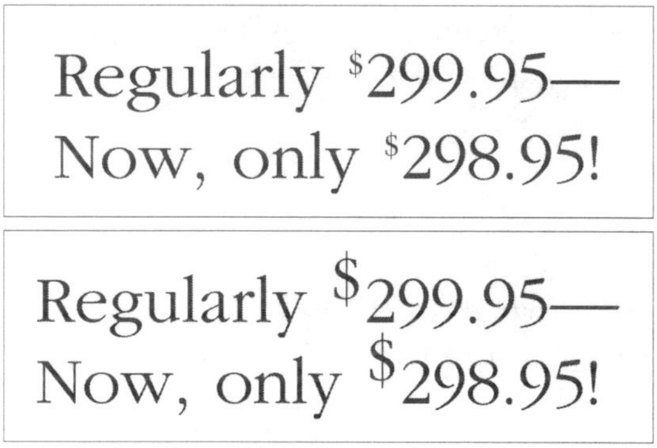

Regularly $299.95—
Now, only $298.95!

Regularly $299.95—
Now, only $298.95!

Figure 11.22 In QuarkXPress, the Superior type style raises the position and reduces the size of text such as dollar signs (top). InDesign doesn't have a Superior type style, so it applies the superscript style instead. While this maintains the raised position of the text, it does not reduce the size (bottom).

- QuarkXPress color profiles are ignored.

- Outlined text takes on a .25-point stroke.

- Line endings such as arrowheads may not match the originals in QuarkXPress.

- Artificially emboldened or italicized text takes on a true bold or italic font if it's available. If the correct font (or style within a font) is not available (for example, bold and italic styling applied to Impact, which can't get any bolder and has no italic face), the text will sport an unattractive pink highlight indicating a missing font or font style.

- Text shadows created by selecting the S in the Measurements panel are deleted.

- By default, text wrap in InDesign is created irrespective of stacking order. A frame carrying text wrap affects text frames above *and* below it in stacking order, even across layers. Modifying text in a converted file makes it subject to InDesign's rules. So if a neighboring frame is set to create text wrap, the text in your just-selected frame will feel compelled to play along and will reflow (or seem to disappear). Select the text frame whose text you don't want responding to text wrap, and then choose Object > Text Frame Options. Select the Ignore Text Wrap option, and then click OK.

Note that you can change the InDesign text-wrap preference to behave like QuarkXPress. Select Preferences > Composition, and then choose Text Wrap Only Affects Text Beneath.

- Up through InDesign CS, there were occasional conversion errors resulting in images being set to be nonprinting as a result of the file conversion. A quick way to check for this is to activate Preview mode (press W on your keyboard). Toggle Preview on and off by repeatedly pressing W, and watch for images to disappear. Think of it as a crude video game. If you find any problem images, open the Attributes panel (Window > Attributes), select the images with the Direct Selection tool (white arrow), and then clear the Nonprinting check box in the Attributes panel. This problem seems to have been fixed since InDesign CS2.

- Some Quark XTensions leave a bit of residue in a QuarkXPress file; most don't prevent or corrupt the conversion. But you may occasionally encounter a QuarkXPress file that fails to convert (as evidenced by the fact that InDesign crashes every time you try to convert). See if the file originator can disable the XTension and resave the file. If not, you may be completely out of luck.

Cleaning Up

After you've tuned up your line breaks and massaged any errant images, don't forget to delete the PDF layer you created for checking the conversion.

To ensure that you're working with a healthy file from this point forward, it's a good idea to export the file as InDesign Markup (File > Export to IDML). Then open up the resulting IDML file, save it as an InDesign file, and work in that file. Think of it as a voodoo ploy to remove any memory of the file's previous incarnations.

When *Not* to Convert Legacy Files

If you're simply reprinting an old job, it's saner to just keep it in its original PageMaker or QuarkXPress state. Unless you don't have a computer that can launch the necessary originating application, there's no true advantage to converting it and, as you can see, the conversion is likely to require additional work and the risk of errors that you might not catch.

When creating templates that will be used as the basis for many documents, we strongly recommend building a new template in InDesign rather than working with a converted file. It's the healthiest start you can have. Besides—you need the practice. However, if you loathe the thought of having to create lots of swatches and styles from scratch, you can do this: Convert the old file to InDesign, but just use it as a donor file from which you import swatches and styles for the new document you're creating from scratch.

MISCELLANEOUS DOCUMENT TIPS

These short topics are just little factoids that you should know about; they're not all pit-falls—some, like Automatic Recovery, are actually good news.

IDLK Files

When you have an open InDesign document, there is an additional file with a similar name that magically appears in the same directory as the file you have open. For example, if you have opened a file named Chapter_1.indd, you'll see a companion file named ~chapter_1~p965so.idlk in the directory. The tilde (~) in front of the name and the file extension .idlk tell you that this is an InDesign lock file. Its purpose is to prevent multiple users from simultaneously opening an InDesign file across a network. Instead, they'll see an alert informing them that they do not have permission to open the document.

Don't delete .idlk files—InDesign cleans up after itself. The files will evaporate when you save and close the open file. If InDesign should crash while a document is open, it won't have time to delete the .idlk file, but just leave it anyway. InDesign will take care of the housekeeping the next time you open, save, and then close the file.

Automatic Recovery

As you work, InDesign keeps track of what you're doing; without impeding performance, it keeps a private version of your working file. This is the same mechanism that gives you unlimited undo capability, and it can be a real lifesaver.

If your system crashes for any reason—power outage, corrupt font, system crash—let InDesign recover as much of your document as it can. Resist the panicked urge to reopen your original file. Instead, reopen InDesign and marvel as your document reappears. You may lose the last few things you did, but you won't lose everything you did in that session. That's because InDesign keeps your most recent operations in memory so you can quickly undo, and it may not have time to write those to disk as it crashes. But it's better than losing the whole shebang. You can't turn off Automatic Recovery—and why would you want to? You can change where InDesign keeps the recovery information by choosing Preferences > File Handling and selecting a directory.

Going Back in Time

If you need to backsave an InDesign CS4 document for use in InDesign CS3, you'll find that backsaving is not available through File > Save. Instead, you must export an InDesign Interchange file (File > Export). In order to open this file from the future, the users of InDesign CS3 must first update their software to the most current version. If they've let all automatic updates install during the life of the product, they're current. To check if software is current, choose Help > Updates, or check the Updates listings in the Downloads section of the Adobe site.

Cautions About Backsaving

It's not ideal to collaborate with someone who isn't using the same version of software that you are, but sometimes it's unavoidable; this caveat is not limited to InDesign. Just be aware that some content created in InDesign CS4, such as cross-references or conditional text, won't have an equivalent in CS3. While the trip through InDesign IDML should keep the content as regular text, these features are no longer "live" if the file is saved in CS3 and then reopened in CS4; cross-references no longer connect to their targets, and text conditions are no longer defined. If your document contains such features, consider the Interchange procedure as a one-way trip. And it's not a bad idea to include a PDF of the document with the Interchange file, so that your recipient can double-check the content.

Reducing File Size

InDesign files are fluffy by nature. Even a simple file is larger on disk than an equivalent QuarkXPress file; it's just a fact of life. But you can economize a bit by performing a File > Save As at the end of the job. When you just choose File > Save, InDesign appends any new data to the existing file on disk. It's faster than rewriting the entire contents of the file, but it results in a larger file size. However, when you choose File > Save As, InDesign completely rewrites the file and does a bit of housecleaning. As a result, you should see a reduction in file size, especially in a document with a lot of large graphics. For example, the file for this chapter had ballooned to 13.4 MB. Performing a Save As reduced that to 8.4 MB. Enormous disk capacities have made us lax about taking up space—*I have a 250 GB hard drive. Why should I ever throw anything away?*—but you may find that document performance improves as a result of using Save As instead of Save.

Let It Bleed

When you create a new InDesign document, you're given the option to create a dedicated bleed zone (**Figure 11.23**). In the New Document dialog, click the More Options button and you'll see the Bleed and Slug options. Entering a value in the Bleed fields does more than just provide spiffy red bleed guides. It earmarks a special *bleed area* so you can easily invoke it with one click when you print or export the file.

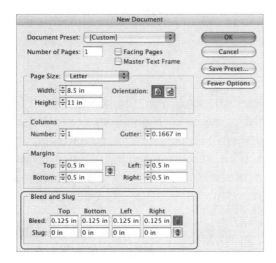

Figure 11.23 Click the More Options button (not shown, because it's already been clicked) and InDesign allows Bleed and Slug entries. Creating a dedicated bleed area in this manner makes it easy to invoke bleed as you print or export.

It's important to note that InDesign makes a distinction between this official bleed *area* and any bleed you *manually* create by extending frames beyond the trim edge of the page, and this fact can bite you. During print or output, if you select Use Document Bleed Settings, InDesign looks for the dedicated bleed value entered in the Bleed options fields of document setup. If you haven't entered values in these fields, InDesign sees a zero value and obligingly gives you zero bleed (**Figure 11.24**). So keep an eye on the bleed value fields; don't just blindly click the Use Document Bleed option.

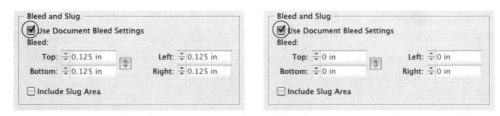

Figure 11.24 If you select Use Document Bleed Settings and see the correct value in all the Bleed fields (left), you're in good shape. But if you see all zeroes (right), you'll have *no* bleed on printed or exported output, regardless of any manual bleed you add.

If you forgot to designate the official bleed area when you created the document, you can still do so at any time by choosing File > Document Setup and then clicking the More Options button in the resulting dialog to create the bleed area. When the Use Document Bleed Settings check box is selected, you will get the desired result during output.

One Size Fits All: Layout Adjustment

If you've (oops) built a document with the incorrect page size or need to change margins, the world has not ended. InDesign's Layout Adjustment can save your proverbial bacon. Choose Layout > Layout Adjustment (**Figure 11.25**), and then change the document size or margin settings. The default settings will do all the right things. Guides will move as will objects snapped to those guides. Text frames created by autoflowing text will expand or contract as necessary, adhering to shifting margins. Radical changes in page size or margin settings may require some massaging after the treatment, but you may be surprised by how good the initial results are.

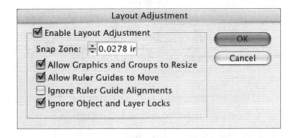

Figure 11.25 So what if your evil twin built the document the wrong size? Select the Enable Layout Adjustment check box to give InDesign permission to fix it.

Checking Out of the Library

InDesign libraries are a great way to have a ready repository of commonly used elements, including text, graphics, and page geometry. These elements can then be quickly dragged into a page without having to re-create them each time. Libraries can be stored locally or on a server (although they must be locked on a server for multiple users to have access).

If you're missing graphics that are required by the library content, you get no warning when you open the Library. For example, if you place an image in a page, and then drag the image frame to the Library, the Library entry represents the geometry of the frame and the directory path of the image in the frame at the time it was placed in the Library. If you subsequently delete that image from your hard drive or server, the Library doesn't warn you that it contains obsolete content.

However, when you drag an obsolete Library item onto a page, it appears as a gray frame with no graphic content, which is your hint that there's nobody home. One workaround for this dilemma is to embed the graphic in InDesign before dragging it to the Library. In the Links panel, select the link name, and then select Embed File from the Links panel menu. Then you can safely drag the graphic or a group containing it to the Library panel. When you drag the Library item onto another page, the embedding is maintained, and there's no need to hunt for the original artwork. One caveat: This is most appropriate for small artwork, since embedding increases the InDesign file size by the amount of the graphic. Embed a 2 MB image in an InDesign file, and you have increased the InDesign file size by 2 MB. Do this for 20 images in a document and—well, you get the idea.

Why Is My Text Two Sizes?

You select text with the Type tool and discover that the text size in the Character panel or Control panel shows a second size in parentheses. You highlight the contents of the font size field and type a new value, but the text becomes a size you didn't expect, and you still see a second value in parentheses (**Figure 11.26**). What's going on?

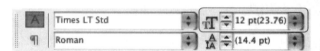

Figure 11.26 How can text be two sizes? It's a combination of an incorrect preference and scaling a frame.

InDesign is trying to tell you the original font size, and the font size as the result of the frame being scaled; it's another case of too much information. InDesign CS3 rectified this aggravation, so if you're experiencing this, one of two things has happened:

• You've inherited a pre-CS3 file in which someone scaled a text frame, probably as part of a group.

• Someone (not you, of course) has changed a preference to reawaken this old behavior.

In either case, the cure is the same. Check the preferences to make sure this doesn't happen again: In the General Preferences, make sure that When Scaling is set to Apply to Content (**Figure 11.27**). This is the default setting, and it prevents the double font size problem. However, you should know that if you change to Adjust Scaling Percentage, you'll see double font sizes, but scaled graphics frames will then display their correct scale factor in the Control panel. So you have to decide which annoys you the most: double font sizes or lying scale fields.

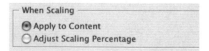

Figure 11.27 Apply to Content is the correct (and default) setting. Adjust Scaling Percentage results in two values for font size in a scaled frame.

To fix the double text value in the font size field, select the text frame (you may have to ungroup first if the text frame is part of a group), and then choose Redefine Scaling as 100 percent from the Transform panel menu (Window > Object & Layout > Transform; **Figure 11.28**), or from the Control panel menu. Switch to the Type tool, select some text, and check to see if you now have a single value for the font size. Heave a sigh of relief.

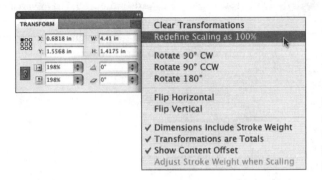

Figure 11.28 To fix double font sizes, select the text frame (not the text), and choose Redefine Scaling as 100 percent from the Transform panel menu, or from the Control panel menu.

Getting Smart

Neatness counts in page layout; that's why we have ruler guides and measurement read-outs to four decimal places in the Control panel. But with the Smart Guide features in InDesign CS4, you may find that you can forget creating ruler guides, but still keep your ducks (well, objects) in a row.

Smart Guides

The gray "flag" containing measurement information appears when you create a frame (**Figure 11.29**). At first it may seem annoying, but you quickly learn to ignore it if you don't need its information. When you create a frame near an existing frame, Smart Guides really shine: Subtle green arrows indicate when you've matched the height and width of a nearby frame. It's more intuitive than it sounds, and you'll soon grow fond of the guidance system.

As you're positioning objects in the page, subtle Smart Guides appear to let you know when you've arrived at the center of the page, or when the center of the object you're dragging aligns with the center of a nearby object. The Smart Guides aren't overwhelming; they're polite, not pushy.

Smart Guides can even help you rotate a frame to match the angle of an adjacent frame: Angle indicators appear in both frames when you've hit the mark (**Figure 11.30**).

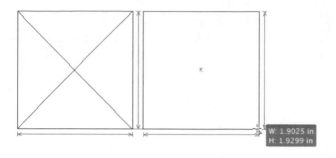

Figure 11.29 Smart Guides display width and height values, as well as subtle dimension hints to tell you when you've created a new object that aligns with an existing object. They even indicated when you've created an object of the same height and width as a nearby object.

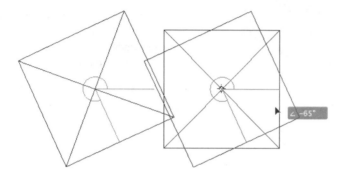

Figure 11.30 Smart Guides indicate when you've rotated an object to the same angle as a nearby object.

Smart Spacing

As you position objects near other objects, the Smart Spacing indicators kick in. If you want to position objects in a row so they are equal distances apart, of course, you can use the Distribute controls in the Align panel (Window > Object & Layout > Align). But the Smart Spacing indicators are more fun because they appear while you are positioning objects: When they show that the object is properly positioned, release the mouse button (**Figure 11.31**).

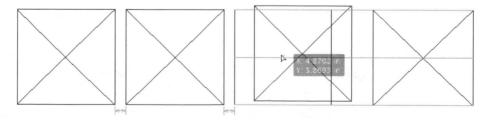

Figure 11.31 Smart Spacing indicators let you know when you've positioned an object so that its distance from an adjacent object is equal to spacing between nearby objects. This can actually become entertaining.

Smart Guide Preferences

To turn Smart Guides on or off, choose View > Grids & Guides > Smart Guides. A check by Smart Guides means they're turned on; click again to toggle Smart Guides off. You can control the behavior and appearance of Smart Guides in Preferences, under Guides & Pasteboard. By default, the Smart Guide indicators are Grid Green, but you can change the color of Smart Guides, selecting from a list that includes Lipstick and Cute Teal (who says software engineers don't have a sense of humor?).

You can also turn on or off the Align To Object Center, Align To Object Edge, Smart Dimensions, and Smart Spacing options, although we think you'll want to leave these options on. Smart Guides are merely visual assistants; they don't force you to snap to them, so they're useful without being intrusive.

Smart Text Reflow

While it isn't part of the Smart Guide arsenal, Smart Text Reflow is, well, smart. It allows InDesign to add new pages when a threaded story is threatened with overset text. By default, Smart Text Reflow only works with text frames based on master page text frames, but you can change that in Preferences. For Smart Text Reflow to become activated, your last text frame must be threaded to at least one other text frame (on a preceding page). If you're working in a long document, it might take a few seconds for the new page to be created and the text to be threaded to a new frame on the page. For those few seconds, you may see an error in the Preflight status indicator at the lower-left corner of the document window, but be patient; that will pass.

TRANSPARENCY

InDesign's ability to create transparent effects has great appeal for designers. It's easy to make objects translucent, feather the edges of vector components, and add drop shadows to *anything*. But the introduction of transparency in InDesign 2.0 caused printers to grumble. The short story is that transparency effects, such as blend modes and opacity settings, utilize an imaging model that goes beyond what PostScript understands. And since PostScript has long been the native tongue of imagesetters, platesetters, and many of our desktop printers, this presents a challenge. (While the increasing use of the Adobe PDF Print Engine in output devices solves transparency issues, not all devices are using the PDF Print Engine yet.) InDesign converts new-fangled transparency content to a form that can be correctly handled by PostScript devices by performing transparency flattening.

Flattening occurs during any of the following procedures:

- Choosing File > Print and then selecting a desktop printer or PostScript file as the target.

- Choosing File > Export and then selecting the EPS format.

- Choosing File > Export to create a PDF and then selecting Acrobat 4 (PDF 1.3) compatibility.

Transparency Flattening

Nothing *within* InDesign is flattened by Transparency Flattening. Your layers remain intact, and all transparency effects are still live. Instead, it's the output stream that is flattened. Content is cut apart, re-created, and reassembled in a form acceptable to PostScript (**Figure 11.32**). And this jigsaw puzzle will image as you expect—if you provide the correct ingredients and the right recipe.

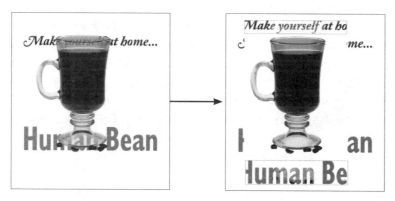

Figure 11.32 During print or export, InDesign starts with transparency involving graphics and text (left), then takes it apart, creating opaque stunt doubles (right) that look like the original effect. Note where the glass cup interacts with text: A text-shaped clipping path is created, which contains a generated image to portray the color interaction of the cup with the text.

Taking some relatively simple precautions when you build a document containing transparency will ensure that it produces predictable results when flattened and processed by a PostScript RIP. And there are some changes that print service providers must make to correctly handle transparent content. The following sections present some best practices for handling transparency as you create documents.

Put Text on Top

When text and vector elements fall beneath transparent elements in InDesign, those elements may be rasterized or converted to outlines during printing or exporting. Bring text and vector elements to the top of the pile, and they'll be safe from rasterization (well, until they hit the RIP). Putting such elements at the top of the stacking order should be sufficient. But it's not a bad idea to think in layers, just as a reminder of the issue (**Figure 11.33**).

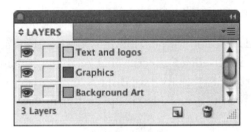

Figure 11.33 Placing text and vector art on a topmost layer ensures that such content will not be rasterized by interaction with any transparent content.

Choose the Appropriate Transparency Blend Space

As InDesign flattens transparent overlapping objects, it must create new objects to replace the overlap area (**Figure 11.34**). While this may sound like extra work, it's necessary as part of creating an output file that PostScript understands. To create the most faithful color in the replacement area, InDesign looks to the Transparency Blend Space setting to determine how it should do the color math. To control the Transparency Blend Space settings, choose Edit > Transparency Blend Space.

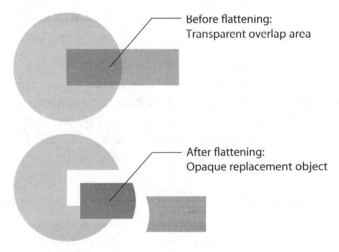

Before flattening:
Transparent overlap area

After flattening:
Opaque replacement object

Figure 11.34 It's easy to create interesting effects by using opacity settings and blend modes (top, before flattening). During the transparency-flattening process, InDesign creates replacement objects for overlapping areas (bottom, after flattening). The Transparency Blend Space needs to match the color space (RGB or CMYK) of the objects so that InDesign can properly match the color of the overlapping areas. It may look messy, but it's easily digested by devices that speak fluent PostScript.

The default setting for Transparency Blend Space is CMYK, and you should leave it that way for print. When generating a PDF for the Web or an onscreen presentation, you can reduce file size by choosing a PDF preset such as Smallest File Size, which uses the RGB color space. In that situation, change the Transparency Blend Space to RGB in keeping with the fact that content will become RGB in the outgoing PDF. This will result in a more satisfactory rendering of the color in overlapped areas in the resulting PDF.

Choose the Appropriate Transparency Flattener Preset

As InDesign performs flattening, it needs a recipe for generating two important components—rasterized text and vector art and soft-edged effects. That recipe is contained in the Transparency Flattener Preset (**Figure 11.35**). Before we discuss appropriate flattener settings, it's helpful to consider some of the functions that take place during flattening.

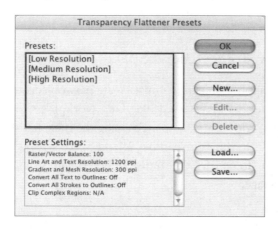

Figure 11.35 Transparency flattener presets are invoked during output or export to govern the generation of shadows and feathered effects. They also govern any necessary rasterizing of text and vector art. The default flattener presets in InDesign are only a starting point. Custom presets are necessary for proper imaging.

Rasterizing Text and Vector Content

The interaction of transparent images with text and vector art is one of the most challenging combinations to image. Text and vector content must sometimes be rasterized during export or output to satisfy PostScript requirements. While it may be disturbing to hear the words *rasterize* and *text* in the same sentence, rasterizing text is not inherently a bad thing (you are no doubt gasping in distaste as you read this). In truth, this rarely happens in most InDesign documents during export or print currently, but it's still helpful to know the rules.

But consider this: Your text and vector content *will* be rasterized eventually when it is processed by a RIP—a raster image processor. The RIP ultimately converts *everything* to pixels, but at such a high resolution (usually 2400 ppi or above) that pixels are not apparent in the output. So it isn't the rasterization process itself that's problematic. It's the choice of incorrect resolution during rasterization that can lead to undesirable results.

Similarly, when you scan signatures, maps, or drawings, you set the scanning resolution to a high value, such as 1200 ppi, to smoothly render drawn lines. Pixels are not apparent in the final artwork because of the high resolution. See? Pixels aren't a problem, as long as the resolution of an image is sufficient to fool the eye into seeing a smooth line.

Generating Shadows and Feathered Edges

All those festive drop shadows you're tempted to create in InDesign must be expressed in pixels. Similarly, feathering effects (Object > Feather) applied to InDesign objects or placed artwork are also accomplished with pixels. The feather and drop shadow aren't *literal* pixels until you export or print—they're just live effects for display until output makes them real. And the resolution of those effects is determined by the flattener preset chosen at the moment of export or print.

Appropriate Flattener Settings

To create and edit flattener presets, choose Edit > Transparency Flattener Presets. The dialog offers three default flattener presets, but since you're creating content for print, the Low and Medium resolution settings are fairly useless. To create a worthwhile flattener preset for print, select the High Resolution option as a starting point, and then click New (**Figure 11.36**).

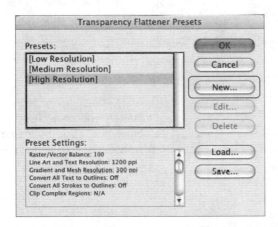

Figure 11.36 The default flattener presets are a bit like the Goldilocks fairy tale, except there's no "just right" setting. Start with High Resolution and then select New to create a custom style.

The two key values in the flattener options dialog are Line Art and Text Resolution and Gradient and Mesh Resolution. There isn't a one-size-fits-all transparency flattener setting. The settings should be dictated by the resolution of the output device.

The Line Art and Text Resolution option governs the rasterization of text and vector content. It should equal the resolution of the output device. For example, if you're printing to a desktop printer with a resolution of 600 ppi, set the Line Art Resolution to 600 ppi. On the other hand, a prepress technician preparing to generate PostScript for a 2400 ppi imagesetter would choose 2400 ppi, and so on. If you're creating PDF/X-1a files to send to a print service provider, ask them to give you specific instructions for creating a flattener preset. Be concerned if your contact responds, "Oh, I don't know. Just make a PDF." Push your way past that person, and ask to speak to a prepress technician for guidance.

The Gradient and Mesh Resolution value governs the generation of drop shadows and soft feathered edges created in InDesign. A prepress technician would usually choose 300 ppi for general output, although lower resolutions might be sufficient for low line-screen jobs such as newspaper work.

If you're printing to your 600 ppi desktop printer, 150 ppi is probably a sufficient gradient setting for printing comps. By the way, this setting has no effect on the resolution of placed images—only on the shadows and feathered edges generated by InDesign (**Figure 11.37**).

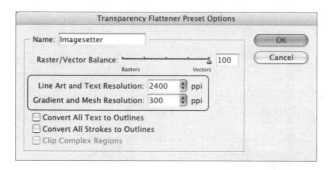

Figure 11.37 Flattener options should be in keeping with the resolution of the output device. For output on an imagesetter or platesetter, a typical setting might be 2400 ppi for line art and 300 ppi for gradients (top).

For a desktop printer with an imaging resolution of 600 ppi, the line-art resolution should be 600. Setting the gradient resolution to 150 saves a little time in the print process.

Invoking Transparency Flattener Presets

Although you may have created custom flattener presets, they don't actually *do* anything until you invoke them during print or export. You'll need to pick the proper flattener preset when you print, export an EPS, or generate a PDF with Acrobat 4 compatibility (**Figure 11.38**). Flattener presets are located in the Advanced section of print and export dialogs.

Figure 11.38 When exporting a PDF with Acrobat 4 compatibility, such as PDF/X-1a, select the appropriate flattener preset in the Advanced section of the Print and Export dialogs.

Chances are, you'll be invoking flattener presets in one of two situations—printing to your desktop printer and generating PDFs for submission to the print service provider. Revisit Figure 11.37 to see suggested settings for both of those situations: Your *actual* settings will depend on output resolution. We'll wait here while you look up your desktop printer resolution or while you're on hold, waiting to talk to a technician in the print service provider's prepress department so you can inquire about their RIP resolution.

Special Case: Spot Color Content

In addition to performing the jigsaw trickery of flattening during output or export, InDesign instructs some components to *overprint* in order to output objects using blending modes and other transparency effects, such as Multiply.

What is overprint? Here's a simple example: Create a solid yellow square, and then place a solid cyan circle on top of the yellow square. The cyan circle *knocks out* (covers up) the portion of the yellow square underneath it, because shapes are usually opaque in PostScript reality. Like pieces of construction paper, they completely cover up anything underneath them. However, if you set the cyan circle to overprint, it's no longer opaque. It allows the yellow square underneath to show through, and the overlap area becomes green (cyan plus yellow, as shown in **Figure 11.39**).

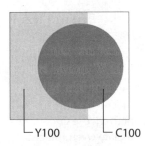
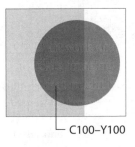

Y100   C100   C100–Y100

Figure 11.39 By default, opaque shapes knock out everything underneath (left). Overprinting allows a shape to intermix with everything underneath (right).

Overprint is not a complicated concept, and it's been part of PostScript forever. InDesign counts on the RIP and other applications to understand overprint in order to properly image transparency effects. If you display a flattened PDF containing a drop shadow (or other transparency effects) on top of spot-color areas in Acrobat, you'll be alarmed to see that the shadow has disappeared. Don't panic: Just turn on Overprint Preview in Acrobat and the display will be correct. Also, many desktop printers don't implement overprint, which is why you may see discolored boxes around drop shadows that fall on spot-color areas when you print on a desktop printer (**Figure 11.40**). It's just one of those things—you're just subject to the limitations of the device.

Figure 11.40 A drop shadow on a spot-color background (left) will not display correctly when a flattened exported PDF is viewed in Acrobat (center) if Overprint Preview is not turned on in Acrobat. If the InDesign document is printed on a desktop printer, it may show a discolored area around the shadow (right). This should not appear on film or plate output, and there are workarounds to eliminate the problem when printing to a desktop printer.

To eliminate (or at least subdue) this problem, make some changes in the Output tab of the Print dialog. Choose Composite CMYK and select the Simulate Overprint option (**Figure 11.41**).

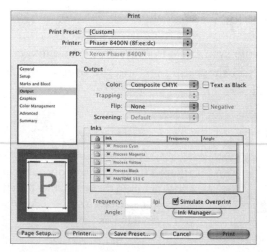

Figure 11.41 To subdue the dreaded discolored-box-under-a-shadow syndrome on a desktop printer, choose Composite CMYK and select the Simulate Overprint option.

Spot Colors and Transparency: Overprinting at the Print Service Provider

InDesign exploits the overprint capability of PostScript to allow shadows and other transparency effects to interact correctly with spot-color content. If you intend to print spot colors, you certainly don't want to convert spot colors to process on your final print job to avoid problems in output, and you don't have to. To correctly render shadows and other transparency effects that interact with spot-color areas, the print service provider will have to enable PostScript overprint on the RIP (in the past, it was usually turned off). This isn't something you can do from within InDesign. It's the responsibility of the prepress department to make this change. But it's helpful for you to know, so that you can communicate with the print service provider. Different RIP vendors label the function slightly differently, but the gist of it is, "Hey! Honor any PostScript overprint instructions!"

Note that, just as correct rendering of overprinting is crucial to imaging transparent effects correctly, being able to *preview* overprinting is necessary for correct display of such content on a monitor. By default, Adobe Acrobat does not show overprinting effects, but you can turn on this feature in Acrobat 9 Professional by choosing Advanced > Print Production > Output Preview, and then selecting the Simulate Overprint option. Adobe Reader also offers overprint preview, but the setting is lurking in Preferences > Page Display. Note that the Macintosh OS X application Preview cannot display overprint in PDF files. By default, Acrobat 9 Professional will automatically display overprinting objects if the PDF meets PDF/X-1a specifications or if the Acrobat preferences have been set to automatically display overprint, regardless of the PDF spec of the file.

Drop Shadows: The Sun Never Moves

In the real world, if you rotate a box sitting on a table, the shadow doesn't rotate with the box because the light source remains stationary. The same rules apply in InDesign; its imaginary sun doesn't move either. If you rotate objects, their shadows do not rotate with them. In home-brewed imposition, for example **Figure 11.42** a shadow's relationship with its parent object will change. In the example, the SmithcoMatic logo is supposed to have a drop shadow that's positioned down and to the right of the logo. However, rotating the art 180 degrees causes the shadow to be positioned *up* and to the *left* of the art. Oops.

Figure 11.42 This looks fine, doesn't it? Try standing on your head, and you'll see what's wrong with this picture: The shadow's relationship with the logos is incorrect in the rotated artwork.

The only cure is to manually change the position of the shadow by choosing Object > Drop Shadow, and then entering a new value for the shadow position (**Figure 11.43**). In the example, the correct shadow position is .04 of an inch for both X and Y offsets. To correct for the rotation, the shadow for the rotated artwork is set to -.04 of an inch for both X and Y offsets (that's a minus sign in front of the number, indicating a negative value).

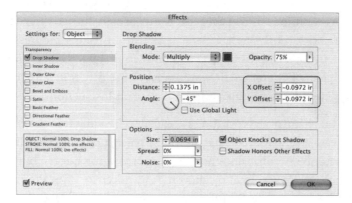

Figure 11.43 To compensate for InDesign's single-sun approach to drop shadows, you may have to alter the X and Y Offset values for rotated objects (for example, during manual imposition).

FINDING & FIXING PROBLEMS

InDesign provides a number of tools that are useful when you're playing "What's wrong with this picture?" before you send your job to the print service provider. Several tools help you spot problems visually, and the new Live Preflight feature can alert you to problems the instant they arise.

Forensic Tools

However careful you might be while you're creating an InDesign document, it's easy to develop blind spots when you're trying to find mistakes. Let InDesign help you find problems that are easy to overlook.

Preview Mode (View > Screen Mode > Preview) simplifies your view of the document, hiding any nonprinting objects such as guides, frame edges, and hidden text characters so that you can concentrate on content. You can toggle the Preview mode among four states: Normal, Preview, Bleed, and Slug. But you can easily toggle between the two most common states, Normal and Preview, just by pressing the W key on your keyboard. In addition to simplifying your view, Preview mode will hide any images or other elements that have been assigned a nonprinting attribute in the Attributes panel (Window > Attributes). If you've set an object to nonprinting while you experiment with your design, its disappearance in Preview mode serves as a reminder to fix the attribute or delete the object.

Overprint Preview (View > Overprint Preview) can be used to confirm that you've set objects to overprint. But perhaps more importantly, you can use it to catch common problems. For example, white objects set to overprint will disappear during output, and they'll disappear during Overprint Preview as well. Why is this? W*hite* in illustration and page layout applications just signifies "this is blank paper—no ink prints here." The rare exception would be a literal white ink created for printing on metallic surfaces or clear substrates. What kind of a fiend would set a white object to overprint? Oh, nobody does it intentionally. It's usually the result of creating a black object, such as a logo, in a drawing program and then setting it to overprint. Subsequently changing the object's fill to white does not turn off the overprint attribute. Illustrator displays a tiny yellow alert triangle in the Attributes panel if you change an overprinting object to white, but it's easily overlooked.

Overprint Preview also provides a more realistic representation of blending modes applied to spot-color objects. The default view mode in InDesign doesn't always correctly represent the effect of blending modes (**Figure 11.44**).

Activating Overprint Preview also turns on High Resolution Display, so you may experience slower performance in a graphics-heavy document. When you're finished using Overprint Preview, you may want to turn it off to speed up performance.

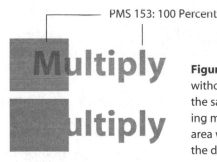

PMS 153: 100 Percent

Figure 11.44 It's impossible to have 200 percent of a single ink without a second printing plate. But if you create two objects with the same 100-percent spot fill, and then apply the Multiply blending mode (top), InDesign's display implies that the overlapping area will be darker. But turn on Overprint Preview (bottom), and the display tells the true story.

Flattener Preview (Window > Output > Flattener Preview) uses red highlighting for text and vector content that may be rasterized during the output process (**Figure 11.45**). Notice the word *may*. During printing or a direct export to PDF, InDesign performs engineering feats to avoid rasterizing such content. However, some workflows that break imaging files into separate linework and image components, such as Scitex or Rampage systems, may treat text areas as image content if the text interacts with transparency effects.

Figure 11.45 The Flattener Preview uses red highlighting (here, represented by solid black) to indicate potential text and vector rasterization.

The **Component Information** dialog (**Figure 11.46**) provides a peek under the hood of your copy of InDesign, as well as a glimpse of a document's life story. In Windows, hold down the Control key as you choose About InDesign from the Help menu. On the Macintosh, hold down the Command key and choose About InDesign from the InDesign menu.

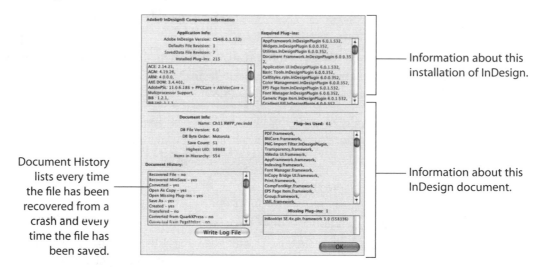

Information about this installation of InDesign.

Information about this InDesign document.

Document History lists every time the file has been recovered from a crash and every time the file has been saved.

Figure 11.46 The Component Information box provides details about the application itself as well as the currently active open document.

The top part of the dialog shows information about the current version of InDesign (Figure 11.46 shows version 6.0.1.532) and the active plug-ins. This may be useful if you need help from Adobe tech support, since you'll need to provide the current version and other environmental information when you call.

The bottom part of the dialog displays information about the active InDesign document, including the very useful Document History, which constitutes a personal diary of the document. You'll see whether the document was converted from QuarkXPress or PageMaker, whether it's been recovered after a crash, and how many times it's been saved (including the versions and platforms in effect during the saves). Would you ever be this nosy about a file? Well, if it's neurotic—crashing frequently or just plain acting strange—take a look at the Document History. If the file has had a traumatic childhood, it may be worth exporting it to InDesign Interchange or InDesign Markup (IDML) as a purification ritual. Then, open the Interchange or IDML file and make a new start.

Info Panel

Often overlooked, the Info panel (Window > Info) provides valuable information about image and text content (**Figure 11.47**). Select an image frame, and the Info panel displays color space such as RGB, CMYK, or Grayscale, along with the effective resolution in ppi. *Effective* resolution is the *actual* resolution of the placed image, which is a product of the original scanned resolution and any scaling. For example, a 300 ppi image scaled to 200 percent in InDesign has an effective resolution of 150 ppi, which would be inadequate for standard 133–150 lpi printing.

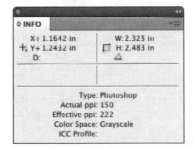 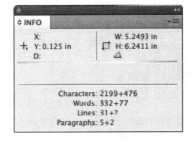

Figure 11.47 The Info panel shows the color space and resolution of a selected image (left) and alerts you if there is overset text for a selected story (right). Numbers after the plus sign indicate overset text.

You can click in a text frame, and the Info panel will tell you if there is overset text at the end of the story, even if the end of the story text is many pages downstream. In Figure 11.46, the entry "Words: 332+77" indicates that there are 77 words in overset text. The entry "Lines: 31+?" indicates that there are 31 lines of visible text, but InDesign declines to speculate on the number of lines in overset text, since that text is "frameless." However, it does report the number of overset paragraphs.

Live Preflight

The Preflight feature was completely revamped for CS4, and now constantly monitors the state of the document, checking it against a set of user-specified preflight rules. InDesign ships with a basic, bare-bones preflight profile, but you might want to create a more ambitious custom profile. If your print service provider or a publication gives you a custom preflight profile, use that profile to ensure that you're meeting their requirements.

Since preflight is dynamic, you can fix problems as soon as they occur if you'll train yourself to keep an eye on the constantly updated Preflight status in the lower-left corner of the document window (**Figure 11.48**).

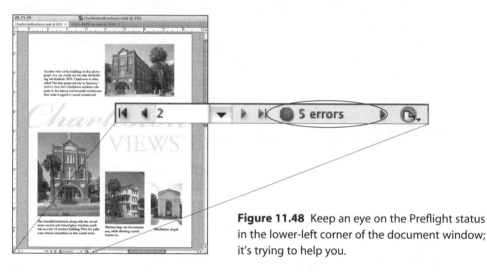

Figure 11.48 Keep an eye on the Preflight status in the lower-left corner of the document window; it's trying to help you.

Our habit is to just pay attention to what's going on in the center of the screen, but it's worth developing the habit of glancing down to make sure the light's still green. If the light turns red, stop working, and check the report in the Preflight panel. You can double-click the status area in the corner of the document window, or choose Window > Output > Preflight.

The Preflight panel (**Figure 11.49**) details all violations of the current preflight profile. Click on a hyperlinked page number to jump to the error in the document.

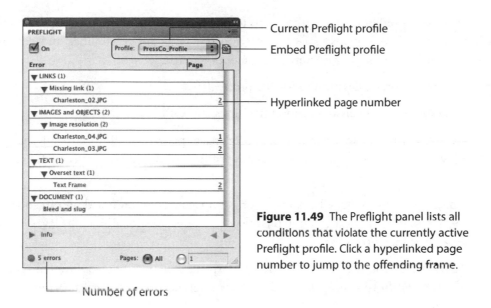

Current Preflight profile

Embed Preflight profile

Hyperlinked page number

Figure 11.49 The Preflight panel lists all conditions that violate the currently active Preflight profile. Click a hyperlinked page number to jump to the offending frame.

Number of errors

Creating a Custom Preflight Profile

The basic preflight profile is sort of anemic: It only checks for missing or modified links, missing fonts, and overset text. You can't modify the default basic profile, so if you want to customize the preflight options (and you should), you have to create a custom profile.

Open the Preflight panel (Window > Output > Preflight), and then choose Define Profiles from the panel menu. Click the plus icon under the left column of the dialog, name the new profile, and begin modifying the settings (**Figure 11.50**).

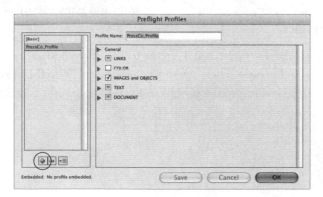

Figure 11.50 Click on the "plus" icon to create and edit a new custom preflight profile.

The extensive preflight options allow you to be very granular when creating the preflight recipe. Explore the options to familiarize yourself with the possibilities and determine what's appropriate for your document. The options include:

- **General:** Enter a description for the profile.

- **Links:** Check for missing or modified links and OPI links.

- **Color:** Check for transparency blending space; plates not allowed; color spaces not allowed; overprinting in InDesign; overprinting white objects; warn if Registration color has been used.

- **Images and Objects:** Check for incorrect image resolution based on thresholds you specify (color, grayscale, and 1-bit images); nonproportional scaling; layer visibility overrides; bleed/trim hazard.

- **Text:** Check for style overrides; dynamic spelling errors; nonproportional type scaling; minimum type size; out-of-date cross-references; conditional text indicators set to print.

- **Document:** Check for page size/orientation; blank page status; bleed and slug setup. Note, however, that you will not be warned if an object has insufficient bleed; you're only warned if no bleed is defined for the document.

Once you've set up the preflight options, click OK to save the profile. Then, in the main Preflight panel, choose the new profile from the Profile drop-down menu to make it the active profile. You can even embed a profile in a document to ensure that the recipient is playing by the correct rules, by clicking the embedding icon next to the Profile drop-down menu in the main Preflight panel window. To delete a preflight profile, choose Define Profiles from the Preflight panel menu, select the profile name, and click the minus sign icon underneath the list of profiles.

Choose Preflight Options from the Preflight panel menu to specify whether to use the prevailing profile or the embedded profile when opening a document; whether Preflight should check all layers, just visible layers, or just visible and printable layers; and whether nonprinting objects should be included.

Importing and Sharing a Preflight Profile

If your print service provider sends a custom profile, import it and use it as your working preflight profile. You might want to supply a custom profile to collaborators or contributors, to help them submit healthy files (or at least to remove any excuse for not doing so). To import a new preflight profile, choose Define Profiles from the Preflight Profiles panel menu, choose Load Profile from the easy-to-overlook tiny drop-down menu beneath the list of profiles, and navigate to the new profile; look for a file with the file extension *.idpp*. To export a preflight profile, select the profile name in the list and choose Export Profile from the drop-down menu. You can also choose Embed Profile to embed the selected preflight profile in the current document (**Figure 11.51**).

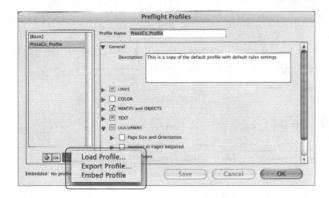

Figure 11.51 To import or export a preflight profile, choose Load or Export from the small drop-down menu beneath the list of profiles.

Packaging the File

InDesign's Package function (File > Package) copies all necessary fonts and art files into a folder for job submission—under most circumstances. However, if you're using Multiple Master fonts, you'll have to manually package any font instances you've created, because InDesign packages only the parent font. For example, if you've created and used Myriad MM 700 BD 600 NO, InDesign packages only the Myriad MM. While Multiple Master fonts were a great concept, this sort of challenge may inspire you to avoid them. You're also warned in the Package dialog that InDesign will not package CJK (Chinese, Japanese, Korean) fonts.

If you've created any text layers in Photoshop and placed the image as a native PSD into InDesign, fonts will not be packaged. It's preferable to save such images as Photoshop PDF files anyway, since fonts can be embedded, and vector edges remain sharp when imaged from Photoshop PDFs placed in InDesign.

It's a good idea to check the Preflight status of the document before you package. While the Package dialog will highlight any errors, it's easier to jump to errors from within the Preflight panel report. Once you've cleaned house, launch the Package function. InDesign copies fonts and artwork rather than moving them. The resulting package folder contains:

- A new copy of the InDesign file.

- A Fonts folder containing the necessary fonts (with the above Multiple Master, CJK, and Photoshop exceptions).

- A Links folder containing all linked graphics files. Note that InDesign will not package any images linked to a placed Illustrator file; you'll have to gather those manually or embed them in the Illustrator file.

- An Instructions text file that lists contents of the Links and Fonts folders.

You should add one more thing: Create a PDF/X-1a from the InDesign file and include that in the package folder as a reference for the print service provider.

PDF CREATION METHODS

There are multiple methods for generating PDF files from InDesign files.

- **Export to PDF:** You'll be happy to know that the easy way is usually the best way—how often does *that* happen? A PDF file generated via InDesign's direct export (File > Export, and choose Adobe PDF as the export format) is as digestible as one created by distilling PostScript. And, most important, there's less chance of vector and text content being rasterized during a direct export. Like Illustrator and Photoshop, InDesign contains the necessary resources to create PDF files without invoking Acrobat Distiller. Unless your recipient instructs you otherwise, use File > Export, and then choose the PDF/X-1a setting.

- **Print to Adobe PDF:** By default, this approach uses Distiller as the target printer, following the PDF job options last used by Distiller. However, you can change those settings by clicking the Printer button at the bottom of the Print dialog. In the dialog that follows, change Printer to Adobe PDF, and then click the Copies & Pages list and select PDF Options. Then you'll be able to choose from the full range of Distiller job options from the Adobe PDF Settings list. There's rarely a reason to use this method to create a PDF: Transparency is flattened, and it's the long way around.

- **Acrobat Distiller:** Generate PostScript by selecting File > Print, and then selecting PostScript File for the printer. For PPD (PostScript Printer Definition), choose Adobe PDF unless instructed otherwise. Use Acrobat Distiller to convert the PostScript to PDF. Whereas this long-winded approach was previously recommended to minimize CID (Character ID) font encoding, you'll achieve equivalent results by exporting from InDesign. You may still encounter instances of CID font encoding in a directly exported or distilled PDF, since some glyphs must be CID-encoded regardless of the method of PDF creation. Current RIPs shouldn't have any difficulty with the fully compliant PDFs created by using File > Export.

- **Save As PDF (Mac only):** The Macintosh operating system offers a built-in approach to creating PDF files. You'll encounter a Save As PDF option in Print dialogs in OS X 10.3.9 and earlier. In 10.4 and later, you'll see just a PDF button. While this method is acceptable for PDF files intended for a quick-and-dirty email attachment, it does *not* offer appropriate controls for making a print-ready PDF file.

To sum up, direct export from InDesign is the preferred method unless the file recipient specifically instructs you otherwise. And it's worth asking "Why?" if they ask that you go the PostScript-and-Distiller route. You may find that they're open to changing their old-fashioned thinking once they discover that their systems fully support directly exported PDFs.

PDF CREATION SETTINGS

If you're asked to submit PDF files, that request should be accompanied by specifications for creating an appropriate PDF for the recipient's workflow. If you're told, "Uh, I don't know. Just make a PDF," the person on the other end of the phone may not be of any help.

It's important to know that the P in PDF stands for *portable*, not for *perfect*. It's possible to make a bad PDF, so barring any specific guidance, it's good to know that InDesign provides reliable recipes for common circumstances:

- **Smallest File Size** is appropriate for PDFs that are to be emailed or posted online. This setting resamples raster images to 100 ppi, applies aggressive compression, and converts all images to RGB while retaining spot colors. This generates a file that is inappropriate for commercial printing and results in color shifts that may adversely alter the appearance of the PDF onscreen. The PDF is compatible with Acrobat 5.0—transparency is not flattened.

- **High Quality Print** is meant for printing on a desktop printer. Images are down-sampled to 300 ppi and compressed with the Maximum quality setting. RGB images are not converted to CMYK, but existing CMYK and spot-color content is maintained, and the PDF is compatible with Acrobat 5.0.

- **Press Quality** is similar to High Quality Print, but it uses InDesign's current color management settings to convert any RGB content to CMYK on the fly, while retaining any spot content. While this setting generates a healthy PDF, its compatibility with Acrobat 5.0 may cause some problems with older devices. It places you at the mercy of someone else's approach to transparency flattening.

- **PDF/X-1a:2001** is your best choice when you're given no specifications for PDF file creation. Any RGB images are converted to CMYK during PDF generation, spot-color content is maintained, and the compatibility with Acrobat 4.0 will render the PDF well behaved on a wide variety of devices.

- **PDF/X-3:2002** is intended for use in a color-managed workflow. Color profiles are embedded in the PDF, and RGB content is not converted to CMYK. Don't use this setting unless specifically instructed to do so. These PDF files are compatible with Acrobat 4.0—any transparency content is flattened in the process of generating the PDF.

- **PDF/X-4:2008** is intended for use in a color-managed workflow that supports live, unflattened transparency. If the print service provider is using RIPs that implement the Adobe PDF Print Engine, they should support this flavor of PDF. Going forward, you can expect more service providers to accept this more modern format.

CHAPTER TWELVE

Acrobat Production Tips

In 1991, Dr. John Warnock, one of the cofounders of Adobe Systems, proposed Project Camelot, in which he suggested using the graphics and imaging operators of PostScript to create portable documents that could be displayed and printed on any computer, regardless of the originating application. These documents would contain all the resources necessary to represent the original document for display and printing. Images and vector art would be crisp. Regardless of operating system or computer platform, fonts would be embedded, ensuring that text would be readable and line breaks would be preserved—even if recipients didn't have the same fonts as the document's creator. Sound familiar?

Thus, what came to be known as Adobe Acrobat was intended to create what might be called digital carbon copies for office document interchange and storage. But a funny thing happened in the graphic arts world. We discovered that converting stubborn documents to Portable Document Format (PDF) files often made them more manageable as print jobs. For example, while Microsoft Word allows you to add festive clip art and other decorative bits such as Word Art to documents, it's really intended for word processing. Turning a Word file into something suitable for printing in two spot colors might require that you generate a PDF, then open that PDF in Adobe Acrobat Professional and use the PitStop plug-in from Enfocus (*www.enfocus.com*) to deconstruct the artwork, fix the things that fell apart during the conversion, and then assign the correct printing colors. It may seem like the long way around, but at least you'd have something that could be printed as intended.

Fast-forward to current day. Many publications and print service providers request that you submit your jobs as PDF files to eliminate the need to send a combination of page-layout files, support artwork files, and the necessary fonts. While this simplifies job submission, it also shifts the responsibility for more of the job's quality control to the shoulders of the person making the PDF file. That would be *you*.

ACROBAT PRODUCT LINE

Currently the Acrobat family consists of four products, each having a specific target audience:

- **Acrobat 9 Standard** is intended primarily for creating PDFs from office applications. Consequently, it lacks the print-oriented preflighting and repair tools found in the professional product. However, it does allow users to participate in comment and review processes, and allows users to rights-enable PDFs for commenting and form-filling by Reader users. Acrobat Standard also includes Acrobat Distiller for converting PostScript to PDFs.

- **Acrobat 9 Pro** provides extensive tools for creating PDF files from images, text files, Microsoft Office files, and Web pages. When you install Acrobat 9 Pro, it adds PDF export functionality to Microsoft Office applications, so you can create PDF files from within an open Microsoft Word file, for example. Acrobat 9 Pro enables you to initiate and participate in comment and review cycles, and contains tools for creating forms and adding interactivity to PDF files. The print production tools make it valuable in design and prepress environments. It's the most popular and widely used version of Acrobat. Acrobat 9 Pro also includes Acrobat Distiller for converting PostScript to PDFs.

- **Acrobat 9 Pro Extended** (available for Windows only) includes all the features of Acrobat 9 Pro and adds PDF export functionality to 3D applications such as SolidWorks. It also supports drag-and-drop PDF creation for many CAD files. Acrobat 9 Pro Extended includes Adobe Presenter, for converting PowerPoint content to Flash-based presentations, and Adobe 3D Reviewer.

- **Adobe Reader 9** is the free PDF viewer. Previously, Reader users could do only what the name implies—read (and print) PDFs. But now they can participate in comment–and–review processes, and save filled-out Acrobat forms if a PDF has been specially rights-enabled from within Acrobat 9 Pro. Reader cannot create PDF files.

Don't be confused by the selections in the Acrobat family. For those of us in the graphic arts who need to manipulate PDF files, the appropriate version to use is Acrobat 9 Pro.

WHERE DO PDFS COME FROM?

Acrobat isn't like drawing or page-layout applications; it's intended for modifying PDFs. PDF files begin life somewhere else, outside of Acrobat. While Acrobat enables you to create PDFs from a scanner, an existing image, or a Web page, they're often exported from other applications such as Adobe InDesign or Illustrator. They may be the result of generating a PostScript file and feeding that to Distiller, or they may be created by some other proprietary process, such as the Global Graphics Jaws interpreter used by QuarkXPress 6.0 and later.

Although Adobe Systems originated the PDF concept and its specifications, anyone is allowed to use the information in the publicly available PDF Reference to write software that creates, reads, or edits PDF files. Given that the PDF Reference is in excess of 1000 pages, it's clearly not a trivial undertaking.

All PDF-creation solutions are not the same. Some third-party implementations of the PDF specifications, such as those used to generate PDF files from non-Adobe applications, may not fully utilize all the features possible in a PDF file. This is not to imply that non-Adobe methods of creating PDFs are inferior. On the contrary, some commonly used PDF creation tools, such as the Global Graphics Jaws Interpreter, create perfectly good PDF files. But non-Adobe applications may have slightly different controls or options, which makes it challenging to generalize about how, exactly, to go about making a PDF file. For that matter, not all Adobe applications use the same approach when making PDFs, although they all share the common PDF Library.

CREATING PDF FILES

The chapters on Illustrator, InDesign, and Adobe Photoshop have offered some suggested PDF-creation settings, but it may be helpful to consider what's important regardless of the tool you're using to create PDF files.

Determining Which Type of PDF You Should Create

To use a very basic definition, a document consists of images, text, lines, and color areas on a page of a certain size. The purpose of creating a PDF is to retain all of these components of the document across multiple operating systems and to ensure that it can be printed as intended. It all sounds so simple, doesn't it? However, there isn't a single, one-size-fits-all recipe for creating PDF files. Broadly speaking, there are several types of PDF files you're likely to create.

- PDF files to be submitted to a print service provider should be generated from page–layout or drawing applications after carefully checking content and job requirements. Images need to be high resolution, which can result in large file sizes. Fonts must be embedded correctly, and it's important to properly define your colors as CMYK, color-managed RGB, or spot color. Think of this as a hermetically sealed, final job file, and don't count on editing it to perfection later.

- PDFs for email (for example, for commenting and review) will require that you sacrifice image quality in the interest of smaller files, but font embedding must still be handled correctly to ensure accurate display and printing.

- PDF files that will be posted online need to be small enough for downloading, but documents such as product brochures or instructional manuals should contain enough image detail to make them satisfactory resources. You'll have to reach a compromise between desired image quality and reasonable file size. You might consider breaking larger documents into smaller chapters, and then hyperlinking the files together to aid the end user in finding their way.

- PDF files intended for distribution on CD/DVD can be larger files since downloading isn't an issue, so you don't have to compromise image quality. You might even consider adding multimedia content and extensive hyperlinking to enrich the files. While such features take you beyond a purely print environment, you can easily start with print-ready PDF files, and bring them to life with Acrobat's built-in multimedia capabilities. For more on the lively possibilities of adding movies, sounds, and interactivity to PDFs, check out *Dynamic Media: Music, Video, Animation, and the Web in Adobe PDF* by Bob Connolly (Peachpit Press, 2006).

PDF Settings and Some Important Standards

The default PDF-creation settings that are available in the Creative Suite applications include a wide spectrum of presets for generating PDF files (**Table 12.1**). Settings such as Standard, Smallest File Size, and Press Quality give some hint of what kind of PDF file they're intended to create. The PDF/X and PDF/A settings are based on standards intended to ensure that a PDF behaves as expected. The X in PDF/X-1a stands for "exchange," signifying that a PDF complying with one of the PDF/X standards can be exchanged between the PDF's originator and recipients with some assurance the recipient will get a usable file. The PDF/A settings are based on standards geared toward long-term archiving and retrieval of electronic files (hence the "A").

A core set of PDF settings is stored in a common repository and shared among all Adobe applications: A new PDF setting created in InDesign will also be available in Illustrator, Photoshop, and Distiller automatically. But there are a few settings that are available only to a single application, such as Illustrator's Default setting or Distiller's Oversized Pages setting.

Table 12.1 PDF Creation Settings Across the Creative Suite.

Setting	PDF Version	Downsample/ Threshold[1]	Compression Image Quality	Color Policy	Available to Application				Description
					Illustrator	Photoshop	InDesign	Distiller	
Smallest File Size	5.0	100/150	Low	Convert to sRGB	✔	✔	✔	✔	Onscreen display and email
Standard	5.0	150/225	Med	Convert to sRGB				✔	Viewing and printing business documents
High Quality Print	5.0	300/450	Max	Leave Unchanged	✔	✔	✔	✔	Viewing and printing design documents
Press Quality	5.0	300/450	Max	Convert to CMYK	✔	✔	✔	✔	For prepress
PDF/X-1a:2001	4.0	300/450	Max	Convert to CMYK	✔	✔	✔	✔	For prepress. Defines TrimBox,[2] BleedBox[3]
PDF/X 3:2002	4.0	300/450	Max	Leave Unchanged	✔	✔	✔	✔	Use in color-managed workflows
PDF/X-4:2008	5.0	300/450	Max	Leave Unchanged	✔	✔	✔		Use in color-managed workflows. Retains live transparency
PDF/A-1b:2005 (RGB)	5.0	300/450	Max	Convert to sRGB				✔	For archive
PDF/A-1b:2005 (CMYK)	5.0	300/450	Max	Convert to CMYK				✔	For archive
Oversized Pages	7.0	150/225	Med	Convert to sRGB				✔	Supports engineering drawings larger than 200" by 200"
Illustrator Default	6.0	None	ZIP	Leave Unchanged	✔				Maintains layers; can roundtrip to Illustrator

[1] Downsampling reduces image resolution. Threshold is the resolution above which Distiller will downsample image content.

[2] TrimBox is the trim edge of the document, based on the originating file.

[3] BleedBox is the edge of defined bleed, based on information in the originating file.

The Digital Distribution of Advertising for Publications (DDAP) association established requirements for print-ready PDFs for advertisement submission, which were then implemented by the Committee for Graphic Arts Technologies Standards (CGATS) as the basis of the PDF/X standards. (Was that enough acronyms for you?) With the constant increase in the numbers of PDF files submitted for advertising, the PDF/X standards are intended to streamline file submission.

The most commonly requested PDF format for print in the United States is PDF/X-1a. (The *2001* appellation you see in Acrobat 9 Pro is added because PDF/X is an evolving standard.) To comply with the PDF/X-1a specification, a PDF file must meet the following requirements:

- Images must be CMYK or spot color (no RGB or LAB images).

- Fonts must be embedded and subset. Subsetting embeds only the characters needed in the PDF file and assigns a special name to the font content so that an output device will not substitute another font for it.

- The trim edges of pages must be explicitly defined. Internally, a PDF file refers to this information as *TrimBox*.

- The bleed limits must be explicitly defined. Internally, this is called *BleedBox*.

The PDF/X-3 is a specification intended for use in a color-managed workflow: It's more common in Europe than in the United States. The stipulations are similar to those for PDF/X-1a, with the exception that image content can be RGB or Lab tagged with color profiles. Unless you and your print service provider are using color management, you're unlikely to be asked to submit PDF/X-3 files. PDF/X-4 allows color-managed RGB content, and retains live transparency: This type of PDF would be appropriate in a workflow that is based on the Adobe PDF Print Engine. And PDF/A-1b indicates an emerging PDF standard for archiving documents for reference long into the future. The *A* represents *archive*.

Export vs. Distiller

Because all of the Creative Suite applications speak fluent PDF, it's possible to directly export PDF files from InDesign, Illustrator, and Photoshop without using Distiller. If you wish to retain layers, live transparency, or interactivity, you *have* to export rather than use Distiller. Some print service providers or publications may insist that you take the Distiller route, but that sentiment is largely built on old wive's tales about creating PDFs. Since exporting is faster and easier than using Distiller, it's worth having a conversation with file recipients to find out why you're being asked to take the long way around. Ask them to test an exported PDF created to their specifications, and then you'll both know what really works.

Acrobat Distiller

Distiller's purpose is to convert PostScript to PDF. Period. Create a PostScript file by printing or exporting PostScript from an application (using Adobe PDF as the target printer), and then drag and drop the PostScript file onto the Distiller window. Distiller uses the settings currently selected in the application. You can also open a PostScript file through File > Open on the Distiller menu. Distiller will process EPS files as well, provided you have the necessary fonts on your computer (or they're embedded in the EPS file). If you've fed a healthy PostScript file to Distiller and chosen the correct job option, you'll watch the progress bar fill up, and soon you'll have a PDF file. If you've dragged multiple PostScript files into Distiller, they'll be listed in the queue box at the bottom of the Distiller window, in which you can reorder, cancel, or pause queued jobs.

Distiller isn't very flashy. When you launch the application, all that appears is a floating window that looks like a disembodied dialog (**Figure 12.1**). There are no tool panels or other obvious controls. But there's much more than meets the eye. Some of the menu commands are way up at the top of the monitor on the Macintosh in the standard location for menu commands in Macintosh applications, but they are seemingly completely separate from the floating window that you see. Distiller's presentation on Windows is a bit more sensible—the menu commands are right on the top rim of the Distiller window.

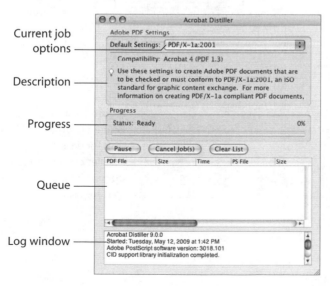

Figure 12.1 Acrobat Distiller may not look complicated when you open it, but there's a powerful PDF-generating engine under the hood. Select a preset PDF recipe from the Default Settings list, or create your own job options by choosing Settings > Edit Adobe PDF Settings from the menu at the top of your computer screen on the Macintosh (not shown here) or the top edge of the Distiller window (Windows).

As each PDF is created, a small PDF icon appears next to its name in the list. Double-click the entry in the queue window, and the PDF file opens in Acrobat (great if you're not sure where you saved the file). If Distiller can't create a PDF file, the log at the bottom of the Distiller window will contain an explanation of the problem, although it doesn't contain any suggestions to help you.

There are two other doorways into Distiller…

First, if you need to convert more than the occasional PostScript file, you may wish to create what's called a *watched folder*, which allows you to batch-distill multiple PostScript files. This is especially useful if you need to convert many PostScript files with the same Distiller settings. Note that the software license for Distiller dictates that you are to use it to process PostScript files only for yourself or for others who also own a license for Distiller.

To create a watched folder, first create a folder to be used as the target folder. Then, choose Settings > Watched Folders from the Distiller menu (remember, it's way up at the top of your monitor on the Mac). In the Watched Folder window (**Figure 12.2**), click Add Folder, and then navigate to the folder you created to earmark the folder to be watched by Distiller.

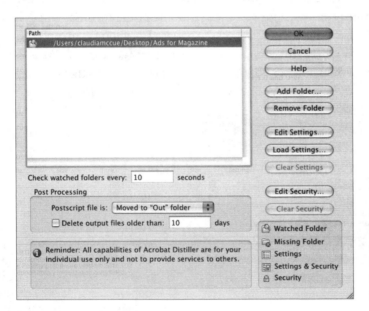

Figure 12.2 The Watched Folder window includes controls for designating folders for Distiller processing as well as options for editing the settings that are used.

By default, the PostScript files will be processed using the current settings in Distiller. However, you can modify these settings by clicking the Edit Settings button and then modifying the settings options. You can choose to delete the PostScript files once they're converted to PDF files or have Distiller move the PostScript files into another folder after processing. When you click the OK button, Distiller will create two folders inside your watched folder. One is the *In* folder, where you'll drop the PostScript files to be processed. The other folder created is the *Out* folder, where Distiller will place the finished PDF files (and the processed PostScript files, if you choose that option). Note that you must drop PostScript files directly into the *In* folder, not just loose into the enclosing watched folder.

The other doorway to Distiller is the Acrobat "printer," named Adobe PDF 9, that's created on your system during Acrobat installation. (Depending on the version of Acrobat installed, the name you see may be slightly different, but you should be able to recognize it easily.) Printing to this target printer generates PostScript and immediately awakens Distiller (albeit hidden in the background) to process it using the last settings that were selected in Distiller. However, depending on the application from which you are printing, the Print dialog may allow you to select other job options without opening Distiller first.

How do you select the right settings for a print-ready PDF? It's best if your print service provider gives you definite specifications for creating a PDF that fits their workflow. Better yet, if your print service provider supplies preferred PDF settings, import the settings into one of the Creative Suite applications to make the settings available to all the applications.

Lacking such guidance, you're almost always safe choosing PDF/X-1a as a start, and then making one minor modification: Make sure that you choose to retain any bleed. Double-check the Marks and Bleed options when generating a PDF from Illustrator or InDesign to ensure that sufficient bleed is included. Photoshop will automatically include the entire image; it doesn't have a concept of bleed.

Even If You're Not Using Distiller…

However you're creating PDF files — whether you're exporting, using Distiller, printing to the Adobe PDF printer, or using some other, proprietary solution — the issues are the same. You have to know how to handle image compression and resampling, font embedding and subsetting, color space, and Acrobat version compatibility. So, although the next few sections are geared toward using Distiller to create PDFs, please view the following pages as a general roadmap to PDF creation issues regardless of the method you're using.

All the Creative Suite applications offer PDF/X presets. But if the PDF-export function in a non-Adobe application doesn't offer named versions of PDF settings, how can you create a PDF that is compliant with the PDF/X-1a specification? It's not difficult, but you need to stick to some basics:

- Set compatibility to Acrobat 4.0. While this may seem old-fashioned given that Acrobat at this writing is at version 9.0, the PDF/X-1a specification stipulates Acrobat 4.0 compatibility. This is to accommodate the capabilities of older RIPs, many of which prefer Acrobat 4.0-flavored PDF files. Since Acrobat 4.0-compatible PDF files don't contain live transparency, there's less chance that a RIP that is not PDF based will incorrectly process the file.

- Set image resolution to 300 ppi for typical 150-line screen work, and to 200 ppi for 133-line screen jobs (more about image handling in a moment). Consult with your print service provider to find out the line screen that will be used on your job. If you don't know, you're safe using 300 ppi.

- Set image compression to Automatic (JPEG).

- Ensure that all image content is CMYK or spot or some combination thereof. Convert any RGB content to CMYK.

- Set font embedding to embed fonts. Enable subsetting, and set the subsetting threshold to 100 percent.

Handling Image Content

The primary cause of a PDF file's size is image content, so if you want to make a smaller PDF, that's where you have to squeeze. It's a bit of a juggling act. You have to balance the size of the PDF with the results of compressing and resampling images and decide whether to compromise image appearance to create a more petite file. When making decisions about image compression and resampling, you have to consider the nature of image content as well as the intended use for the PDF file. If the document's text is the most important content, and images are just incidental accents (such as gauzy, out-of-focus photographs of soft clouds), then you can be more liberal when compressing images. However, when the images are key elements—for example, in a technical manual wherein it's crucial to differentiate between small details—you'll have to be willing to accept a larger PDF so you can maintain important detail.

Image compression and resampling options can look overwhelming in Distiller and other applications' PDF creation dialogs. There are so many fields and menu choices. But in most cases, you're just being asked the same question about different types of image content. What should happen to color images? How should it handle grayscale images? And what about bitmap images (also called bilevel—black and white with no shades of gray)? Being able to control the fates of color, grayscale, and bitmap images separately gives you some flexibility. For example, you might want to maintain higher resolution in color images, but not mind reducing the resolution of less-important grayscale images. Separate controls allow you to do that.

Resolution Settings

If you want to more aggressively reduce the file size of a PDF, you can set the base resolution and downsampling threshold to the same value (**Figure 12.3**). *Downsampling* is the process of reducing the number of pixels in an image. An image downsampled from 300 ppi to 72 ppi is much smaller, because it's constituted of smaller, coarser pixels. The downsampling threshold is the resolution above which Distiller will downsample image content. A setting that downsamples images to 300 ppi if they're above 450 ppi ignores images whose resolution falls between 300 and 450 ppi, leaving their resolution unchanged. Setting both downsampling and the threshold to the same value forces images between 300–450 ppi to also be downsampled. You're discarding pixels, but at this level, it shouldn't result in an obvious loss of detail.

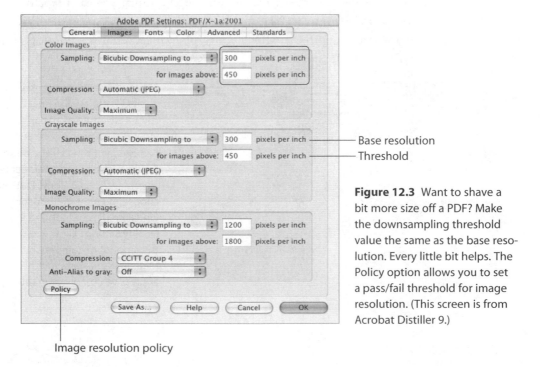

Base resolution
Threshold

Image resolution policy

Figure 12.3 Want to shave a bit more size off a PDF? Make the downsampling threshold value the same as the base resolution. Every little bit helps. The Policy option allows you to set a pass/fail threshold for image resolution. (This screen is from Acrobat Distiller 9.)

Compression Settings

Besides allowing you to resample image content to economize PDF size, Distiller and some other PDF-creation processes provide options for compression. Compression involves methods of re-expressing the image content in a more economical way, usually by eliminating redundant information. Overly aggressive JPEG compression, however, can cause a noticeable erosion of an image, resulting in effects such as rectangular artifacts. But don't be terrified of the JPEG compression option in Distiller. Careful compression levels can reduce image size without visibly degrading the image.

Acrobat Distiller and most other PDF-creation applications use both ZIP and JPEG methods of compression. ZIP compression is *lossless*, meaning that it does not discard image information—it just describes the image in a more compact way. ZIP can reduce the size of flat-color image content such as cartoons or maps. JPEG compression achieves better file-size reduction with photographic image content, because photographs can contain a wide range of colors with smooth transitions. The correct choice of a compression method seeks to reduce the size of the resulting PDF file without unnecessarily impairing its appearance.

What do you do if you have both kinds of content? Good news—choose the Automatic (JPEG) option in Distiller or other Creative Suite applications, and each type of content is handled appropriately (**Figure 12.4**). It's worth noting that, since ZIP compression is lossless, it's also perfectly appropriate for photographic images, but it will not produce as small a file as JPEG compression can.

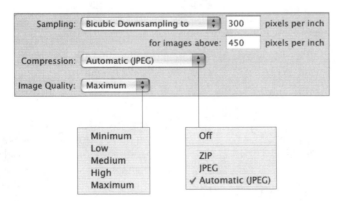

Figure 12.4 ZIP compression is a lossless compression method that can reduce the size of flat-color images such as cartoons; JPEG compression can achieve better results with photographic content. Automatic (JPEG) allows Distiller to choose the right method for individual image content. The Image Quality settings allow you to choose the amount of compression, with Minimum quality being the most aggressive compression setting.

Font Embedding

The purpose of embedding fonts is to ensure that the PDF file looks and prints like the original document. Keep in mind that you're allowed to embed fonts only if the font vendor's End User License Agreement (EULA) allows you to do so—see Chapter Six, "Fonts," for more on font licensing EULAs.

If you embed a font in a PDF, things can still go awry once the file leaves your hands. If you just embed a font (without subsetting), font substitution can still take place if the RIP is already using a font of the same name. Imagine a RIP thinking, "Why should I bother to pry open this PDF to get its Helvetica Bold, when I already have one warmed up?" It sounds harmless, just substituting one Helvetica Bold for another. But not all Helvetica Bold versions are the same. There may be subtle differences in font metrics that can result in loss of fidelity to the original file. Additionally, fully embedding larger fonts such as OpenType fonts (which can have over 65,000 glyphs) can add to the size of the PDF file.

One solution to these issues is to *subset* font information. Subsetting embeds only the characters used in the document, which reduces file size. If your PDF consists of one line of text reading "ABC123," only the characters A, B, C, 1, 2, and 3 are embedded, rather than packing up the entire font. Beyond the file-slimming aspects, subsetting gives each font a unique name. For example, a PDF file containing an *embedded* version of the font, Skia, describes the font as *Skia-Regular.* But a PDF file containing a *subset* version of Skia refers internally to the font by a unique name such as *AMIIKI+Skia-Regular*, eliminating any chance that a RIP will be tempted to use a font named *Skia-Regular* instead.

There are disadvantages to subsetting, however. If multiple PDF files containing subset versions of a font are combined (whether by Acrobat or some other process such as imposition), conflicts can arise, resulting in dropped characters or odd spacing. Consult with your print service provider to see if they'd prefer that you simply embed rather than subset fonts, and supply the fonts themselves along with the job (if the font license allows this). This may allow some flexibility during later parts of the workflow.

EDITING PDF FILES

Since one of the primary purposes of the Portable Document Format is to maintain document integrity, you shouldn't be surprised that the ability to edit PDF files in Acrobat is rather limited—that's not an accident. We're not supposed to pick at PDF files once they're created. They're supposed to be finished files, ready to ship.

Of course, little things happen—a missing comma, a blemish in an image, the wrong spot color—and desperation drives you to start prying at the corners of a PDF file. That's when you find the limitations.

Acrobat offers three editing tools in the Advanced Editing toolbar (**Figure 12.5**). Choose Tools > Advanced Editing > Show Advanced Editing Toolbar to display the tools. Use the TouchUp Text tool for selecting and editing text (assuming you have the correct font, and it allows editing). Use the TouchUp Object tool to select images and vector objects for editing in imaging applications such as Photoshop and vector-editing applications such as Illustrator. You may never use the

Figure 12.5 TouchUp tools: TouchUp Text (left), TouchUp Reading Order (center), TouchUp Object (right).

TouchUp Reading Order tool, which allows you to modify object attributes to create more accessible files for visually impaired users. *Accessible* PDF files have specialized underlying structure enabling them to be displayed in a way that makes them more easily read by visually impaired readers. Text in such a PDF file reflows as the reader zooms in, and line breaks are altered so that the reader is not forced to move the file onscreen to see a complete line of text. (This reflow is just a display effect: The PDF file cannot be saved or printed in the reflowed state.) Accessible PDF files are also more easily read aloud by applications called *screen readers*. Screen readers are specialized utilities that read onscreen content so that sight-impaired users can hear what they cannot read. Acrobat 9 Pro and Standard, as well as the free Reader product, contain a rudimentary built-in screen reader. If you want to experiment with it, choose Read Aloud > Activate Read Out Loud from the View menu in one of the Acrobat products. Once the Read Out Loud option is activated, choose one of the options (but be sure to first make note of the keyboard shortcut for "Stop" so you can shut it up).

Editing Text

To edit text (or attempt to), use the TouchUp Text tool to highlight text and change it. It's important to note that the purpose of font embedding is to ensure that a PDF file displays correctly and prints as intended. The fonts embedded in the PDF are not available for you to use in any other way—and that includes editing text. Consequently, you do need to have the necessary fonts active on your system to add or delete text in a PDF file. If you attempt to edit text using an unavailable font, you'll receive a warning alert (**Figure 12.6**).

If you do have the necessary fonts active on your system, you can edit text, although you may find that Acrobat refuses to embed some fonts after editing. It's honoring the limitations of the font's licensing, which in some cases allows embedding, but forbids editing.

It can be frustrating when you encounter these roadblocks, but Acrobat offers no way around it in some cases. You may be forced to go back to the originating application to make the changes and then export a new PDF file (which is the best approach anyway). Of course, if you don't have the original file, this option isn't available.

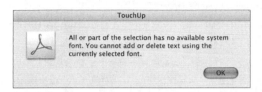

Figure 12.6 You can't edit text in a PDF if you don't have the necessary fonts active on your system. Font embedding is for display and printing purposes only — it doesn't make the font available to you for any other use.

Even if you have the correct font, and it allows editing, you can only edit one line of text at a time. Text won't wrap as it would in a page-layout program. To make extensive text edits, go back to the original application if possible, or use PitStop to perform surgery.

Even without PitStop, you may be surprised to discover that although you may be prevented from adding or deleting text, you can still change attributes such as size, fill color, stroke attributes, and baseline position of existing text. To change attributes of the text, select it with the TouchUp Text tool and then right-click (Control-click on the Mac) and choose Properties from the context menu. Don't get too excited: You can't assign spot colors, and while you can create a CMYK color on the Macintosh, you're limited to choosing RGB values on Windows.

Are you starting to take all this bad news as a sign that you're not supposed to tinker with text in PDF files? Good. Hold that thought. It will keep you out of all kinds of trouble.

Editing Graphics

Surprisingly, you can alter graphic content in a PDF file more extensively than you can edit text. Using the TouchUp Object tool on the TouchUp toolbar, you can select graphic content for manipulation in Photoshop or Illustrator. When you install Acrobat, it searches for the locations of the newest versions of Photoshop and Illustrator on your computer and opens them when you embark on a TouchUp edit.

TOUCHUP TIP #1: Although Acrobat will allow you to designate external editors other than Photoshop and Illustrator, the lines of communication don't work both ways. You'll be able to extract the content, but you can't write the corrected content back into the PDF file.

Choose the TouchUp Object tool, select the desired graphic content in the PDF, and then right-click (Control-click on the Mac) to view the context menu, and then select Edit Image or Edit Object, depending on the type of content you've selected (**Figure 12.7**). The appropriate external application will launch and open a temporary file of the graphic for editing. For example, if you've selected vector content, Illustrator is opened. If you've selected an image, Photoshop is opened. The title bar of a TouchUp image in Photoshop or Illustrator displays a name such as *Acro1143710152.pdf*, indicating that it's a TouchUp file.

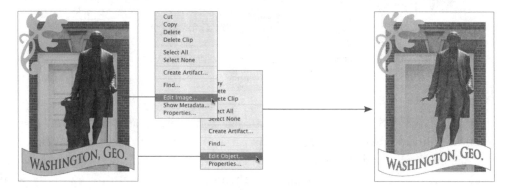

Figure 12.7 Select an image (left) with the TouchUp Object tool, and then right-click (Control-click on the Mac) to select Edit Image. Then the image is available to modify in Photoshop. Make your changes, and then choose File > Save, and the corrected image is saved back into the PDF (right). Select vector content, and then right-click (Control-click on the Mac) to select Edit Object from the context menu to open the vector content in Illustrator. Make your changes, choose File > Save to send the modified content back to Acrobat, and then save your corrected PDF file.

The goal in using the TouchUp Object tool is to sneak into the PDF file, extract the graphic content (whether vector or raster) for the external editing application, make the necessary edits in Photoshop or Illustrator, and then slip the corrected image or vector art back into the PDF. To pull this off, you have to play by the rules that limit the extent to which you can change TouchUp content, especially in Photoshop. Note that you can't add layers in Photoshop and sneak an image back into the PDF. You can create layers as necessary to accomplish the corrections, but you'll have to flatten before returning the image to Acrobat. But you can still do more than you might think. You can fix blemishes, change color modes—even convert to a duotone. You can't add transparency or blending modes, however. If you scale the image, it will be distorted when it's written back into the PDF. When you're done, choose File > Save in Photoshop, and the corrected image is saved back into the PDF file.

Using the TouchUp Object tool to select vector content takes you to Illustrator to modify the selected content. As with images, you can make your edits and then choose File > Save to write the vector content back into the PDF file. There are fewer limitations when editing vector content. For example, you can add layers and even rotate and scale content in Illustrator. When you choose File > Save, Illustrator communicates the changes back to Acrobat and modifies the PDF file accordingly.

> **TOUCHUP TIP #2:** *Need to extract an image or vector component from a PDF file for use in another job? Has the client lost the original vector artwork for the company logo? If she has a PDF file containing the logo, you can use the TouchUp tool to extract the content so you can use it outside of Acrobat. When you have a TouchUp image or vector object open in Photoshop or Illustrator, you can choose File > Save As and select another format (such as PSD for images or AI for vector objects) to save as a file on disk rather than saving it back into the PDF file. This is a great way to extract artwork from a PDF file if you've lost the original artwork. Understandably, it wouldn't be polite to extract artwork you have no rights to use.*

While the TouchUp tools may bail you out of problems as deadlines loom, it's often safer to go back to the original file to make corrections, if you can. Sometimes PDF files just fall apart during editing (nature's way of saying don't mess with them). You should watch carefully for shifted content or unwanted changes. If you're required to frequently edit PDF files because your customers send you PDFs with problems, you should consider adding the dedicated editor Enfocus PitStop to your Acrobat arsenal.

COMMENT AND REVIEW

When you collaborate with other content creators, you may find it saner to send PDF files for them to review, rather than clogging their in-boxes with InDesign, Photoshop, or Illustrator files. And rather than suffer through faxing marked-up copy ("Is that a blob or a comma?") or the cost of couriers, you can streamline the collaborative process by using the commenting and review features built into Acrobat.

Acrobat 9 Standard, Pro, and Pro Extended all contain extensive mark-up tools, which mimic real-life markup tools such as sticky notes, highlighters, and markers. You can choose a single tool by selecting Tools > Comment & Markup, or choose Tools > Comment & Markup > Show Comment & Markup Toolbar (**Figure 12.8**).

Figure 12.8 The Comment & Markup tools work much like their real-world counterparts. Note that the Text Edits tools, like real red pens, don't actually make text corrections; they just indicate what should be fixed.

You can dock the toolbar by dragging it up to the toolbar area, or let it float freely. Hover over a tool in the Comment & Markup toolbar for a moment and a tool tip will appear, providing a bit of guidance for using the tool. Here's an overview of the tools:

- **Sticky Note:** Click to "stick" a note to the PDF; type your comments in the note-like area that appears. Right-click (Control-click on the Mac) on the note icon and choose Properties to change the note icon, to select a new color for the note and its icon, or change the author name. To reposition the note icon, just drag it. By default, the open note appears at the edge of the document page, but you can drag it anywhere in the page.

- **Text Edits:** Despite the tool name, the group of Text Edits tools don't change text in the PDF; they just indicate desired changes. To indicate text change or deletion, pretend you're typing: For example, select the main Text Edits tool, click and drag across text you'd like to delete, and press the Delete or Backspace key on the keyboard. A strikethrough appears throughout the text. To indicate replacement text, highlight a range of text, and then type the replacement text. The existing text is struck through, and a pop-up note appears, containing the new text you've typed. You'll find that you most often use the Text Edits tool this way, and you'll rarely use the other options hidden in the drop-down menu, available under the Text Edits button.

- **Stamps:** The Dynamic stamps pick up the user name and, in some cases, the date from the system. The Sign Here stamps are like those little stick-on guides you've seen on contracts. The Standard Business stamps include Void, Confidential, Draft, and the one you'll rarely see in the wild: Approved. You can also create your own custom stamps from Illustrator AI files, PDFs, or JPEGs. To apply a stamp, either click in the page or click and drag to size the stamp as you apply it.

- **Highlight Text tool:** Click and drag across text to highlight it. Right-click on the highlighted area and choose Properties to select a new color or open a pop-up note.

- **Callout tool:** This creates a type-in "balloon" anchored to an arrow. Click where you'd like to anchor the arrow (for example, at the corner of a photograph on which you want to comment), and then drag to where you'd like the rectangular balloon to appear. When you release the mouse button, you can begin typing text in the balloon; as you type, the balloon expands vertically. Right-click to open the context menu; you can spell check selected text in the balloon, or select from text styles such as Bold, Italic, and Underline. You can also change the color, style, and weight of the callout balloon outline.

- **Text Box tool:** Click or click and drag to create a text area, and then type or paste content into the container. As with the Callout tool, you can spell check and apply limited formatting.

- **Cloud tool:** Click (don't drag) in a connect-the-dots fashion to create a polygonal cloud. When you've closed the shape, you can right-click to change the properties or open the pop-up note.

- **Arrow and Line tools:** These two tools are fairly intuitive: The arrow appears where you first click, and the line continues from that first point. As with most of the other markup tools, right-click to change the properties or open the pop-up note.

- **Rectangle and Oval tools:** Click and drag to create these geometric shapes; hold down the Shift key to constrain the shape to a circle or square. By now, you know the right-click drill.

- **Pencil tool:** Draw as you would with a real pencil or marker. Right click to change properties.

You'll probably find that the Sticky Note, Text Edits, and Pencil tools are the most intuitive and easy to use. All markups except the Callout and Text Box markups can have a pop-up note attached; just right-click (Control-click on the Mac) on a markup icon on the document to choose Open Pop-Up Note from the context menu.

Want more? Choose Tools > Customize Toolbars, scroll down to the Comment & Markup Toolbar section. You can add a Pencil Eraser tool, as well as options for attaching a file as a comment. You can also record an audio comment if you have a microphone attached to your computer.

> **TIP:** Explore the options in the Customize Toolbars environment. You can add quite a few optional tools to toolbars, and eventually fill up the top third of your application window with all the little knickknacks. If you want to go back to the factory settings, choose View > Toolbars > Reset Toolbars.

To delete a comment, select it with the Hand tool and press the Delete key. To customize the properties of future markups of a certain type, or to modify the properties of an existing markup, select the markup, and then right-click and choose Make Current Properties Default.

Reader Users Can Play, Too

While markup features have been available since Acrobat 3.0 (when they were called Annotations), potential collaborators had to purchase a retail copy of Acrobat to participate. But that changed when Acrobat 7.0 Professional added the ability to enable a PDF so that users of the free Reader application could create, import, and export comments and markups. Acrobat 8.0 added the option to enable Reader users to save filled-out forms (previously, form data would vaporize when a Reader user saved a filled form—very frustrating).

Since its introduction in Acrobat 7.0, the "enable for Reader" feature has changed names and menu locations, bouncing between the Documents, Comments, and Advanced menus. To enable a PDF in Acrobat 9 for Reader users to comment, choose Advanced > Extend Features in Adobe Reader. In addition to being able to add markups to the PDF, users of Reader 8.0 or later will be able to save filled-out forms, sign in a signature field, or digitally sign the document anywhere in the page. However, enabling these features for Reader users actually disables some functions: Acrobat Pro users can no longer edit text or graphic content, nor can they insert or delete pages (**Figure 12.9**).

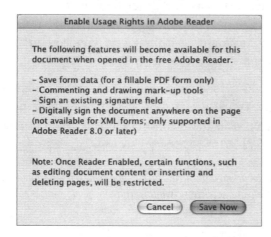

Figure 12.9 Enabling usage rights for Reader users *disables* some functions for the PDF when it's reopened in Acrobat Pro.

If you wish to make edits to an enabled file using Acrobat 9 Pro, you will have to save a copy of the file, and make the edits to the copy (**Figure 12.10**).

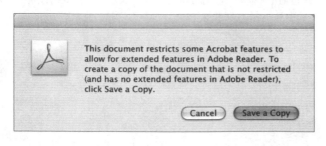

Figure 12.10 A rights-enabled PDF can't be edited. However, you can save a copy of the file and work on the copy.

When Reader users open an enabled PDF, they will see a new entry in the toolbar — a Comment button. They now have the full markup functionality of Acrobat 9 Pro, including all the markup tools and the ability to import and export markups.

Collaborating with Others

Now that everyone can mark up your PDF, what do you do next? You have to disseminate the PDF to multiple reviewers and figure out a way to retrieve their comments and view them in context so you know what corrections to make to the original file. Of course, there's a chance that everyone will just use the Approved stamp and leave it at that. In your dreams.

Email-based Reviews

It's easy to email the PDF to recipients, instruct them to add their markups, and then ask them to send the marked-up PDF (or just the comments) back to you. Reviewers can't see each other's markups, so there may be some redundancy or conflict between their requests. The originator of the review (that would be you) will probably want to combine all the harvested markups on a single PDF to see them all at once.

To initiate an email-based review, choose Comments > Attach for E-mail Review. Acrobat launches a setup wizard that walks you through the process. You can select the currently open document or another file, and then choose participants by entering their email addresses manually or selecting them from your address book. The wizard generates an email message instructing recipients how to participate, but you can customize the message. Users with Acrobat 6 or later, or version 7 and later of the free Reader, can participate.

Shared Reviews

A Shared Review requires that you store a PDF in a central location, such as a workgroup server, a WebDAV-enabled server such as Apple's MobileMe iDisk, or Acrobat.com. To start a Shared Review, choose Comments > Send for Shared Review and choose one of the two options in the drop-down menu:

- Automatically download & track comments with Acrobat.com. (You'll need to sign up for the free Acrobat.com service if you haven't already done so.)

- Automatically collect comments on my own internal server. (Specify the directory path to your internal server, or the URL of the Web server.)

The Shared Review wizard will walk you through the remaining steps. Once you've set things in motion, the recipients you choose will receive an email with a link to the URL so they can download the PDF for reviewing. If you're using Acrobat.com, participants will have to create a login for Acrobat.com before starting their reviews (it's free). A copy of the PDF will automatically be created on their computer with "_review.pdf" appended to the name.

When the PDF is opened a yellow bar appears across the top with instructions to add comments and publish them. Participants can comment with Reader or Acrobat, and then click the Publish Comments button in the yellow bar to upload their comments. They can check for other reviewers' comments by clicking the Check for New Comments button in the yellow bar. This makes it possible for all reviewers to see each other's markups and perhaps avoid redundancy.

Collaborate Live

If you'd like to replicate the experience of sitting around a conference table viewing proofs with your collaborators—but have to accommodate the far-flung locations of two participants—Collaborate Live may be the answer. When you install Acrobat 9 Standard or Pro, you also install a doorway to free collaboration features through Acrobat.com. Up to three participants can sign in and view documents together—for example, you and two clients. The views are synchronized; if one participant zooms or moves the view of the document, the screens of the other two participants reflect this. There is also a chat window, but you'll probably just have a conference call (not an Acrobat.com feature; you'll have to use your own teleconferencing solution).

To launch a Collaborate Live session:

1. Choose File > Collaborate > Send & Collaborate Live. The Acrobat.com screen displays; click the Next button.

2. Sign in with your Adobe ID and click Sign In. If you don't yet have an Adobe ID, click the Create Adobe ID hyperlink to create one.

3. Acrobat displays a form containing email text and fields for recipients' email addresses. Enter recipients' addresses in the To and CC fields, and modify the email text if you wish.

4. By default, the PDF is sent as an attachment to the email. Alternatively, you can select the option to store the file on Acrobat.com and just include a hyperlink to the file.

Acrobat adds "_collab.pdf" to the filename, saves this PDF in the same directory as the original file, generates an email (which you can edit), and launches your default email program. Recipients must have Acrobat 9 Pro or Adobe Reader 9 to participate.

A collaborator opens the PDF attachment (alternatively, the email can just include a hyperlink to the file hosted on Acrobat.com). An Adobe ID is not required for collaborators; they can just sign in as a guest. This is not a presenter/client arrangement: All three participants can change the view and others will be led along with them. (This is why the conference call is a good idea: "Hey! Hold still for a minute!")

While each participant can use markup tools during the Collaborate Live session, those markups are not visible to other participants. Each participant can save a copy of the PDF with his or her own markups, however. The big advantage of Collaborate Live is that you can quickly and easily conference with two other participants—for free.

Collecting and Summarizing Comments

When it's time to gather everyone's markups into one place, you can use one of several methods. If you've used the Shared Review approach, you can just open your review copy of the PDF (that's the one with "_review.pdf" appended to the filename) and click the Check for New Comments button in the yellow bar to download and apply everyone's markups.

Exporting Comments

If you have sent the PDF as an email attachment to reviewers, you could have them send back their marked-up PDFs. But if you're dealing with large, multipage PDFs, this could clog your in-box; paging through multiple copies of a long document to make note of all the markups would be time-consuming and tedious. So, rather than ask reviewers to send back the complete PDF, have them just send the markups: It's sort of like having them peel up a marked-up overlay and send that. Instruct Acrobat users to choose Comments > Export Comments to Data File. In Reader, they'll choose Document > Comments > Export Comments to Data File. Once the markup data file is created, they can just email that much smaller file (usually just a few kilobytes) to you.

Importing Comments

Once you've received all the reviewers' markups, open your "master" PDF in Acrobat 9 Standard or 9 Pro, choose Comments > Import Comments, and navigate to the data file sent by a reviewer: You can select multiple data files and import them simultaneously. The comment data file has an .fdf (Forms Data Format) file extension. Since the reviewers made comments on a copy of your original PDF, you may see an alert as you import the data files, warning you that the comments are from a different version of the document. Just ignore the warning.

Summarizing Comments

After all the comments are imported into your copy of the PDF, you may have a bit of a mess: Multiple reviewers may complain about the same things, and their markups could be stacked on top of each other. It can be confusing and aggravating to try to sort through, so make it easy on yourself: Choose Comments > Summarize Comments. The Summarize Options dialog gives you options for layout (we like "Document and comments with connector lines on single pages"), font size (we recommend Large), and the color of connector lines (**Figure 12.11**).

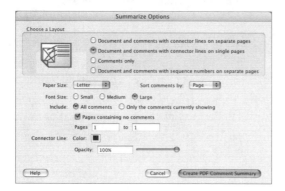

Figure 12.11 Choose a layout for the comments summary, as well as font size and connector line color, and then click Create PDF Comment Summary.

The summary is generated as a PDF. The "single pages" option recommended above yields a thumbnail of the document, with a list of comments labeled by name and type of markup, along with the text of all pop-up notes (**Figure 12.12**). It can serve as a great roadmap as you perform the requested alterations.

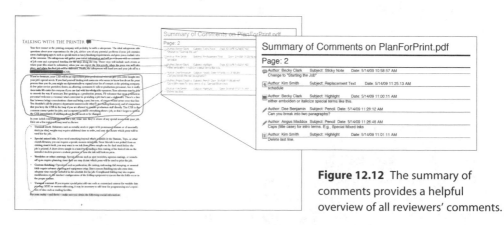

Figure 12.12 The summary of comments provides a helpful overview of all reviewers' comments.

The summary PDF exists only in computer memory until you save it. Then, it's like any other PDF: You can view and print it, and even put comments on it (although that somehow seems wrong).

ConnectNow

When you install Acrobat 9 Standard, Pro, or Extended, you are automatically entitled to free use of Adobe ConnectNow, a Web-conferencing and screen-sharing service. ConnectNow is not limited to displaying PDF files; you can share the view of any document or application on your computer. It's helpful for teaching software or providing technical support, or collaborating during the design process. As with Collaborate Live, you are limited to a total of three participants; for larger groups, you'll have to upgrade to Connect Pro, which isn't free. For more information on Connect Pro features and pricing, visit *www.claudiamccue.com/go/yU7Bf*.

Sharing Your Screen with Adobe ConnectNow

To use Adobe ConnectNow, all you and your collaborators need is a Web browser. Attendees log in to the meeting space from their own computers by going to the URL you provide. If the meeting is their first visit to a ConnectNow meeting, they will be prompted to download and install the required Adobe ConnectNow Flash plug-in (it's quick and painless). By the way, this same functionality is available in all other Creative Suite 4 applications: Just choose File > Share My Screen and follow the instructions.

To initiate a meeting:

1. Choose File > Collaborate > Share My Screen in Acrobat (or choose File > Share My Screen from within any other Creative Suite 4 application). Adobe ConnectNow launches; if you don't have the necessary Flash plug-in, you will be prompted to permit its installation. Enter your Adobe ID and password, or create a new ID.

2. Invite participants. The URL for the meeting room is automatically displayed, and you can even send email invitations to participants by clicking the Send Email Invitation Now link in the Welcome screen.

To join the meeting, participants click the meeting URL in the email they've received (or they can just type the meeting URL in the address bar of their browser). They can identify themselves with their Adobe ID if they have one, or just sign in as guests. Once the two attendees have joined the meeting, you can share your computer screen, use the chat module, take notes in the Shared Notes module (all participants can save the shared notes), and use other meeting features, such as the whiteboard feature.

Acrobat.com

As an owner of Acrobat 9 Standard, Pro, or Extended, you have access to all the free online services of Acrobat.com, including file sharing and storage, online PDF conversion from many file formats, and use of the Buzzword collaborative online word processor, in addition to ConnectNow Web conferencing. Services include:

- **Share:** Rather than emailing large attachments, you can make files available online at Acrobat.com.

- **Adobe Buzzword:** Collaborate online with the free Buzzword word processor.

- **My Files:** Free online storage (up to 5 GB) you can access from anywhere. Think of it as a giant USB drive you don't have to carry with you.

- **Create PDF:** Upload up to five files for online conversion to PDF. File types include Microsoft Word, Excel, and other common file formats. This is great if you don't own the application but need to make a PDF from a supplied application file. Once you've used up your five-file limit, you can subscribe to the online service for unlimited online conversions for $9.95/month or $99.99 per year.

PRINT PRODUCTION TOOLBAR

If you receive PDFs from collaborators and other suppliers, it's important to find problems in those PDF files and fix them (**Figure 12.13**). To display the Print Production tools, choose Advanced > Print Production > Show Print Production Toolbar. If it's necessary to perform any major surgery, you'll still need to repair the original file and create a new PDF, or use Enfocus PitStop to perform the corrections. But you can accomplish quite a bit just by using Acrobat's built-in tools.

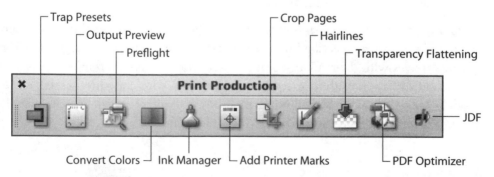

Figure 12.13 The Print Production toolbar in Acrobat 9 Pro provides tools to find and fix problems without returning to the application that created the PDF file.

The Print Production tools fall into two major categories: *Forensic tools* help you find problem areas in a PDF file, and *repair tools* alter content to fix problems. As with other toolbars in Acrobat, this toolbar can float anywhere in the document window, or can be docked in the toolbar area at the top of the application.

Forensic Tools: What's Wrong with This PDF?

Acrobat 9 Pro contains two great forensic tools: Output Preview and Preflight. The two tools take different approaches, because they're meant to call attention to different problems.

Output Preview (Advanced > Print Production > Output Preview) takes a visual approach, selectively displaying content according to parameters you choose. You can highlight such elements as RGB images, spot-color content, overprinting elements, and rich black areas.

Some problems aren't so easily found visually, which is where the Preflight tool comes in. The Preflight tool tests a PDF file against a preflight profile to determine problems. The preflight process then generates a report to tell you what's wrong. A Preflight profile can determine such things as whether a PDF file complies with the PDF/X-1a standard, and can check for such problems as insufficient image resolution, incorrect page size, font embedding issues, and much more, based on the rules of the preflight profile used.

Output Preview

Select the Output Preview tool, and then use the controls to show and hide objects in the PDF by various criteria. You'll see a list of inks used in the PDF file, and you can selectively show and hide individual plates to easily see where the inks are used in the page. As you move your cursor over the document, the Output Preview displays percentage values for each ink, as well as a total area coverage value for the current cursor location. You can choose a cursor sample size ranging from point sample (do you really care about a single pixel? probably not) to 5 by 5 average.

Choose the option to highlight Total Area Coverage, pick a highlight color, enter a value for the maximum ink value, and areas in violation of the value are highlighted in the page. The appropriate value depends on the printing press, ink, and stock being used; you'll have to ask your print service provider to tell you what's correct for your job. If you have large areas carrying more ink than your print service provider recommends for your job, you'll have to go back upstream and alter image content and other artwork so the job will print acceptably. If you're doing your own conversions of RGB images to CMYK, you can factor in this value in your color separation setup.

As you view the PDF, use the check boxes next to ink names to view and hide individual plates, so you can check for incorrect or extraneous inks (**Figure 12.14**).

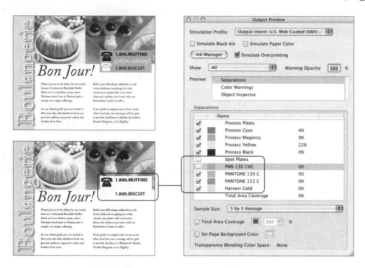

Figure 12.14 Use the Separations controls in the Output Preview dialog to toggle plates on and off. Here, one rectangle uses an ink named PMS 130 CVC (right). But there's another spot color named PANTONE 130 C, and another named Harvest Gold. That can't be right.

Select Show in the Output Preview dialog to view options for isolating RGB content (**Figure 12.15**) and other types of color space such as grayscale, CMYK, and spot color.

Figure 12.15 From the Show list, choose RGB, and any RGB objects are displayed while everything else is hidden. It's a quick way to isolate images that are using the wrong color space.

As with all the Output Preview options, it's up to you to pay attention and take note of what's displayed. In Figure 12.15, one image is displayed when the Show > RGB option is selected. Now we've discovered that we have one problem image, which must be converted to CMYK for output. As you'll see shortly, this is a problem you can fix in Acrobat.

Object Inspector

New to Acrobat 9 Pro, the Object Inspector doesn't select objects for interrogation; it just displays everything that's true where you click in the PDF. Think of it as sort of a core sample that reveals everything underneath. The Object Inspector reports on color space, color values, image resolution, overprint attributes, font information, and more (**Figure 12.16**).

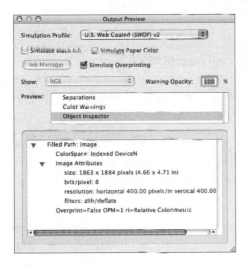

Figure 12.16 The Object Inspector displays information about everything underneath where you click in the document. Here, it displays the color space and resolution of an image.

 Preflight

A preflight profile includes one or more *checks* (an inspection of a PDF) or *fixups* (repair procedures), or sometimes both checks and fixups. You can check for problems such as image resolution, spot colors, font embedding, or compliance with a standard such as PDF/X-1a. Depending on the rules that constitute the profile you select (and there's quite a variety of preflight profiles supplied with the program), Acrobat can display an error, provide information, fix a problem, or just ignore the results.

To view preflight options, choose the Preflight tool from the Print Production toolbar, or choose Advanced > Print Production > Preflight. Be patient; it takes a moment for the Preflight dialog to appear. The Preflight dialog (**Figure 12.17**) consists of four tabs across the top (Profiles, Results, Standards, and Options), and the main options window beneath them. Profiles are organized in groups such as PDF analysis, PDF standards compliance, and so on. Click the triangle next to a group name to display the profiles within that group.

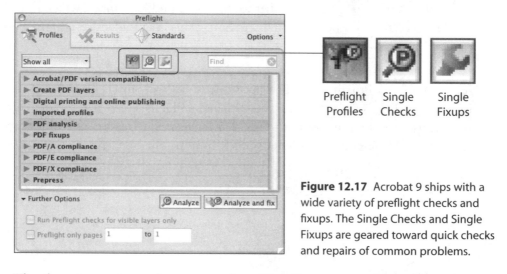

Preflight Profiles   Single Checks   Single Fixups

Figure 12.17 Acrobat 9 ships with a wide variety of preflight checks and fixups. The Single Checks and Single Fixups are geared toward quick checks and repairs of common problems.

The three icons above the groups of profiles allow you to choose from the group list (Preflight Profiles), Single Checks, or Single Fixups. Single Checks are preset checks that look for a single common problem, such as RGB content or fonts that aren't embedded. Single Fixups fix a single common problem by performing repairs such as RGB to CMYK conversion.

Once you've selected the preflight profile to run, click the Analyze button below the list of profiles. If there's a long list of problems in the preflight report, Acrobat offers a quick way to find the problem visually. Select the item in the preflight report window, and then click the Show in Snap button (**Figure 12.18**). The item is displayed in a floating window so you can identify it. Why is it called Snap? As your mother would say, "Well, it just *is*."

Figure 12.18 To easily locate a problem, highlight the item in the preflight report, and then select Show in Snap, which will display the selected item in a floating window.

While Acrobat ships with an extensive set of prefabricated preflight profiles, you may still want to create a custom profile for your needs. The easiest way to do this is to select an existing profile, duplicate it, and then modify it to suit your needs. Select a profile that gives you a good start and then choose Duplicate Preflight Profile from the Options drop-down menu. Name the new profile, and then modify its settings (**Figure 12.19**).

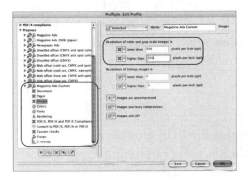

Figure 12.19 To edit a custom profile, choose a topic from the profile's list of tests, modify the parameters to fit your needs, and then save as a new profile.

If you need to preflight multiple files with the same profile, you can automate the process by creating a Preflight Droplet. In the main Preflight dialog, select a profile, and then choose Create Preflight Droplet from the Options menu.

In the Droplet Setup dialog, you can designate Success and Error folders, allowing Acrobat to sort the preflighted PDF files into separate folders so you can quickly determine which ones passed the preflight criteria (**Figure 12.20**). Acrobat creates a Droplet icon to represent the batch process. To start the process, shift-click to select multiple PDF files, and then drag the whole bunch on top of the Droplet. Caution: If you drag a *folder* to the Droplet, it won't process the files inside. You can only drag PDF files to the Droplet icon. The preflight-and-sort process doesn't change the PDF files to Acrobat 9 files. It just peeks inside the files and sorts them according to the assigned preflight profile without resaving the PDF.

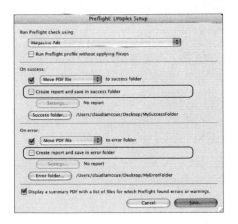

Magazine Ads

Figure 12.20 To set up a Preflight Droplet, choose a profile and then specify handling for PDFs that pass and those that fail. Here, the Droplet will move the passing PDFs to the MySuccess folder, whereas the failing PDFs will go in the MyError folder. Click the Save button, and Acrobat creates a Droplet like the one above wherever you specify.

Repair Tools

Once you've found all the problems with a PDF file, how do you fix them? Some problems —such as missing fonts, text reflow, and low-resolution images—are best fixed in the originating application. But you can still fix some common problems without leaving Acrobat by using the built-in repair tools (and the fixup functions in the preflight profiles).

Ink Manager

If the Output Preview display has shown that the PDF file contains extraneous spot colors, rather than return to the original application, you can repair the problem with the Ink Manager. Choose an incorrect spot ink in the list, and then select the correct spot ink from the Ink Alias list at the bottom of the dialog. This converts all content that is in the wrong spot color so that it will be output on the correct plate (**Figure 12.21**).

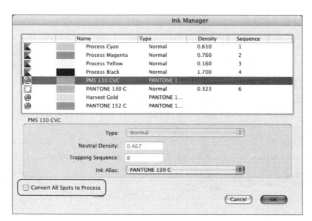

Figure 12.21 Use the Ink Manager to map one spot color to another spot color. Select the errant spot color in the list, and then use the Ink Alias list to choose the target ink. You can also convert all spot colors to process with one click (lower left), or map a spot ink to a process ink.

But there's a catch: By default, Ink Manager settings only affect the PDF temporarily. If you were to output the job directly from Acrobat (which almost never happens), the output would correctly reflect the Ink Manager settings. But if you save, close, and then reopen the file, you'll be appalled to see that the extraneous spot colors, like zombies in cheap B-movies, have returned.

There's good news, though: You can make Ink Manager settings permanent in a PDF by using the Convert Colors tool.

Convert Colors

If you've discovered that you have RGB images in a PDF, and you have no access to the original file to generate a PDF, you can select the Convert Colors tool on the Print

Production toolbar to convert RGB content to CMYK. You can specify a document profile as well as a destination space to ensure an appropriate conversion (**Figure 12.22**). Also, the Convert Colors function can make Ink Manager choices permanent, which is very good news. When you click OK in the Convert Colors dialog, you are warned that the changes cannot be undone. But the file is not automatically saved. If you have performed a Change Color operation in error, just choose File > Revert to start over.

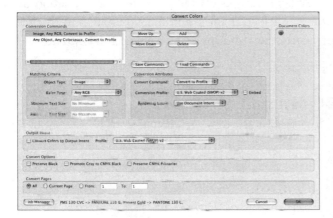

Figure 12.22 Select Convert Colors to make color-space changes such as RGB to CMYK, CMYK to grayscale, and so on. This also makes any Ink Manager choice permanent in the file.

Add Printer Marks

If you need to add trim and crop marks to a PDF file, you can specify trim and bleed marks, as well as color bars and page information by using the Add Printer Marks tool. You can also select from several styles or printer marks, including those comparable to the ones generated by InDesign and QuarkXPress. For the position of such marks to be correct, the PDF file must contain properly defined TrimBox and BleedBox information from the originating application. But when you add marks, they will initially fall outside the visible edge of the page, which will make you think you've done something wrong. You haven't. You just have to follow up by expanding the document's dimensions so the marks show. For that, you need the Crop Pages tool. Acrobat even politely informs you to follow up with the Crop Pages tool (**Figure 12.23**).

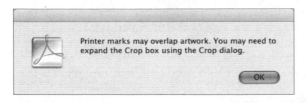

Figure 12.23 When you add printer marks, Acrobat prompts you to expand the page dimensions with the Crop Pages tool.

 Crop Pages

The Crop Pages tool is a multipurpose tool. Think of it as the change-document-dimensions tool, because it can crop as well as increase page size (**Figure 12.24**). While increasing the page size actually changes the dimensions of the PDF page, cropping with the Margin Controls just visually masks out the area outside the margin dimensions. Page content still exists. It just doesn't show. That's why cropped PDF files show no reduction in file size. Everything is still there, lurking. Since cropping isn't final, you may find that some other applications ignore cropping instructions and show the original full content.

If you've used the Printer Marks tool, the Crop Pages tool is your next stop. You'll need to add sufficient new material on the page to allow the marks to be visible. Adding one inch in both directions will usually do the trick. For example, if you've added marks to a page that's currently 8.75 by 11.25 inches, set the new page dimensions to 9.75 by 12.25 inches.

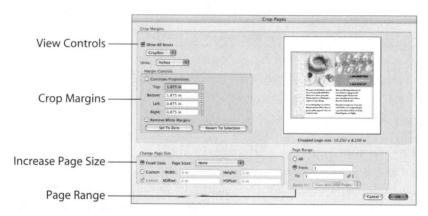

Figure 12.24 In the Crop Pages controls, Margin Controls crop the document. Change Page Size increases the document's page size, but does not scale the content.

The Crop Pages function, like the Ink Manager, only affects the PDF while it is open in Acrobat. But you can create a permanent page crop by using a customized fixup. It's a bit clunky, but here's how:

1. Choose the Crop tool (Tools > Advanced Editing > Crop Tool).

2. Click and drag to create a rectangle the size of the intended final crop.

3. Right-click and choose Set ArtBox from the context menu. This defines the rectangle as the ArtBox for the document; you'll need that in a minute.

4. Open the Preflight dialog (Advanced > Preflight). From the Options drop-down, choose Create New Preflight Single Fixup.

5. In the left column, choose the Page category.

6. Set the Fixup options as necessary: Assign a name, select the Set Page Geometry Boxes option in the Type of Fixup column, and modify the settings as shown in **Figure 12.25**. Click OK, and then save the fixup.

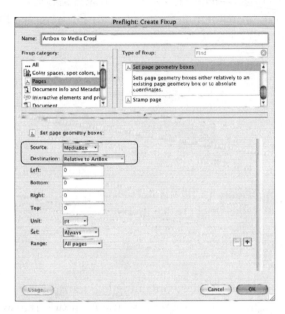

Figure 12.25 Tell Acrobat to recognize the ArtBox you defined manually, and to convert it to a MediaBox, which will truly crop the file.

When you run the fixup by clicking the Fix button in the Preflight dialog, you'll be prompted for a new filename, because this fixup will permanently alter the file, deleting all content outside the newly defined trim and resetting the trim definition as you have specified.

As you can see, this is not an exact process, and it's difficult (if not impossible) to create the crop you need. If you can't persuade the file creator to send a new PDF of the correct size, you may find it saner to place the PDF in an InDesign page of the correct size, turn on High Resolution Display, and position the PDF so it will be cropped correctly when the document is exported to PDF.

Fix Hairlines

Thin lines can come from CAD artwork or from vector art that's been greatly reduced in a page layout. While direct-to-plate imaging and newer press controls provide the ability to image and print small details that might have disappeared in transit 20 years ago, a line of extremely thin width can benefit from a little fluffing up to ensure imaging.

The Fix Hairlines tool allows you to increase the weight of stroked lines using a threshold value (**Figure 12.26**). It also offers options for padding Type 3 fonts (which can contain patterned or gray components) or pattern fills. Note that exercising these options may add more complexity to the PDF file, since this could result in a large number of elements in the file being modified. A pattern fill could contain hundreds (or thousands) of lines which would have to be modified during the hairline fixing process. But in a typical PDF file, the hairline fixing should just take a few seconds.

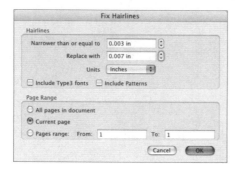

Figure 12.26 The Fix Hairlines tool adds weight to thin strokes.

Transparency Flattener Preview

If your print service provider can't accept PDF files containing live transparency, such as PDF files that are generated by InDesign or Illustrator, you can use Acrobat's Transparency Flattening controls to manage the flattening process (**Figure 12.27**).

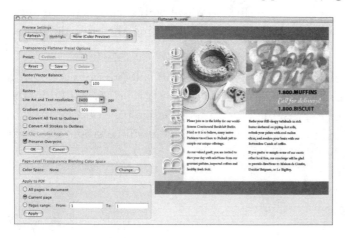

Figure 12.27 The Transparency Flattening options enable you to see what areas will be affected by flattening. You can control the process rather than being at the mercy of a RIP that can't handle live transparency in PDF files.

Drag the Raster/Vector Balance slider all the way to the right. You should see 100 in the Raster/Vector value. Use the resolution of the print service provider's RIP for the Line Art and Text resolution value, and set the Gradient and Mesh resolution to an appropriate image resolution, such as 300 ppi. Don't select the options for converting text or strokes to outlines, so you can avoid any thickening of text or rules.

PDF Optimizer

To make a lower-resolution PDF from an existing PDF file, or to save for a previous version of Acrobat, use PDF Optimizer rather than going all the way back to the originating application and generating a new PDF. The PDF Optimizer also produces better results than the old-fashioned method of printing to PostScript from Acrobat and then using Distiller to process the new PostScript file — a process referred to as *refrying*. That method carries the risk of losing font embedding or introducing color errors. In addition, PDF Optimizer offers much more granular control over file-size reduction than the Reduce File Size option available under the File menu, which just uses a default setting with no visible controls.

If you frequently have to create low-resolution PDFs from high-resolution PDFs, consider purchasing a dedicated solution that can streamline that process. Both PDF Enhancer and PDF Shrink from Apago, Inc. (*www.apago.com*) can accomplish surprising reductions in PDF file size while retaining reasonable appearance quality.

Trap Presets

It's unlikely that you'll be required to use the Trap Presets features in Acrobat 7, since trapping is a complicated undertaking that's best left to the knowledgeable folks at the print service provider. The Trap Presets feature in Acrobat doesn't actually create traps within the PDF file: It lets you specify trap settings that are subsequently used as instructions by a RIP that uses the Adobe In-RIP Trapping engine. The trap settings you choose only affect the print stream out of Acrobat—no trapping instructions are stored in the PDF. However, the presets you create are available as presets in Acrobat for future use.

JDF

Job Definition Format (JDF) information may not mean much to you right now, but watch this acronym. The ability to generate an electronic job ticket and store it within a PDF file has the potential to streamline workflows and reduce job errors. JDF information can contain details such as page size, number of colors, binding requirements, and even contact information for people involved in the job. It's an electronic version of the old job information sheet that traveled with a physical job jacket as job materials traveled through a printing plant. The appearance of JDF functionality in Acrobat is a hint that the road is being paved for JDF to be increasingly important in the way we define and track jobs. Unless your print service provider is currently using JDF-based job ticketing, you won't be required to explore this part of Acrobat.

USING EXTERNAL PDF EDITORS

PDFs are much more complex than they look. Under the hood, they're a spaghetti-like network of things such as XObjects, Arrays, Page Tree Nodes, and Optional Content Groups. That's why some edits can't be undone in Acrobat (**Figure 12.28**). You'd break the spaghetti.

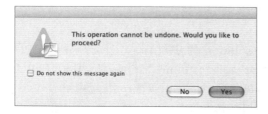

Figure 12.28 There is no Undo command for many operations in Acrobat. This is nature's way of letting you know that PDF files are more complicated than you might think. At least you're warned.

Even if you're using some of the excellent, third-party add-ons for Acrobat to perform edits, it's advisable to work on a copy of your file just in case things fall apart.

As for using Adobe Illustrator to edit PDF files...*don't*. We all have, ah, friends who have done this in desperation in the olden days before PitStop and other PDF-editing software. There was no viable alternative back then, and deadlines will drive you to do such unseemly things. But if it wasn't generated by Illustrator, opening a PDF file in Illustrator without the necessary fonts available will wreck font embedding, and manipulating objects may cause unexpected loss of content. It's OK to edit PDFs saved directly from Illustrator, however. They're special files: The original Illustrator file is contained within the PDF, and that's what you'd actually be editing, provided you use the default option to retain Illustrator editing capabilities. But you're risking the possibility of file damage when you use Illustrator to edit PDF files created by other applications. It's preferable to return to the originating application to make edits. Then create a new PDF file and go on with your life.

APPENDIX
Print Production Resources

When you enjoy what you do for a living, your education never stops. And if your education never stops, there's a good chance that you'll get more enjoyment out of what you do for a living. I once worked with a guy who didn't understand my fondness for learning new software. He once said to me, "If you learn that, they'll just make you do it all the time." Understandably, he couldn't fathom why I'd go to trade shows and conferences for fun. I'm sure he was really disturbed by the fact that I referred to the now-defunct Seybold Seminars in Boston as "Spring Break."

If you consider yourself an avid, life-long learner, and you'd like to add to your arsenal of printing knowledge, I hope you'll find the resources in this appendix useful. I've included information about organizations, online resources, books, and publications, and even some print-related tourist destinations. Really.

ORGANIZATIONS

Organizations related to the graphic arts industry vary in structure and offerings. Some are small, loosely knit, informal user groups that meet for snacks and presentations (not necessarily in that order of importance). Some larger organizations are more like corporations with regional chapters, and they often hold annual international conferences that include extensive seminar offerings, exhibit booths, and awards banquets.

Some organizations consist only of a Web presence and perhaps online forums. Regardless of the type of group that appeals to you, it's helpful to join organizations in order to see how other people approach design and print. Meeting other professionals in the industry, and seeing their work, is inspirational as well as educational.

User Groups

Unlike groups geared toward general design or printing industry members, user groups are usually devoted to a single software program or a suite of programs. The Adobe Acrobat and InDesign user groups hold chapter meetings in various cities around the world. While these two groups are supported by Adobe, they are funded and run by the group members themselves. A typical user group meeting might include demonstrations of software features, opportunities to have questions answered and technical issues solved by expert users or guest speakers, and a chance to win software, books, and other door prizes. And don't forget those snacks.

- **Adobe Acrobat User Community**   *www.acrobatusers.com*

  Started in 2006, the Acrobat User Community is growing rapidly. The Web site offers links to the individual chapters, as well as tips, tutorials, and video presentations.

- **Adobe InDesign User Group**   *www.indesignusergroup.com*

  The InDesign User Group Web site is a rich portal to all things InDesign, including chapter information, useful plug-ins, and tutorials. It's also an easy doorway to the Adobe forums and the great InDesign Secrets site. Check out the InDesign Secrets podcast!

Online Communities and Forums

Joining online communities and forums is sort of like raising your hand and having the entire world answer you. Post a question in an online forum, and the answers arrive in your in-box. Strong emotions and priceless information make the online communities like lively little villages, including the inevitable family squabbles.

Some forums (fora? forii?) are sponsored by software vendors and feature the expected product announcements and sales pitches in addition to useful resources. Some forums are maintained strictly by enthusiasts and are free of any corporate influence.

- **Adobe Forums**   *www.adobe.com/support/forums*

  Adobe forums are available for all Adobe products. While the forums are predominantly user-to-user in nature, they are moderated for civility, and Adobe staff are frequent contributors. The topics are a mix of general software issues and printing issues.

- **Community MX**   *www.communitymx.com*

  Community MX contains news about Adobe (formerly Macromedia) products, including Dreamweaver, FreeHandMX, Fireworks, and ColdFusion, as well as online tutorials.

- **National Association of Photoshop Professionals**   *www.photoshopuser.com*

  The National Association of Photoshop Professionals (NAPP) is a national organization that provides online tutorials, publishes a bimonthly magazine, and hosts regional seminar events, in addition to its yearly Photoshop World conference. Members are also eligible for discounts on software and hardware.

- **PDF Zone**   *www.pdfzone.com*

  A service of Ziff Davis Media, PDF Zone contains PDF-related industry news, as well as tips, tricks, and tutorials. Not all of the content is print-related, though.

- **Planet PDF**   *www.planetpdf.com*

  Planet PDF is a service of Nitro PDF Software, a software development company devoted to Acrobat solutions. The searchable Planet PDF store offers a huge variety of plug-ins and software related to Acrobat. The online content also includes tips, tricks, and PDF-themed articles about a wide spectrum of industry uses for Acrobat.

- **PrintPlanet**   *www.printplanet.com*

  Created and maintained by Dave Mainwaring, the PrintPlanet forums are some of the most lively and most useful printing resources on the Web. Forums are devoted to individual topics, including prepress, digital printing, print technology, packaging, and fonts. And there are great training resources available in the associated PrintPlanet University, a service of PrePress Training Solution.

- **Typographica**   *http://new.typographica.org/*

  Typographica is home to lively discussions of font designs, readability issues, and tutorials on font creation, that should give you some deep respect for the efforts of font designers.

Printing Industry Organizations

You may consider yourself to be purely a designer, with no interest in pursuing the technical end of the printing trade. But the online educational resources provided by these printing industry organizations can be very helpful when you want to understand more about printing processes.

- **Association of Graphic Communications** *www.agcomm.org*
  An affiliate of GAIN, the AGC provides print-oriented training for graphics software in the northeastern United States.

- **IDEAlliance (International Digital Enterprise Alliance)** *www.idealliance.org*
  IDEAlliance offers seminars (including some that are available online) on highly technical topics such as XML.

- **International Prepress Association** *www.ipa.org*
  The IPA offers a great variety of online seminars on a wide range of topics ranging from graphics software to PDF creation to print processes.

- **Pacific Printing and Imaging Association** *www.pacprinting.org*
  The PPIA offers training and print-oriented seminars in the Pacific Northwest.

Packaging Organizations

Packaging adds another dimension to the printing process, both literally and figuratively. These packaging organizations offer extensive educational resources.

- **Flexographic Technical Association** *www.fta-ffta.org*
  The FTA Web site offers industry news, online articles, and information on upcoming flexography-related events and training sessions.

- **Institute of Packaging Professionals** *www.iopp.org*
  The IOPP Web site provides access to an extensive bookstore, comprehensive links to industry resources, and information on packaging conferences and training events.

- **Paperboard Packaging Council** *www.ppcnet.org*
  Devoted to the folding-carton industry, the PPC Web site provides numerous informational pieces in PDF format, as well as links to publications and industry events. Additional, premium content is available to PPC members.

Technical Education Organizations

The printing industry contains a number of organizations devoted to education and providing reference materials.

- **Graphic Arts Educational and Research Foundation**   *www.gaerf.org*

  GAERF was created by the National Association for Printing Leadership (NAPL), the Association for Suppliers of Printing, Publishing and Converting Technologies (known as NPES for some ancestral reason), and the Printing Industries of America, Inc. (PIA). These three associations own the Graphic Arts Show Company, (GASC), which is responsible for a number of industry trade shows, including the huge annual GraphExpo event in Chicago. GAERF finances educational programs and provides information about these programs on its Web site.

- **Graphic Arts Information Network**   *www.gain.net*

  A joint effort of Print Industries of America and the Graphic Arts Technical Foundation, GAIN sponsors publication of an extensive library of print-related books, available through the GAIN Web site. There is also an online job bank and links to industry events.

- **Specialty Graphic Imaging Association**   *www.sgia.org*

  The SGIA focus is on printing processes that fall outside of offset printing. It offers coverage of a diverse range of imaging and printing processes, including screen printing, large-format inkjet printing, and textile printing.

- **The National Council for Skill Standards in Graphic Communications**
  www.ncssgc.org

  The National Council for Skill Standards offers educational resources and certification programs for printing-industry professionals.

CONFERENCES AND TRADE SHOWS

Perhaps because the Internet has become such a rich source of information, some graphic arts and printing conferences have evaporated. It's no longer necessary to make a pilgrimage to a trade show for the sole purpose of cornering someone in a booth to get answers to questions about equipment or software. Instead, it's easy to go to a vendor Web site and scroll through posted information. The venerable Seybold Seminars became a casualty of this shift in recent years, a victim of declining attendance. However, there's still a market for the large shows such as DRUPA and On Demand Expo, which feature running presses printing live jobs and finishing equipment spewing out pocket folders.

Printing Industry Events

In addition to featuring fully operational equipment, most printing exhibitions, conferences, and trade shows offer seminars on printing issues. Some exhibitors provide hands-on educational demos. And don't forget to fill up your bag with all those cute tchotchkes such as promotional light-up pens, squeezable software mascots, and company T-shirts.

- **Digital Print World**   *www.digitalprintworld.co.uk*

  Geared toward digital printing (as opposed to offset or letterpress printing), the annual Digital Print World is a predominantly British show, but it attracts attendees from all over the European Union.

- **DRUPA**   *www.drupa.com* (English-language site); *www.drupa.de* (German-language site)

  Held every even-numbered year, DRUPA is enormous. That's why it's a two-week event. Featuring nearly 2,000 vendors and welcoming nearly 400,000 attendees, DRUPA is a truly international print show. Attendees can see everything from software vendors to bookbinding machines.

- **Graphics of the Americas**   *www.graphicsoftheamericas.com*

  This Miami-based trade show is oriented toward Latin American printing consumers. While many exhibitors speak Spanish, and many of the educational sessions are presented in Spanish, it is a fully bilingual show.

- **IPEX**   *www.ipex.org*

  Held in England, IPEX is very much an international print show, with large attendance from the United States and Europe.

- **On Demand Conference and Exposition**   *www.ondemandexpo.com*

  Focusing on digital, on-demand printing solutions, the On Demand Expo includes exhibits and educational sessions devoted to variable-data printing issues.

- **Print/GraphEXPO/Converting Expo**   *www.gasc.org*

  The GraphEXPO shows in Chicago occur annually, but every four years (2001, 2005, 2009, 2013, and so on), they kick it up a notch and present the even larger PRINT show. The PRINT shows include actual operating printing and finishing equipment and occupy the massive McCormick Place convention center from the floors to the rafters. Wear comfortable shoes.

Design Conferences

Many design-oriented conferences are worth attending for the hands-on training sessions that are presented by software sponsors or training consultants. Don't forget to leave extra space in your suitcase for those tempting paper samples, too.

- **AIGA National Conference**   *www.aiga.org*

  Because the AIGA partners closely with Adobe and Aquent, conferences often include training sessions.

- **HOW Design Conference**   *www.howconference.com*

  Software companies such as Adobe, Quark, and Extensis are sponsors and exhibitors at the HOW Design Conference. Take advantage of their hands-on training sessions as well as the software demonstrations in exhibit booths.

- **InDesign and Creative Suite Conferences**   *www.mogo-media.com*

  Both the InDesign Conference and the Creative Suite Conference are well attended by designers and printers. The informal atmosphere encourages real-world questions and the opportunity to network. Periodic smaller regional seminars complement the larger conference offerings.

- **Photoshop World Conference and Expo**   *www.photoshopworld.com*

  Fill your brain with seminars from the best photographers, instructors, and authors on the art of capturing and manipulating images. Rest up first, though.

- **The Cre8 Conference**   *www.cre8summit.com*

  Sessions focus on a wide range of topics, from branding, marketing, and management to application skills.

DESIGN AND PRINTING BOOKS

I know. We can read PDF files onscreen. But there is still no substitute for the tactile joys of ink on paper. Maybe I'm just old-fashioned, but I still feel that books are the most portable, shareable, tangible way to store information. Besides, how could you fill all those bookshelves with the impressive, leather-bound spines of PDFs?

Desktop Publishing

- ***Inside the Publishing Revolution: The Adobe Story,*** by Pamela Pfiffner (Adobe Press, 2002)

  This book is a rousing account of the huge upheavals in design and printing that have sprung from Adobe Systems. It introduces you to Adobe cofounders John Warnock and Charles Geschke and many of the inspired Adobe minds, and provides a fascinating timeline for the developments in software and technology that made desktop publishing possible.

- ***The Non-Designer's Scan and Print Book,*** by Sandee Cohen and Robin Williams (Peachpit Press, 1999)

  This concise and very readable book is not just about scanning. It's full of tips about prepress and print production, with many examples to explain the concepts.

- ***Desktop Publishing Primer,*** by Hal Hinderliter (Graphic Arts Technical Foundation, 2004)

- ***From Design Into Print: Preparing Graphics and Text for Professional Printing,*** by Sandee Cohen (Peachpit Press, 2009)

  A great sequel to *The Non-Designer's Scan and Print Book*, it's updated to reflect changes in technology and printing processes—now in full color.

General Design

While there are hundreds of books on all aspects of design, from color to type to visual concepts, three books stand out for capturing important basics. No fluff, just concise and effective at illuminating concepts to make you think differently about aspects of design that are easily taken for granted.

- ***Before & After,*** by John McWade (Peachpit Press, 2003)

  John McWade makes design and production look so easy. Along with his examples of great design solutions, he explains printing requirements and suggests design approaches that allow you to deal with printing limitations.

- *Before and After Graphics for Business,* by John McWade (Peachpit Press, 2005)

- *Professional Design Techniques with Adobe Creative Suite 3,* by Scott Citron (Adobe Press, 2007)

  Although the book is written for CS3, the design guidance is not application-specific, and the step-by-step instructions make sense even if you're using a later version of the software.

- *The Mac Is Not a Typewriter,* Second Edition, by Robin Williams (Peachpit Press, 2003)

  One of the classic guides for desktop publishing, this book helps you learn the rules for creating professional-looking type. Topics range from avoiding amateur mistakes, such as double spaces and straight quotes, to typographic niceties, such as kerning and hanging punctuation.

General Printing

Some of these printing tomes are encyclopedic and can be measured by the pound as well as page count. Some are more instructional in nature. It's difficult to single out any of the books in this list—they're all quite good. But I've earmarked several as being essential guides for designers wanting to deepen their understanding of printing.

- *The Basics of Print Production,* by Mary Hardesty (Graphic Arts Technical Foundation, 2002)

- *The Complete Guide to Digital Color: Creative Use of Color in the Digital Arts,* by Chris Linford (Collins Design, 2004)

- *Fold: The Professional's Guide to Folding,* (2-Volume Set), by Trish Witkowski (Finishing Experts Group, 2002)

  A painstakingly researched and wonderfully detailed (and readable) encyclopedia of folding techniques.

- *A Field Guide to Folding,* by Trish Witkowski (Finishing Experts Group, 2007)

  A condensed version of the FOLDRite system, highlighting 85 of the most common folding styles used in the industry today.

- *Forms, Folds, and Sizes: All the Details Graphic Designers Need to Know But Can Never Find,* by Poppy Evans (Rockport Press, 2004)

  The title says it all: This is a great guide to important printing issues, and an essential reference for designers.

- *The GATF Guide to Desktop Publishing,* by Hal Hinderliter and Jim Cavuoto (Graphic Arts Technical Foundation, 2000)

- *Getting It Printed,* Fourth Edition, by Eric Kenly (HOW Design Books, 2004)

- *Getting It Right in Print: Digital Prepress for Graphic Designers,* by Mark Gatter (Harry N. Abrams, 2005)

- *A Guide to Graphic Print Production,* by Kaj Johansson, Peter Lundberg, Robert Ryberg (John Wiley and Sons, 2002)

- *Handbook of Digital Publishing, Volume I and II,* by Michael L. Kleper (Prentice Hall, 2001)

- *Makeready: A Prepress Resource,* by Dan Margulis (Henry Holt and Company, 1996). This book is out of print, but is worth searching for on used-book sites.

- *Official Adobe Print Publishing Guide,* Second Edition, by Brian P. Lawler (Adobe Press, 2005)

  This book covers print processes from offset to digital, with excellent examples explaining such concepts as duotones, trapping, and proofing.

- *Pocket Pal,* 20th Edition, by Michael Bruno, Frank Romano, Michael Riordan (Graphic Arts Technical Foundation, 2007)

  The *Pocket Pal* was first published by International Paper Company, and it is updated every few years. It's small but mighty and includes a glossary and great, short explanations of printing processes. You should have a copy in your backpack at all times.

- *Printing Technology,* by J. Michael Adams and Penny Ann Dolin (Thomson Delmar Learning, 2001)

Typography

Desktop publishing put typesetting into the hands of many eager typists, who often lacked the instincts or training for typographic finesse. But enhancements to design software and the enticing possibilities afforded by OpenType fonts have inspired a return to the art and craft of typography. If you love beautiful typography, or you want to learn more about how typography works as part of designing and printing, here are some books that are part reference, part inspiration.

- *The Complete Manual of Typography,* by James Felici (Adobe Press, 2002)

- *The Elements of Typographic Style,* by Robert Bringhurst (Hartley and Marks Publishers, 2004)

- *Thinking with Type: A Critical Guide for Designers, Writers, Editors, and Students,* by Ellen Lupton (Princeton Arch, 2004)

- *U&lc: Influencing Design and Typography,* by John D. Berry, editor (Mark Batty, 2005)

SOFTWARE-SPECIFIC BOOKS

Somehow, the original software manuals are never enough, are they? They're either arcane, or a bit skimpy. And some of them appear to be written by engineers who are proud of the features, but who may have no idea how their software is used in the real world.

Acrobat

- *Adobe Acrobat 9 How-Tos: 125 Essential Techniques,* by Donna Baker (Adobe Press, 2008)

- *Adobe Acrobat 9 PDF Bible,* by Ted Padova (John Wiley and Sons, 2008)

- *Adobe Acrobat 9 for Windows and Macintosh: Visual QuickStart Guide,* by John Deubert (Peachpit Press, 2008)

Adobe Creative Suite

- *Sams Teach Yourself Adobe Creative Suite 4 All in One,* by Mordy Golding (Sams, 2009)

- *Adobe Creative Suite 4 Bible,* by Ted Padova and Kelly L. Murdock (John Wiley and Sons, 2008)

Illustrator

- *Real World Adobe Illustrator CS4,* by Mordy Golding (Peachpit Press, 2008)

- *The Adobe Illustrator CS4 Wow! Book,* by Sharon Steuer (Peachpit Press, 2009)

- *Illustrator CS4 Bible,* by Ted Alspach (Wiley, 2008)

- *Adobe Illustrator CS4 How-Tos: 100 Essential Techniques,* by David Karlins (Adobe Press, 2008)

InDesign

- *Exploring InDesign CS4,* by Terry Rydberg (Delmar Cengage Learning, 2009)
  A wonderful textbook to teach yourself (or someone else) how to be productive and creative in InDesign. In addition to teaching software techniques, Terry Rydberg weaves in design advice, production knowledge, and subtle hints to do things the right way.

- *InDesign Type: Professional Typography with Adobe InDesign CS2,* by Nigel French (Adobe Press, 2006)

- *Real World Adobe InDesign CS4,* by Olav Martin Kvern and David Blatner (Peachpit Press, 2009)

- *InDesign CS4 for Macintosh and Windows: Visual QuickStart Guide,* by Sandee Cohen (Peachpit Press, 2008)

- *Adobe InDesign CS4 One-on-One,* by Deke McClelland and David Futato (Deke Press, 2008)

Photoshop

Because Photoshop is important to users across a broad spectrum of industries—from hobbyists and office users to professional photographers, industrial designers, Web designers, video artists, scientists, and medical professionals—there is a tidal wave of books for learning and exploring the application. You could probably add a room to your house constructed solely of Photoshop books (of course, check your local building codes first).

- ***Adobe Photoshop CS4: Up to Speed,*** by Ben Willmore (Peachpit Press, 2008)

  Upgrading from a previous version? Want to hit the ground running? Ben's thorough but easy-to-read style hits the mark. It focuses on what's changed and what's new. And, given the substantial interface changes in CS4, the "Where's My Stuff" section at the start of each chapter is a sanity saver.

- ***Adobe Photoshop CS4 for Photographers: A Professional Image Editor's Guide to the Creative Use of Photoshop for the Macintosh and PC,*** by Martin Evening (Focal Press, 2008)

- ***Real World Camera Raw with Adobe Photoshop CS4,*** by Bruce Fraser and Jeff Schewe (Peachpit Press, 2008)

Photoshop Specialty Topics

There are a few indispensable resources that can greatly improve your mastery of Photoshop in production.

- ***Adobe Photoshop Restoration and Retouching,*** Third Edition, by Katrin Eismann and Wayne Palmer (New Riders Press, 2006)

- ***Photoshop LAB Color: The Canyon Conundrum and Other Adventures in the Most Powerful Colorspace,*** by Dan Margulis (Peachpit Press, 2005)

- ***Photoshop Masking and Compositing,*** by Katrin Eismann (New Riders Press, 2004)

- ***Professional Photoshop: The Classic Guide to Color Correction,*** Fifth Edition, by Dan Margulis (Peachpit Press, 2006)

- ***Real World Color Management,*** Second Edition, by Bruce Fraser, Chris Murphy and Fred Bunting (Peachpit Press, 2004)

- ***Photoshop Studio with Bert Monroy: Digital Painting,*** by Bert Monroy (New Riders, 2008)

  Even if you don't aspire to creating digital confections like Bert Monroy's astonishing photorealistic pieces, you can learn valuable techniques for creating something out of nothing when you're called upon to retouch challenging images.

- ***Photoshop CS4 Down & Dirty Tricks,*** by Scott Kelby (New Riders, 2009)

  The "Down & Dirty" series is great fun; learn special effects for the entertainment value, and pick up useful techniques along the way.

PUBLICATIONS

If you agonize over the prospect of killing trees to print magazines, note that some of these publications are available electronically. Highly recommended electronic versions include *Before and After Magazine*, *Design Tools Monthly*, and *InDesign Magazine* (which includes QuickTime movies).

Desktop Publishing

- *Design Tools Monthly*   *www.design-tools.com*

  Great tips, bug alerts, and industry news condensed into one valuable resource. In addition to the monthly newsletter, you receive shareware and freeware software and fonts. Available in both print and downloadable PDF versions.

- *InDesign Magazine*   *www.indesignmag.com*

  Despite the name, InDesign Magazine is about more than just InDesign. Published six times a year as an electronic magazine (there is no printed version), this engaging publication includes great tips and tricks, information about bug workarounds, and articles about printing issues, plug-ins, and design in general.

Design

- *CMYK Magazine*   *www.cmykmag.com*

- *HOW Magazine*   *www.howdesign.com*

- *I.D. Magazine*   *www.idonline.com*

- *Print Magazine*   *www.printmag.com*

- *Communication Arts*   *www.commarts.com*

Printing Technology

- *American Printer*   www.americanprinter.com
- *Graphic Arts Monthly*   www.gammag.com
- *Package Design Magazine*   www.packagedesignmag.com
- *Printing Impressions Magazine*   www.piworld.com

Tutorials

- *Before and After Magazine*   www.bamagazine.com
  Succinct but enjoyable, *B&A* is a combination of tutorials and good design sense.
- *Layers Magazine*   www.layersmagazine.com
- *Photoshop User Magazine*   www.photoshopuser.com/magazine.html

DESTINATIONS

Maybe I'm the only person who would go to a printing-themed museum on vacation.

Oh, I'm not? Good! I'll see you there!

- **Robert C. Willliams Paper Museum**   www.ipst.gatech.edu/amp/
  Institute of Paper Science and Technology
  Georgia Institute of Technology
  500 10th Street NW
  Atlanta, GA 30332-0620
- **Ben Franklin's Courtyard and Print Shop**   www.ushistory.org/tour/tour_fcourt.htm
  318 Market Street
  Philadelphia, PA 19106
- **Crane Museum of Papermaking**   www.crane.com/about/museum
  30 South Street
  Dalton, MA 01226

- **Hamilton Wood Type and Printing Museum**   *www.woodtype.org*
  1619 Jefferson Street
  Two Rivers, WI 54241

- **International Printing Museum**   *www.printmuseum.org*
  315 Torrance Boulevard
  Carson, CA 90745

- **Museum of Printing History**   *www.printingmuseum.org*
  1324 West Clay Street
  Houston, TX 77019

- **Museum of Printing**   *www.museumofprinting.org*
  800 Massachusetts Avenue
  North Andover, MA 01845

- **Center for Book Arts**   *www.centerforbookarts.org*
  28 West 27th Street, 3rd Floor
  New York, NY 100015

3D effects, 185–186
4-Color Process Guide, 34

A

AAs (artist alterations), 13
accessible PDF files, 272
Acrobat, 259–296
   books on using, 307
   collaborating with, 279–282
   collecting comments in, 281
   Comment & Markup tools, 275–279
   ConnectNow service, 283
   Distiller feature, 257, 260, 265–270
   editing PDF files in, 271–275, 296
   enabling Reader features from, 278–279
   font embedding in, 271
   forensic tools, 285–289
   handling image content in, 268–270
   online services included with, 284
   Overprint Preview option, 246
   preflighting files in, 287–289
   previewing output in, 285–287
   Print Production toolbar, 284–296
   product line for, 260
   Professional version, 8, 260
   Read Out Loud option, 272
   repair tools, 290–296
   Simulate Overprint option, 247
   summarizing comments in, 282
   User Community, 298

Acrobat.com Web site, 284
activating fonts, 108, 113–114, 115
Add Printer Marks tool, Acrobat, 291
adjustment layers, 148, 149
Adjustments panel, Photoshop, 148
Adobe Acrobat. *See* Acrobat
Adobe Bridge, 205
Adobe Buzzword, 284
Adobe ConnectNow, 283
Adobe Creative Suite, 307
Adobe forums, 298
Adobe FreeHand, 98
Adobe Gamma, 48, 49
Adobe Graphics Model, 180
Adobe Illustrator. *See* Illustrator
Adobe InDesign. *See* InDesign
Adobe Lightroom, 80
Adobe Paragraph Composer, 229
Adobe Partner Web site, 187
Adobe PDF Print Engine, 11
Adobe Photoshop. *See* Photoshop
Adobe Photoshop Elements, 80
Adobe PostScript. *See* PostScript
Adobe Reader, 260, 278–279
Advanced Editing Toolbar, Acrobat, 272
AI files, 198, 218–219
Aldus PageMaker. *See* PageMaker
alpha channels, 159, 167
Alsoft MasterJuggler, 114
Aperture, Apple, 80
Appearance panel, Illustrator, 183–185
Apple Aperture, 80

Apple desktop computers, 3
  See also Macintosh computers
Apple iPhoto, 80
Apple LaserWriter, 3
application files
    platform issues with, 135
    submitting to printers, 134–136
aqueous coating, 18, 41, 42
Arrow tool, Acrobat, 277
Artboard Options dialog, 172
Artboard tool, 172, 173
artboards (Illustrator), 170–174
    bleed settings, 174
    creating, 172–173
    deleting, 173
    hiding, 173
    modifying, 173–174
    page layout and, 174
    saving files with multiple, 198–200
    trim size and, 53
artist alterations (AAs), 13
artwork
    InDesign files as, 219–220
    PDF files as, 220
Attributes panel, InDesign, 249
automatic font activation, 115
Automatic (JPEG) compression, 270
Automatic Picture Replacement (APR), 84
Automatic Recovery, InDesign, 232

B

backsaving InDesign files, 233
baseline, 18
basic imposition, 59–60
Bézier shapes, 104
Bicubic Sharper resampling, 144

bindery, 18
binding, 16, 65–69
    case, 66
    coil, 16, 18, 68
    comb, 16, 19, 67–68
    custom, 69
    perfect, 16, 23, 66
    post, 69
    saddle stitched, 16, 25, 65
    wire, 16, 26, 69
    See also finishing
bitmap images, 81
black
    duotone, 160–161
    rich, 39–40, 139
black-and-white printing, 27–29
blanket, 18
bleed
    Illustrator settings for, 174, 200
    importance of providing, 54, 128
    InDesign settings for, 234–235
    vector artwork and, 131
Blend tool, Illustrator, 190–191
blended objects, 190–191
blending modes, 151, 152
blind embossing, 20, 74
bluelines, 2, 12, 18, 140
BMP file format, 95
books
    desktop publishing, 304
    general design, 304–305
    printing information, 305–306
    software-specific, 307–309
    typography, 306–307
    See also magazines
Bridge, Adobe, 205
bump plates, 161
Buzzword word processor, 284

C

calibrating monitors, 48–49
Callout tool, Acrobat, 276
Camera RAW format, 79
cameramen, 2, 18
camera-ready art, 3, 18
canvas area, 171
case binding, 66
CDs
    distributing PDF files on, 262
    submitting jobs on, 136
CEPS (color electronic prepress system), 2, 18
channels, 158–159
characters, 111
chase, 18
choking, 38
CID (Character ID) font encoding, 257
Clean Up dialog, Illustrator, 177
Clipping Masks, 150–151
clipping paths, 155, 156
Cloud tool, Acrobat, 277
CMYK color
    adding spot color to, 161–162
    color printing and, 30–31
    Illustrator options for, 170, 191–192
    limitations of, 33–34
    RGB color conversion to, 94–95, 146
    screen captures converted to, 93–94
    specifying color values for, 33
    spot color approximation with, 35–36,
        191–192
coated paper, 35
coatings, 42–43, 127
coil binding, 16, 18, 68
collaborating over PDF files, 279–281
    Collaborate Live sessions, 280–281
    email-based reviews, 279
    shared reviews, 279–280
Collect for Output feature, QuarkXPress, 134

color
    checking, 137
    CMYK, 30–34
    fill, 184
    naming, 130
    spot, 34–36
color break, 4, 18, 23
color corrections
    layers for making, 147–149
    performing in RGB color space, 145
color electronic prepress system (CEPS),
    2, 18
Color Formula Guides, 34
Color Key proofs, 2, 19
color management, 47
color mode, 170
Color panel, InDesign, 220
color printing, 30–36
    CMYK inks for, 30–34
    spot colors for, 34–36
color proofs, 12
color separations, 2, 19
color space, 129, 145, 167
color temperature, 19
colorimeter, 48
colorizing images, 226–227
comb binding, 16, 19, 67–68
Comment & Markup tools, Acrobat, 275–277
comments
    adding to PDFs, 277–278
    collecting and summarizing, 281–282
    deleting from PDFs, 277
Committee for Graphics Arts Technologies
    Standards (CGATS), 264
Component Information dialog, InDesign,
    250–251
compressed files, 133, 136
compression settings, 270
comps, 19

computer-to-plate (CTP), 8, 13, 19, 50
conferences and trade shows, 302–303
Connect Pro service, 283
ConnectNow service, 283
continuous tone, 19
contract proofs, 12, 14, 19, 50
conversions
    Illustrator text, 195–197
    PageMaker legacy files to InDesign,
        227–229, 231
    QuarkXPress legacy files to InDesign,
        227–229, 230–231
    RGB to CMYK color, 94–95, 146
    screen capture to CMYK, 93–94
    spot color to CMYK, 191–192
    text to outline, 102–103, 118
Convert Colors tool, Acrobat, 290–291
corrections, 13, 140
Create PDF service, 284
Cromalin proofs, 2, 20
Crop Pages tool, Acrobat, 292–293
cropping
    images, 85
    PDF pages, 292–293
crossover art, 139
cross-platform issues, 119–124
    filenaming, 120–122
    fonts, 123
    graphics formats, 124
    progress made in, 119–120
CTP (computer-to-plate), 8, 13, 19, 50
curing process, 20
Curve Precision setting, 178–179
custom binding, 69
customer alterations, 13
customer service representative (CSR),
        6, 126–127
Customize Toolbars option, Acrobat, 277
custom-mixed inks, 20, 42, 127

D
DCS files, 162
debossing, 20, 74
deleting
    artboards, 173
    comments, 277
    layers, 167
    paths, 167
design
    books on, 304–307
    conferences on, 303
    magazines on, 310
desktop publishing
    advent of, 3–4
    books on, 304
    magazines on, 310
dfontifier utility, 112
dfonts, 111–112
DIC guide, 34
die cutting, 2, 16, 20, 72–73
digital cameras, 20, 79
Digital Distribution of Advertising for
        Publications (DDAP), 264
digital photography, 9
digital press, 20
digital printing, 15, 43–46
    advantages of, 43–44
    limitations of, 44–46
Direct Selection tool, InDesign, 213, 214
Distiller, Acrobat, 257, 260, 265–268
document profiles, 169–170, 183
Document Raster Effects settings, 181–183
dot etchers, 2, 20
dot gain, 20, 28
double spaces, 131
Douma, Mark, 112
downsampling, 269
dpi (dots per inch), 29
drag-and-drop into InDesign, 205–207

Drop Shadow effect, 179
drop shadows
    Illustrator filter for, 179
    InDesign handling of, 214–215, 219, 243, 247–248
    Photoshop creation of, 152
Droplet, Preflight, 289
drying agents, 41
duotones, 160–161, 226–227
DVDs
    distributing PDF files on, 262
    submitting jobs on, 136
Dynamic Media: Music, Video, Animation, and the Web in Adobe PDF (Connolly), 262

E

Edit Original button, InDesign, 212
editing
    graphics in Acrobat, 273–275
    graphics in InDesign, 212
    PDF files in Acrobat, 271–275, 296
    text in Acrobat, 272–273
    text in Illustrator, 196–197
effective resolution, 251
effects
    Illustrator, 176, 179–183
    Photoshop, 180
emailing PDF files, 262, 279
embedded fonts, 101–102, 117, 133, 271
embedding
    graphics in InDesign, 207–208
    images in Illustrator, 189–190
embossing, 2, 20, 74–75
EMF file format, 100
Encapsulated PostScript. *See* EPS
Enfocus PitStop, 8
environment controls, 48–49

EPS (Encapsulated PostScript)
    drop shadows and, 219
    opening in Photoshop, 165
    raster vs. vector, 88
    saving in Illustrator, 198, 200
    vector graphics and, 97–99
estimators, 7, 20
EULAs (End User License Agreements), 116–118, 271
exporting
    comments from PDF files, 281
    InDesign files to PDF, 256
    PDF files from applications, 264–265
    preflight profiles, 255
Extend Features in Adobe Reader option, Acrobat, 278
Extensis Suitcase, 108, 114

F

fake duotones, 226–227
feathering effects, 243
file extensions, 120, 122
File Handling & Clipboard preferences, Illustrator, 207
File Transfer Protocol (FTP), 136
files
    backsaving, 233
    compressing, 133, 136
    flattening, 151
    naming, 120–122, 130
    reducing size of, 233
fill colors, 184
film strippers, 2, 21
filters, 179–180
finishing, 15–17, 21
    building files for, 52–55, 69–71
    die cutting, 72–73

finishing (*continued*)
  discussing with printers, 127
  embossing, 74–75
  foil stamping, 75
  folding process and, 56–58
  imposition process and, 58–64
  printer specifications for, 55
  trimming and, 52–55
  See also binding
Fix Hairlines tool, Acrobat, 293–294
flatbed scanners, 78
flatness settings, 155
flats, 2, 21
Flattener Preview option, InDesign, 249
flattening
  layers, 151
  transparency, 188–189, 240–248
flexography, 14, 21
FlightCheck Designer, 132, 133
FlightCheck Professional, 8, 132, 133
fluorescent inks, 41–42
FM (frequency modulation) screening, 32
foil stamping, 2, 21, 41, 75
folders, watched, 266
folding, 15
  configuring jobs for, 56–58
  InDesign plug-in for, 58
folding dummy, 21, 62
Font Book utility, 110, 113–114
Font Explorer X, 114
FontAgent Pro, 108, 114
FontDoctor, 115
FontLab, 116
fonts, 107–124
  activating, 108, 113–114, 115
  conflicts between, 115
  converting to outline, 102–103, 118
  cross-platform issues, 123
  embedding, 101–102, 117, 133, 271

  licensing issues, 116–118
  Macintosh OS X system, 111–112
  management programs, 114–115
  multilingual, 110
  Multiple Master, 112–113, 255
  OpenType, 109–111
  PostScript (Type 1), 107–108
  screen, 107–108
  sending to service providers, 118
  substituting, 113
  TrueType, 108
  vector artwork and, 130–131
  Windows system, 112
Fonts control panel, 114
forensic tools, Acrobat, 285–289
FPO images, 8–9, 21, 83, 84
Free Transform tool, InDesign, 213
FreeHand, Adobe, 98
frequency modulation (FM) screening, 32
FTP (File Transfer Protocol), 136
fulfillment, 17

G
ganged content, 15, 21
GIF file format, 95
glazed embossing, 74
Global Graphics Jaws Interpreter, 261
glossary of printing terms, 18–26
glue flap, 71
gluing, 17
glyphs, 109, 111
Goe System, 34, 36, 193
graphic arts tasks
  desktop publishing's redistribution of, 3–4
  historical division of, 1–3
graphics
  Acrobat editing of, 273–275

dragging and dropping, 205–207
embedding/unembedding, 207–208
extracting from PDF files, 275
InDesign editing of, 212
placing in InDesign, 203–205
replacing existing, 211
transforming, 213–214
updating missing/modified, 208–211
See also images; vector graphics
graphics formats. *See* image formats
gravure printing, 14, 21

H

hairline fix, 293–294
halftone dots, 28
halftones, 21
    black-and-white, 28–29
    color, 30–31, 32, 33
hiding artboards, 173
High Quality Print option, InDesign, 258
Highlight Text tool, Acrobat, 276
hinting, 102, 130
hot type, 2, 21

I

IDLK files, InDesign, 232
IDML (InDesign Markup) format, 222, 231
Illustrator, 169–202
    3D artwork in, 185–186
    AI files in InDesign, 218–219
    Appearance panel, 183–185
    artboards in, 170–174
    bleed options in, 174, 200
    blended objects in, 190–191
    books on using, 308

capabilities of, 105
CMYK approximations in, 191–192
color mode in, 170, 176
document profiles, 169–170, 183
drag-and-drop into InDesign from, 206–207
editing PDF files in, 296
EPS files in, 98–99, 200
font management, 110
linked and embedded images in, 189–190
live effects in, 176, 179–183
native file format in, 99
opening PDF files in, 202
Overprint Preview option, 186, 187, 192
PDF file creation, 200–201
PSD files used in, 89, 167
saving files from, 198–201
Scoop plug-in, 101, 174, 190
Separations Preview panel, 194
simplifying complex artwork in, 177–179
spot color options, 191–194
symbols used in, 175–177
templates, 183
text features in, 195–197
transparency effects in, 186–189
trim size in, 53
version issues, 194–197, 199
image formats
    appropriate for print, 87–95, 97–100
    cross-platform compatibility of, 124
    features comparison chart, 90
    inappropriate for print, 95–96, 100–101
image proofs, 137–138
image work, 10
images
    bitmap, 81
    colorizing, 226–227
    cropping, 85
    downsampling, 269
    editing, 212

images (*continued*)
  embedding, 189–190
  finding missing, 211
  linking, 189
  retouching, 129
  rotating, 86
  scaling, 81–83, 130
  transforming, 213–214
  See also graphics; raster images
imagesetters, 22, 46
imaging software, 79–80
importing
  comments from PDF files, 281
  preflight profiles, 255
imposition, 2, 12, 22, 58–64
  basic, 59–60
  multipage, 60–64
InDesign, 203–258
  Automatic Recovery, 232
  backsaving files in, 233
  bleed settings in, 234–235
  books on using, 308
  Color panel, 220
  colorizing images in, 226–227
  Component Information dialog, 250–251
  drag-and-drop into, 205–207
  editing graphics in, 212
  embedding/unembedding graphics in,
      207–208
  files as artwork in, 219–220
  finding and fixing problems in, 248–256
  Flattener Preview option, 249
  FOLDRite plug-in, 58
  font management, 108, 110
  IDLK files, 232
  Illustrator files in, 198–199, 218–219
  Info panel, 251
  Ink Manager, 224–226

Layout Adjustment feature, 235
legacy file conversion in, 227–231
Library used in, 235–236
Links panel, 208–211
Object Layer Options dialog, 216–218
Overprint Preview option, 249
Package function, 134, 255–256
page size setup, 52
PageMaker legacy file conversion,
      227–229, 231
PDF creation in, 256–258
PDF files as artwork in, 220
placing graphics in, 203–205
Preflight feature, 252–255
Preview mode, 248–249
PSD files used in, 89, 167, 214–218
QuarkXPress legacy file conversion,
      227–229, 230–231
reducing file size in, 233
Separations Preview panel, 223–224
silhouettes in, 156–157
sizing text in, 236–237
Smart Guide features, 237–239
Smart Text Reflow, 239
Snippets in, 208
Swatches panel, 220–222
text frame scaling in, 236–237
tips for using, 232–239
transforming graphics in, 213–214
transparency effects in, 239–248
updating graphics in, 208–211
User Group Web site, 298
InDesign Interchange (INX) format, 222, 233
InDesign Markup (IDML) format, 222, 231
Info panel, InDesign, 251
information resources. *See* print production
    resources
Ink Aliasing, 224

Ink Manager
    Acrobat, 290
    InDesign, 224–226
inks
    custom-mixed, 42, 127
    fluorescent, 41–42
    large coverage areas, 39–43
    metallic, 41
    problem, 40–41
    process color, 30, 33, 35–36
    rich black, 39–40
    spot color, 34–35
interpolation, 82
INX (InDesign Interchange) format, 222, 233
iPhoto, Apple, 80

J

Job Definition Format (JDF), 6, 295–296
job flow diagram, 5
job jacket, 6, 22
job submission, 4, 125–142
    application files for, 134–136
    page-layout file check, 131–132
    PDF files for, 133
    planning process, 128–132
    preflighting your job, 132
    preparing designs for, 125–126
    press check following, 140–142
    proofing cycles following, 136–140
    providing printouts in, 132
    raster image check, 129–130
    sending job files, 132–136
    talking with CSRs about, 126–127
    vector artwork check, 130–131
job ticket, 6–7, 22
JPEG compression, 270
JPEG file format, 79, 95–96

K
kiss plates, 161
knock out, 22, 245

L
Lab Values, 225
laminate, 22
layers, 146–151
    adjustment, 148, 149
    Clipping Masks and, 150–151
    color corrections with, 147–149
    deleting, 167
    flattening, 151
    InDesign handling of, 216–218
    layer masks and, 147
    merging, 151
    Smart Objects and, 149–150
Layout Adjustment, InDesign, 235
leading, 21, 22
legacy file conversion, 227–231
    clean up following, 231
    PageMaker conversion issues, 229
    preparing files for, 227–228
    QuarkXPress conversion issues, 230–231
    what to expect from, 228–229
letterpress printing, 14, 22
Library, InDesign, 235–236
licensing issues for fonts, 116–118
lighting considerations, 48, 50
Lightroom, Adobe, 80
line shots, 2, 22
Line tool, Acrobat, 277
linen tester, 22
linking images, 189
Links panel, InDesign, 208–211
Linotype Font Explorer X, 114
lithography, 22

live effects, 176, 179–183
loaded-graphics cursor, 204
loupe, 22
lowercase, 22
lpi (lines per inch), 28, 29

M

Macintosh computers
    cross-platform issues, 119–124
    Displays utility, 48, 49
    file associations fix, 212
    filenaming conventions, 120–122
    font activation, 113–114
    OS X system fonts, 111–112
    Save As PDF option, 257
magazines
    design, 310
    desktop publishing, 310
    printing technology, 311
    tutorial, 311
    See also books
Magic Wand tool, Photoshop, 153
Make Work Path tolerance setting, 153–154
makeready, 2, 14, 22
"marching ants" indicator, 153, 159
Markup tools, Acrobat, 275–277
masks
    clipping, 150–151
    layer, 147
    nondestructive, 159–160
MasterJuggler, 114
Matchprint proofs, 2, 23
mechanical, 1, 23
mechanical color, 4, 23
merging layers, 151
metallic inks, 41
missing graphics, 211

mockups, 19
modified graphics, 211
moiré effect, 31, 137, 139
monitor considerations, 47–50
    calibration, 48–49
    color management, 47
    environment controls, 48
multilingual fonts, 110
multipage imposition, 60–64
Multiple Master fonts, 112–113, 255
Multiply blend mode, 187
museums, 311–312
My Files service, 284

N

naming files, 120–122
National Association of Photoshop
        Professionals (NAPP), 299
native file formats, 99
native PSD format, 88–89
New Document Profiles folder, 183
nondestructive mask edits, 159–160

O

Object Inspector, Acrobat, 287
Object Layer Options dialog, InDesign,
        216–218
objects
    blended, 190–191
    silhouetted, 153–159
    Smart Objects, 149–150
offset printing, 14, 23
online communities/forums, 298–299
on-press imaging, 14
opacity, 151

OpenType fonts, 109–111, 123
OPI (Open Prepress Interface), 23, 84
optimizing PDFs, 295
organizations, 297–301
    online communities/forums, 298–299
    packaging organizations, 300
    printing industry organizations, 300
    technical education organizations, 301
    user groups, 298
Outline view, Illustrator, 176
outlining text, 102–103, 118
Output Preview tool, Acrobat, 285–287
Oval tool, Acrobat, 277
Overprint Preview option
    Acrobat, 246
    Illustrator, 186, 187, 192
    InDesign, 249
overprinting, 245–246, 247

P

Package function, InDesign, 134, 255–256
packaging organizations, 300
page creep, 63, 64
page proofs, 2, 23, 138–139
page size, 52–53
page-layout files
    checking for job submission, 131–132
    collecting elements of, 134–135
page-layout programs, 3
PageMaker
    desktop publishing origins and, 3
    legacy file conversion to InDesign,
        227–229, 231
Pantone Color Bridge, 34, 36
Pantone Color Formula Guide, 34
Pantone Goe System, 34, 36, 193
Pantone Matching System, 34

paper
    digital presses and, 46
    press check and behavior of, 141
    special orders for, 127
Paragraph Composer, 229
path designation, 120
paths
    clipping, 155, 156
    creating, 153–155
    deleting, 167
    flatness settings, 155
    simplifying, 104–105
PDF Enhancer, 295
PDF files
    accessible, 272
    Acrobat Distiller, 265–268
    adding comments to, 277–278
    artwork from, 220
    collaboration using, 279–281
    collecting comments on, 281
    compression settings, 270
    creation of, 261–271
    early conception of, 259
    editing, 271–275, 296
    emailing, 262, 279
    exporting from applications, 264–265
    external editors for, 296
    extracting graphics from, 275
    font embedding in, 117, 271
    forensic tools, 285–289
    Illustrator files saved as, 170, 200–201, 296
    image content and, 268–270
    InDesign files saved as, 256–258
    markup features for, 275–279
    opening in Illustrator, 202
    origin of, 260–261
    Photoshop PDF, 89, 165–166
    preflight process, 8, 133
    repair tools, 290–296

PDF files (*continued*)
  resolution settings, 269
  RIP conversion of, 11, 87
  saving vector art as, 100
  settings for, 257–258, 262–264
  submitting to printers, 133, 261, 267
  summarizing comments on, 282
  types of, 261–262
PDF Optimizer, Acrobat, 295
PDF Options dialog, Photoshop, 166
PDF Print Engine, 11
PDF Reference, 261
PDF Shrink, 295
PDF/X-1a, 201, 258, 264, 268
PDF/X-3, 258, 264
PDF/X-4, 258, 264
PDF/X Checkup, 8
Pen tool, Photoshop, 154–155
Pencil Eraser tool, Acrobat, 277
Pencil tool, Acrobat, 277
perfect binding, 16, 23, 66
personalization, 4, 23
PGF file format, 199
Photoshop, 3, 80, 143–167
  books on using, 308–309
  color space issues, 145
  drag-and-drop into InDesign from, 206
  duotone creation, 160–161
  effects, 180
  EPS file format, 88
  font management, 110
  image use considerations, 143–145
  layers used in, 146–151
  native PSD format, 88–89
  PDF file format, 89, 165–166
  PSD files in InDesign, 214–218
  resolution issues, 145
  RGB to CMYK conversions, 93–94, 146
  saving files in, 165–167

screen capture conversions, 93–94
silhouetting objects in, 153–159
spot colors added in, 161–162
spot varnish plate creation, 162–163
transparency effects in, 151–152
vector elements in, 163–165
Photoshop.com service, 80
Photoshop Elements, 80
picas, 23
PitStop editor, 202, 259, 273
pixels, 77, 181
PlaceMultipagePDF script, 220
planners, 7, 23
plates, creating, 13–14
platesetters, 24, 46
PNG file format, 95
pocket folder, 69–71
points, 24
post binding, 69
PostScript, 24
  conversion to PDF, 265–267
  desktop publishing and, 3
  encapsulated, 88
  RIPs and, 11
  See also EPS
PostScript Printer Definition (PPD) files, 257
PostScript (Type 1) fonts, 107–108
potential pixels, 181
PPD files, 257
ppi (pixels per inch), 29
preflight, 8, 24
  Acrobat tool for, 287–289
  creating custom profiles for, 253–254
  importing/sharing profiles for, 255
  InDesign feature for, 252–255
  prior to job submission, 132, 133
Preflight Droplet, 289
Preflight panel, InDesign, 252–253
Preflight tool, Acrobat, 287–289

prepress, 8–13, 24
Preserve Spot Colors option, Illustrator, 185
preset, Transparency Flattener, 242, 243–245
press check, 2, 14, 24, 140–142
press issues, 36–43
    large ink coverage areas, 39–43
    registration, 36–37
    trapping, 37–38
press proof, 24
Press Quality option, InDesign, 258
pressroom, 14
Preview mode, InDesign, 248–249
previewing documents
    in Acrobat, 285–287
    in InDesign, 248–249
print production resources, 297–312
    conferences and trade shows, 302–303
    design and printing books, 304–307
    magazines, 310–311
    museums, 311–312
    organizations, 297–301
    software-specific books, 307–309
Print Production toolbar (Acrobat), 284–296
    Add Printer Marks tool, 291
    Convert Colors tool, 290–291
    Crop Pages tool, 292–293
    Fix Hairlines tool, 293–294
    forensic tools, 285–289
    Ink Manager, 290
    JDF information, 295–296
    Output Preview tool, 285–287
    PDF Optimizer, 295
    Preflight tool, 287–289
    repair tools, 290–296
    Transparency Flattening options, 294–295
    Trap Presets feature, 295
print service providers
    application file submission to, 134–136
    discussing print jobs with, 126–127

fonts sent with jobs to, 118
PDF file submission to, 133, 261, 267
press check with, 140–141
proofing cycles with, 136–140
sending job files to, 132–136
Print to Adobe PDF option, 256
printable area, 171
printer alterations, 13
printer marks, 291
printer profiles, 49
printer's spreads, 24, 60, 133
printing
    black-and-white, 27–29
    books about, 305–306
    coatings used in, 42–43
    color, 30–36
    digital, 43–46
    glossary of terms for, 18–26
    image formats for, 87–95, 97–100
    ink coverage issues, 39–42
    magazines on, 311
    museums related to, 311–312
    press check during, 140–142
    registration issues, 36–37
    trapping issues, 37–38
printing industry
    events, 302–303
    organizations, 300
printing plants
    job flow diagram for, 5
    overview of departments in, 4–17
printouts of job, 132
problem inks, 40–41
process colors, 30
production, 8–9
profiles
    document, 169–170, 183
    monitor, 48
    printer, 49

Progressive Graphics Format (PGF), 199
Project Camelot, 259
proofing process, 12, 136–140
   correction check, 140
   image proof check, 137–138
   imposed blueline check, 140
   page proof check, 138–139
   signing off on proofs, 140
proofs, 24
   contract, 12, 14, 19, 50
   image, 137–138
   page, 2, 23, 138–139
PSD files, 88–89, 165, 167, 214–218
publications. *See* books; magazines

Q

Q2ID utility, 227
quadtones, 160
QuarkXPress
   Collect for Output feature, 134
   font management, 110
   legacy file conversion to InDesign,
      227–229, 230–231
   PDF file creation, 261
   PSD files used in, 89, 167

R

random proofs, 12, 137–138
raster image processors (RIPs), 10–11, 24
   halftone dots and, 29
   PDF Print Engine in, 11
   proofs based on data from, 50
   rasterization process by, 242–243
   transformations performed by, 87
raster images, 77–96

cropping, 85
digital photos and, 79, 85
file formats for printing, 87–95
imaging software and, 79–80
inappropriate formats for printing, 95–96
placing into vector graphics, 103–104
pre-job submission check of, 129–130
programs for transforming, 86–87
raster effects and, 181–183
resolution issues with, 80–84, 129
retouching work on, 129
RGB to CMYK conversion of, 94–95
rotating, 86, 130
scaling up/down, 81–83, 130
scanners and, 78, 83–84
screen captures as, 91–94
Smart Objects as, 150
vector graphics vs., 97
RAW images, 79
Read Out Loud option, Acrobat, 272
Reader, Adobe, 260, 278–279
reader's spreads, 132–133
Ready, Set, Go!, 3
Real World Color Management (Fraser, Murphy,
   and Bunting), 47
Rectangle Frame tool, InDesign, 203
Rectangle tool
   Acrobat, 277
   InDesign, 203
Reflex Blue ink, 40–41
refrying, 295
registered embossing, 74
registration, 24
   digital printing and, 45
   printing inks and, 36–37
Relink button, InDesign, 211
remapping spot colors, 224–226
repair tools, Acrobat, 290–296

resizing. *See* sizing/resizing
resolution
    approaches to working with, 83–84
    determining for images, 80–81
    digital presses and, 46
    effective, 251
    PDF settings for, 269
    Photoshop considerations, 145
    scaled images and, 82–83
    screen captures and, 91–92
resources. *See* print production resources
retouching images, 129
RGB color
    color correction in, 145
    converting to CMYK, 94–95, 146, 191–192
    digital photos and, 9
    screen captures converted from, 93–94
rich black, 39–40, 139
RIPs. *See* raster image processors
ROOM (RIP Once, Output Many), 25
rotation
    checking layout files for, 132
    of raster images, 86, 130

S

saddle stitching, 16, 25, 65
salesperson, 6, 126
Save As command, 233
Save As PDF option, 257
saving
    files with multiple artboards, 198–200
    Illustrator files, 198–201
    Photoshop files, 165–167
    symbols in Illustrator, 176
    vector art as PDFs, 100
Scale tool, InDesign, 213

scaling
    checking layout files for, 132
    graphic frames, 213
    raster images, 81–83, 130
    text frames, 236–237
scanners, 2, 25, 78
scanning
    artwork, 9
    FPO, 8–9, 84
scatter proofs, 137–138
schedulers, 7, 25
Scoop plug-in, 101, 174, 190
scoring, 25, 72
screen angle, 31
screen captures, 91–94
    converting to CMYK, 93–94
    resolution of, 91–92
screen fonts, 107–108
screen printing, 14, 25
screen readers, 272
screen ruling, 28, 46
screen values, 33
Selection tool, InDesign, 213, 214
sending job files, 132–136
    application files, 134–136
    PDF files, 133
    See also job submission
Separations Preview panel
    Illustrator, 194
    InDesign, 223–224
service bureau licenses, 117, 118
Share service, Acrobat.com, 284
Shared Review feature, Acrobat, 279–280
sharing
    PDF files, 279–280, 284
    preflight profiles, 255
sheetfed presses, 25
shingling, 64

shipping, 17
short print runs, 44
signatures, 16, 25, 60
signing off on proofs, 140
silhouettes, 25, 138, 153–159
    alternative silhouetting methods, 157–159
    paths used for creating, 153–157
Simplify dialog, Illustrator, 178
Simulate Overprint option, 246, 247
Single-Line Composer, 229
size considerations
    for file size, 233
    for print planning, 128
    for trim size, 52–53
sizing/resizing
    artboards, 173
    raster images, 81–82
slang terms, 52
Smallest File Size option, InDesign, 257
Smart Guides (InDesign), 237–239
    setting preferences for, 239
    Smart Spacing indicators, 238
Smart Objects, 149–150
Smart Text Reflow, 239
Snippets, InDesign, 208
soft proofs, 12
software-specific books, 307–309
special effects, 139
specialty inks, 41–42
spell check, 131
spiral binding, 18, 68
spot colors, 34–36
    3D artwork and, 185, 186
    adding to CMYK images, 161–162
    approximating with CMYK, 35–36, 191–192
    digital presses and, 45–46
    guides for choosing, 34

Illustrator options for, 185, 186, 191–194
    remapping with Ink Manager, 224–226
    transparency and, 245–247
spot varnishes, 42–44, 162–163
spreading, 38
Stamps tool, Acrobat, 276
Sticky Note tool, Acrobat, 276
stitching, 16
stochastic screening, 32
strokes, 184–185
styled text, 131
subsetting fonts, 271
substituting fonts, 113
Suitcase Fusion, 108, 114
Summarize Options dialog, Acrobat, 282
summarizing comments on PDFs, 282
SVG filters, 180
Swatch Options dialog, Illustrator, 192
swatches
    Illustrator, 192
    InDesign, 220–222
Swatches panel, InDesign, 220–222
Symbol Options dialog, Illustrator, 175–176
symbols, Illustrator, 175–177
system fonts
    Macintosh OS X, 111–112
    Windows OS, 112

T

technical education organizations, 301
templates, Illustrator, 183
text
    avoiding styled, 131
    converting to outlines, 102–103, 118
    editing in Acrobat, 272–273
    Illustrator features for, 195–197

InDesign frame scaling and, 236–237
rasterization of, 242
transparency flattening and, 241
vector graphics and, 101–103, 130–131
Text Box tool, Acrobat, 277
Text Edits tool, Acrobat, 276
TIFF files, 87, 99, 167
toner-based printing, 44–46
touch plates, 161
TouchUp Object tool, Acrobat, 272, 273–275
TouchUp Reading Order tool, Acrobat, 272
TouchUp Text tool, Acrobat, 272, 273
Toyo Color Finder, 34
trade shops, 2, 25
trade shows and conferences, 302–303
transforming graphics, 213–214
transparencies, 25
Transparency Blend Space, 241–242
transparency effects
    Illustrator, 186–187
    InDesign, 239–240
    Photoshop, 151–152
Transparency Flattener Presets, 242, 243–245
transparency flattening
    Acrobat and, 294–295
    drop shadows and, 247–248
    Illustrator and, 187–189
    InDesign and, 240–248
    layer stacking order and, 241
    spot colors and, 245–247
Trap Presets feature, Acrobat, 295
trapping, 11, 25, 37–38, 139
trimming, 15
    bleed provided for, 54
    printer specifications for, 55
    trim size and, 52–53
tritones, 160
TrueType fonts, 108, 123

TRUMATCH Colorfinder, 36
tutorial magazines, 311
two-color job, 27
typesetters, 2, 26
typography books, 306–307

U
uncoated paper, 35
Unicode, 109
UPC (universal product code), 26
Update Link icon, 211
updating graphics, 208–211
uppercase, 26
user groups, 298
UV (ultraviolet) coatings, 42

V
variable data, 15
variable data printing (VDP), 11, 26, 44, 127
varnishes, 42–43, 127, 162–163
vector graphics, 97–105
    color naming for, 130
    file formats for, 97–101
    inappropriate formats for printing, 100
    incorporating images into, 103–104
    Photoshop images and, 163–165
    pre-job submission check of, 130–131
    programs for creating, 105
    raster images vs., 97
    rasterization of, 242–243
    saving as PDF, 100
    simplifying, 104–105
    Smart Objects as, 150
    text handling in, 101–103, 130–131
viewing booth, 26

W

Warnock, John, 259
watched folders, 266
web presses, 26
Web resources. *See* print production resources
Web-based PDF files, 262
Windows computers
    cross-platform issues, 119–124
    filenaming conventions, 120–122
    font activation, 114
    system fonts, 112
wire binding, 16, 26, 69
WMF file format, 100

Z

Zig Zag effect, 179
ZIP compression, 270

WATCH
READ
CREATE

Meet Creative Edge.

A new resource of unlimited books, videos and tutorials for creatives from the world's leading experts.

Creative Edge is your one stop for inspiration, answers to technical questions and ways to stay at the top of your game so you can focus on what you do best—being creative.

All for only $24.99 per month for access—any day any time you need it.

creative
edge

peachpit.com/creativeedge